MW00459680

Ambitious Honor

Ambitious Honor

George Armstrong Custer's
Life of Service and Lust for Fame

James E. Mueller

University of Oklahoma : Norman

This book is published with the generous assistance of the
McCasland Foundation, Duncan, Oklahoma.

Parts of chapters 3 and 4 were published as "'Custar' in the News: George Armstrong Custer in the Gettysburg Campaign," in *A Press Divided: Newspaper Coverage of the Civil War*, edited by David B. Sachsman (Piscataway, N.J.: Transaction Publishers, 2014).

Library of Congress Cataloging-in-Publication Data

Names: Mueller, James E., 1960– author.
Title: Ambitious honor : George Armstrong Custer's life of service and lust for fame / James E. Mueller.
Description: Norman : University of Oklahoma Press, 2020. | Includes bibliographical references and index. | Summary: "A biography of George Armstrong Custer that argues he had the soul of an artist rather than a soldier. This artistic passion for creativity and recognition drove Custer to success—and, ultimately, to the failure that has overshadowed his notable achievements."—Provided by publisher.
Identifiers: LCCN 2020014496 | ISBN 978-0-8061-6720-6 (hardcover)
Subjects: LCSH: Custer, George A. (George Armstrong), 1839–1876. | Generals—United States—Biography. | United States. Army—Biography.
Classification: LCC E467.1.C99 M84 2020 | DDC 973.8/092 [B] —dc23
LC record available at https://lccn.loc.gov/2020014496

The paper in this book meets the guidelines for permanence and durability of the Committee on Production Guidelines for Book Longevity of the Council on Library Resources, Inc. ∞

Copyright © 2020 by the University of Oklahoma Press, Norman, Publishing Division of the University. Manufactured in the U.S.A.

All rights reserved. No part of this publication may be reproduced, stored in a retrieval system, or transmitted, in any form or by any means, electronic, mechanical, photocopying, recording, or otherwise—except as permitted under Section 107 or 108 of the United States Copyright Act—without the prior written permission of the University of Oklahoma Press. To request permission to reproduce selections from this book, write to Permissions, University of Oklahoma Press, 2800 Venture Drive, Norman, OK 73069, or email rights.oupress@ou.edu.

1 2 3 4 5 6 7 8 9 10

For Cathy

"In years long numbered past, when I was merging upon manhood, my every thought was to be great. I desired to link my name with acts and men, and in such a manner as to be a mark of honor, not only to the present, but to future generations."

George Armstrong Custer to Libbie Custer, 1867

Contents

Preface

Custer's Eyes

George Armstrong Custer did not have the eyes of a soldier, at least in the opinion of James E. Kelly.

And Kelly would have known, because the artist and sculptor made a career of doing sketches and statues of military heroes, especially Civil War generals, usually based on studies he did from life. Kelly was a boy during the war and had been a self-confessed hero worshiper of Union soldiers ever since a family friend visited their New York home in his shiny blue uniform.[1]

Kelly went to art school after the war and established a career as a magazine illustrator. He did a sketch of Sheridan's famous ride at Winchester that was published in a history of the United States. He turned the sketch into a statue and then devoted much of his career to interviewing generals like Sheridan and making meticulously designed sketches and statues, incorporating details they remembered about their most famous battles. No detail was too small for Kelly, who measured their heads and facial features with calipers to make his statues look as near to real life as possible. While working with Theodore Roosevelt, Kelly made the future president grab his fingers in the way he held his horse's reins so he could make the best bronze recreation of him charging up San Juan Hill.[2]

Custer's eyes came up in a conversation Kelly had with Winfield Scott Hancock in 1880. Kelly had convinced the reluctant Hancock to pose for a painting of the council of war of the top Union generals at Gettysburg. Over the course of several sittings, artist and subject chatted about the war and various Union generals.

In one sitting, Hancock, squeezed into his uniform and, concerned about the fullness of his chin, held his military pose so long that sweat began rolling down his face. Making conversation, he asked Kelly to define the artist's phrase "a soldier's eye."

Kelly explained that it was a hooded look where the skin hangs down from the eyebrow over the upper eyelid. He'd noticed it not only in generals but also in sailors and Indians—something he thought was handed down through generations who had lived the outdoor life.

"It isn't necessary that a man should be a soldier because he has it, but I have noticed, as a rule, our successful soldiers have it," Kelly said. "Sheridan, Grant, and Sherman have got it. You have got it. Custer did not have it, but he was not necessarily a soldier—I think the pictorial, the romantic part of War appealed to him as much as the fighting. He had more of the artist's or literary eye."

Hancock's grandson, who was not yet school age, came running in and climbed on the old general's lap, distracting the men from their conversation about what soldiers are supposed to look like. Kelly finished the sketch while Hancock hugged the boy.[3]

Custer not necessarily a soldier? One wonders what Hancock thought of that. He had seen Custer join a charge in a desperate fight at Williamsburg in 1862. Yet after the war he had seen Custer leave his command during an Indian campaign to make a mad, romantic dash across Kansas to be with his wife. Which was the real Custer?

It is the contention of this book that Kelly's observation is the key to understanding Custer's life. Custer fought with abandon and was one of the most successful cavalry commanders of the Civil War. He had a remarkable talent for war, but it was a career he was thrust into because of the times in which he lived. Custer had an artistic temperament and as such was drawn to creative endeavors like writing and performing. Those talents drew him to fields such as education, journalism, entertainment, and politics. Custer's first professional job was schoolteacher, and he quit to attend West Point, mainly to get an education. While he was in the army, he wrote a book and numerous magazine and newspaper articles, and at the time of his death he was writing another book and planning a speaking tour. While Custer never ran for office, he spoke at a political convention and went on a campaign tour with President Andrew Johnson. Had he survived his last battle, he might well have retired from the U.S. Army to pursue a career in one or more of these areas. In addition to a writing career, he could have given lectures like Mark Twain or performed in shows like Buffalo Bill Cody.

All of this is not to say Custer hated the army or was a reluctant soldier. He was a true Jacksonian Democrat who loved America and believed in the causes to which he devoted his life—the preservation of the Union and the expansion of the country across the continent. He also enjoyed the excitement and the pageantry and fame that his great martial success won for him. But his creative side chafed at regulation and conformity. Like a novelist who resists editing, Custer at times resisted the orders of his superiors, preferring to write his life story his way.

On the way to his last stand at the Little Bighorn in 1876, Custer famously refused the offer of additional troops in part because he wanted his regiment—the Seventh Cavalry—to get sole credit for the great victory that he and everyone involved anticipated. His shocking defeat and death, along with that of every man under his direct command, was huge news for a month or so but was then eclipsed by the presidential election and other concerns.

As those concerns have passed away (who but a historian remembers the contenders in the 1876 election?), Custer's name remains ever current. MIT researchers who developed a tool to measure the fame of historical figures from 4,000 B.C. to 2010 ranked Custer as the ninety-first most famous military figure *in the history of the world*. In the top one hundred, headed by Alexander the Great and including such varied leaders as Spartacus, Horatio Nelson, and Erwin Rommel, only one of Custer's contemporaries is listed—Robert E. Lee, at No. 90. In a list of only the most famous American military figures, Custer is ranked fourth behind Lee and World War II heroes Douglas MacArthur and George S. Patton. Of Custer's peers, William Tecumseh Sherman, at No. 9, is the only man besides Lee in the top ten famous American military figures.[4]

Why did Custer so capture the imagination? This biography suggests one answer by looking at Custer not as a born soldier predestined to military glory but as a man who had the soul of an artist, who viewed life as a romantic journey. The journey ended in a battle that on its own is quite interesting but would never have become so famous had it not been for the death of its star player. Custer's artistic sensibility compelled him to create a life story that has fascinated both historians and the public for generations—a story that ends with a battle that has become a central part of the myth called variously the American Frontier, the Wild West, or simply, the West.

Myths, according to historian Richard Slotkin, are the stories that explain national character. They transmit the worldview of a country's ancestors to its modern descendants. Slotkin started writing about the Frontier Myth in 1965 and finished about thirty years later, having produced three volumes of about eight hundred pages each, concluding that through all of the changes in U.S. history, the Frontier Myth was a durable explanation of American character. In particular, Slotkin argued that Custer and his last stand were key to understanding the myth because they fit the American self-image of being on a mission to fight the enemies of civilization.[5]

Custer's life story is thus a crucial part of American history because of the overriding importance of the Frontier Myth to the nation's character. Furthermore, the Frontier Myth has proved adaptable as the country has changed, and Americans have used historical figures like Custer to represent different things at different times. "The stories changed as the larger society changed, and different groups recast the stories to create new meanings," wrote historian Richard White. "The West became, in this sense, something of a national mirror. When Americans looked into the imagined West for images of themselves, their own present situation determined what was reflected back."[6]

Custer has proved to be one of the most enduring images seen in the mirror even though the Little Bighorn as a battle was not terribly important to the conquest of the West. Custer biographer Louise Barnett noted the slaughter of the buffalo, the construction of railroads, and the gradual settlement of land by homesteaders as being more important than military actions. But Custer's dramatic life and death make a more compelling and simple story of westward expansion than the "thousands of small events" that settled the frontier. "His death speaks to the contradictory needs of the national psyche more than to the contradictory realities of his life—to our desire in a less self-reflective era for the sharply etched image of the hero charging into battle and more recently to our critical reassessment of the violent conquest of our country."[7]

Indeed, Custer's rich but brief life has more than enough material to provide countless interpretations of his life story and his last battle. Barnett made Custer's wife, Libbie, a key focus of her book, while historian Jeffry Wert emphasized Custer's Civil War career. Nathaniel Philbrick, most famous for his books about sea adventures, compared Custer and Sitting Bull to ships' captains leading their followers on two voyages that met in a tragic conclusion.[8] Most recently, T. J. Stiles argued in his 2016 Pulitzer Prize–winning *Custer's Trials* that Custer should be understood as a man living on a chronological frontier more than on just a geographical one. Custer, Stiles wrote, was a man out of place in a time that completely reordered American life with industrialization and other societal changes that diminished the importance of the individual, the romantic, and the heroic. Custer helped to create this modern country through his military service, but he was never able to adapt personally to that change, an inner conflict that contributed to instability.[9] Custer's ambivalence to change spoke to many of his contemporaries, and that ambivalence continues to speak to succeeding generations about their own attitude toward their time in the history of their country.[10]

It is my contention that Custer's ambivalence was not about the time he lived in but the roles he played during that time. He spent most of his life as a soldier, and he enjoyed aspects of that life, but he always yearned for more. Custer, who was an artist at heart, reveled in the performance of the various roles he took during his life. A reporter who observed him take over a political rally with his charisma and perfect sense of timing wrote in awe, "He is the thing he does."[11] Custer expertly chose his own costumes for his roles, wearing the outfit of a cavalier while he fought in the Civil War, the buckskins of a frontiersman during his Plains service, and the suit and top hat of a dandy on his trips to New York. He was comfortable in all of these roles because of his artistic temperament. What Stiles called Custer's instability—a better word would be "complexity"—came from his constant struggle between showmanship and duty. He wanted to be a heroic officer, but as an artist he was frustrated whenever he felt that his creativity was stifled by military rules or that he was not recognized for his achievements.

Custer's artistic temperament is, ultimately, what made him an enduring figure in the Frontier Myth and American history. Because he was a performer and a writer, he created a public figure that could not but be immortalized by his dramatic death. As Slotkin noted, because Custer understood the media and publicity, he was an author of his own myth.[12]

Indeed, Custer's artistic skills place him in another category of American—the storyteller. Custer was raised in frontier Ohio, where the teller of tall tales was admired as an entertainer and embellishing a story was an accepted practice. Like Mark Twain writing about prospecting in Nevada, or Lincoln talking about his adventures in rural Illinois, Custer made his experiences in the West come alive for his audience. It's a tradition that has continued to our times, where writers such as Hunter Thompson do not just write the story but become the story.

Custer's story is the tale of a soldier who was an artist first. As such, his story properly begins as a young man studying to be a teacher but dreaming of an undefined greatness. . . .

Acknowledgments

Writing a biography of a man as famous as Custer requires much research and thinking to create some new angle worth writing about. It would take another book to list all of the great Custer scholars who have informed my understanding of his life. As the saying goes, I stand on the shoulders of giants. But I would like to mention a few, in alphabetical order, whose work has been particularly helpful: Stephen E. Ambrose, Sandy Barnard, Louise Barnett, James Donovan, Brian Dippie, Lawrence Frost, Paul Hedren, Paul Andrew Hutton, Shirley A. Leckie, Jay Monaghan, T. J. Stiles, Robert M. Utley, and Jeffry D. Wert.

Sandy and I share a common career as journalism professors as well as an interest in Custer, and he has always been extremely generous in sharing research and ideas. Jim Donovan has been a regular participant in the Mayborn Literary Nonfiction Conference at my professional home—the University of North Texas—and also has always been willing to discuss ideas and offer encouragement.

The book has, of course, required much research from a variety of sources. I would like to thank the staffs at the Monroe County Historical and Museum Association Archives and the Monroe County Library System. In particular I would like to thank Charmaine Wawrzyniec, Custer curator at the library, and Caitlyn Reihle, curator of collections for the museum.

This is the second book I have written with the University of Oklahoma Press, which is an outstanding publishing house. Chuck Rankin, who edited my first OU book, *Shooting Arrows and Slinging Mud*, was instrumental in helping me develop the concept for this biography and getting it started. Adam C. Kane took over after Chuck retired and has been a tremendous help in completing the book. Stephanie E. Evans, senior manuscript editor, has done an outstanding job shepherding the manuscript through the publication process. Tim Bryant caught errors with his sharp copyediting and offered many suggestions to improve the clarity and flow of the writing.

But most importantly, I would like to thank my wife, Catherine Mueller, for her strength, wisdom, and love. Cathy, a professional writer with her own demanding career, helped me with research, ideas, and editing in addition to making countless trips to Montana, Michigan, and other Custer sites. I could not have done it without her.

CHAPTER ONE

What Is Ambition?

When George Armstrong Custer was a sixteen-year-old student at the McNeely Normal School in Hopedale, Ohio, he copied a verse about ambition in his notebook. The verse, which was part of a poem by a popular author named N. P. Willis, didn't seem to have any connection to his lessons. It just seemed to be something he found interesting, something that hinted Custer was dreaming of being more than a schoolteacher, which was itself a big dream for a small-town blacksmith's son.

> What is ambition
> Tis a glorious cheat
> It seeks the chamber of the gifted boy
> And lifts his humble window and comes in[1]

Ambition had crept in Custer's window, all right. Custer, a rambunctious boy who was the center of attention of his family, craved more than the ordinary life of physical labor of his old man. Custer dearly loved his father, but he did not want to spend his life standing over a hot forge pounding out horseshoes like Emanuel Custer did in the village of New Rumley, Ohio.

This ambition had been handed down from Emanuel, who as a young man had sought more for his own life, moving from his home in Cressaptown, a small community in western Maryland, to New Rumley in 1824, when he was eighteen years old. Emanuel came to practice blacksmithing with his uncle Jacob and took over the business when Jacob became a farmer. That left Emanuel as the proprietor of one of three major businesses in town, the others being a tavern and a general store. Emanuel married Matilda Viers, and they had three children before she died in 1835.[2]

Maria Kirkpatrick, a twenty-nine-year-old woman in the village, lost her husband the same year, leaving her with three children of her own. Maria was the daughter of James Ward, who had moved from Burgettstown, Pennsylvania, to New Rumley around 1816 and opened the village tavern. Ward had died about a dozen years earlier, so when Maria's husband died, she was left with no father or grandfather to help support and raise her family. There were only about a dozen families living in New Rumley, so it was only natural the two grieving parents would find solace in each other. They married about a year after they lost their spouses, and they started their own family. Their first two sons, James and Samuel, both died within a year of their birth. George Armstrong Custer, the first child to survive to adulthood, was born on December 5, 1839. The family and close friends called him Armstrong or "Autie," which was the way George pronounced his name when he first learned to speak. Four more children followed: Nevin in 1842, Thomas in 1845, Boston in 1848, and Margaret in 1852.[3] Along with Emanuel's first three children and Maria's first three, the family comprised a blended family of eleven children.

It was a loving family that made no distinction between the parentage of the children. Maria was a thin, frail woman who would look over her half-glasses while knitting to watch the happy chaos of the household. Occasionally she would have to be, as she said, "unpleasant" to make the children mind, but her actions were never so harsh that she regretted them later. Maria did feel frustrated that the Custers were not wealthy enough to have her great desire—a beautiful home for her children. But she tried to make up for it with kindness. When the children were pleased with her cooking, it brought her joy.[4]

Emanuel was louder and more boisterous than his fragile second wife, and one of his greatest joys was playing with his children. The Custer patriarch was confident in his religion and his politics, the latter of which consisted of devotion to the Democratic Party and a worshipful patriotism. His eldest son, George, observed and quickly demonstrated a talent for performance, echoing his father's views in dramatic ways and earning the satisfaction of making the adults laugh approvingly. When George was five, Emanuel took him to the dentist to have a tooth pulled. He told him to be a good soldier, and if it bled a lot, that meant it would heal quickly. It took the dentist two tries with the forceps to yank it out. Walking out of the office, despite the pain in his mouth, George burst out, "Father, you and me can whip all the Whigs in Ohio, can't we?" Emanuel was so pleased that he stopped people on the way home to regale them with the story.[5]

George got to perform for a larger audience when his father took him to meetings and drills of the New Rumley Invincibles, the local militia company. The Invincibles, in contrast to their name, had a reputation as a loosely structured group with outlandish uniforms and musters that featured drinking, dancing, fiddling, and cursing. During the United States' dispute with Mexico, which led to war in 1846, the Democrats supported hostilities, while the Whigs, including Congressman Abraham Lincoln, were for peace. Militia units throughout the country debated the international crisis, with several taking mock votes on the 1844 presidential election between Whig Henry Clay and Democrat James K. Polk.[6] At an Invincibles meeting, George took center stage. Decked out in a uniform his mother made and armed with a wooden musket, he declared to his father's unit that like the Democrats, "My voice is for war!" George's performance was so funny and perfectly timed that people talked about it for years afterward.[7]

Everyone could laugh because the Invincibles were not going to fight in Mexico or anywhere else. Under U.S. militia law, these types of units could not be deployed outside of the United States. The danger of any kind of war inside of Ohio was also negligible because the local Indian tribes had long since been subdued. Dating from the times of the Pilgrims, American militia gatherings like those of the Invincibles had always been a social event, often combined with church services, festivals, and shooting matches. "Traditional militia service had come to appeal primarily to those who loved parades, pageantry, martial music, and ceremony," wrote one historian. "Most militia functions had little to do with military preparedness. They allowed an amateur to enter show business and join the circus."[8] In fact, the militia of Custer's boyhood represented the same civic function that professional sports teams serve in the modern era: an entertaining spectacle that provides something identifiable for the community to rally around.[9]

Young George saw that his father, as a member of the militia, was somebody important in the community, somebody who wore a uniform and had fun putting on a show for the town. The local militia's loose structure suited Emanuel's fervent Jacksonian politics with its mix of patriotism, independence from formal authority, and respect for the common man. Emanuel's family had been Whigs back in Maryland, but he admired an old man in the town, a local character who played war songs on a fife and was a veteran of both the Revolution and the War of 1812. When Emanuel found out the veteran of two wars was a Democrat, he decided to switch parties. He cast his first vote for Andrew Jackson, the first president who represented working men such as blacksmiths.[10]

Emanuel became a Democratic committeeman and was frequently listed as such in the local newspapers before the Civil War. On occasion he led meetings and gave speeches urging support for the party's ticket. During the 1856 campaign he participated in an assembly of what the *Cadiz Sentinel* described as "the unterrified yeomanry" of New Rumley, who raised a 160-foot hickory pole—the symbol of Jacksonianism—in honor of Democratic candidate James Buchanan. They flew a thirty-foot-long flag from the pole. The *Sentinel* noted approvingly that the flag had thirty-one stars "emblematic of the *whole Union*"—the italics emphasizing that the Democrats, unlike the northern Republican party, represented the entire country. The group, some four hundred strong, then marched to a platform erected at the end of town. The group elected Emanuel president, and he gave a speech and presided over the rest of the festivities.[11]

By 1856, George had moved away from home, but he would often have witnessed such scenes while he was growing up. Emanuel took him to political meetings just like he took him to militia musters. George observed that like the militia musters, elections were passionate yet entertaining. He saw that his father, despite his strong beliefs, was friendly with everyone and resolved disputes with humor. At home Emanuel was fun-loving with his children, engaging in pranks and roughhousing, and in town he was a popular figure, welcome at the homes of people of all political beliefs.[12]

Emanuel at first envisioned George following in his footsteps, learning a trade and perhaps owning his own business. He apprenticed George to a carpenter when he was nine. When he was given the job of making a piano stool that could also serve as a living room stand, he created a piece that a local family used for years, referring to it as "Custer's First Stand" after he became famous. But the boy only occasionally got to practice the artistry of the profession. He spent most of his time working a giant lathe to grind posts for large four-poster beds. It was not a future that would allow him to express himself.[13]

George's parents, too, recognized he was something special. Perhaps he could be the first in the family to go beyond a workingman's life. They sent the boy to live with his older half-sister Ann in Monroe, Michigan, which is about 220 miles from New Rumley. Ann had married David Reed, who operated a drayage business in Monroe. She was lonely and needed help with her family, and Custer, who at age thirteen had completed the six years of schooling that was typical for children in Ohio, could get more education. Custer worked for the Reeds to earn his room and board while he attended Alfred Stebbins' Young Men's Academy, which was cheaper than the high schools in Ohio yet promised to prepare students for any college in the United States.[14]

Custer grew very close to Ann and referred to her as his second mother. He proved to be a reliable babysitter but an indifferent student, who got top marks without trying too hard. He was more interested in the arts than the sciences, reading novels about knights and soldiers such as *Ivanhoe* and *Charles O'Malley, The Irish Dragoon*, which he hid behind his geography text during lessons. O'Malley, who was a rascally cavalryman serving during the Napoleonic Wars, was a logical hero for Custer because Monroe was the site of a battle during the War of 1812, an event within living memory and which had occurred at about the same time as O'Malley's adventures. O'Malley's fictional experiences were like those of the Invincibles—military service was fun, theatrical, and patriotic.

John Barry, who attended Stebbins' Academy with Custer and served with him during the Civil War, said Custer had a keen sense of humor and a tender heart but was also impulsive and craved adventure. One time, they were both unprepared for a recitation they had to give before a special visitors' day, where student achievements were demonstrated for the guests.[15] An hour before their presentations, Custer asked Barry if he was ready. Barry was not. How did Custer feel about his speech? "Badly, horrible," Custer said. "But I think I see a way out." Custer cooked up a plan that he and Barry would walk out of school with the large grammar class when it was dismissed and simply be gone when the instructor called on them to give their speeches in the next period. The infuriated Stebbins suspended them for the rest of the term, but Custer said he didn't care because the fishing was good that time of year.[16]

The pranks were part of Custer's nature, but they belied the ambition within. Custer's family had sent him to Stebbins' Academy because they wanted big things for him, and he wanted the same for himself. He decided to become a teacher. In the 1850s, education was a career that, if not necessarily high-paying, promised a certain prestige. American fiction at the time portrayed teachers as civilizers—a common trope was the young schoolmaster coming to a rural area and having to face down the bullies who resisted education. The schoolmaster was a force for morality, fighting the ignorance and vice common to the frontier.[17]

In his unfinished memoirs, Custer never wrote about his motivation for a career in education, but the early history of Ohio provides a clue. Admitted to the Union in 1803, Ohio was a young, rapidly growing state during Custer's youth, going from a population of 45,000 in 1800 to 1.52 million in 1840 and 1.98 million a decade later.[18] The early settlers, like Emanuel, tended to be patriotic believers in the greatness of America. As descendants of the Revolutionary War, they believed that power should come from the people, not top-down from a monarchy, so the people had to be educated and be loyal to each other, not to a king. Public culture, including schools and newspapers, would help people overcome their natural instincts to pursue their own interests at the expense of others. Freedom had obligations, such as the obligation to educate yourself, read newspapers, and engage in public conversation.

This desire for improvement helped make the Ohio of Custer's time intellectually vibrant. "By the 1830s, nearly every village had at least a handful of residents who made reading and writing a major part of their lives," wrote historian Andrew Cayton. "Men and women were scribbling furiously in diaries and journals, reading newspapers and magazines, listening to sermons and public lectures, composing poems and short stories, painting and designing, and attending public meetings and parties. Romantic and sentimental, they emphasized emotion as much as reason, feelings as much as logic. Describing rivers and forests, lamenting the passing of Indians, detailing the deaths of children, cataloguing the vagaries of love, they were often melodramatic." Such creative work was a way of self-improvement, and the conversation was about how the world worked: the rules of existence.[19]

For Custer, the profession of teaching was a way to enter this intellectual life. He would be a learned man carrying out the patriotic duty of educating the populace. Custer didn't keep a diary of his teaching career, but John Roberts, a schoolmaster in Madison County, Ohio, about 160 miles from New Rumley, chronicled his own experiences, which no doubt were similar to those of Custer. Roberts considered teaching to be a privilege and one of the highest callings. "Let the old despots of Urope [sic] tremble in their seats," he wrote, "for the sons of enlightened America will scatter the mists of ignorance from the face of the habitable globe. [Czar] Nicholas may look out if America takes him into hand & uses not cannons but the schoolmaster, & his pen will come down upon their old antiquated notions & dispel them like the sun does the morning fogs of July."[20]

Roberts also wrote for the local newspaper, which he said was another schoolhouse because it enlightened the public and promoted democracy. Roberts believed that a free press and free schools were essential to democracy, and the party most committed to this idea was the Democratic party.[21] It was a philosophy shared by most Ohio Democrats; certainly, it was the philosophy Emanuel tried to pass on to his children.

Custer absorbed that lesson, but he struggled against his impulse to show off, to perform, to be one of the ignorant ones who didn't care about education. He was one of those students who made life hard for the schoolmaster, disrupting class through humor, pranks, and simply lack of effort. The little boy who got attention at the militia meetings later helped lock his teacher out of the one-room schoolhouse he attended.[22] But the ambitious side of Custer wanted to be among the favored few who would get an education and in turn teach others, filling an important role in a glorious new nation. A teacher would also be doing creative work with his mind, studying a variety of topics and preparing lessons. At the same time, a teacher would have fun, performing before the students and roughhousing with them in much the same way Emanuel did with his rambunctious tribe. Teaching would be a perfect fit for a gregarious, ambitious young man like Custer.

A career in education in Ohio in the 1850s was fairly simple to establish. Ohio had a tradition of local autonomy for public schools, although quality varied from community to community. The Ohio school law of 1849 institutionalized the practice of boards of education to run local districts supported by property taxes.[23] Most school districts required only a certificate from a county examining board, which was awarded after completion of a written test.[24] In 1855, Custer enrolled in the new McNeely Normal School in the village of Hopedale, which is only about twelve miles from New Rumley. The school was started by Cyrus McNeely, the founder of the village, which he had named Hopedale because he had hopes for the school he had established. He donated ten acres of his land for the school, which was to be a teacher training institute—normal schools teach "norms" or standards.[25] The local newspaper praised the faculty and compared the school's purpose to that of West Point: "Our best and most accomplished military men are those who serve a regular term at an institution, where they are taught both the duties of the soldier and the officer. So it is with the young lady and gentleman who graduate at a Normal School. There they are taught fully the duties of the scholar and the teacher.— And with the present able crop of instructors at the McNeely Normal School, no better institution can be found in the country to impart this useful knowledge than the excellent one at Hopedale."[26]

Custer lived in a boarding house with other students, both male and female, while he studied how to teach and also learned more about the subjects he would be teaching his students.[27] In effect, Custer was going to a coeducational college.

He took his studies seriously judging by his seventy-seven-page notebook, which included carefully copied notes with some drawings and snatches of poetry like the one about ambition. Custer made the notebook his own by writing his last name in large script on the cover with a dramatic curl of the "C" stretching down the page and doubling the size of the letter.

Custer filled the inside of his notebook with detailed lessons about how to secure and hold the attention of students by using the "eye, ear and feelings." For example, the teacher could use his appearance and gestures to capture the students' eyes. The teacher, Custer noted, captured the ear of the students by using a variety of tones, and he should focus on the quality and quantity of his voice—not just being loud, but also speaking plaining and briefly. Custer, who even as an adult tended to stammer and speak rapidly when he got excited, wrote a note to himself to "study to improve this." Custer noted that a teacher should use his feelings to get the students' attention by emphasizing "sympathy, cheerfulness and goodness," the last defined by "kindness, gentleness, generosity and zeal for the right."[28]

Custer also took detailed notes on how to get students to conduct good recitations—the very assignment he skipped out on when he was a boy at Stebbins' Academy. According to Custer's notebook, a teacher should teach recitation in three stages: leading the student, accompanying the student, and finally letting the student do the recitation completely on his own. The best recitations, Custer learned, began with "thrilling incidents and facts," questions and answers, or "vivid descriptions of animals and persons." The teachers were also supposed to work on how students delivered the recitation, focusing on their posture, loudness, and clarity.[29]

Custer's lessons on history, politics, and society encouraged a reverence for the United States and its people. They reinforced what he had learned at home and provided what at the time was considered the main purpose of education: to create good citizens. In an editorial the *Cadiz Sentinel* argued that both the head and heart should be educated: "The highest objects of a good education are to reverence and obey God, and to love and serve mankind: everything that helps in attaining these objects is of great value, and everything that hinders is comparatively worthless. When wisdom reigns in the head, and love in the heart, the hand is ever ready to do good: peace smiles around, and sin and sorrow are almost unknown."[30]

Any society, Custer learned at McNeely, passed into various stages— "savage, barbarous, half civilized, civilized and enlightened," and the

United States had achieved the latter stages. Custer's notes listed the greatest achievers in various fields, and all of them were Americans. The greatest philosopher was Benjamin Franklin, the greatest lexicographer was Noah Webster, the greatest ornithologist was James Audubon, and the world's greatest inventors were Samuel Morse, Eli Whitney, and Robert Fulton. "The greatest man, take him all in all, of the last hundred years—George Washington an American," Custer wrote carefully in his notebook.[31]

Custer's detailed notes showed he was enthusiastic about his role as a teacher in contributing to the civilizing force of America. When he was working on his lessons, the fun-loving Custer could be violently serious. Once, when Custer and another student attended a spelling bee at a nearby school, a youth who had some disagreement with Custer stood at the window, making faces. Custer punched the boy right through the glass. He cut his hand, but he demonstrated that he would not let anyone interfere with his work.[32]

Custer wouldn't put up with interruptions from his roommates, either. One night Custer was in the loft trying to sleep, but his roommate was entertaining some girls, and they were making too much noise. Custer stuck his bare legs through the floor opening, pretending he was going to come down undressed. The girls ran out in a panic, and Custer was able to get his sleep.[33] Another roommate went to bed too early for Custer's tastes. In mid-winter he filled the roommate's boots with water and set them outside. When the roommate got up, he found them on the porch, frozen stiff to the tops.[34] On the one hand, these were boyish pranks, but on the other hand they were a way Custer asserted leadership and focused on the task at hand. In his room, things were done his way.

Custer might have chased his roommates' girlfriends out of the house, but he did plenty of his own chasing of girls when it suited him. Custer and a friend named Joe Dickerson arranged a sleigh ride one winter for the local girls, with straw and buffalo robes making a warm nest in the wagon. Custer kept urging Dickerson to pick up one more girl until Dickerson was forced out of the wagon and onto one of the horses. Dickerson tried to get even by racing around a sharp turn, which knocked the sleigh into a snowbank with a pile of girls and Custer underneath the robes. Custer took a long time getting out from under the pile, and Dickerson realized he had been played by his friend.[35] Like the way he handled his schoolwork, Custer would not take interference in his dating. While Custer was escorting a young lady around Hopedale, another student knocked Custer's hat off. Custer immediately thrashed the student with his umbrella.[36]

As an attractive and outgoing youth, Custer had no trouble getting dates. He had several girlfriends and was having such a good time that he regretted leaving McNeely when he completed the course of study in 1856. But he had earned certificates in a couple of different school districts, and it was time to start his professional career. Custer wanted to work in a school near his home, but the superintendent thought that Custer, as a not fully grown sixteen-year-old, was too small to handle the large farm boys in the one-room schoolhouse. Some of the "schoolboys" were eighteen, close to two hundred pounds, and hardened by field work.[37] The superintendent was right about Custer's size but didn't recognize his determination to succeed, as soon became evident.

Custer quickly learned teaching would not be easy, and he fell victim to some of the same pranks he had pulled on his own teachers. A Christmas tradition at the time called for students to lock their teacher out of the school until he gave them treats. John Roberts, the Madison County teacher, had heard about such incidents at other area schools, and he gave his charges two pounds of candy and one pound of almonds one New Years' Day to avoid any trouble. During Custer's first Christmas of teaching, some of the boys went in the schoolhouse after he left and stayed all night, intending to keep the young teacher out of the school the next day. When they went outside in the morning to get wood for the stove, they found Custer waiting and he slipped inside the school. The older boys wrestled Custer outside and locked the door. Custer didn't give in but instead got the school directors to come reopen the building.[38]

Discipline was the most difficult job for the young teacher on the frontier. Roberts found that it was hard to strike a balance between being too lax and being too strict. Although the older students were sometimes bigger than the teachers, and could be a physical threat, the little boys were the hardest to deal with. "It takes a great deal of patience & forbearance to govern a lot of little chaps," Roberts wrote in his diary. "I would rather undertake a large regiment of men than a large school of five-year-old schoolboys. They so soon forget your admonitions. Still, I am very fond of the business and do not complain of it as a nuisance but rather like it, as it puts a man to working his wits sometimes and stirs him up and makes him lively. . . ."[39]

Custer, too, enjoyed the creative challenge of matching wits with his charges. His lessons at McNeely included school "governance," which was the vernacular of the time for managing the classroom. Custer dutifully wrote in his notebook that the purpose of school government was to reform the offender, protect the school, and vindicate authority. The teacher accomplished this by "rewarding the good, punishing the bad, and deterring others from vice."[40] Rather than focus on the punishment of miscreants, Custer's artistic side preferred to control by entertaining and rewarding his charges. For students who were exceptional, he gave out elaborately printed awards that looked like a cross between a diploma and a stock certificate with the heading "Reward of Merit" made out to the pupil and signed by himself. He played the accordion to get them going in the morning and roughhoused with the young boys. He had such fun that his enthusiasm was contagious. One girl recalled that "When he was present, he was so jovial and full of life that everyone enjoyed themselves."[41]

Custer was enjoying himself in general with the typical life of a young man in frontier Ohio, which included a lot of drinking and carousing. Roberts's diary makes frequent mentions of the drunkenness and parties among young people, even during religious revivals, which he noted sometimes featured more whiskey than prayer. Roberts confessed that he was glad he had a weak stomach or else he might have succumbed to the evils of drink. Roberts for a time was worried he had gotten a girl pregnant and had thus ruined his career. Unwanted pregnancies, no doubt fueled by the heavy drinking, were frequent in Ohio in the 1850s, with the couples sometimes marrying and other times the father leaving town.[42]

Custer dabbled in both drinking and fornicating. At one time he was going to a Methodist meeting where he was supposed to talk about temperance. He stopped at a friend's, and their little girl caught a whiff of his breath and said sarcastically that he smelled like temperance. Like the punchline of an old joke, Custer was also having a good time with a farmer's daughter, in this case his landlord's pride and joy, Mary Jane (Molly) Holland. While he was teaching, Custer was boarding with a wealthy farmer named Alexander Holland, whose home was only about a hundred yards from the schoolhouse. After a time, Holland came to know of Custer's reputation and didn't want him dating his daughter. In addition to the drinking, Holland didn't approve of Custer because he was two years younger than Mary and was the son of a noisy, hardcore Democrat. He told Custer that he had to find other lodgings and was no longer welcome at the Holland farm.[43]

Custer, however, was not someone who took "no" for an answer, especially when he was in love. He and Molly kept up their affair by meeting at neutral sites and through an explicit correspondence. The forbidden aspect of the intense relationship sparked Custer's artistic nature. He wrote his love a poem about the agony of separation:

To Mary
I've seen and kissed that crimsoned lip
With honied smiles o'erflowing.
Enchanted watched the opening rose,
Upon thy soft cheek glowing.
Dear Mary, thy eyes may prove less blue,
The beauty fade tomorrow
But Oh, my heart can ne'er forget
Thy parting look of sorrow.[44]

The parting sorrows did not keep Custer from pursuing his career. In fact, he found quite a bit of joy in it, especially his first paycheck for $26, which he promptly took home and put in his mother's lap. He later wrote a heartfelt letter to his father telling him he appreciated all his parents had done for him; teaching him right from wrong and sacrificing so he could get an education. "I know but few if any boys are so blessed as I have been, by having such kind, self-sacrificing parents to train and guide them as I have. I know I might heap millions of dollars at your feet, and still the debt of gratitude would be undiminished."[45]

At around this time, Custer began setting his sights on West Point, but not necessarily to pursue a military career. It's true that Custer was steeped in American patriotism and Revolutionary War lore—he had a great-grandfather who served in the militia in Pennsylvania.[46] And his adopted hometown was the site of a famous War of 1812 battle called the River Raisin Massacre. But Custer's main exposure to the military was his father's militia unit, which emphasized the amateur and fun side of soldiering and not the martial aspects of the profession.

Custer instead was considering a teaching career beyond one-room schoolhouses, perhaps at a university, or else entering other fields such as law and business. If he couldn't get admitted to West Point, he planned to head East and try to work his way through one of the great universities. In antebellum America, there were no government grants or loans to help poor students. West Point, however, provided a free education, the only real option for the son of a blacksmith teaching in a rural district. Custer wrote his sister Ann that he wanted to go to West Point and that although his mother was opposed, his father was in favor of it. "I think it is the best place that I could go," Custer wrote. "I will get $28 per month for five years and be getting a good education at the same time and when I get out I will get 5 years pay ahead and besides what I get while I am there but if I go there I expect to go in the Army when I am through." He added that another man from Cadiz went to West Point and was "worth upwards of two hundred thousand dollars now which he had made in the Army." Custer did not explain how an army officer could make so much money, but his naiveté is understandable. The military academy provided a wonderful education for its graduates, who played an outsized role in American institutions, particularly education. By 1879, more than 140 of Custer's fellow graduates would be college professors. Many wrote textbooks or were college presidents. In 1879, a list of West Point alumni included ninety-one authors, eighteen clergymen, and three artists.[47]

In order to join that elite Corps of Cadets, Custer would need an appointment from his local congressman, John A. Bingham, a Republican. Since Custer was the son of a vocal Democrat, the appointment seemed like a long shot. Custer, however, was more tolerant of other ideas than his father was. His work for the public schools exposed him to people of different beliefs and the importance of keeping his own views in check when necessary. In the classroom, he was honest with his students, talking about his own politics but not to the point of intimidating them from expressing their own. When the Democrat

Custer assigned an essay about Democratic president James Buchanan, one girl wrote a critical piece about him called "10 Cent Jimmy," which was a popular Republican insult of Buchanan after he had made the gaffe of claiming 10 cents was a fair wage for manual laborers. Custer didn't mark her down for her challenge of his opinion.[48]

Custer's plan for convincing Bingham to appoint him was to use the same disarming honesty. His first letter to the congressman respectfully asked him to send information about the appointment process if he could find time to write him back. Bingham responded that the appointment had already been made and another man was in line for the next slot, but he did enclose the qualifications for the academy. Custer, never to be deterred from his goals, thanked Bingham, laid out his own qualifications and said he wanted the appointment if the other boy dropped out. In the meantime, Custer participated in a Republican rally in Cadiz so he could shake Bingham's hand.

Custer's public relations tactics worked. When the next year came around for the appointments, Custer received a form letter from Jefferson Davis, the secretary of war, admitting him to West Point. Some historians suggest Bingham was influenced by Alexander Holland, who was a prominent local Republican and likely saw the appointment as a way of separating Custer from his daughter Mary. But in a speech at the Cadiz Methodist church, Bingham said Custer was one of the most honorable and truthful men he had ever met. Writing in his memoirs years later, Bingham recalled he had been impressed by Custer's honesty, particularly because he told him he was a Democrat so there would be no misunderstanding.[49] The appointment made local news. The *Cadiz Sentinel* reported that "Mr. C. is a young man of more than ordinary ability, and we believe that he will make a creditable military officer."[50]

Although Custer's mother was still against him going to the military academy, Custer's father was proud. Emanuel sold his farm and gave Custer the $200 down-payment for his expenses at the academy.[51] But it was with a mix of pride and fear that he sent his oldest son off to become a professional soldier and all the uncertainty that career meant. Almost a decade later, after four years of college and about an equal amount of time in the Civil War, Emanuel admitted to his son how worried he was. In a letter written in the plain style of a blacksmith,

Emanuel effusively praised George, who had been an indifferent churchgoer, for his recent profession of Christianity. Emanuel wrote that he had "prayed daily yes I may say hourly only when I have been a sleep for you ever since you went to west point and Bless the Lord I have not prayed in vain."[52]

Custer needed all the prayers he could get just to stay in the academy. Custer's record featured a legendary acquisition of "demerits," which were infractions against the rules, and he hovered at the bottom of the academic rankings. The academy dismissed any cadet with more than one hundred demerits in a six-month period. Custer earned ninety-four in one period and ninety-eight in another. He finished with 812—dramatically close to the 835 that mandated dismissal. Custer's academy record of demerits is an incredible list of foolishness, sloppiness, arrogance, and a mindless challenge to rules apparently for no other reason than to fight authority. In other words, he was the sort of fun-loving college student recognizable on campuses today. Even more, he was a student with an artistic spirit who rebelled against conformity. How else to explain a list of offenses that included such easily avoidable items as buttoning his coat, talking in ranks, and "hair out of uniform"?[53]

Custer also entered West Point in 1857 with a Jacksonian militia attitude toward the military. His greatest military heroes, Washington and Jackson, were not professional soldiers, but rather citizen soldiers who had led largely volunteer armies, even if they did have a cadre of professional soldiers among their troops. Many West Point graduates didn't stay long in the military but used it as ticket to advancement. Jefferson Davis, who had signed Custer's admittance letter, was a West Point graduate who had left the military to become a planter and a politician. And Custer's own experience with the military growing up had been the New Rumley Invincibles and their carousing musters. Why shouldn't the drills at West Point be punctuated with drunken pranks and camaraderie?

They certainly were for Custer. One of his favorite scams was to ride his horse so slowly on marches outside the campus that he would fall well to the rear and out of sight of the commander. He would then water his horse at the trough in front of the local hotel and water himself inside at the bar, returning to the column before the march ended.[54] He also frequently slipped off the post to Benny Havens, a nearby tavern immortalized in song by the cadets.

One of Custer's classmates, Peter Michie, who later became a brigadier general, recalled that Custer was in trouble so often that he was the usual suspect when anything bad happened. "He never saw the adjutant in full uniform that he did not suspect that he was the object of his search for being placed in arrest, and then to have five minutes more freedom he would cut and run for it. . . . He had more fun, gave his friends more anxiety, walked more tours of extra guard, and came nearer being dismissed more often than any other cadet I have ever known."[55]

And Custer had a lot of friends because he was so much fun to be around. His antics kept his classmates constantly amused. Once he asked the Spanish instructor to translate "class dismissed." The professor did so, and Custer led the class out of the room. When a cadet from Indiana named Jasper Myers showed up for his first day with a bushy beard, Custer took one look at him and told him to go back home and send his son, as the government wanted the boy to have the appointment, not the old man.[56]

Another prank solved a noisy problem for the cadet. A lieutenant kept a rooster that strutted below the cadets' barrack windows. Its crowing annoyed the cadets, but only Custer acted. He snuck out the window one night and soon had the bird boiling over the gas burner in his room. "West Point has had many a character to deal with," wrote Morris Schaff, one of Custer's classmates, when recalling the rooster feast years later. "But it may be a question whether it ever had a cadet so exuberant, one who cared so little for its serious attempts to elevate and burnish, or one on whom its tactical officers kept their eyes so constantly and unsympathetically searching as upon Custer. And yet how we all loved him; and to what a height he rose!"[57]

Schaff acknowledged that Custer, as was the norm at the academy, engaged in the hazing of younger cadets. For Custer it was a way to have fun rather than a means of tormenting the freshmen. Schaff gave as an example that a stodgy country boy from Maine had a huge silver pocket watch. Custer, John "Gimlet" Lea, and some of their pals routinely ordered the cadet to take it out and answer all kinds of ridiculous questions about it. They made him check its time against the academy sun dial. When it didn't match the sun dial, they threatened to report him for carrying a timepiece that discredited the official army time. "I can see the crowd around him," Schaff wrote. "And more mischievous countenances never twinkled in a light-hearted group."[58]

Custer's sense of humor was part of his natural charisma. He was a good-looking youth, with reddish-blonde hair that earned him the nickname "Fanny" because it looked feminine, and "Cinnamon" after the hair product he used. Yet the slight schoolteacher had grown into a powerful and athletic young man, nearly six feet tall. The cadets recognized Custer as the strongest man in his class; he could jump to a standing position from lying down, and he made the highest horseback jump recorded at the academy except for U. S. Grant.[59]

Such skills were what counted among his peers, not grades. Money or family background didn't matter either. Custer went to school with men from some of the leading families in America, such as Washington, Du Pont, Vanderbilt, and Breckinridge. Schaff wrote that any cadet who tried to use his social standing would have been scorned by the entire corps. "It was a pure, self-respecting democracy."[60]

The cadets instead judged each other on who they could trust. "Men were rated according to those qualities that youth worships as ideals," Michie recalled. "The grade of good-fellowship was fixed by the unwritten laws of honor, charity, and all that is summed in the word manliness. Though ability in studies and aptitude for the enforced military exercises were the official means of grading the young men in class rank, he who was fearless, outspoken, generous, and self-sacrificing became the leader among his fellows."[61]

Custer was not a leader in academics, and he was at a disadvantage when competing with boys from the East, where the schools were better. Most of the cadets who flunked out were from the South and West, like Custer. (Ohio was considered the West at that time.) The curriculum was astoundingly rigorous, especially when compared to the remedial classes, exam reviews, and multiple-choice tests for college students in twenty-first-century America. Henry A. Du Pont, who had attended the University of Pennsylvania before going to West Point, thought the academy was twice as tough as his old school, and with good reason. West Point students were expected to be ready every day to go to the front of the class and thoroughly discuss any part of the lesson. Final exams were a terror. Questions could be over any part of the class that semester and could be quite detailed. For example, a question for a natural philosophy class in 1855 required the student to draw a cross section of the human eye and explain all the parts and how they worked to produce vision. In 1858 Custer wrote home in relief that he had passed his examinations when so many others had flunked out. "My class which numbered over 100 when we entered in June is now reduced to 69. This shows that if a person wants to get along here he has to study hard." It was an understatement. While preparing for final exams in 1861, he wrote home that he was studying constantly. "I and others only average about four hours' sleep in the twenty-four. I work until one at night, and get up at five. All my classmates are becoming pale and thin. I lost five pounds already!"[62]

The academy's philosophy intentionally fostered competition with a weekly posting of grades and regular ranking of cadets based on grades and demerits. For Custer, however, the ranking meant little. He quickly learned after entering the academy and sizing up the competition that he could not compete academically for one of the top spots in his class. Michie wrote that Custer in fact wittingly aimed for the bottom ranking because it was a form of distinction that he could achieve. If so, Custer's plan fit his artistic temperament to find some way to get the spotlight. In any case, Custer, like many students then and now, did what was necessary to get by while enjoying himself. "I would not leave this place for any amount of money, for I would rather have a good education and no money than a fortune and be ignorant," Custer wrote Ann.[63]

One thing the artistic Custer really enjoyed was writing. He wrote many letters to family and friends when he moved out to attend McNeely, but at West Point he began to write obsessively, violating academy rule rules to stay up late, hiding a candle under his blanket to write letters that could stretch for dozens of pages. In one eight-page letter to a friend, Custer wrote about life at West Point and then switched topics by writing that he would say a few words about politics. He wrote for two and half more pages. It was a habit he would maintain for the rest of his life, writing on trains, in hotel rooms, and regularly in the field during his campaigns. Custer developed a fast but wordy style that he would continue to struggle with when he started to write professionally for newspapers and magazines, and editors would ask him to cut back on his prose. Custer couldn't help himself. As biographer Stephen Ambrose noted, writing was an integral part of his character, and he became addicted to it while at West Point.[64]

Despite his love of writing, Custer's grades in English were only average, like most of his school record. The academy considered mathematics the most important subject because it was the foundation of engineering, and Custer himself later said English was one of the most useless subjects he studied. Nevertheless, the curriculum required students to write essays, many on moral or ethical issues as West Point strove to develop character and graduate Christian gentlemen. As he had at Stebbins, Custer continued to read adventure novels, including the *Leatherstocking Tales* by James Fenimore Cooper. It inspired a romantic notion of the Indian, a contradiction to the tales of the brutal massacre of American prisoners by Indians at the River Raisin battle in Monroe—a story Custer had heard often as a boy. But Custer the college student, with his growing artistic sensibility, could empathize with the plight of the Indian, which he wrote about in a melodramatic essay called "The Red Man." According to Custer, the Indians had lived an idyllic life before civilization came. "When we first beheld the red man; we beheld him in his home, the home of peace and plenty, the home of nature. Sorrows [*sic*] furrowed lines were unknown on his dauntless brow." The woodsman and hunter chased him out of his ancestral home. Now he lived in caves, frightened and alone in his misery. "We behold him now on the verge of extinction, standing on his last foothold, clutching his bloodstained rifle, resolved to die amidst the horrors of slaughter, and soon he will be talked of as a noble race who once existed but have now passed away." Custer was so proud of the essay he mailed it home.[65]

His studies were distracted by thoughts of family. He never tired of talking to the cadets about his old home, and he subscribed to the *Cadiz Sentinel*, which allowed him to keep up with his father's political activities and other news of the area. Privately, he worried about his family—it would be a concern that would trouble him the rest of his life. Once he was admitted to West Point, it was clear that Custer was the hope of the family, and he felt that responsibility keenly. After two years at the academy, he got his first furlough home and persuaded his parents to move to Monroe, where they rented a house. A year later, however, they moved to Tontogony, Ohio, near Toledo, apparently because his father's horse was stolen in Monroe. Custer continued to fret about his parents, and those worries distracted him at West Point. He wrote to Ann and her husband that "I would feel much more contented and could attend to my studies much better because I am continually thinking of them and always have an anxiety and fear that they will not be able to buy a farm where they can get along comfortably." (In 1863, Custer finally persuaded them to move back to Monroe after he told them he would pay to send his little sister Margaret to the Boyd Seminary, a prominent school for young women in Monroe.[66])

But the problems of the Custer family paled next to the situation in the country, which seemed to be plunging toward civil war. After Lincoln's election, Southern states started seceding, and Southern cadets started resigning from West Point. In response to the crisis, President Buchanan ordered the cadets to the chapel on February 22, 1861, to honor Washington's Birthday by hearing a reading of his Farewell Address, which warned against the dangers of sectional jealousy and urged the preservation of the national union. After the morning ceremony, cadets had the day off. In the evening, as was customary, the band played the evening tattoo. Every window in the cadet barracks was lit, but the cadets were to remain quiet. When the band played the "Star Spangled Banner," Schaff was amazed to see Custer lead a thunderous cheer of the Northern cadets for the patriotic song. The band then played "Dixie," and Thomas Rosser, a Southern cadet, led his side in an equally loud cheer. Custer, in his element as an entertainer, then led a cheer for the Stars and Stripes, and the Southerners answered as the evening took on the spirit of a pep rally. "Ah, it was a great night," Schaff recalled.[67]

As Lincoln's inauguration grew near, disputes between Northern and Southern cadets became frequent and threatening. Just before the inauguration, some cadets were reading aloud a *New York Herald* story that quoted Ben Wade, a radical Republican senator from Ohio known for his abolitionist views. A Southern cadet sneered that they should not listen to Wade. The Ohioan Schaff, even though he was a Democrat,

resented the insult to his senator. Angry words were exchanged, and
Schaff feared he would be beaten by the Southerner, who was much
bigger and had a violent reputation. When Custer heard about the
incident, he told Schaff, "If he lays a hand on you, Morris, we'll maul
the earth with him."[68]

Custer had many friends, and as a Democrat, he was no abolitionist.
But in the looming secession crisis he stood with the North in favor of
preserving the Union. "In case of war, I shall serve my country according to the oath I took," Custer wrote his sister on April 10, 1861.[69] Two
days later the South fired on Fort Sumter.

The normal course of study at West Point was five years, but because
of the war, Custer's class was pushed through in four. He studied like
never before and graduated with his class on June 24, 1861. Watching
the class clown get his diploma stood out for Michie: "When Custer,
the foot man [i.e., lowest-ranked man] of his class, stood before the
superintendent to receive his diploma, the latter looked at him steadily
for a moment, no doubt immensely relieved that his task of disciplin-
ing this spirited youth was happily ended; while Custer, on the other
hand, was equally happy, as with a very low and apparently humble
bow he received the coveted prize for which he had endured four years
of precarious existence."[70]

The *Cadiz Sentinel* claimed Custer graduated "with the highest honors of his class."[71] Most likely it was Emanuel Custer, whom the Democratic paper often mentioned as "our old friend," who gave the editor
the news with the exaggeration of a proud father. Bragging, after all,
was "the motto of everyone" and viewed as the way to success on the
Ohio frontier, according to schoolteacher diarist Roberts.[72] And coming from his background and with his artistic temperament adjusting
to a military culture, graduating at all was for George Custer indeed
a high achievement. Now he would be tested in ways neither he nor
his proud father could imagine. This would be no drunken militia
muster.

The former schoolteacher Custer claimed he was ready, writing with
bravado to his sister that he would not come home for a furlough before
he headed to the front. "It is my duty to take whatever position they
assign me," he wrote with the heroic drama that characterized much of

his writing. "It is useless to hope the coming struggle will be bloodless or of short duration. Much blood will be spilled and thousands of lives lost. If it is to be my lot to fall in the service of my country and my country's rights I will have no regrets."[73]

While awaiting assignment, Custer as a new second lieutenant had some duties at West Point. A few weeks after graduation, Custer was acting as officer of the guard, which meant he was responsible for discipline and supervising cadets. He heard a disturbance among some tents and found two cadets fighting while a crowd gathered. Instead of obeying his duty to stop the fight and report the cadets, Custer responded with his artistic propensity to make everything a show. He yelled, "Stand back boys; let's have a fair fight!" The crowd, however, began to melt away. Custer was intensely watching the fight and didn't notice that two officers, lieutenants William B. Hazen and W. E. Merrill, were approaching. Hazen asked, "Why did you not suppress the riot which occurred here a few minutes ago?" Taken by surprise and confused by the accusation that the fight was a riot, Custer was unusually speechless. Hazen ordered him to his tent under arrest. A few hours later, his class received its list of orders for duty. Custer's name was not on it.[74]

While he was awaiting court-martial, Custer asked to see his successor as officer of the guard, Milton B. Adams, and warned him to study the academy regulations like a prayer book to avoid what happened to him. Too late, Custer realized that his dramatic side that favored showmanship had betrayed the part of him that focused on duty.[75]

Custer was charged with failing "to suppress a riot or disturbance." Custer pled guilty but in his appeal argued that such scuffles were common and did not injure the participants. The best way to solve such disagreements and keep them from festering was to have a fair fight. He called as his witnesses the two cadets who were fighting to prove that neither was injured.[76]

With the country's pressing need for trained officers to fight in the looming war, it would have been incredible if the government had booted Custer from the army for enjoying a good fight when he had just graduated in an accelerated program designed to create more officers. The court on July 16 slapped Custer's wrist, sentencing him to be "reprimanded in orders." It explained the lenient sentence was due to

Custer's defense and his "general good conduct testified by Lieutenant [William B.] Hazen, his immediate commander."[77] The trial had taken hardly more time than the fight that generated it. After it was over, Custer was given his orders to report to Washington immediately.[78]

Custer had entered the academy in peacetime as a frontier-schooled youth who had never traveled outside his region. He had escaped that provincial background—the first in his family to do so—and graduated from the toughest college in the country, and he did it while competing against boys who had more advantages in education, wealth, and connections than he did.

Custer had demonstrated a talent for politics by persuading a Republican to appoint a dyed-in-the-wool Democrat to West Point in an era when those appointments were basically spoils for a congressman to use for the members of his own party. He had shown he could get along with people from a variety of backgrounds, and he had used his sense of humor and theatricality to do it. He had developed a lifelong habit of writing, which he had used to carry on a passionate affair with a girl. The affair had ended, but for the romantic Custer, it was part of his journey and the first example of his creative writing—poetry. He demonstrated his showmanship with his pranks at West Point, gaining friends and establishing a reputation for entertaining people.

Custer had entered West Point for advancement, not necessarily for a martial career. He had found much to like—the uniforms, the sense of belonging to something bigger than himself, the mental and physical challenges. However, he never lost the sense of fun and the Jacksonian contempt for rules that he had learned at the musters of the New Rumley Invincibles. It would take the cauldron of combat service to impress the necessity of discipline on Custer and the thousands of citizen soldiers soon to enter the military.

Custer was twenty-one when he graduated. A military career was still not a given. In fact, an argument could be made for the opposite. Many of the men who would enter the service for both North and South had graduated from West Point but entered civilian life after varied success in the army. Ulysses Grant had wound up working at his father's tannery as a last resort after failing in several jobs. George B. McClellan was a railroad executive. William T. Sherman and Thomas

Jackson (who would become Stonewall Jackson in the war) were college educators. All of them returned to the military because of the war.

But instead of serving in the army for a few years and using his degree for a springboard to another profession, fate decreed that Custer would graduate at the start of what would become his country's bloodiest war. He was thrust onto the biggest stage of his era.

CHAPTER TWO

Staff Officer

Learning the Profession

The legend of Custer began with a plunge into a muddy river. It was May 22, 1862, and Custer had been at war for about a year. He had seen combat, but most of his experience so far had been as an aide for generals who used the junior officer for a variety of tasks. Custer was up for any assignment that would bring him the attention his artistic nature craved. He had even flown in an observation balloon to take notes about Southern troop movements as the Union army invaded Virginia to try to capture the rebel capital of Richmond.

On this day, Brig. Gen. John Barnard, the Army of the Potomac's chief engineer, had grabbed Custer to help him examine the Chickahominy River for a possible crossing place. Barnard, forty-seven, was a Mexican War veteran famous for constructing the defenses of Tampico and ensuring the security of the supply lines for the invading American army. After the Mexican War, he had served as superintendent of West Point from 1855 to 1856, just missing Custer. After the Civil War he would continue his engineering career and later cofound the U.S. National Academy of Sciences. But on that hot spring day in 1862, Barnard sat on his horse, considering the question of the depth of the Chickahominy, which was a problem for him to solve. Next to him was a junior officer that through the military grapevine Barnard likely knew was the goat of the class of 1861. The scholarly Barnard looked at Custer and said, "Jump in!"[1]

Another soldier might have thought Barnard was joking. Certainly that soldier would have looked at the water and wondered about cotton-mouths. If he had seen combat like Custer had, he would have looked at the treelined opposite bank and considered the odds that rebel pickets watching from the woods would snipe him. He might have taken the order to mean jump in with his horse.

Custer, however, said nothing but slid off his horse and waded into the river. He kept his left hand on his sword and with his right hand carried his pistol over his head as the water swirled up to his armpits. Custer kept wading until he reached the enemy bank. He had found a crossing, so Barnard called him back. But Custer had the spotlight, and he wasn't giving it up. He clambered up the other bank and disappeared into the woods. He only returned after he found the location of the enemy pickets.

When Barnard told George B. McClellan, the commander of the Army of the Potomac, about the reconnaissance, McClellan wanted to meet Custer. The army commander was an immaculately uniformed officer who placed much stock in appearances. Custer, his uniform caked with the mud of the Chickahominy, was embarrassed to be seen. But the dirty uniform was a costume of authenticity. McClellan thanked Custer for his performance and asked if there was anything he could do for him. "He seemed to attach no importance to what he had done, and desired nothing," McClellan recalled years later. But McClellan saw that Custer would get things done, and he offered him a promotion to captain and a job as aide-de-camp on his staff.[2]

Custer had authored a fantastic story. He did his duty—and more—and did it with panache. It was like a play; a junior officer attracts the attention of the army commander with his daredevil actions. Who could resist repeating such a tale? Not the press, which made Custer a minor celebrity. Alfred Waud, the combat artist for *Harper's Weekly*, sketched a determined Custer wading across the river while the general sits on his horse, watching from the safety of shore. Waud could spot a star in the making. He would sketch Custer frequently throughout the war, and he was the only journalist Custer took with him on a raid behind rebel lines in 1864. Major newspapers like the *New York Herald* picked up the story and embellished it, placing McClellan at the scene. "He deliberately plunged into the stream at New Bridge," the

Herald reported, "and in the face of the rebel sharpshooters waded to the other side, establishing the fact that the stream was fordable. The commanding General at once made him captain." Custer, who kept his subscription to the *Cadiz Sentinel*, could even read about himself in his hometown newspaper, which reported breathlessly that Custer was promoted for being the first Union soldier to cross the Chickahominy, "which he did *alone*, while the enemy's pickets lined the opposite shore and ours were a half a mile from this side."[3]

The episode also became the talk of the army. James Harrison Wilson, who knew Custer at West Point, recalled years later that he had heard Custer rode his horse into the river. In Wilson's version, McClellan was at the river and said he wished he knew how deep it was. Nobody in McClellan's retinue said a word. But Custer spurred his horse into the river and said, "I'll damn soon show how deep it is." He swam his horse to the far shore and back. He said, "That's how deep it is, General," and took his place in the back of the group.[4] As so often happens in life, the factual story is more interesting that the fictional versions. But in any telling of the story, Custer had an instinctual knack for performance, for taking center stage and holding it. He was in the right place at the right time—what came to be called Custer's Luck among his comrades in the army, some of whom were jealous of his success. But he always took advantage of the time and place in which he found himself. He thrust himself completely into the situation and made people notice him.

Custer had been doing that from the time he left West Point about a year earlier, barely escaping expulsion from the army. His court-martial proved to be a lucky break that allowed him to arrive in Washington just in time to be invited to carry dispatches from the commander of Union forces, Winfield Scott, to the front. Custer had taken the train from New York, where he stopped to get his picture taken and buy his lieutenant's outfit, including a saber, revolver, and spurs. Years later, when he started writing his memoirs, he still recalled the enthusiasm of the crowds, the people who offered lavish refreshments, and the kisses from women young and old. Custer realized he was part of something bigger than himself, that these strangers were counting on him and his comrades to defend the country.[5]

He arrived in Washington early in the morning and went to the hotel of his old West Point roommate, James Parker of Missouri.

Custer rousted Parker and was shocked to find he had left the service to join the Confederate army. The two boys had a lot in common. They were Westerners whose fathers had emigrated from slaveholding Eastern states—Emanuel Custer from Maryland and Parker's father from Virginia. They were big, physical kids who focused more on fun than studies, and both finished at the bottom end of the class. After hearing Parker's decision, Custer pondered that the two had lived, eaten, and struggled together every day for years at the academy. Now they would fight on opposite sides of the greatest war the country had ever known. Custer told him goodbye with a fondness based on their close friendship. He left quickly, as he wrote later, to "report for such duty as might be assigned me in the great work which was then dearest and uppermost in the mind of every loyal citizen of the country."[6]

Custer headed to the War Department, where he waited until 2 o'clock to report to the adjutant general's office for his orders. Before assigning Custer's orders, the officer in charge asked if he wanted to be presented to Scott. The commanding general was imposing in both his reputation and physical presence. Scott had entered the army in 1807 and had been promoted to general during the War of 1812 when he was only twenty-seven years old. He had led the American army to victory during the Mexican War and had been a general longer than McClellan had been alive. He had run for president in 1852, and despite losing big, he had remained a national hero.[7]

For junior officers like Custer, who had seen him only from a distance at West Point, the meticulous "Old Fuss and Feathers" was an awesome figure. It was like being asked to meet Washington or Napoleon. Custer was escorted to the room where Scott and several congressmen were seated around a table covered with maps and other military documents. The aide interrupted their conversation to introduce Custer and ask if Scott had some special orders to give him. Scott was seventy-five, but still a dominating presence—six foot five and about three hundred pounds: a big man in the twenty-first century, and a giant in Custer's time.[8]

"Well, my young friend, I am glad to welcome you to the service at this critical time," Scott said. "Our country has need of all her loyal sons in this emergency." He asked if Custer wanted to put his education to work training volunteers or going to the front. For the former schoolteacher, the training assignment might have been appealing, but Custer always wanted to be where the action was. He gave the right answer, requesting assignment to his cavalry unit at the front.

"A very commendable resolution, young man," Scott said. He told Custer to find a horse and return at 7 o'clock to take some dispatches to the army commander, General Irvin McDowell. "You're not afraid of a night ride, are you?" Scott asked. Who would not have been a little anxious about riding all night with dispatches from the commanding general to the man in charge of the first great battle of the war? Custer would never admit fear and lose such a grand opportunity. He took the assignment.

However, in Washington on the eve of the war's first major battle, a horse was almost impossible to find. Custer visited most of the major stables and had no luck. By chance he met an enlisted man who had been stationed at West Point but was now with McDowell's army. The soldier had been sent to Washington to bring an extra horse back to his unit. Custer could ride that extra horse. "Here was my opportunity, and I at once availed myself of it," Custer wrote later.

In a further stroke of Custer's Luck, the horse was Wellington, an animal Custer had ridden often at the academy. It made the ride to the front easier as the soldier regaled the excited Custer through the night with stories of the army's first skirmish two days earlier at Blackburn's Ford. They arrived about 3 in the morning, the roads around the army so filled with sleeping soldiers taking a break from their march that Custer had trouble riding around them. When they reached headquarters, Custer hoped to give the dispatches to McDowell, but a staff officer took them and then invited Custer to have breakfast.

"I was very hungry," Custer wrote later. "And rest would not have been unacceptable, but in my inexperience I partly imagined, particularly while in the presence of the white-haired officer who gave the invitation, that hunger and fatigue were conditions of feeling which a soldier, especially a young one, should not acknowledge." Custer declined breakfast for himself but let Wellington be fed. When another officer later offered Custer a breakfast of steak, cornbread, and coffee, he couldn't refuse again. It was a good thing, because he wouldn't eat for another day and a half. The battle of Bull Run would start soon, and Custer was about to get his first experience of combat.[9]

After Custer finished breakfast, he remounted and headed off to join his unit, Company G of the Second Cavalry. He arrived before dawn, making introductions with his fellow officers in the dark, with only the outlines of horses and riders visible in the early morning. They sat on their horses awaiting orders for their role in the battle.[10]

For many men, combat is a test of manhood, and they volunteer for service and look forward to war with excitement. Only the veterans approach the conflict with the fear born of knowing what combat is like. But as the prospect of combat gets closer, the new soldiers begin to get anxious. As the ultimate moment arrives, most men have a physical reaction—sweating, dry mouth, chattering teeth, or clenching jaw— not a few soil themselves. The typical soldier is afraid of two things— that he will be killed or maimed, and that he will be a coward in front of his comrades.[11]

What emotions did Custer feel? He did not provide graphic details in his memoir, preferring to make a funny story out of his experience. But he did hint at the fear and confusion he felt. For much of the battle, Custer's unit did not have a lot to do. Eventually, they were ordered to move forward to support an artillery battery. The rebels fired at the battery, and at Custer.

"I remember well the strange hissing and exceedingly vicious sound of the first cannon shot I heard as it whirled through the air," Custer recalled. "Of course I had often heard the sound made by cannon balls while passing through the air during my artillery practice at West Point, but a man listens with changed interest when the direction of the balls is toward instead of away from him. They seemed to utter a different language when fired in angry battle from that put forth in the tamer practice of drill."[12]

Rebel soldiers were moving forward to attack the battery. Custer's unit was ordered to the top of a hill to repel the attack, and he knew they would probably be told to charge. Custer wondered how he would react. He had never done anything more dangerous than jumping his horse over an obstacle in training. He had never used his sword on any- thing other than a dummy stuffed with bark. "It may be imagined that my mind was more or less given to anxious thoughts as we ascended the slope of the hill in front of us," Custer wrote later with consider- able understatement. "At the same time I realized that I was in front of a company of old and experienced soldiers, all of whom would have an eye upon their new lieutenant to see how he comported himself under fire." Riding next to him was another junior officer, Leicester Walker, who had not gone to West Point. He looked to Custer as an academy graduate for guidance.

Custer determined to act the part of the experienced soldier. When Walker asked him what weapon to use, Custer replied firmly, "The saber," because it is what he had always imagined would be used in a charge. He drew his sword from the scabbard. But as they rode their horses at a walk up the hill, he began to worry over his choice. He would have to get close to the enemy to use the saber. If he swung and missed, the rebel cavalrymen would likely kill him. Since this was his first battle, wouldn't it be better to use a pistol, which had six shots? He could start shooting before he had to get alongside his enemy. Custer sheathed his saber and pulled out his pistol. Walker, watching Custer, did likewise. They approached the crest of the hill. Custer continued his mental argument with himself. In the heat of battle, he might miss all six shots and then be in hand-to-hand combat with an empty gun against a rebel with a saber. Custer holstered his pistol and drew his saber. So did Walker. The comedy routine ended only when they reached the top of the hill and anticlimactically found the battery was safe. They returned to their original position without firing a shot or swinging a blade.[13]

The two inexperienced armies fought hard all day while Custer's unit waited in anxious tedium. Finally, reinforcements arrived for the rebel army and they broke the Union lines, sending them running in a panicked, humiliated mob, with many soldiers throwing away their weapons. Custer's unit, which had not broken, acted as a rearguard. A heavy rain added to the misery of the retreat, and the army made its way back to Washington in the night. When they reached camp, Custer was so exhausted that he stretched out under a tree and slept in the mud and rain for hours. He woke to the depressing reality that the Union had lost the first major battle of the war despite all its high expectations. It was, he wrote years later, the lowest point of the war that he could remember. Still his faith in the Union cause and ultimate victory was not shaken. His sense of duty would compel him forward.[14]

In the days after the battle, Custer sought out his Ohio patron, John A. Bingham. He showed up at Bingham's place without the usual custom of sending a card. Custer's filial relationship with Bingham did not require such formalities. Bingham recalled Custer was breathless with either excitement or embarrassment. The junior officer, although now a veteran, spoke hesitantly to Bingham. He started what seemed to be a rehearsed speech about Bull Run. Custer told the congressman he had tried to do his best. He wanted to thank Bingham, he said, because he was responsible for getting him into West Point.

But Bingham had already heard of Custer's heroic participation in covering the retreat. He interrupted him and shook his hand. "I know. You're my boy Custer!"[15]

It was a pattern Custer would follow throughout his life, developing close mentor-pupil relationships with politicians, officers, and businessmen whom he emulated and tried to impress. Like dismissing the pain of a toothache to tell his father they could beat all the Whigs in Ohio, Custer was eager to share his success with Bingham. And in the same way that he observed his father's leadership in the militia and local politics, Custer would study how these new role models became successful.

For the first two years of the war, Custer was fortunate to serve as a staff officer for five different generals, all of whom had different styles and abilities. Custer learned something from each, and his duties included leading reconnaissance missions, which taught him the problems of command and tactics. In a sense, Custer was getting his advanced degree in military science.

His first professor was Philip Kearny, forty-six, a wealthy New Yorker who had lost his left arm to grapeshot during a cavalry charge he led at the battle of Churubusco in the Mexican War. Kearny had inherited a fortune from his family, who made him study law—a suitable gentlemanly pursuit—at Columbia College (now Columbia University). Kearny had always dreamed of being a soldier and entered the military after his grandfather, who was his guardian, had died. He quickly made a name for himself, and Winfield Scott had called him "the bravest man I ever saw, and a perfect soldier."[16]

Kearny's military career had included fighting Indians in Oregon and Algerians in North Africa, the latter while studying cavalry tactics with the French army. After the Mexican War, he resigned his commission to fight with the French against Austria, winning the Legion d'Honneur for a cavalry charge at Solferino. When the Civil War started, Kearny returned to the United States and was given command of the First New Jersey Brigade. Custer's company of regulars was attached to it. Kearny needed a staff officer and wanted a West Pointer, so he took Custer, who was junior enough to be spared from active command.[17]

Kearny emphasized organization, discipline, and esprit de corps. Custer thought Kearny was the strictest officer he ever served under, although his wrath was usually directed at the senior officers rather than subalterns like Custer or enlisted men. Custer recalled admiringly that Kearny was a master of the use of profanity. When he chewed out somebody, he used "such varied and expressive epithets, that the limit of the language seemed for once to have been reached." Some officers on the receiving end of one of Kearny's blistering critiques resigned rather than risk facing such scolding again.[18]

Yet Kearny could adjust his style to the occasion and the type of men he commanded. When he first assumed command, he noticed the men violating orders by stripping a nearby apple orchard. He profanely chastised the officers in charge. But they were new volunteers, not West Pointers, and in the spirit of freeborn Americans they told him they didn't appreciate being talked to that way. Kearny then invited them to an elaborate dinner party and persuaded them during the evening that for the honor of the regiment they had to exert more discipline over the men.[19]

Custer, with his artistic sensibility, would have appreciated Kearny's stress on the importance of style. Kearny was immaculately uniformed and well-mounted, and he expected the same of his officers. For the blacksmith's son from frontier Ohio, it must have been amazing to serve with the wealthy Kearny, who had traveled the world as a civilian and liked the finer things in life. He splurged on luxuries like a fancy carpet for his tent, a camp bed imported from Europe, and a field kitchen to always provide him with hot meals served with imported wine and brandy. But he also worried about his men. He made a habit of sampling the food in the troops' mess, and if it was bad or the kitchen was dirty, he let those in charge have one of his famous tongue-lashings.[20]

To increase unit spirit, he invented the Kearny patch, a red flannel diamond that the troops wore with pride and which became the nickname of his division. A system of patches was later adopted for the other divisions and is in fact a precursor of army decorations in use today. "I found him ever engaged in some scheme either looking to the improvement of his command or the discomfiture of his enemy," Custer recalled.[21]

The latter led to Custer's first participation in a nighttime raid. Kearny ordered three hundred men to capture some Confederate pickets at an outpost about five miles from his headquarters. He sent Custer along as his liaison. Custer used his storytelling skill to recall the episode in his memoirs as a tense ride that got ever more frightening the closer they got to their goal.

"The cracking of a twig in the distance, or the stumbling of one of the leading files over a concealed log, was sufficient to cause the entire column to halt, and with bated breath peer into the darkness of the forest in a vain endeavor to discover a foe whose presence at that particular time and place was not desired." Every tree or cow in the darkness looked like a rebel soldier, necessitating a halt to see if they were being watched. Finally, they heard voices near a farmhouse. They stopped to listen.[22]

Someone yelled, "Who comes there?" Three musket shots were fired at Custer's column. "It was a sorrowful waste of ammunition to fire three muskets when one would have answered as well," Custer remembered. "I am sure that while we may all have been facing toward the house when the first shot was fired, we were not only facing but moving in the opposite direction before the sound of the last one reached our ears."[23]

Shortly afterward Custer was ordered off Kearny's staff because a new army directive mandated that no regular army officer could serve on the staff of volunteer officers such as Kearny. Custer was sent back to serve as a junior officer with his cavalry company. He wrote later that he found the service under Kearny to be "agreeable and beneficial" although he thought Kearny was a peculiar mix of gallantry, haughtiness, and violent temper. He was severe yet had a charisma that endeared him to his men. He could be domineering yet put on a courtly manner when he chose to do so. "And whether it was the attack of a picket post or the storming of the enemy's breastworks, Kearny was always to be found where the danger was greatest."[24] Custer could have been describing himself. Certainly in Kearny he found an officer who made a lasting impression.

An impression of a different sort was made when Custer became ill and went home to Monroe on sick leave from October 1861 till February 1862.[25] The nature of his illness is not known, but his West Point classmate Tully McCrea wrote that at one point Custer was near death. One day he celebrated with some old friends in a saloon and then walked home to his sister's house, leaning on one of his friends as they staggered along, taking up the whole sidewalk. They passed the house of a prominent judge, Daniel Bacon, who, along with his daughter Libbie, witnessed the debauchery. Custer's friends left him on the front porch of his sister's home. When she found him, she took him inside into her room and locked the door behind them. No one knows what she said. But Custer returned to the army a teetotaler.[26]

McClellan, who was now commander of the Army of the Potomac, began his campaign to take Richmond in March 1862. Custer's outfit, as part of the cavalry, was assigned to scout for the location of the enemy and gather other information. They came across impressive abandoned fortifications that upon close inspection turned out to be armed by "Quaker guns"—logs painted to look like cannons. Again, Custer was learning that much of warfare was show—looking ferocious. But soon enough they saw real rebels—pickets in force about a mile away. The column halted as they waited for orders from headquarters. The men joked among themselves; reporters came up sniffing for a story and joined the conversations. Finally, the regiment received orders to attack and drive the pickets across the river and out of the way. By chance the captain and lieutenant of Custer's company were absent from duty that day, putting Custer in command of the unit. He saw the opportunity and immediately volunteered to lead his company in a charge.

Permission having been granted, Custer led his company to the base of the hill, where the rebels were waiting. He yelled "Charge" for the first time in combat. The rebels took off in a hurry, crossed the bridge, and set fire to it. Custer's troop pursued them to the edge of the water, exchanging gunshots along the way. Since they couldn't cross the burning bridge, Custer ordered his command to return to the column, his mission accomplished.

The only causalities on the Union side had been a wounded horse and a grazing head wound to a private named John W. Bryaud. The wound was so slight that Custer joked years later in his memoirs that Bryaud might have suffered more from all the inquiries of the reporters, who were anxious to get the details about the first blood shed on the expedition. Custer was famous when he was recalling the episode, but at the time he was much more serious about the press coverage. He wrote his sister Ann the day after the skirmish that he had been interviewed by reporters from the *New York Tribune*, the *New York Times*, the *New York World*, and the *Philadelphia Inquirer*—all among the leading newspapers of the day. About two weeks later while sailing south on the *Adele Felicia* Custer wrote, "All the New York, Philadelphia and Washington papers have an account of my skirmish in which I am mentioned in a highly flattering manner."[27] He saw a Southern newspaper story and noted the exaggerated number of Union troops and casualties.

Custer might have been exaggerating, too, making himself seem the star to his family. The reporters interviewed Bryaud and Custer, but stories in most papers relegated the affair to a couple of sentences and featured General George Stoneman, who was head of the cavalry and the most newsworthy figure. Custer, like a young actor scouring reviews for a mention of his name, was carefully reading his clippings. Perhaps he would have more chances when McClellan finally engaged the rebel army.[28]

McClellan had decided to move his army by water down the coast to Fort Monroe, Virginia, where his troops would have a shorter march to Richmond than going overland. McClellan, thirty-five, was, like Kearny, from a prominent family. His father was a Philadelphia surgeon who had founded Jefferson Medical College, and his grandfather was a general in the Revolutionary War. McClellan was a prodigy, entering the University of Pennsylvania to study law when he was only thirteen, then entering West Point at fifteen with a waiver for his age secured with the help of a letter from his father to President John Tyler.[29]

Like Kearny, McClellan was a combat veteran of the Mexican War, but instead of leading cavalry charges, he served as an engineer. He learned the value of flanking movements and siege operations rather than frontal assaults. He also studied Winfield Scott's balancing of politics and war as he worked with the administration of President James K. Polk. McClellan noticed how Scott stressed good relations with the civilian population by keeping American soldiers from destroying property. A rising star, McClellan was sent to Europe to study foreign armies as an observer during the Crimean War.

McClellan left the army in 1857 to become a railroad executive and was active in Democratic Party politics, supporting Stephen Douglas for president in 1860. He rejoined the army after Fort Sumter and led his command to several small victories in western Virginia while McDowell struggled at Bull Run. Lincoln made him commander of the army because he was the only winner to be had at the time.

McClellan used his skill at organization to train and equip the army, which had been defeated at Bull Run. He often visited individual units to review the troops and encourage them. His charisma and attention won the adulation of the men. McClellan provided Custer with another role model who was wealthy, well-traveled, and sophisticated. McClellan was an experienced soldier, but unlike Kearny he added the understanding of politics to Custer's lessons.

The young officer, like most of his fellow soldiers, admired McClellan, writing to Ann that victory was certain. "The greatest expedition ever fitted out is going south under the greatest and best of men, Genl. McClellan," Custer wrote.[30]

After landing at Fort Monroe, Custer was soon transferred from the Fifth Cavalry to serve on the staff of General William F. (Baldy) Smith, who was in charge of building fortifications to begin a siege of Yorktown. Smith needed West Point–trained engineers like Custer, who once again considered himself fortunate for the opportunity to get more varied experience.

Smith, thirty-eight, was a Vermonter who had graduated fourth in his class at West Point. He had spent much of his career before the war doing surveys for the Topographical Corps of Engineers in the Midwest, South, and Mexico. He had served two appointments as an assistant professor of mathematics at the academy.[31]

The studious Smith was a fan of one of the newest military technologies—observation balloons. About six months earlier he had requested that a balloon be permanently attached to his division. He didn't get his request at that time, but he had access to the Union's balloon corps during the Peninsula campaign. Another general, Fitz-John Porter, had almost been captured when the balloon in which he was sailing broke from its moors and drifted over Confederate lines. He could hear the rebel soldiers yelling at him, but a lucky breeze blew him back over Union lines. Porter, who was an enthusiastic balloonist, knew how to operate the ship and he opened the gas line. He told a *New York Herald* reporter that he wasn't sure how fast he came down, but it was a speed he didn't want to try again. He landed on top of an unoccupied tent, which collapsed under the weight of the basket. Porter emerged from a pile of silk and tent canvas. He was unhurt and joked with the cavalrymen who found him that "You ought to have sent the flying artillery after me." The *Herald* editorialized that Porter's coolness showed he was the right man to lead troops in battle.[32]

Porter was the right man to lead, but not to fly. Smith decided a junior officer would be a better, or perhaps more expendable, aeronaut, and he assigned Custer observation duty, telling him to get binoculars, a compass, and a notebook to scout the rebel lines from the air.

Custer was anxious, having never even seen a balloon except from a distance, and he had heard about Porter's wild ride. As he approached the balloon before his first flight, he studied its construction. The balloonist, the famous inventor and scientist Thaddeus C. S. Lowe, thought Custer looked completely unnerved.

"Well, Captain, do you wish to go up with me?" Lowe said.

"Yes," was all Custer said. Lowe, who had taken up many officers in his balloon, thought Custer had the "courage of impulsiveness"—that he had to act immediately to overcome his fear. "When he was up, he was physically white and shivering like an aspen leaf," Lowe recalled.

Custer's reaction was not that unusual. McClellan, too, had trembled and changed color when he flew with Lowe, and he asked if the bottom of the basket would come out.[33]

The basket was a rectangle about four feet by two feet on the sides and two feet tall. On his first flight, Custer sat on the bottom holding tightly to the ropes attaching the basket to the balloon. He thought the basket seemed fragile and asked the balloonist if it was safe. "He began jumping up and down to prove the strength of the basket, and no doubt to reassure me," Custer recalled. "Instead, however, my fears were redoubled, and I expected to see the bottom of the basket giving way, and one or both of us dashed to the earth."[34]

But Custer gradually got used to being aloft and was able to take some good notes. At his own suggestion, they began making night flights so he could count the enemy campfires and better guess the number of troops. After he had flown several times, he wrote home that "I had the finest view I ever had in my life. I could see both armies at once. I was up in the balloon nearly all night while the rebels were evacuating Yorktown and was the first one to discover the retreat of the rebel army."[35] Early on the morning of May 4, Custer noticed heavy fires and flashes suggesting explosions in Yorktown. He noticed there were fewer rebel campfires than usual. He descended and told Smith the rebels had evacuated during the night and were retreating toward Williamsburg.[36]

Smith's division joined the pursuit of the rebels. Custer received permission to leave headquarters and ride with Winfield Scott Hancock's brigade as they closed on the Southern army. He wanted to be where the action was. Hancock, thirty-eight, was a West Pointer who had been wounded during the Mexican War. Unlike Kearney and McClellan, Hancock had remained in the army his whole career, serving in Florida and Kansas between the wars. In the battle of Williamsburg, Custer, serving as one of Hancock's aides, would for the first time see a career officer in a desperate fight.[37]

As part of the Union attack, Hancock's brigade had advanced and occupied some abandoned Confederate fortifications. Hancock thought it was a strong position from which to launch an assault, so he sent couriers to request reinforcements and permission to attack. The messengers went back and forth for much of the day. First Hancock was told to hold his ground, then he received an order to fall back. Hancock was so convinced of the strength of his position that instead of retreating, he sent yet another call for reinforcements. Two more hours went by, but there was no word from headquarters. Meanwhile Confederate troops kept arriving until Hancock's force was outnumbered.[38]

Writing about Williamsburg years later, Custer realized that Hancock faced personal dishonor if he lost the battle because he had disobeyed orders in not falling back. He would be court-martialed and disgraced. "Death upon the battled field was far preferable," Custer concluded. He admired Hancock's coolness in the situation. All of his aides but Custer had been sent back one at a time to request reinforcements. Hancock rode up and down the line, his hat in his hands, urging his men to do their duty and be sure to aim low. They could see the rebels advancing to the attack. "Do not be in a hurry to fire until they come nearer," Hancock said again and again.[39]

The Confederate infantry charged screaming their unnerving rebel yell, the first time Custer had heard it. Hancock's troops responded to his orders with a steady fire that broke the rebel attack when they were only twenty paces away. Hancock, Custer wrote, was never at a loss for expletives when things were going badly. But with the rebel attack broken, Hancock returned to the excessive politeness that characterized his manner. Custer wrote that Hancock gave his next order as if talking to guests at a banquet: "*Gentlemen,* charge with the bayonet."[40]

Custer joined the charge, which routed the rebels. A rebel captain and five men surrendered to Custer, who also picked up a large white silk flag with a red cross in the center. It was a rebel battle flag—the first taken by the Army of the Potomac. Custer was cited for gallantry in the action—the second time that day. (Earlier that day Custer had rushed under fire to stamp out the flames rebels had set on a bridge the federals needed to cross.)[41]

But Custer's day of triumph was tinged with sorrow. Among the prisoners Custer found his friend from West Point, John Lea, who had been badly wounded in the leg. In happier times, Lea and Custer had good-naturedly teased the cadet from Maine about his huge pocket watch. Now they hugged each other and wept. They chatted over old times and exchanged information about their classmates. Custer brought Lea his meals and gave him some cash and socks—an important garment for a foot soldier. Lea in turn wrote Custer a note describing how well he had been cared for. Lea thought Custer could use it to get good treatment if he were captured by the rebels. When they parted, Lea's final words were "God bless you, old boy!" Bystanders afterward asked Custer if Lea was his brother.[42]

Custer wrote to his sister Ann about Lea, and all of his other adventures, including flying in balloons and being the first to report the evacuation of the rebels. He proudly wrote that the captured flag was sent by McClellan to the president in Washington. "The battle of Williamsburg was a hard fought battle much harder than Bull Run."[43]

Williamsburg was actually a smaller battle than Bull Run in terms of causalities, but Custer's role was bigger, and his letter reflected his experience. Custer continued the practice he had started at West Point of writing exhaustive letters, often of a half dozen pages, to family and friends. The writing provided a great outlet for his need to create something artistic. His letters were often humorous and dramatic, and through them he was developing an authorial persona that would show up later in his magazine writing and memoirs. He wrote to entertain and inform, telling the story of the war with the eye for detail of a journalist. He did not try to spare his loved ones' feelings about how much danger he experienced.

He wrote Ann about a close call that happened while he and another officer were scouting rebel lines. They left their troopers to crawl on their hands and knees to peer at the enemy artillery through spyglasses. Custer and his comrade thought they were safe hiding behind the chimneys of a burned-out house. But the rebel gunners spotted them and fired a shot at them. "We fell flat on our faces in order to avoid it. This shell passed over us and exploded over our party beyond, one of the fragments struck one of our men tearing off his arm. We allowed no grass to grow under our feet after that."[44]

The reality of war was forcing the West Point prankster to grow up. With his artist's temperament he stood outside himself and observed the man he was becoming. He wrote to Ann that he discovered he was a person who could be happy no matter the circumstances. He was in good health and had no wants. "It is said that there is no real or perfect happiness during this life," he wrote. "This may be true but I often think that I am perfectly happy. I know that I am happier than those around me, not because I have more cause to be but simply because my disposition enables me to look on the bright side of everything."[45]

Yet in the same letter he could describe a burial with the emotion of a novelist. He was riding to visit friends in the camp of the Seventh Michigan when he came across soldiers digging graves for their comrades killed in a skirmish the day before. Custer had participated in the hour-long fight, and he knew the Union casualties were heavy. He dismounted and hitched his horse to a tree so he could witness the burial. He noticed they were buried without coffins; their shrouds were their blankets.

"Their duty was done, no more will they start at the sound of the drums, no more will they sit around the camp fire listening to stories of home, never again will they respond to their names at roll call," Custer mused, and then as he often did, quoted literature—this time Hamlet: "They have gone to that bourne from which no traveler returneth."

As he studied the dead soldiers, he was drawn by one in particular. "I was struck by his youthful appearance together with something handsome about his face which even death had not removed." Custer questioned some of the bystanders from the man's regiment and learned he was a popular soldier. He had married a beautiful girl the day before he left Vermont to join the army. "I at once thought of the severe shock that awaited her when the news of his death should reach her." Custer knew she would want some token of memory, so he took a knife and a ring from the soldier's pockets. "I then cut a lock of his hair off and gave them all to one of his comrades who was from the same town and who promised to send them to her. I then turned away, mounted my horse and continued on my road to the camp of the 7th Michigan."[46]

Custer saw some of his own friends killed in battle, and he wrote his family about his grief. "They all died in the discharge of their duty, and were I to have my choice I would prefer their fate to that of many who live and are unhurt—it is better to die an honorable death than to live in dishonor. There are many who are known to me for whom it would have been far better to have been slain on the battle field than to survive by acts of cowardice."[47]

Custer had witnessed bravery by wounded Union soldiers who had to be abandoned, when McClellan, stymied by Robert E. Lee, retreated. Custer was assigned to urge the walking wounded to try to get across a bridge and warn them that the army would destroy the bridge to delay the rebels' pursuit. One soldier couldn't make it in time. "I told him there was now no chance for him and he must make up his mind to be taken prisoner," Custer wrote. "He received the announcement as became a soldier and asked for my little order book to write a few lines to his mother and to his sweetheart. After he had finished he gave the book back with the request that I would copy his notes in ink and forward them to their addresses. I then bade him farewell and told him to 'keep a stiff upper lip.' I cannot describe everything that occurred during our 'flank movement' to the James River."[48]

Custer did describe everything else he was experiencing, from his dreams to a dog he adopted. Every anecdote, every detail, was sensational in Custer's telling. The dog he adopted, a Newfoundland that was sleeping at his feet while he wrote his letter, was white except for a black head. "I never saw a prettier dog in my life." He described how hard he was working, at one point spending night and day in the saddle for four days in a row, with only time for a breakfast of coffee with hardtack broken up in it. "I was never very hungry nor did I become weary or fatigued. The excitement was probably the cause."[49]

Even the way he wrote his letter emphasized his role at the center of the action. While describing how well his black horse performed under fire, Custer broke the narrative to write "the general desires to see me so I must leave my letter for a short time. . . ." Then he picked up the story, writing, "I have been busy all day since when I went to see the General. He sent me to Kearny & [General Joseph] Hooker's to carry some orders and acquire information, this occupies the entire day. I can now finish my letter."[50]

Custer finished by describing a dream he had, although he admitted he was not a big believer in their significance. He dreamed he was in his tent when someone called him to look at the balloon, which had ascended. He got his telescope and spotted two of his female friends from Monroe in the basket. He was magically transported to the basket, but when he arrived, the basket was empty, much to his disappointment. Custer didn't interpret the dream, but one meaning is obvious—

he was worried about the war coming between him and girlfriends back home—a concern of soldiers throughout history. Custer's artistic temperament required him to be on center stage. He couldn't stand to be away from the action, whether at the front or at home. He asked his family to forward the *Monroe Commercial* to him and to send him news of the girls.[51]

Custer's family didn't just send him the news. Their letters were filled with advice and warnings, often in a lecturing, almost hectoring tone.

His father expounded on his views on the war in a letter that must have made his son wonder whether he was doing the right thing by fighting. Emanuel wrote that he was for the Union, but not for abolishing slavery. If the war was made about slavery, he told his son, he would urge all the soldiers to lay down their arms and let the abolitionists and rebels fight it out. "I would like to be rid of both and then we might look for a lasting Peace."[52] It was a common thought among Democrats in the upper Midwest. John Roberts, the Ohio schoolmaster diarist, wrote in 1862 that both secessionists and abolitionists were to blame for the war. Once the war was over, "Set the press and the school master to work in their midst to renew the old regard for the old flag," Roberts concluded.[53] Custer no doubt had similar thoughts. As a former teacher, Custer would have agreed with Roberts on how to handle the postwar settlement.

Custer's father also asked for details about the current war. Was it true the rebels had used Quaker guns? He wrote that Custer's mother was worried all the time about him and that he shouldn't be too adventurous. Emanuel counseled him to follow the example of Maj. Robert Anderson at Fort Sumter—to ask the Lord for wisdom every day. "I hope that you will follow his example if the lord is on our side none can hert. Writ soon and often soon and often soon and often my dear son. Good by my dear son hopeing to here from you soon Foreever your affectionate parents."[54]

Custer's sister Ann also pressured him about religion and his behavior, telling him she prayed for him every day. She chided him to be sure to put the correct date on his letter because the last one seemed misdated. She said a Monroe man named Albert Strong had a presentiment that he would be killed in his first battle, and then he was. They had the funeral in town and the crowd was so large that the church couldn't hold it. Another local man had his horse shot out from under him and was seriously wounded. "This war is a dreadful thing," she wrote. "O how many homes will be made desolate and how many hearts will bleed." Throughout the letter, she urged him to write and told him that their mother was worried so much about him and his brother Tom that she was sick. "My Dear Brother I want you to be vary careful of yourself. Don't expose yourself you know how much your parents depend on you and how much we all love you." She couldn't resist mothering him, closing with "Be a good boy Armstrong. Try and take good care of yourself."[55]

Ann likely intended the description of the town funeral to scare Custer into being more careful. But for a man like Custer, who thought it would be better to die on the field than live as a coward, it would have had the opposite effect. If he died on the battlefield, he would be the star of a ceremony in his hometown. Certainly the letters did not change his risky behavior, which so far had led to rewards. Custer continued to seek danger and went beyond his duty, such as when he jumped in the river on the scouting mission: Instead of being shot by rebel pickets, he got a dream job on McClellan's staff.

One of Custer's first major missions for McClellan was to accompany a cavalry unit of about 350 men on a scout. After surprising and capturing a rebel camp, Custer and about ten men went chasing stragglers. For the first time, Custer killed a man in close combat. He had been in combat several times before, but this episode affected him enough to write a moment-by-moment story about it for Ann.

He told her it started when he heard a young bugler call to him: "Captain! Captain!"

Custer couldn't see him because he was behind some bushes. He asked him what was the matter.

"Two Secesh are after me!" the boy yelled.

Custer spurred his horse toward the boy. He drew his revolver as he got closer. He saw the bugler fighting off rebel cavalrymen with his carbine. When the rebels saw Custer, they took off. Custer chased one of them, an officer on a slower horse than Custer had. He got to within about ten steps of the officer and yelled at him to surrender. Custer fired two shots at him but missed. The rebel stopped and faced Custer.

He had a short rifle and looked like he was unsure whether to fight or surrender. Custer pointed his revolver at him and told him to surrender or he would kill him. The rebel gave up.

Custer turned the prisoner in and then joined the chase of another group of rebels. His pistol reloaded, he chased an officer mounted on a strong horse. Again Custer closed to within a few steps. He could have shot the man, but he saw that the rebels were heading toward a rail fence.

"I reasoned that he might attempt to leap it and be thrown, or if he could clear, so could I," Custer explained to Ann. "The chase was now exciting in the extreme. I saw as he neared the fence that he was preparing for a leap, and what was more, I soon saw that the confidence he had in his horse was not misplaced, for he cleared the fence handsomely." In his panic, the rebel looked back at Custer. He rode his horse over soft ground, which made him run slower. Custer meanwhile kept his horse on firmer ground and got close enough to capture the rebel.

Custer warned the man to surrender or he would shoot. The rebel rode on. Custer aimed as carefully as he could and fired, but the rebel kept riding. "I again called on him to surrender, but received no reply," Custer wrote. "I took deliberate aim at his body and fired. He sat for a moment in his saddle, reeled and fell to the ground. His horse ran on, and mine also."

Custer captured another rebel who had lost his horse and was running on foot to the woods. Custer heard the bugler sound the rally and returned to the command. On the way back he saw Union troops rounding up riderless horses. He recognized the horse of the man he had shot because it was wearing a distinctive red morocco breast strap. He took the horse for his own and noticed that it had a beautiful black morocco leather saddle highlighted with silver nails. "The sword of the officer was fastened to the saddle, so that altogether it was splendid trophy."

But the trophy had come at a price. In the excitement of battle, Custer didn't see what had happened to the rebel officer. He wasn't even sure he was dead. Another Union officer, Richard Byrnes, filled him in. "Lieutenant Byrnes told me that he saw him after he fell, and that he rose to his feet, turned around and fell to the ground with a stream of blood gushing from his mouth. It was his own fault; I told him twice to surrender, but was compelled to shoot him."[56]

Custer didn't have long to muse over Byrnes's story. The command had to ride twenty miles back to Union lines, and they might have to fight again before they reached safety.

Once in camp, Custer read a letter he received from Ann and then wrote his description of the raid, including shooting the rebel officer, in his reply to her. He concluded the letter by praising his horse for getting him through the fight. He would send home a souvenir—a double-barreled shotgun he had taken from one the rebels—to their younger brother Boston.[57]

Custer's letter reflected the confused reaction that many men have to combat. Most men are reluctant to kill, even after being trained to do so. Killing someone close enough to call for his surrender is much more difficult than shooting at anonymous soldiers seen indistinctly across the battlefield—something Custer had done before. On the other hand, not pulling the trigger in combat can cause guilt or feelings of unworthiness among soldiers, especially those professionally trained like Custer. They disparage themselves because they think they should be able to kill in battle. Custer delayed shooting his adversary as long as he could, then he fired. Like many soldiers, Custer probably felt a sense of euphoria at first. He had killed. He took a trophy. Ever the showman, Custer had also acquired things he particularly valued—a good-looking horse, a saddle, and a sword for his outfit.[58]

Custer the artist had also written a story as vivid as anything appearing in the press at the time. But in addition to telling a dramatic tale, Custer was working through his own guilt. It is a feeling that many combat veterans have after the euphoria of battle has passed. Now he had to get something off his chest. He told the tale of the kill in clinical detail to his sister—as he had surely repeated it many times back in camp—in order to accept what he done.

Ann, fourteen years older and like a second mother, understood. "You[r] vary welcome letter was I was going to say read with much pleasure," Ann replied. "[But] it made me feel sad to hear that you had to kill that man and I think you was in a vary dangerous position yourself. I am afraid the next thing I hear you will get shot. You are so venturesome. O the horrors of war when will this cruel war be over and many loved ones return home?"[59]

In between battles, however, the cruelty abated and soldiers on opposing sides could be friendly. Most soldiers are reluctant to kill, but they also have a remarkable ability to socialize with each other, trading gossip and goods during informal truces. This phenomenon has been recorded in most wars but was a distinctive feature of the Civil War because of the common heritage of the men in the opposing armies. Custer, who had many Southern friends, took the practice to an extraordinary degree.

When Custer found out that Lea had been paroled and was recuperating at a home in Williamsburg, he rode over to visit him. To Custer's pleasure, two young Southern ladies were staying at the home. Although everyone was, as Custer wrote Ann, "strong 'secesh,'" they had a pleasant visit and insisted when he left that he return and spend the night. Incredibly, McClellan granted Custer permission to stay with an enemy soldier. But the story got even stranger because during the return visit Lea told Custer he was going to marry one of the young ladies and would move up the wedding to the next day if Custer would be the best man.

Custer relished being part of the unusual circumstances and the romantic story of Lea's courtship and wedding. Lea had met his future fiancé and mother-in-law when the two had gone to the Williamsburg battlefield to bring food to the wounded rebel soldiers, who were scattered in buildings throughout the area. "In visiting the different places containing the wounded, *they for the first time met L.*," Custer wrote, underlining the shocking—for that time—fact that they had met without the usual introductions of the courting ritual. "She had him carried to her home, took care of him, etc., etc., and he fell in love with her, courted and married her. I never heard nor even read of a wedding so romantic throughout."

The enthusiastic Custer saw everything as superlative—the bride and the bridesmaid were two of the prettiest girls he had ever seen. The groom and best man wore their dress uniforms—one gray, the other blue. "It was a strange wedding," Custer wrote. "I certainly never heard of one like it."

Both he and Lea marveled at the coincidences that had brought them together, but which didn't stop them from having fun. When the bridesmaid cried after the wedding, Lea teased her that she shouldn't be sad that she didn't have a husband—Custer was available.

"Captain L, you are just as mean as you can be," she replied, but nevertheless took Custer's arm into dinner, telling him he should be in the Confederate army.

The next morning Custer returned to his own army, but McClellan gave him permission to go back and stay as long as he liked. Custer stayed for about two weeks. The girls played the piano and sang patriotic Southern songs, and Lea and Custer played cards, each representing his own country in the games. Custer left only when the Union army started pulling out. "I never had so pleasant a visit among strangers," he wrote Ann.[60]

Even though fraternization occurred throughout the war, and McClellan gave Custer permission to do so, his behavior seems extreme. But for Custer the artist, the episode was like living in a romantic novel. It was a great story that he enjoyed telling his sister. It was daring, it was exciting, it was something he had never heard done before.

But he would still do his duty. Custer closed his letter by writing that "L. has been exchanged, and is now in the rebel army, fighting for what *he supposes* is his right." Left unsaid was the obvious—Custer was fighting for what he believed was right, and he would reluctantly put aside the friendship if they met on the battlefield.

Custer was far angrier at those who, from the comforts of home, criticized his hero McClellan. Lincoln had briefly fired McClellan after he failed to capture Richmond, but then reinstated him when Gen. John Pope was soundly whipped at the Second Battle of Bull Run. Custer remained on McClellan's staff during the subsequent campaign, in which McClellan fought Robert E. Lee to a draw at the battle of Antietam. The battle stopped Lee's invasion of Maryland, but Lincoln fired McClellan for good after he failed to destroy Lee's army and continued to dither rather than fight.

Custer defended McClellan. His enemies, Custer wrote Ann, were unpatriotic, or cowards, or both. They were the type who stayed home instead of serving. The editor of one of the Monroe papers was such a type to Custer, and in his rage he could not recall the man's name: "If I could meet him I would horsewhip him."[61]

After a year of war, mostly spent as an aide to generals, Custer had learned the importance of the media in garnering support from the public and politicians. Much of what he had seen also reinforced what he had learned growing up, and it fit his natural instincts for performance. If you want to be recognized, you have to be big in the moment, you can't just sit on your horse, you have to jump in the river. You have to put on a show.

CHAPTER THREE

Gettysburg

Saving the Union

While the Army of the Potomac was engaged in a bitter fight at Fredericksburg, Custer was out of the show, back home in Monroe, in military purgatory.

McClellan had been banished to Trenton, New Jersey, and then to New York to "await orders." Custer, as a captain on McClellan's staff, was also awaiting orders.

It wasn't how Custer wanted to spend his time at that point in his life. Several months earlier, in October 1862, he had been present when Lincoln visited McClellan at the Antietam battlefield. One of the most famous photographs of the war, showing McClellan and Lincoln standing with other officers in front of a tent, includes Custer standing way off to the side, as befits a junior officer. Sometimes, when the photo is reproduced in history books, Custer, who wore longer whiskers at the time and looks nothing like his popular image, is cropped out of the photo. A close look shows a ghosted second Custer and multiple images of his boots. The young aide had moved closer to the presidential group while the photo was taken, and the slow exposure time of Alexander Gardner's camera caught Custer's need to be on stage.

Just being near the conversation between the president and his top commander was an amazing achievement for a young officer who scarcely a year before had almost been dismissed from the army. Even though he had seen the carnage of war and grieved for those hurt by it, the war was exciting for him. He tried to explain the conflicting emotions in a letter to his cousin Augusta Ward written at about the time of Lincoln's visit. He was writing in response to her question about whether he would be glad to see the war end. Custer replied that he wished for peace for the country but for himself he would be glad to see a battle every day. "Now do not misunderstand me," Custer wrote, searching for an explanation. "I only speak of my own *interests* and *desires*, perfectly regardless of all the world besides, but as I said before, when I think of the pain & misery produced to individuals as well as the miserable sorrow caused throughout the land I cannot but earnestly hope for peace, and at an early date. Do you understand me?"[1]

Instead of seeing battle, Custer, like his mentor, had to go home. He made the most of it. Custer was a dashing figure in his uniform and a local celebrity since he had been mentioned in a few paragraphs in the New York newspapers. He saw old friends, went to parties, flirted with girls, just like he did when he was a teacher.[2] On Thanksgiving Day he went to a party at Boyd's Seminary, a Monroe girls' school. For Custer, who liked to ride in a sleigh packed with girls, it must have been a dream come true. Then he met the school's valedictorian, Elizabeth Bacon, and life changed.

Elizabeth, twenty, was not only book-smart, but a quick-witted woman who, like Custer, had an indefinable charisma that drew people to her. She was cornered at the party by a luckless swain named Conway Noble, who was having no success impressing her. He asked her if he could introduce her to Captain Custer, and she agreed just to get rid of Noble.

"I believe your promotion has been very rapid," Libbie said, indicating she was aware of Custer's record.

"I have been very fortunate," Custer replied.[3]

It was the briefest of meetings, but that was all it took to start a love so intense that they would devote the rest of their lives to each other. They came from different backgrounds, but their differences complemented each other, making them a successful team. They shared a love for adventure and an artistic sensibility that proved a unifying passion.

Libbie, like Custer, was the child of an immigrant to the Midwest who was involved in local politics. Daniel Bacon, her father, was a sixty-one-year-old circuit court judge who had left Onondaga County, New

York, some forty years earlier to find a place where he could buy cheap land and make a political career. Like Custer, he had earned a teaching certificate as a young man. He had supported himself by teaching while he studied law at night. He opened a law office, bought property, and entered politics, serving in a variety of positions, including inspector of schools and Whig representative to the territorial legislature.[4]

After establishing his career, Bacon married Eleanor Sophia Page, the daughter of a wealthy Grand Rapids nursery owner. Eleanor was about fifteen years younger than Bacon but she was sophisticated, with a taste for fashion and knowledge about the latest, more lenient child-rearing techniques, which she got from *Mother's Magazine*. The Bacons had four children, but Libbie was the only one to live beyond age seven and was essentially raised as an only child. Her parents doted on her and sought to raise her as a Christian and a lady. But the young mother caught dysentery and died suddenly in 1854 when Libbie was only twelve. For a while, Libbie was shuffled around to boarding schools and lived with relatives until her father married Rhoda Pitts, who became a loving stepmother to Libbie and reestablished a home in Monroe.[5]

Despite the turmoil in her young life, Libbie thrived in school. She grew into a pretty girl, attracting the attention of grown men when she was only a teenager. By the time she met Custer, Libbie had several serious suitors, including a minister and a businessman. Like Custer, she was also a bit of a local celebrity, and for more than just being the daughter of a politician and lawyer. Her valedictory speech had been reviewed in the *Detroit Free Press*, which called it one of the best at her graduation ceremonies.[6]

On the surface, Libbie and Custer seemed to have little in common other than being two good-looking young people who were big frogs in their small-town pond. Many biographers of Libbie or Custer make much of their different backgrounds—she the spoiled only child of a rich Republican judge, he the social-climbing son of a loud-mouthed Democratic blacksmith/farmer. It's as if they were Sandy and Danny from a nineteenth-century version of *Grease*.

Deeper reflection shows that their backgrounds were more similar than different. Both fathers came to the Midwest from the East, dreaming of improving their lives and being independent from their families. True, Bacon became a lawyer and Emanuel Custer a blacksmith, but both were businessmen. Furthermore, both were champions of the American idea, leaders of their respective political parties, and involved in their communities. Both wanted more for their children, sending them to the best schools they could afford.

Libbie would have been able to see her father in Custer. Like his future father-in-law, Custer had been a schoolteacher, and he used that as a springboard to a better life. And Libbie, like Custer, wanted adventure. She could have married any of several prominent men, including a widowed Presbyterian minister who called at her home frequently and chased her around the room for a squeeze. She was flattered, but the future of a minister's wife held little appeal to a girl who read avidly of the wider world, who had spent time with relatives in upstate New York, and who had the heart of an artist. Instead, Libbie dreamed at night of marrying a Union soldier. In one dream, which in a strange coincidence was similar to a scene from *Gone with the Wind*, Libbie killed a rebel soldier, much like Scarlett O'Hara killed a Yankee deserter. Unlike Scarlett, however, Libbie felt guilty for killing the soldier, and her dream hero rescued her.[7]

Her dreams illustrated one of the main things she had in common with Custer—an artistic sensibility. They were both imaginative, dramatic people who loved performing and creating. Libbie's father had given her a diary for her ninth birthday, and after a year's hesitation to start writing because she was afraid of not writing neatly enough, she started recording her thoughts when she was ten. As one of her biographers noted, Libbie wrote with the keen eye of a journalist, describing events around town, such as the suicide of a German immigrant, the local reaction to the California Gold Rush, and the arrival of P. T. Barnum's Traveling Museum—complete with Tom Thumb. Libbie noted that a crowded stand had collapsed, breaking the leg of one spectator and the jaw of another.[8]

Custer did not keep a journal, but his voluminous letters were an equally adept way to practice storytelling. Custer the schoolteacher also liked to perform, and he learned from the classroom how to manipulate an audience. Libbie had similar skills. For her graduation speech, she talked about crumbs, explaining that there was greatness in small things as well as in large ones. She chose the bizarre topic because she guessed its very oddity would engage the crowd. It did. Most of the listeners knew her personal story of being the only surviving child of a widowed father, and the emotional speech left a tear-filled assembly.[9]

She met her match in Custer, however. He was smitten after the Thanksgiving Day party and pursued her as if she were a rebel picket he was going to take prisoner. Custer scouted her routine and began showing up around her home and church so he could escort her on walks. He invited her to a concert, but she turned him down in favor of going with her father. By the end of the holidays, he had proposed, but she declined.

At one party, Custer and Libbie wandered off to a small room. Noticing their image in a mirror, Libbie blurted out that it looked like a scene from a book. She had seen them as an image from a romance novel. Custer must have thought the scene called for the hero to kiss the girl, just like Charles O'Malley would have done in the Irish dragoon novels that he favored. Thus, he tried to embrace her, but she pushed him off, reminding him that she was not that kind of girl.[10]

The young cavalryman also knew how to play the Victorian dating game. Custer increased his attention to several of those kinds of girls, in particular one named Fanny Fifield, who had a reputation in their circle of friends. After Custer had exchanged daguerreotypes with Libbie, she was flattered to see him in her church. But instead of escorting her after the service, he walked Fifield home. At a party at Fifield's house, Custer said a couple of things to Libbie that she thought were sarcastic. She got angrier when she felt he paid more attention to his card game than to her. To add to the couple's trouble, Daniel Bacon was upset when he discovered Libbie's interest in Custer, thinking the officer who had fallen down drunk in the street the year before was no match for his daughter.[11]

The conflicts only seemed to fuel their romance. They agreed to carry on a hidden correspondence when Custer returned to duty so her father wouldn't know about their relationship. Custer would write Libbie through a mutual friend named Nettie Humphrey. The clandestine nature of the relationship must have added to the excitement for two people who were not only falling in love but were in love with drama.

Part of the drama, of course, was that Custer would be heading back to the war. First, he had to go to New York to help McClellan write his final reports. McClellan was through with commanding troops, but he still had a few things to teach Custer. McClellan showed the junior officer an example of fine living and a way to get there. The black-smith's son was amazed at the fancy four-story brick house McClellan had in one of the best areas in Manhattan. It was the gift of wealthy Democratic party leaders who entertained him and courted him with the object of luring him into politics. With typical enthusiasm, Custer wrote Ann that "It is the most magnificently furnished house I was ever in." Custer himself was living beyond his means at the Metropoli-tan Hotel and talking about buying a new suit of civilian clothes so he could fit in with McClellan's swanky friends. [12]

Custer could not have failed to notice the power of the press and McClellan's ability to communicate and to use journalists for his own ends. When Custer was on McClellan's staff at the front, he had seen the general work reporters. Worried that Lincoln and other Repub-licans would fire him for political reasons, McClellan ensured the support of the Democratic *New York Herald* by providing one of its correspondents exclusive access to his plans—access to details he never shared with Lincoln.[13]

Thus when Lincoln finally relieved McClellan for incompetence, his friends in the press still championed him. McClellan was constantly praised in the city's Democratic newspapers, whose publishers were usually power brokers like Manton Marble of the *New York World* and James Gordon Bennett Sr. of the *New York Herald*.[14] McClellan had failed to capture Richmond in the Peninsula campaign, and he had failed to destroy Lee's exhausted army after Antietam. No matter, the press was powerful enough to tell his side of the story and turn him into a presidential contender for the next election. According to the Democratic newspapers, Lincoln had made a terrible mistake by reliev-ing McClellan. The *Herald*, for example, called McClellan a "genius" and compared him to George Washington in patriotism and military skill. The paper editorialized that McClellan was a young man and eventually he would lead the army again or the nation as president.[15] The New York newspapers began to carry regular features on his doings around the city, even detailing the balls, operas, and dinners he attended.[16] When the Congressional Committee on the Conduct of the War criticized McClellan for being too slow during the Peninsula campaign, the *Herald* took up the cudgel for him, reminding readers that the life of the republic was in the balance: "If the Army of the Potomac had been crushed in any great battle the rebels would have marched into Washington, and the war would have virtually ended in our being compelled to acknowledge the Southern confederacy. . . . And therefore, McClellan, as a prudent and patriotic man, ran no unnecessary risks."[17]

McClellan also burnished his own reputation through his official reports, in which he portrayed himself as the embattled hero of the nation fighting overwhelming odds. Custer learned from a master egotist the use of such reports as career enhancers and political documents. Facts were secondary to the telling of a story that gave you the starring role. Custer, as a staff officer, was present and privy to the intelligence reports McClellan had and he knew when McClellan was exaggerating the numbers of rebels he had faced.[18] Custer, raised in the brag culture of frontier Ohio, would not have been shocked at McClellan's exaggerations; he would have simply absorbed the lesson as the way things were done.

Years later, when writing his own memoirs, Custer attempted to explain why official reports from different officers writing about the same battle could be so unlike each other and from memoirs like the one he was writing. Battles, Custer wrote, were so complicated, ever-changing, and spread out over such large areas that a battlefield looks like "an immense series of animated kaleidoscopes, the number of which is only limited by the number of observers, no two of the latter obtaining the same view, and no individual probably obtaining the same view twice." In an understatement, Custer admitted that sometimes battles were poorly planned, but the military culture was such that officers had to obey their orders without question, as Tennyson wrote in his poem of the Light Brigade's disastrous charge. "Then, when official reports became the order of the day, they were usually so framed as to touch lightly if at all upon the blunders committed and disasters suffered, and to make the most of successes gained, whether these were the result of accident or design."[19] Custer knew the official reports were only one version of reality, and it was understood in the military that the version you wrote would reflect to your credit.

Custer's lessons under McClellan were reinforced under his next commander. Soon after finishing his work with McClellan, the army sent Custer back to his old cavalry company at his former rank of first lieutenant. Custer's unit was in the division of Gen. Alfred Pleasonton, who invited Custer to join his staff. Pleasonton had been two years ahead of McClellan at West Point, and like him had served with distinction in the Mexican War, earning two brevets for gallantry. And like McClellan, he knew how to use the press and promote himself in reports. Although most generals played those games, Pleasonton had developed an outsized reputation for politicking in the army. Charles Francis Adams Jr., who served under Pleasonton, despised him as a mediocre officer who made his career through good press: "He is pure and simple a newspaper humbug," Adams wrote to his mother. "You always see his name in the papers, but to us who have served under him and seen him under fire he is notorious as a bully and a toady. He does nothing save with a view to a newspaper paragraph. At Antietam he sent his cavalry into a hell of artillery fire and himself got behind a bank and read a newspaper, and there, when we came back, we all saw him and laughed among ourselves."[20]

Adams was right that Pleasonton worked the press, but it was unfair to call a man who earned two brevets for gallantry a coward. Pleasonton believed a general's job was to direct the battle, and he tried to impart that lesson to his Michigan protégé. "I used to tell him: 'Don't be so anxious to fight yourself—fight your command,'" Pleasonton told an interviewer years after the war. "He was so anxious to fight himself he would forget his command."[21]

Pleasonton showed Custer another example of how to promote your career through official reports. In his report of his actions at the battle of Chancellorsville, he claimed his outfit halted an attack by Stonewall Jackson, saving the Union army from destruction. The exaggerated claim was persuasive enough that he was promoted from division commander to corps commander. Pleasonton's promotion meant that his aide—Custer—would be promoted, too—and thus Custer's rank was restored to captain.[22]

Pleasonton, like Phil Kearney and McClellan, enjoyed fancy uniforms and fancy living. He wore a whip on his wrist, and most of his staff did the same to emulate him.[23] Custer got one too, slapping it against his oversized cavalry boots, the sound reassuring to the men in line. But he especially enjoyed the band music Pleasonton had played every evening and the fine meals that included delicacies the general had shipped to camp from Baltimore.[24]

Custer also enjoyed the responsibility that Pleasonton gave him. The senior officer sent Custer as his representative on a raid behind rebel lines to catch a party of Southern civilians who were reported to be traveling from Richmond with a lot of money and important documents. The raiding party of about seventy-five men traveled down the Potomac River into Chesapeake Bay on steamboats, then rode overland to snatch their quarry. At one point Custer left the main party with nine other men in a small boat so they could chase another rebel boat. After capturing it, Custer led four men ashore to scout around the area. They came to a plantation house, and Custer spied someone lying down on the veranda, reading a book. As they got closer, he saw it was a Confederate officer.

"At first, I thought we were in a trap, that others might be near, perhaps in the house" Custer later wrote to Nettie Humphrey, who would of course pass the letter secretly to Libbie. Custer knew that with only four men, he couldn't fight a large force. But he snuck up on the rebel officer and told him he was his prisoner. "He replied very coolly, 'I suppose so.'"

Custer interrogated him and found there were no other rebels within six miles. The officer had just come home for a short visit.

Custer was again struck by the odd circumstances of the war. When he went inside the house, he met the officer's sisters. They tried to put on a brave front at first, but then showed their grief at their brother's capture. Custer immediately thought of his own sister and imagined how she would have felt had the roles been reversed. Uncomfortable in what he had to do, he apologized for his "painful but imperative duty." Nevertheless, Custer the writer could also see the absurd humor in the situation. The rebel had just begun reading Hamlet's soliloquy when Custer captured him. "To be, or not to be" seemed perfect for such a situation. "On our march back he and I had a hearty laugh over his literary pursuits."[25]

The raid was a brilliant success. They captured twelve prisoners and thirty horses, and they burned two boats and a bridge—all without losing a man. Maj. Gen. Joseph Hooker, now commander of the Army of the Potomac, commended Custer for his role in the expedition. Two of the horses stood out. Custer kept one, which was a beautiful black stallion worth $900 that he named Roanoke. Always with an eye for costume, Custer planned to ride Roanoke only in parades; he would not risk losing a show horse in battle. He gave the other valuable horse to Pleasonton.[26]

As he did with most of his superiors, Custer developed a warm relationship with Pleasonton, writing that he was more like a father than a general. Custer typically admired his leaders and took some bits of their style to add to his own. The leaders in turn saw Custer as a talented student, someone whom they could watch grow as an officer and a man. During a break in the campaigning, while the soldiers were occupied with fixing their quarters, Custer felt free to ask Pleasonton for two favors: to appoint his Monroe friend, George Yates, to his staff and to recommend himself to Michigan Governor Austin Blair for command of the Fifth Michigan Volunteer Cavalry. Pleasonton agreed to do both.[27]

Custer also wrote to John Bingham, the Republican congressman who had appointed him to West Point, and Isaac Christiancy, associate justice of the Michigan Supreme Court and owner of the *Monroe Commercial*. Custer had written letters trying to help Christiancy's son, Henry, get a staff appointment with an infantry division. The support of his friends was not enough, however, to obtain the command of the Fifth Michigan. The Republican Blair refused Custer, writing that he was a McClellan man and that his family were well-known Democrats.[28]

In the meantime, Custer concentrated on his staff work and took every opportunity to make an impression in combat. In June, Hooker ordered Pleasonton's command to scout Lee's army to find out if they were moving north to invade Pennsylvania. Pleasonton sent Custer to ride with Col. Benjamin F. Davis and the Eighth New York Cavalry, which would be in the lead. The day was foggy, and as they approached a ford in the Rappahannock River, they could not be sure if rebels were nearby.

They heard someone order them to halt. Custer and Davis fired their pistols and led a charge across the river. The Yankee cavalry roared past the startled Confederate picket and into a camp of enemy cavalry—part of Jeb Stuart's famed Invincibles, the same name as Emanuel Custer's militia outfit, but a much more professional fighting unit. The Invincibles, who were just waking up, had been preparing for a review for Lee and had no idea they would be attacked. But more rebels were gathering beyond the camp. In the subsequent melee of charges and countercharges, Davis was killed. Custer led at least one other charge and was thrown from his horse at a stone wall. Some accounts said Custer took command after Davis's death on the field; others downplayed his role. But most agree that at one point he found himself surrounded and fighting hand-to-hand as he led his men out of a trap. Pleasonton cited Custer to Hooker for gallantry.[29]

Pleasonton noticed Custer, but the press did not. Northern papers covered that skirmish and others as the cavalry sparred with the rebel horsemen, but Custer was usually mentioned only briefly, if at all. The *Chicago Times'* coverage was typical. On June 11, it devoted two columns to what it called "The Great Cavalry Battle at Beverly Ford," describing the battle as "a desperate hand-to-hand encounter." It mentioned a number of officers by name, including the unfortunate Davis, but not Custer. Another story credited the victory to Pleasonton, whom the paper described as one of the most "dashing and brave" officers in the service."[30]

The cavalry clashed with the rebels again at Aldie, Virginia, on June 17, and again Custer played a dramatic role even though he was assigned only to carry dispatches for Pleasonton. Late in the battle, Custer joined the troopers at the front lines, and his skittish horse took him on a "charge" into the Confederate lines. Custer killed one rebel with his sword and managed to escape by the flank, circling the field to make it back to Union lines. A Michigan newspaper provided thrilling details. "Outstripping his men in pursuit of the enemy, one of them turned, fired, but missed, his revolver being knocked by a sword blow that sent the rider toppling to the ground. Another enemy trooper tore alongside, but Custer, giving his horse a sudden check, let the man go shooting by."[31]

However, most major newspapers ignored Custer's role, focusing instead on Pleasonton or Brig. Gen. Judson Kilpatrick, a brigade commander. One widely reprinted story described Union troopers retreating before the advancing rebels when Kilpatrick ordered a charge. "There was a little hesitancy at first, when General Kilpatrick, accompanied by Colonel [Calvin] Douty, of the 1st [M]aine, and Captain Costar [sic] of the Gen. Pleasonton's Staff, went to the front and called upon the troops to follow. There was no hesitancy then. The Maine boys gave three cheers for Gen. Kilpatrick, and the whole column made a dash up the road in the face of a terrible fire from carbines, rifles and cannon, sweeping everything before them. This virtually ended the fight. The rebels, after a little more skirmishing, fell back, and our forces to-night occupy their position." The story made no mention of "Costar's" solo charge into the rebel lines.[32]

The reporters might have ignored Custer or misspelled his name, but Pleasonton saw in him great potential for combat command. The general always studied the actions of his aides under fire. Many bright junior officers would get flustered and ask Pleasonton to repeat his orders. Custer could always look him in the eye and repeat the order exactly, no matter what chaos was going on around him.[33] Pleasonton got the chance to promote Custer to a command slot in late June, when Lincoln replaced Joseph Hooker with George Gordon Meade as commander of the Army of the Potomac. Pleasonton used the change in command to push for a reorganization of the cavalry, along with the promotion of several promising young officers, including Custer.

Then-Captain Custer learned of his promotion after returning to his tent wet and miserable from a ride around the camp inspecting pickets. He tentmates greeted him as "General Custer," which infuriated the sensitive junior officer, who had once punched a boy for teasing him during a class exercise. He declared that he would be a general one day. His comrades knew when to give up the joke and pointed him to an envelope on the table addressed to Brig. Gen. George A. Custer, U.S. Vols. Amid the congratulations of his tentmates, Custer sunk down in a chair, forcing himself to keep from crying.[34]

At twenty-three, Custer was the youngest general in the Union army and among the youngest in American history, period. Custer was assigned command of the Second Brigade of the Third Cavalry Division, which was commanded by Kilpatrick. Custer's command included the Fifth Michigan, which Blair had refused to give to the Democrat Custer.[35] The promotion was all the sweeter because Custer had earned it on merit, not from pulling strings or cultivating reporters, but by impressing his mentor, Pleasonton.

Now that he was a general, Custer was faced with the task of acting like a general—a job made all the more difficult because of his youth and inexperience as a commander. He had jumped over a number of older veterans—men such as a major named Marcus Reno, who had been ahead of him at West Point. Reno was later to figure prominently in the Battle of the Little Bighorn. Custer was aware of the resentment, jealousy, and mistrust of his subordinates.[36]

What to do? Custer did what he had first learned as a boy showing off for the New Rumley Invincibles and had relearned serving under Scott, Kearny, McClellan, and Pleasonton. In order to command, you had to look like a commander. You needed the costume, and you needed to perform. Like an actor doing improv, Custer rummaged around through his trunks and cobbled together an outfit including a light blue wide-collared shirt he got from a Potomac gunboat sailor and a velveteen jacket with gold braid on the sleeves. His orderly Joseph Fought found silver stars from a camp peddler and sewed them on the collar. Custer topped it off with a wide-brimmed hat he got from a Confederate officer. With his long golden hair and Van Dyke whiskers, he looked more like an English cavalier than a modern officer.[37]

His outfit surprised and mystified the men in his command.

"Do you know anything of this Popinjay who has been put in command of our Brigade," one officer asked Capt. Alexander C. M. Pennington, who commanded an artillery battery in the brigade. Pennington had been a classmate of Custer's at West Point.

"I suppose you refer to Gen. Custer?" Pennington said. "In the next fight we get into, you stick close to this Popinjay and then let me know what you think of him."[38]

James K. Kidd, a captain with the Sixth Michigan, wrote that initially it was hard to see beyond Custer's gaudy appearance to the fighting spirit underneath. Kidd first encountered his new commander when he heard an unfamiliar voice giving orders as the brigade deployed for action at Hanover, Pennsylvania. He wrote of Custer's startling appearance, "Looking back to see whence it came, my eyes were instantly riveted upon a figure only a few feet distant, whose appearance amazed if it did not for the moment amuse." The outlandish costume drew his attention, but he noticed that Custer, sitting on his beautiful horse, looked like he was born to command. Kidd recalled years later that Custer's self-styled uniform would be the distinguishing characteristic that the men under his command would always look for in the heat of battle, where they would find the reassurance of their leader's presence.

America's Civil War produced many colorful characters—Stonewall Jackson, Jeb Stuart, and William T. Sherman—but none like Custer. Kidd wrote, "George A. Custer was, as all agree, the most picturesque figure of the Civil War."[39]

Custer stood out with his looks, but he also needed the air of command. He assumed the gruff attitude he had learned from Kearney and started from his first day as a general riding through camp and enforcing regulations. Officers had to turn out for stable call instead of detailing the duty to noncommissioned officers; baggage limits were enforced; and salutes had to be given and returned.[40]

Still, Custer would have to do more than sound and look like a general. He would have to prove himself in combat to his men and to his mentor—and to the press, which was vital to advancing his career and the need of his artistic temperament for recognition. He was no immediate sensation. After two years of war, many generals had cultivated reporters and were newspaper heroes. For Custer, becoming a media celebrity would be a gradual process.

The promotion of Pleasonton's three young protégés, skipping several ranks to general, was the first bit of news. The *New York Times*'s E. A. Paul, writing a story about cavalry actions, mentioned Custer's promotion (although he misspelled his name), along with that of the other new generals, Elon Farnsworth and Wesley Merritt. Paul called the trio "dashing and brilliant young officers, who are thus promoted in violation of red tape and regardless of political [i]nfluences, because of their are [sic] fitness to lead cavalry, Maj. Gen. Pleasonton has said that with such officers he can destroy the rebel cavalry; and he will do it. The new Generals are assigned, and already at work." The *Detroit Free*

Press reported native son Custer's promotion in a profile that included the praise that he had rendered "gallant service" at Beverly Ford and Aldie. "The General is the youngest Brigadier in the services, being but twenty three years of age. He styles his command the Wolverine Brigade."[41]

Custer would soon get the chance to lead the Wolverines in the biggest battle of the war. He assumed command of his brigade on June 29, 1863, and that same day the Union cavalry was marching north, assigned to look for the enemy while guarding the Army of the Potomac's flank and rear.[42] On June 30, at the battle of Hanover, Custer led his brigade in combat for the first time and helped drive Confederate cavalry under Jeb Stuart out of that town. Much of the battle was a stalemated artillery duel until Custer led his men in a flank attack on the rebel cannons. Stuart ultimately withdrew, and Kilpatrick cited Custer for gallantry.[43]

Although Custer was now a general, he didn't get much more press coverage than when he was a staff officer. Few papers mentioned Custer's role, and if they did write about him, they didn't provide much detail. The *New York Herald*, for example, wrote only that "Generals Kilpatrick and Castar [*sic*] drove Stuart out of Hanover, after a splendid fight, and they are still pursuing him, part of his force going towards Gettysburg and part towards York."[44]

On July 1, parts of the rival armies collided at Gettysburg, but Kilpatrick's cavalry, including Custer, had bivouacked in the town of East Berlin. General Meade ordered a concentration of his whole army at Gettysburg, so Kilpatrick marched toward the Army of the Potomac with Custer's regiment in the lead. On July 2 they ran into Confederate cavalry near Hunterstown, and Custer once again led his men in a charge on the rebel positions. Custer's horse was shot out from under him, and while he was on foot a rebel aimed his carbine at the new general. A Union private shot the rebel and pulled Custer onto his own horse, taking him to safety.[45]

Kilpatrick's troopers were then ordered to march to Two Taverns, south of Gettysburg. Pleasonton told Kilpatrick to send one brigade to support Brig. Gen. David McMurtrie Gregg's division, which protected the Army of the Potomac's right flank and rear. Kilpatrick in turn sent Custer, who would be in one of the most critical positions of the campaign, although no one knew it at the time.

Lee had been hurling his army at Meade for two days, and both sides were exhausted and near the breaking point. The fate of the country hung in the balance on July 3 when Lee gambled everything on an assault on the Union center—what would go down in history as Pickett's Charge, named for Confederate Maj. Gen. George Pickett. At the same time Stuart's cavalry was heading for the Union rear. If the infantry broke the Union center and Stuart swept through the rear, the Army of the Potomac could have been thrown into a panic and defeated. With Lee free to attack Philadelphia or other Northern cities, Lincoln would have been forced to sue for peace.[46]

Stuart's force of about seven thousand was blocked by about five thousand Union horsemen under the overall command of David Gregg, positioned three miles behind the main Union line. Custer's brigade was not normally under Gregg's command but was serving as reinforcements. The Union horsemen could hear the roar of artillery in the distance that was intended to soften the Union lines for Pickett's Charge. "The earth quaked," Kidd remembered. "The tremendous volume of sound volleyed and rolled across the intervening hills like reverberating thunder in a storm."[47]

The cavalry, too, began fighting. Custer's Fifth Michigan turned back several rebel attacks but was about to be overrun when Gregg ordered the Seventh Michigan to charge. Custer took the lead, shouting "Come on, you Wolverines!" and drove the rebels back until they were stopped by a stone wall. Rebels charged up to the wall and began firing point-blank at the Yankees. The action was so close that men were burned by the fire of each other's guns. After a melee of hand-to-hand combat, Custer withdrew when he saw more rebels were about to attack his flank.[48]

To Kidd, who was watching with a perfect view from his post supporting Custer's artillery, the succeeding pause seemed like both sides had stopped to catch their breath. They had fought back and forth with one side appearing to win, then the other. Stuart's movement toward the Union rear had been checked momentarily. "But the wily Confederate had kept his two choicest brigades in reserve for the supreme moment, intending then to throw them into the contest and sweep the field with one grand, resistless charge," Kidd wrote.[49]

Stuart organized a massive attack with eight regiments. "Squadron after squadron, regiment after regiment, orderly as if on parade, came into view, and successively took their place," Kidd wrote. Pennington's artillery tore holes in the rebel lines, but they closed the gaps and moved forward. "In superb form, with sabers glistening, they advanced. The men on foot gave way to let them pass. It was an inspiring and imposing spectacle, that brought a thrill to the hearts of the spectators on the opposite slope."[50]

The only fresh Union regiment was Custer's First Michigan, led by Col. Charles H. Town, who was suffering from tuberculosis. Gregg sent the order to charge to try to stop Stuart. The odds looked hopeless. For Custer, it was center stage, the role of a lifetime. Embracing the challenge, he rode up to Town, gave him the order to charge, and then led it himself, yelling, "Come on, you Wolverines!"[51]

The rival units of cavalry collided with an explosive force that sent horses and riders flying end over end. The cannons held their fire as the men battled in close combat. "Then it was steel to steel," Kidd wrote. "For minutes—and for minutes that seemed like years—the gray column stood and staggered before the blow; then yielded and fled."[52]

Custer's official report reveled in the success of the attack, which had been made against five-to-one odds. The Yankees' war cry had terrified the enemy, he wrote. "For a moment, but only a moment, that long, heavy column stood its ground; then, unable to withstand the impetuosity of our attack, it gave way in a disorderly rout, leaving vast numbers of dead and wounded in our possession, while the First, being masters of the field, had the proud satisfaction of seeing the much-vaunted chivalry, led by their favorite commander, seek safety in headlong flight."[53]

Custer wrote in a vivid style trying to bring the reader to the scene, but he claimed he could not find the language to express his appreciation for the courage of his men. He concluded, "I challenge the annals of warfare to produce a more brilliant or successful charge of cavalry than the one just recounted."[54]

The action was brilliant, ferocious, and just might have saved the United States from dissolution. It was so ferocious, in fact, that witnesses described the crash of the two forces as sounding like falling timber.[55] But to paraphrase the hoary philosophical question: If a charge sounds like falling timber, but no journalist is around to write about it, did it really happen?

Gettysburg was well-covered by the press with more than forty-five reporters. Many from the major New York papers were present for at least part of the battle, and they were largely free to roam all over the front. In fact, one historian wrote that there were *too many* reporters on the scene. The largest New York papers sent teams of reporters that spread all over the area, used the telegraph constantly without regard to any budget, and transmitted bits and pieces of news without context to the broader story.[56] Unfortunately for Custer and the other heroes of the cavalry fight, no reporters witnessed their action or wrote about it in any detail in the extensive press coverage of the battle.[57]

Almost all of the reporters focused on the infantry portion of the field because that's where the bulk of the fighting was done. The infantry was numerically the largest part of the army, and Meade's headquarters was in view of the infantry fighting. The reporters at Meade's headquarters or following his various corps and division commanders also tended to write from the perspective of those officers, who were their main news sources, and often, like Meade, were lionized for winning battles. One reporter noted that the night after the battle was won, Meade rode up to his headquarters after inspecting another part of the field, and the army band started playing a "significant melody"— "Hail to the Chief." One observer, probably another reporter, said, "Ah! General Meade, you're in very great danger of being President of the United States."[58]

Journalists working on other parts of the field naturally emphasized the actions of the generals they interviewed. A *New York Tribune* correspondent wrote in a story about the decisive third day that he got most of his details of the battle from Winfield Scott Hancock.[59] Without disparaging the courage of Hancock, who was seriously wounded in the battle, it should be no surprise that Hancock was the focus of the story and one of the legendary heroes of the battle. And so it was for the bulk of the Gettysburg coverage. The reporters wrote what they saw, and most of them saw the infantry action and got details provided by the infantry officers.[60]

The cavalry, on the other hand, was overlooked because journalists did not think it would make a major contribution to the outcome of the battle. Military experts and war correspondents alike saw the cavalry as a supporting force best used for scouting and raiding. A reporter who wanted to be at the center of the action would try to find a place to observe the massed infantry attacks.

E. A. Paul of the *New York Times* was one of the few reporters who dedicated himself to the cavalry beat. During Custer's fight on the third day of Gettysburg, Paul apparently stayed with Kilpatrick. He likely assumed that the fiercest cavalry action would be with the man nicknamed "Kill-cavalry."[61]

For most reporters, however, covering the horse soldiers was considered too much action for too little journalistic glory. The cavalry often operated behind the enemy lines and was frequently on the move. The cavalry beat was considered more dangerous and difficult than covering the main army. William Young, a *New York Herald* cavalry reporter, recalled that his immediate predecessor had been killed in action, and the reporter before him had been captured. The editor, anticipating a short future for Young, told him when he was transferred from the infantry beat to the cavalry to write his own obituary just in case. After Young himself had been captured and then escaped, he wrote tongue-in-cheek that he didn't finish the obituary before he took his new assignment because he wanted "time to do full 'justice to the subject.'"[62]

Given the way the press operated, it's no wonder full justice was not done to the cavalry fight at Gettysburg. The stories were short, spare accounts with no context for the fight's connection to the rest of the battle. One of the most frequently published breaking news stories about the cavalry fight was a three-paragraph account of Union horsemen being dispatched to meet Stuart, who "was preparing to make one of his raids on our rear, to cut off our trains and prevent communication with Baltimore and Washington." The story, which had no byline but was datelined from Washington, appeared in papers from Kansas to Pennsylvania as well as in Southern papers like the *Memphis Appeal*. It reported that Meade ordered Gregg to intercept Stuart. "He [Gregg] proceeded to accomplish his mission and met Stuart about two miles from our lines already on his way to execute his designs.

General Gregg charged the rebels and was at first repulsed. He rallied his men and again charged, routing Stuart's force who left his dead and wounded on the field in their hasty retreat." Custer, who led the decisive charge, was not mentioned.[63]

Paul, instead of writing about the defeat of Stuart, filed a brief report on Kilpatrick's ill-fated charge against entrenched rebel infantry on another part of the field that had no relation to Pickett's Charge.[64] Readers of the *Times* had to wait until July 21—long after the narrative of the main battle had been reported and set in the public mind—to read a detailed story about cavalry actions during the Gettysburg campaign. In that issue Paul wrote a story that described fifteen actions that occurred over sixteen days on the march to and from Gettysburg. Unfortunately, in his attempt to summarize the hard work of the cavalry, Paul "buried the lede"—journalese for missing the main point of the story—by putting the Gettysburg fight near the end of the story, not as a climax but merely part of a list of cavalry actions.[65] The story, while providing plenty of statistics on things like the number of prisoners captured and equipment seized, provided no real context or vivid detail.

A *Times* editorial in the same issue bragged about Paul's story, claiming that no one could understand the "brilliant service" of the cavalry without reading it. The *Times* didn't explain specifically what that service included, or how it contributed to winning Gettysburg; it only noted that Paul was wounded while accompanying "the cavalry in all its gallopades" and that he "was a witness, if not a participator, in all the battles." The editorial recommended that more cavalry units were needed as the war "draws to a close," implying they would be needed to harass the retreating rebel armies.[66]

The veterans of the cavalry fight believed the lack of press coverage obscured their role in the battle. "We cavalrymen have always held that we saved the day at the most critical moment of the Battle of Gettysburg, the Greatest Battle and turning point of the War of the Rebellion," wrote William Brooke-Rawle, a second lieutenant with the Third Pennsylvania. "I know that it has not been the custom among historians to give us any credit for having done anything to affect the outcome of the battle."[67] Kidd wrote that twenty years after the battle the cavalry veterans had still not gotten credit for helping to win Gettysburg. He was incensed that even battle maps done by the Corps of Engineers left out the cavalry field. "'History' was practically silent upon the subject," he said, "and had not the survivors of those commands taken up the matter, there might have been no record of the invaluable services which the Second cavalry division and Custer's Michigan brigade rendered at the very moment when a slight thing would have turned the tide of victory the other way."[68]

Subsequent history might not be silent about the cavalry battle, but it never gets much above a whisper in discussing the defeat of Stuart's attack. Although a few recent books have made the argument that Custer's charge "saved the Union" by preventing Stuart from coordinating with Pickett and thus winning the battle, most historians dismiss it as somewhat of a sideshow.[69]

Those who downplay the importance of the cavalry fight argue that it's impossible to know Lee's plans for the cavalry action because no written orders for Stuart exist. It could have been intended as a raid or some other action unrelated to Pickett's attack. Furthermore, participants' accounts vary greatly.[70] The cavalry action was a series of charges and counter-charges, confusing the participants and making it difficult to sort out just what happened.[71] Bruce Catton, one of the most famous of Civil War historians, never mentioned Custer in his book on Gettysburg and dismissed the action as "a sharp but essentially meaningless engagement."[72] After searching through varied histories of the battle to write a biography of Custer, historian Jay Monaghan concluded that opinion on the significance of the cavalry fight to the outcome of Gettysburg "varies with the analysts' prejudices."[73]

Journalism, as the saying goes, is the "first rough draft of history" and plays a significant role in framing how events are interpreted by later generations. And professional historians writing years later usually examine newspaper reports, particularly those of war correspondents who were eyewitnesses and presumably would have a more objective viewpoint of what happened than the participants.

Would the generally understood history of Gettysburg and Custer's actions be different today had the first news stories included substantial information about the cavalry fight on July 3? We'll never know. But it's interesting to consider that a recent history of the Battle of the Bulge in World War II argues that press reports in 1944 overemphasized the actions at Bastogne, distorting our understanding of the role of units other than the 101st Airborne in defeating the German offensive.[74]

Custer and the cavalry got a little more ink as Lee's retreat turned into a running fight in which the horsemen played a larger role. But overall Custer's press coverage during the Gettysburg campaign illustrated the old army cliché about Indian fighting—it consisted of being shot at by someone hiding behind a rock and having your name misspelled in the newspapers. Rebels, rather than Indians, were shooting at Custer, but he certainly had his name misspelled often and in a variety of ways—Castar, Costar, and Coster were some of the versions that were published.[75]

Once tied to the fading star of McClellan, Custer had earned his promotion to general through hard work, audacity, and the instinct of the artist for seizing the moment. He had helped win the biggest battle in American history. Yet his role went largely unrecognized in the media, and when reporters did mention him, they considered him too unimportant to get his name right. The glory went to higher ranks who cultivated the press.[76]

Custer would have to earn his fame on other fields.

CHAPTER FOUR

Boy General of the Golden Locks

After the Battle of Williamsport, also known as Falling Waters, reporters gradually began to notice Custer's leadership and aggressiveness, although he still labored in the shadows of the other cavalry officers. The press, as always, gravitated toward the top commanders as their sources and focus.

Custer, who needed a higher profile in his battle for the respect of Libbie Bacon's father, got a break when Brig. Gen. Judson Kilpatrick was granted a leave until August 4 to deal with kidney ailments.[1] Pleasonton put Custer in temporary charge of the division, and reporters used him for a number of stories to generate copy during a quiet time while both armies recovered from the arduous Gettysburg campaign.

In a recap of the Gettysburg campaign, The *Detroit Free Press* focused on Custer's leadership. "Gen. Custer at once gained the confidence of his brigade. Experienced and accomplished, he has proven himself possessed, in an eminent degree, of those qualities necessary in a cavalry officer. He shuns no danger, avoids no necessary hardships, makes no unnecessary sacrifice of his men, but by his courage, activity and good judgment has already made a proud history for his brigade."[2]

Another *Free Press* story reported that Custer gave "a salutary lesson" to Virginia bushwhackers. An escaped Union prisoner told Custer of a civilian who was acting as an armed scout for rebel cavalry. When they could not find the scout at his house, Custer ordered the house burned. "Experience has proven that the most extreme measures are necessary to put a stop to the murderous and cowardly practices of these men, and that Gen. Custer will adopt such measures there is no room to doubt," the correspondent wrote approvingly. The writer also explained that Custer encouraged slaves to come to his unit, where he would give them safe conduct to freedom. "General C. has, I understand, no negro-worshipping proclivities, but finding these people to be an element of strength to the rebel cause, determined to set them free."[3]

According to the *Free Press*, Custer was also active in negotiations with the Confederates when the rival armies were close enough that the pickets were within speaking distance of each other. "Our men were subjected to a fire from the rebel sharpshooters until a few days ago, when Gen. Custar [sic] went over with a flag of truce and made arrangements to have it stopped. There is now a more friendly spirit manifested between the pickets, and papers are exchanged, tobacco furnished, politics and the war discussed, &c."[4]

Custer, mindful of his image, made sure the story would not support charges that as a Democrat he was overly sympathetic to the South. The *New York Times* subsequently carried a brief denial by Custer that he had any political conversations with the enemy.[5] A Confederate colonel also didn't like what he saw in the papers, and wrote an angry letter stating that he and Custer had only discussed the ceasefire to protect civilians. "The officers of my Staff, as well as myself, were very reticent, and observed unusual caution in our conversation. On the contrary, Gen. Custer and his Staff, all mere youths, branched out extensively, and tried to show us how much they knew."[6]

Custer's youth and his stylish uniform drew the attention of reporters, especially in Kilpatrick's absence. A *New York Tribune* reporter wrote a colorful description of Custer and said he should be getting more attention because of his skill and bravery, which had earned him the jump in promotion:

> With a manly and weatherbeaten face of severe expression, he wears the long flaxen curls of a girl of fifteen, and in lieu of the usual uniform dons a black velvet jacket, embroidered

profusely on the back and arms with gold lace. He is proud of his Michigan men, and they fully return the sentiment. Whenever a charge is made, be it of the brigade, regiment or company, he trots coolly at the head, spurs into a gallop, and the curls, gaily dancing time to each movement as a beacon followed with enthusiasm. Custer, adding to unflinching bravery, has excellent judgment, and is universally esteemed by his brother officers. He is a man of mark; and would shine in any military sphere.

The army needed such fighting generals instead of the kind who "sits on either his horse or a fence, smokes and claps his hands when a thing is handsomely done." [7]

Kilpatrick was considered a fighting general too, and his star still shined brighter. In August, *Harper's Weekly* ran a story on the Union's top cavalry officers with sketches and stories about each: Maj. Gen. George Stoneman, Pleasonton, Maj. Gen. John Buford, and Kilpatrick. *Harper's* gushed about Kilpatrick's latest raid in Virginia and concluded that he was "likely to make his name still more famous before the war ends."[8]

Custer was not mentioned in the story, but in mid-September he got another opportunity to shine as the war heated up. Meade had heard that Lee was moving some of his troops and ordered the cavalry to scout the Confederate positions. The opposing horsemen clashed at Culpeper, Virginia, and Custer led a dramatic charge. Confederate artillery fire hit Custer in the foot and killed his horse.[9]

The *New York Tribune* blared Custer's injury in all caps in the fifth deck of its multiply headlined front-page story about the battle, although the story itself called the injury "a slight flesh wound in the calf."[10] The *Baltimore American* and the *New York Times* acknowledged that Custer "was wounded while gallantly charging a battery of the enemy, in which charge three guns were captured," but gave no other details.[11] A subsequent story about the battle in the *New York Times* showed the usual bias toward top commanders, putting Pleasonton in the lead of the story, but it provided details of Custer's wounding. "Gen Custer charged at the head of his brigade twice, and the second time took guns, limbers, horses, men and all complete. His horse was killed by a round shot, which passed through and killed a bugler behind him. It also touched Gen. Custer's leg, giving him a painful, but not dangerous confusion [sic], which will take him from the field for a short time."[12]

The *New York Times* ran yet another story about the battle about a week later, this time including a description of Custer capturing prisoners:

> Gen. Custer, whose irrepressible gallantry led him far ahead of his command, came up and went with them. Down the hill they went at a gallop—a perfect avalanche of shot and shell crashing above them, and ploughing the ground around them. Dressing the line for a moment at the foot of the hill on which the battery was, they charged up with such impetuosity that everything gave way before them. With great rapidity they dashed around in the rear of the guns, and in a moment they were ours. After the guns were captured Gen. Costar came up armed only with his riding whip, compelling many a man to surrender at discretion.[13]

The *New York Herald* provided the most dramatic account of Custer's charge, although it appeared in the middle of the story and was not mentioned in the five headlines: "The charge is described as having been one of unequalled gallantry. The brigade was obliged to dash through the town, and down a steep hill, through a ravine, and then up a steep and very high hill to the battery, which meanwhile was belching forth its shell and canister upon their ranks. But it could not retard the speed nor daunt the spirit of the 'Boy General of the Golden Locks' and his brave troops."[14] An editorial in the same issue called the fight "not only a brilliant but an important affair." However, it praised Kilpatrick, Buford, and Gregg without mentioning Custer.[15]

Harper's included a sketch of Custer charging the guns and a brief description that called the charge "brilliant." However, Custer is not easily identified in the crowded drawing. The piece was only one among seven in a two-page spread and was by no means the featured illustration. The dominant sketch, which spanned both pages, was of Buford's artillery at Raccoon Ford.[16]

Nevertheless, more people were beginning to take notice of Custer both for his actions and his theatrical appearance. Lt. Col. Theodore

Lyman, an aide to Meade, saw the charge and wrote one of the most often-quoted descriptions of Custer's appearance during the war. Lyman was a wealthy New Englander who had studied zoology at Harvard. He met Meade before the war while Meade was an engineer designing lighthouses and Lyman was collecting marine specimens. Lyman was not a professional soldier, but he was a scientist with an eye for detail. He examined Custer as if he were looking at an exotic fish.[17]

"This officer is one of the funniest-looking beings you ever saw, and looks like a circus rider gone mad!" Lyman wrote in a letter to his wife. "He wears a huzzar jacket and tight trousers, of faded black velvet trimmed with tarnished gold lace. His head is decked with a little, gray felt hat; high boots and gilt spurs complete the costume, which is enhanced by the General's coiffure, consisting in short, dry, flaxen ringlets! His aspect, though highly amusing, is also pleasing, as he has a very merry blue eye, and a devil-may-care style."

Lyman observed Custer ride up to Pleasonton after the battle and immediately ask for a leave to go home.

"How are you, fifteen-days'-leave-of-absence?" Custer said. "They have spoiled my boots but they didn't gain much there, for I stole 'em from a Reb."

Lyman had admired the charge, and he noticed that in addition to the torn boot, Custer's leg was injured. "[S]o the warlike ringlets got not only fifteen, but twelve [additional] days' leave of absence, and have retreated to their native Michigan!"[18]

Lyman wrote with the flippancy of the Harvard intellectual serving in a staff job. Custer was the uncouth Midwestern blacksmith's son who was doing the actual fighting. Tully McCrea, one of Custer's West Point classmates, wrote a more sympathetic description at about the same time.

McCrea ascribed Custer's appearance to his romantic nature and delight for flouting convention. "Last summer when he was in the Peninsula, he vowed that he would not cut his hair until he entered Richmond," McCrea wrote to his cousin, and sweetheart, Belle McCrea. "He has kept his vow and now his hair is about a foot long and hangs over his shoulders in curls just like a girl. He was dressed in a fancy suit of velveteen covered with gold braid, with an immense collar like a sailor's, with his Brigadier star in each corner. Put a fancy cap on his head, and a hearty smile on his face, you then have his 'tout ensemble.' You may think from this that he is a vain man, but he is not; it is nothing more than his penchant for oddity."

Tully, who spent about a dozen years loyally courting Belle, told her that Custer was quite the ladies' man and didn't care whose heart he broke. "What a monster! methinks I hear you say," Tully wrote. "Perhaps he is. But he is a gallant soldier, a whole-souled generous friend, and a mighty good fellow, and I like him and wish him every success in his new role of a Brigadier."[19]

Tully, unlike Lyman, recognized Custer's costume for what it was —a romantic sensibility—but he misread Custer's personal life. Custer loved women. He appreciated beauty and delighted in flirting. Yet he also had a romantic notion of marriage and saw himself in the role of husband and provider. His request for leave was to continue his pursuit of Libbie Bacon.

Custer had asked Libbie repeatedly to marry him, but she had always turned him down. On this leave, Custer came home a celebrity and wounded hero. The breakthrough in their relationship came at a masquerade ball covered by the local newspaper. Custer was dressed as Louis XVI and Libbie as a gypsy playing a tambourine. Louis XVI was a hero for leading France into an alliance with the United States during the Revolutionary War. He was executed during the French Revolution, going to the guillotine bravely at the age of thirty-eight. Custer, always throwing himself into the role he was in, must have played a dashing king with the subtext that he, too, could die young in battle. Libbie as a gypsy would have been a flirtatious seductress.

Their favorite song was "Then You'll Remember Me," a classic sentimental ballad from the opera *The Bohemian Girl*, which featured an exiled Polish nobleman who joins a band of gypsies. He becomes involved in a love triangle with a gypsy queen that ends in tragic death. Libbie promised to sing the song for Custer when he returned from the front. Custer in turn gave her sheet music for it, the first song he ever bought for her.[20]

Custer and Libbie were discovering how well they fit together. They were sentimentalists who could imagine themselves in different places and times, both fans of the romantic novels of their age. Each could easily craft a different persona for various situations: Custer a class clown, a humble aide, or a fearless boy general; Libbie a poor girl who lost her mother, a scholar, or a femme fatale.

The masquerade began at 9 in the evening, supper was served at midnight, and then the revelers danced again, not stopping till morning, knowing they had to find joy when they could with war always hanging over them. When Custer again asked Libbie to marry him, this time in the Bacons' garden, she agreed. She insisted on one caveat, though: They could not be formally engaged or married until her father gave his consent.[21] It seemed a small obstacle since Custer was now a general and a hero. At this point in the war it was evident that veterans would rule the country when it was over. The war was so big that the role a man played in it would dictate his future, not his parents' background.

People were already telling Libbie that Custer would be somebody important after the war. When Custer was promoted to general, Libbie's friend Nan Darrah congratulated her, writing "When I know he is President of the U.S. I shall not be surprised in the least."[22] When Libbie read novels, she imagined the hero in her mind's eye as Custer, confessing to her journal that his image came dashing into her fancy while she was reading. "Every other man seems so ordinary beside my own particular *star.*"[23]

Others around the country were taking note. Custer's friend Thomas Ward wrote from West Point, "I most heartily congratulate you on the very flattering manner in which your name has been mentioned in the New York papers during the last month, and I assure you the natives about these parts are getting to have a high regard for your soldierly qualities."[24]

Christiancy, Custer's friend who was associate justice of the Michigan Supreme Court, took the young general to a political meeting at the Kalamazoo home of Charles S. May, the lieutenant governor. Governor Austin Blair and Charles M. Croswell, a state senator who would be elected governor after the war, were also at the meeting, which occurred while the state fair was going on in Kalamazoo. The crowd of Republican heavyweights must have seen in Custer a future political star for their state—perhaps even the first president from Michigan, as Libbie's friend suggested.

Custer, who missed his own young niece and nephews while he was at the front, left the political conversation to play with May's four-year-old daughter. Custer asked her for a picture to take with him back to the front, and she sassily replied he would have to send her his first. About a month later, May's daughter got a picture from Custer with a letter enquiring after her and her family. May, recalling the incident years later to the *Kalamazoo Telegraph,* said his daughter still cherished the picture, and that the incident, although minor, reflected Custer's character. "Everybody now knows that Gen. Custer was not only a gallant and dashing soldier, but a commander of ability, a hero and a patriot. But was it not because he was a true knight and hero that he could thus turn away from the thoughts and sound of war and carnage and interest himself in a little child?"[25]

Custer was constantly thinking of his family. He carried on a lively correspondence with them, scratching his writer's itch by detailing his experiences as if he were writing an adventure novel. Custer's family worried about him, but they didn't understand the life of a soldier. They made a lot of demands on him: his father argued politics, his mother guilted him about being away from home and describing how poor they were. She did it slyly, through his sisters and father, not writing Custer directly. And always, they worried about his faith and feared that he would be wounded or killed.

Custer's older half sister Ann, acting as his second mother as she usually did, teased him that perhaps he thought he was too good for the family now that he was famous. Their father hadn't received a letter from Custer for a while and couldn't figure out why his son wouldn't write him, she explained. Ann also urged Custer to write her husband, David Reed. "Try and write a few lines home if you possibly can or they will think you have forgot them. You don't know how often we think of you." She apologized for the quality of her own writing and playfully suggested that might be why he didn't write home as much as he should. "You will see a grate many mistakes this evening. I don't know how a General can read such a letter as this. Some of the folks think you will hardly speak to common folks Now. I told them I did not think it would make much difference with you. We see your name in the papers quite often. I do hope you will be careful of your self and not rush into danger."[26]

In another letter she urged him to write several times and asked him when the war would be over. She was worried that he would take too many risks.

> I feel very ancious about you all the time. I don't know what day I may have some bad News from you. I do hope you will be careful of yourself and your life be spared.
>
> My Dear Brother O how much I wish you was a christion. You have often said you was happy. I don't think there is any true happiness in the world with out religion. It sweetens all the cares and trials of this life. Our heavenly father has bin so kind to us and done so much for us we are under obligations to love and serve him. Do try and write often.[27]

Custer's little sister Maggie wrote chattier letters, sounding like the teenager that she was. With the invincibility of youth, she wasn't worried about Custer. She described her scrapbook album and the shininess of the silverware she set on the table, promising her big brother that she would let him use one of her forks when he came home. She told him to let his whiskers grow so she could see how he looked with a beard. In one letter she asked him to send her a feather, and in another some shells to decorate the table. She matter-of-factly told him "Little Tom dog is dead" without further explanation. What reaction this prompted in the dog-loving Custer can only be imagined. But she quickly changed topics to ask him to send $5 (equivalent to about $100 in 2020) to their mother so she could hire a mason to repair an old shed. Their mother, Maggie explained, "hates to ask you for it."[28]

Custer didn't mind sending it. For him, family and friends were the joy of life. His thoughts always returned to his boyhood in Ohio and Michigan. About this time, while Custer was achieving fame and honor, he was reminiscing about Hopedale and he contacted a classmate named David Donovan, who he had not seen in years. Donovan, who had become a lawyer in Ohio after a spell working in journalism, wrote back enthusiastically that he wanted to stay in touch. "Later attachments and friendships may change or pass away, but some of the attachments of earlier years only grow stronger through change and time," Donovan wrote. "I can say with truth, that so far as I am concerned such an attachment was ours."[29]

Perhaps Custer was reminiscing because he had made a more permanent attachment to his hometown by becoming engaged to Libbie Bacon. But like many a young fiancé, he was wary of his father-in-law and had avoided asking him for permission to marry Libbie. Custer went back to the front with the knowledge that he would have to compose a winning letter to convince the judge he was worthy of his daughter. Custer admitted in his letter of October 1863 to the judge that in his youth he had made mistakes, including drinking too much. Custer was only twenty-three, yet he wrote of himself as if he were middle-aged. In a sense, he was, as most of the young men of his generation had been through two years of war. He had killed men and been wounded himself, narrowly escaping death several times. Now he was a general, responsible for the lives of thousands of men.

Ever an artist, he saw his life as a heroic story. Some men are embarrassed by their humble upbringing. For Custer, it was a point of honor, part of his struggle against the odds. "I left home when but sixteen, and have been surrounded with temptation, but I have always had a purpose in life," he wrote to Bacon.[30]

When Custer left home it was to be a schoolteacher—hardly the life of temptation, it would seem. Yet he had a burning ambition to be great at something. He had copied in his teaching school notebook the N. P. Willis poem about ambition—a warning of how all-consuming that particular temptation could be. He also fought against the temptation of drinking, sleigh riding with the girls, being the class clown—in essence, always being the performer, the center of attention. Thus far he had succeeded at reaching for greatness, serving as the army commander's trusted aide when he was barely out of West Point, and now commanding men in the greatest battles in history. But he still was surrounded by the temptations facing a young man away from home in the army—drinking, gambling, womanizing. And as throughout his life, he was trying like a great performer to hone his skills, to be the star, the leader in battle, but not let his personality overwhelm his judgment. Would Daniel Bacon understand?

Waiting for a reply, Custer contented himself by mooning over Libbie, singing "Then You'll Remember Me" around the campfire with his friends."[31]

The judge decided to let Custer twist in the wind a bit, even though he knew his daughter was deeply in love. Bacon exercised his dwindling hold on parental power by addressing Custer formally as "Sir" and writing in October that it would take "weeks or even months" of thought before he could give an answer to Custer's request.[32]

Custer threw himself back into his duty, fighting with a theatrical ferocity that amazed his soldiers and fellow officers alike. The first battle after his leave occurred when Meade sent two cavalry divisions—including Custer's command—to scout rebel movements that looked like an offensive. The Union cavalry crossed the Rappahannock and eventually wound up in a trap as Stuart's cavalry surrounded them while the Union infantry in the area retreated. Custer wrote in his official report about the "heavy masses of rebel cavalry"—more than double his command—that surrounded him.[33]

Should they surrender? Pleasonton and Kilpatrick, who were trapped with Custer, agreed to his suggestion to instead punch a hole through the rebel lines so they could escape across the river. Custer rode to the front of the Fifth Michigan. The moment cried for theater. Custer stood up in his stirrups and shouted, "Boys of Michigan. There are some people between us and home; I'm going home, who else goes?" The men gave three cheers in response. He tossed his hat to an aide, letting his blonde curls float in the breeze. The band struck up "Yankee Doodle"—the song they always played to signal a charge.

As they started at a trot, Custer couldn't resist the scene he had authored, twisting in the saddle to watch the sabers sparkle in the sunshine. Custer turned back toward the enemy. The moment was right. He pointed his blade toward the enemy and shouted, "Charge!" The bugles blared. The men shouted. The hooves thundered.

A witness wrote later, "Custer, the daring, terrible demon that he is in battle, dashed madly forward in the charge, while his yellow locks floated like pennants in the breeze. Fired to an almost divine potency, and with a majestic madness, this band of heroic troopers shook the air with their battle cry."[34]

Custer's horse was shot. He remounted, and his second horse was shot within fifteen minutes. The rebels and the Union troops charged and countercharged all afternoon, but the Yankees under Custer eventually broke through, escaping back to the Union lines.[35]

The press noticed Custer, but most of the glory still went to higher-ranking generals. For example, the *Baltimore American* devoted a paragraph of its battle coverage to Custer's charge. "A charge was ordered, and General Custer's brigade gallantly drove the enemy into a thicket of woods, from which they however recharged in larger numbers, and our cavalry then made a grand charge in their front and flanks, exiting their way through and joined Buford." But most of the rest of story focused on Kilpatrick.[36] Two days later, when the paper had more space to devote to the battle, it used the headline "Gallantry of Kilpatrick," praising his leadership and ignoring Custer completely. The *American* even quoted Kilpatrick as using Custer's favorite battle cry, "Come on, you Wolverines!"[37]

A few days after the cavalry's narrow escape, Meade ordered them forward again to see if the rebel army was retreating. Stuart set a trap and defeated the Union forces at Buckland Mills, capturing a battalion of the Fifth Michigan and Custer's headquarters wagon, which included personal material such as letters and clothes. Custer blamed Kilpatrick, and a number of men in the command agreed.[38]

Northern newspapers, however, tended to put a positive spin on the defeat. One reporter described going through the army camp and hearing how the cavalry "had covered the retreat and suffered terribly." But that was not the whole story, the writer added. "Not till the next day did we hear of that grandest cavalry fight the world has ever witnessed, in which the whole cavalry force of both armies was engaged. Not till the next day did we hear how Gen. Pleasanton, ordered to cover the retreat of the army from Culpeper, held his position until nearly surrounded; how he proved himself the Prince of cavalry officers; how Kilpatrick, surrounded, ordered his division to break their way through, and *how they did it;* how nobly Gen. Custer sustained his former hard earned reputation; how the First Michigan Cavalry charged upon twice their number of the enemy, scattering them like chaff. . . ."[39]

The *Chicago Times* mentioned the heavy Union losses but pointed out that one surrounded brigade had escaped the rebels. "In the engagement on Monday, Gen. Custar was conspicuous, and reports the rebel cavalry were driven beyond Buckland's Mills from Gainesville, where our cavalry encountered rebel infantry and artillery in line of battle, their line extending a mile."[40]

The *New York Times* praised the fighting quality the Union troops showed even after defeat. "Gen. Custer's brigade did not retire from Buckland's Mills until his men had exhausted all their carbine ammunition. The officers and men then held the bridge with their pistols, until the enemy had forded the river and thus flanked the brigade, which then fell back, holding the cavalry in check. . . ."[41] A more detailed story the next day praised Custer and several other officers, but singled out Kilpatrick, who "at a glance" recognized the danger and took appropriate action.[42] The *Times'* final piece on the action claimed the series of battles was so "brilliant" that the action couldn't be described. "It is sufficient to say that Gen. Kilpatrick's division, often flanked, and at one time entirely surrounded, did all that brave men could. The General's eye and voice were always where they were needed. He was most ably seconded in his efforts by Gens. Davis and Custer. Gen. Davis, in his dangerous duty of bringing up the rear, continually exposed himself to the enemy's hottest fire, and seemed endowed with a charmed life."[43]

As with most of the coverage, Custer, while mentioned, played second fiddle to other officers. After the battle of Buckland Mills, the armies entered another stretch of routine duties of picketing, drilling, and camp life.[44] Custer's celebrity was growing; a little more success and he could join the upper ranks of fame.

The success and Custer and Libbie's insistent love were enough to persuade her father to consent to the marriage, although not without some evident hesitation. Bacon wrote that he wished Custer were a Christian but admitted he couldn't judge Custer's morals when his own were "far short" of Custer's when he was his age. Bacon conceded he was proud of Custer's military record. He cautioned Custer that he was not a wealthy man, so Libbie would not have a large inheritance. He agreed to place Custer's gift to Libbie—a photograph of Custer—in her room. It portrayed "the great object of her love and affection. I can anticipate the strength of her lungs when it shall meet her eye in her surprised admiration and loud and hearty laugh."[45]

The wedding reflected the couple's synergistic enthusiasm for fame. Libbie originally wanted a simple afternoon wedding in her home, but as in the case of many weddings, the plans grew more elaborate as the excitement built. She wrote to her cousin Rebecca Richmond in January—about a month before the wedding—that she was going to have her dress made in Detroit and her "underclothes made on a machine." The dress was looped with yellow military braid and her corsage of red roses fit the same theme. In response to Custer's comment that her preparations were elaborate, she reminded her groom that he "was not marrying a girl *entirely* unknown in this state." She told Custer she wanted him in his full-dress uniform.[46]

"I have changed my mind about not wanting ostentation," Libbie wrote. "If we begin by regulating our actions by the opinions of others we shall never have any of our own. I want to be married in the evening, in the church."[47] She got her wish, of course. Custer would have done anything to please his bride, and a man who had designed his own uniform for show would never have turned down an ostentatious wedding.

At any rate, Custer had a professional crisis that would have put wedding plans in the background of his mind. Pleasonton told him there was a rumor that Michigan Senator Jacob M. Howard, who was on the military affairs committee, would oppose his official confirmation as brigadier general of volunteers. Howard's reasoning was that Custer was not a true Michigan man, and that he was a strong Democrat, a McClellan man, and worst of all—a Copperhead sympathetic to the rebels.[48]

Custer, as was his nature, made his case with passionate writing, sending Howard a letter avowing his loyalty to President Lincoln and the Emancipation Proclamation. After three years of bloody war, the politics of men like Custer were changing. They might have Southern friends, they might be against complete equality, but they saw the end of slavery as necessary to win the war and as the right thing to do for those in bondage, whose suffering they had seen firsthand while fighting in Southern territory. "The President . . . as Commander in Chief of the Army and as my superior officer Cannot issue any decree

or order which will not receive my unqualified *support*," Custer wrote
in an eight-page letter to Howard. "But I do *not* stop here . . . All
his acts, proclamations and decisions embraced in his war policy have
received not only my support, but my most hearty, earnest and cordial
approval. . . . . My friends . . . *can* testify that I have insisted that so long
as a single slave was held in bondage, I for *one*, was opposed to peace
on any terms, and to show that my acts agree with my words I can
boast of having liberated more slaves from their Masters than any other
General in this Army." The latter claim would be hard to prove, but
Custer could be forgiven of a little of his native Ohio frontier brag as he
warmed to his peroration. Negotiations with Rebels? "I would *offer* no
compromise except that which is offered at the point of the bayonet,"
he declared.[49]

The letter to Howard, plus a flurry of others to Michigan Senator
Zachariah Chandler, Congressman F. W. Kellogg, and three to his
friend Christiancy, on the advice of Pleasonton, did the job. Just as he
had gotten into West Point through contacting his local congressman,
Custer was able to write his way to securing his promotion. Custer,
Pleasonton, the whole Michigan congressional delegation, and most of
the officers of the Michigan brigade celebrated the anniversary of their
state's admission to the Union at a grand "Sons of Michigan" ball in
Washington. The year before, it had been a stag party, according to a
lengthy story in the *Washington Evening Star*, but in 1864 the daughters
of Michigan were invited to an elegant affair that featured an extravagant supper and dancing until the morning hours. "The pretty women
were not all of Michigan, perhaps, but had an 'affinity' that way evidently, and especially for her young." How much dancing "Custar"
did was not reported—the *Star* could not get his name right it—but
he must have been anxious to head out on his leave to Monroe to get
married.[50]

The wedding, on February 9, 1864, was the event of the season in
Monroe. An overflow crowd at the First Presbyterian Church greeted
the bridal party at about 8 P.M. Custer had cut his curling locks, disap-
pointing some in the crowd, but it fit his and Libbie's vision of what a
military wedding should look like. The cavalier was the look for the
battlefield, the shorn West Point style was for the public ceremony.
About three hundred attended the reception at Daniel Bacon's home,

where they could admire the rich collection of gifts for the famous couple. The First Vermont cavalry sent an engraved silver dinner service,
the Seventh Michigan sent a seven-piece silver tea set, and the Bacons
gave Libbie a gold watch, a Bible, and a parasol. Other gifts included a
chess stand made of Grand Rapids marble, a gold-lined thimble, and a
book of Elizabeth Browning's poems.[51]

The wedding made national news—even in the *New York Herald*—
although only as a paragraph announcement, usually noting that Custer
was the youngest general in the army. The silver set from the Vermont
cavalry was worth a paragraph in the Vermont newspapers. Custer's
marriage was newsworthy and important enough to his men that they
wanted to claim him as their personal star.[52]

Daniel Bacon couldn't help boasting about the wedding in a letter to
his sister Charity. "All went off remarkably well, and no mistake made.
It was said to be the most splendid wedding ever seen in the State.
From one to two hundred more in the church than ever before and as
many unable to enter for want of room."[53]

A few months later Bacon was more reflective in a letter to his sister
about the wedding and the match between his daughter and the young
soldier. "I never engaged in an enterprise with more cheerfulness, and
yet a good deal was useless and largely extravagant." He had agreed to
the marriage "cheerfully" not out of his own judgment but more to
make Libbie happy. "It is not common for a couple to come together
whose highest aspirations are fully gratified. This is emphatically true
in this case, for both feel that they have the highest possible treasure,
and if they think so [then] it be." Bacon wished the war was over and
hoped it would end that summer but worried it would be a bloody
year. "What awaits Custer no one can say. Libbie may be a widow or
have a maimed husband. There is no better way than to put our trust
in Him who governs all things."[54]

For the new couple, the war likely added to the excitement and passion of young love. Richard Holmes wrote in a study of the psychology
of the soldier that war throughout history has heightened the sexual
desires of both men and women. The constant threat of death and the
uprooting of couples adds a frisson to relationships that isn't present in
peacetime. "The whirlwind wartime romance may be a cliché, but it is
a cliché founded in fact," Holmes wrote.[55]

The intensity of their relationship became evident at West Point, which was one of the stops on their train ride through New York state. Custer the schoolteacher loved the academy and wanted to show it to Libbie. Everyone seemed to remember Custer, even the dogs that hung around the college. But Libbie let an old professor kiss her and walked with some of the cadets down a path known to Custer as the Lovers' Walk.[56]

Custer wanted to be her only star, and overcome with jealousy, he sat in silence on the ensuing train ride to New York City. Libbie wrote later she feared he would send her back to Monroe. "I was amazed to see my blithe bridegroom turned into an incarnated thundercloud." Her tearful protestations that the professor was as old as Methuselah and the cadets were mere boys finally got Custer out of his green mood.[57]

Libbie's parents had not let her see plays as a girl. Custer took her to several on their honeymoon, starting a mutual interest they would share for the rest of their marriage. One play was *Uncle Tom's Cabin*, an adaptation of the powerful novel that had fueled support for abolition. For Custer, the play must have reinforced his feelings about fighting to end slavery.[58]

When the Custers arrived in Washington, they saw *East Lynne*, a melodrama made from a popular 1861 British novel by Ellen Wood. It had a convoluted plot involving a cheating wife who abandons her family and is disfigured in a train accident. She then becomes governess to her own children in the house of her former husband and his new wife. Wood wrote thirty novels and was known for her conservative and Christian style—a far cry from the swashbuckling novels Custer favored only a few years before. But he loved the play, surprising Libbie with the depth of his emotion. She recalled that he "laughed at the fun and cried at the pathos in the theatres with all the abandon of a boy unconscious of his surroundings." Libbie herself cried so much she soaked her lace handkerchief by the end of the first act. She turned to Custer to ask for his handkerchief and found him red-faced. "Don't keep it long, Libbie," he said as he handed her his wet handkerchief. "I need it."[59]

On a subsequent leave in Baltimore, they saw the famous comedic actor John Sleeper Clarke. "I laughed till I cried, and I thought Autie would have a fit, he nearly fell off his seat laughing," Libbie wrote her parents, describing in great detail a scene in which Clarke's pants were so tight he had to keep his legs stretched out straight when he sat down. "It was simply killing."[60]

The theater was a welcome but as it turned out short-lived distraction for the honeymooners. Custer received orders to return to his unit. Libbie went with him to the brigade headquarters where, as the general's wife, she was catered to by the staff and Custer's housekeeper, an escaped slave named Eliza Brown.

Custer would soon depart on what would be the first of many separations from Libbie required by his service. Kilpatrick had hatched a daring plan, and Custer, as usual, was set to play a supporting role in his shadow.

CHAPTER FIVE

Then You'll Remember Me

Celebrity

Judson Kilpatrick had created a scheme sure to win glory and fame. The plan, initially rejected by Pleasonton but later approved by Lincoln and Secretary of War Edwin Stanton, called for troops to raid Richmond and free Union prisoners held in the city. Col. Ulric Dahlgren, the son of Union Adm. John Dahlgren, volunteered. The twenty-one-year-old Dahlgren had lost a leg at Gettysburg but was still welcomed on the raid, lending it a powerful patron in addition to a certain cachet. Custer's role was to lead fifteen hundred cavalrymen in a diversionary attack to burn the Lynchburg Railroad Bridge over the Rivanna River some fifty miles behind rebel lines. Custer left Libbie on February 28, 1864.

Alfred Waud, the famous *Harper's Weekly* artist correspondent, chose to ride with Custer rather than with the main attack. Waud, who had sketched Custer's jump in the Chickahominy River in what seemed a lifetime ago, had a reporter's sense of where the real story would be.

He was right. The Kilpatrick-Dahlgren raid was an epic failure. Kilpatrick, normally so reckless, became overly cautious right at the brink of success. He was on the outskirts of Richmond with three thousand troops facing only about five hundred rebels when he inexplicably retreated to the Union lines. Dahlgren, leading a separate column, was waylaid by rebels. His entire command was either captured or killed. Dahlgren was among the dead, and the rebels found documents on his body detailing plans to assassinate Confederate President Jefferson Davis and burn the capital. The news was published widely in Southern newspapers, adding fuel to the rebel spirt to resist the hated Yankees.

Custer, on the other hand, was making good news for the Union. In two days he marched more than one hundred and fifty miles, burned the Rivanna River bridge, destroyed three flour mills and a rebel camp and captured fifty prisoners and five hundred horses. He also liberated more than one hundred slaves, whom he brought back with him. Remarkably, his command suffered no fatalities and only a few wounded. Some of his men were captured, but he freed them in the back-and-forth of the cavalry skirmishes he fought during the raid.[1]

At one point, the rebel cavalry under Stuart appeared to have Custer trapped on the wrong side of the Rapidan River. Some of Custer's subordinates panicked and recommended he abandon his cannons and run. Custer's artistic sense led him to find a solution in pretending. He feinted an attack, drawing the rebels in the wrong direction, and led his men back safely into the Union lines.

Until the raid, Custer had always been second to Kilpatrick and other cavalrymen in the press. Even when Custer led Kilpatrick's division during the latter's extended sick leave, news stories invariably referred to "Kilpatrick's Division, under the temporary command of Custer." But after Custer's stunning success in the raid, he started to emerge from the shadows of his superiors and become a star in his own right.

The raid was front-page news around the country, and the first stories to be reported were about Custer, who finished his mission before Kilpatrick returned. The *New York Herald* filled its entire front page with stories and a giant four-column-wide map of the area of the raid. The *Herald* praised Custer's actions in a headline as a "splendid demonstration," and one story declared it was "one of the boldest and most successful cavalry raids of the war."[2]

Another story told how Custer refused to give up when his escape was blocked by Stuart. "For some time the officers of our little command were at a loss what to do," the *Herald* wrote. "The object of their wearisome and dangerous raid was to draw the rebel cavalry away from the central road to Richmond; but they had no intention of drawing them so far in their rear. All that bothered our troops was the section of Ransom's battery, and that slightly impeded their progress. In general council it was proposed to throw those two Parrot guns into the nearest and deepest ditch; but General Custar, protesting, declared he would fight his way through. He ordered a charge, which was led by himself in person."[3]

But the biggest boost came from Waud's story and illustrations. Many soldiers, including Custer, had their photographs taken in uniform, and these were prized possessions and exchanged with family and friends. However, printing technology had not been developed to the point that photographs could be reproduced in newspapers or magazines. Combat artists like Waud were the Civil War equivalent of war photographers, and their action sketches in illustrated newspapers like *Harper's Weekly* were the source of much of the public's mental image of the war. Custer made the cover of *Harper's Weekly* on March 19 with a drawing of him leading a charge in the classic cavalryman's pose— sword upraised, hatless, and long hair flowing wildly. A double-page spread of Waud's sketches from the raid, headlined "Scenes Connected with General Custer's Late Movement across the Rapidan," followed in the next issue, March 26, and included Waud's story. The correspondent praised Custer's leadership, writing that he had fooled the rebels into taking a wrong road and then easily crossed the Rapidan with minor casualties.[4]

On Custer's subsequent leave to Washington, Libbie noticed the impact of the *Harper's Weekly* coverage. People recognized Custer on the street, and she decided to keep a scrapbook of his clippings.[5] He was a national star, a celebrity in an age when athletes and entertainers did not eclipse the sacrifice of military heroes.

The Custers were not strangers to news coverage. Even on their honeymoon, local papers like the *Cleveland Morning Leader*, for example, would publish a few paragraphs noting that the young general and his new bride had stayed in town while traveling to the East.[6] Custer's own family and his new in-laws kept track of his doings in the military, talking about his mentions in the *New York World*, the premier daily in the United States.[7] But this talk was that of a family excited just to see the name of one of its members in print, much like a twenty-first-century family gets excited when they see one of their own on television. Now, after the raid, Custer's ambitions of greatness that he had dreamed of while a college student were being recognized by the nation.

Custer was conflicted about the fame. On the one hand, he had a boyish excitement about seeing his name in print and shared it with his new bride to impress her. In the first months of their marriage, he sent her a clip of an editorial from the *Detroit Free Press*. "It speaks of me in the most flattering manner," Custer wrote Libbie. Yet he urged her not to show it to others because they might think he was being vain.[8] He knew his duty was to help win the war regardless of individual honors.

On the other hand, the growing fame raised the stakes for Custer. More powerful people noticed him, and more rewards were possible: higher ranks in the military, and a career in politics or some other field after the war. Libbie, like Custer a dreamer and ambitious for a life outside of parochial Monroe, helped further his career.

Part of the time that Custer was at the front, Libbie lived in a boarding house in Washington. She fit in well in Washington society, flirting with congressman and even Lincoln. She enjoyed the attention she and Custer received, writing to her parents that Custer was invited to visit the House of Representatives, and the congressmen swarmed him, wanting to get close to the new star general. Lincoln, too, was impressed by Custer.[9]

"The President knew all about him when Autie was presented to him, and talked to him about his graduation," she wrote. "None of the other generals receive half the attention, and their arrivals are scarcely noticed in the papers. I am so amazed at his reputation I cannot but write you about it. I wonder his head is not turned."[10]

After Custer returned to the front, Libbie, accompanied by Michigan congressman Kellogg and his wife, went to a party at the White House. When Lincoln first met Libbie in the receiving line, he gave her the standard greeting, but then he recognized her last name. He took her hand again. "So this is the young woman whose husband goes into a charge with a whoop and a shout," he said warmly and joked that married life would change Custer's ways. "Well," he said, "I'm told he won't do so anymore."

Libbie replied she hoped Custer would keep doing what he was doing.

"Oh, then you want to be a widow, I see," Lincoln said.

The president and Libbie laughed at his dark humor. Later, Libbie talked with one of Lincoln's secretaries and told him that if women could vote, Lincoln would have hers.

"Was I not honored," she wrote her parents of the reception. "I am quite a Lincoln girl now."

Other politicians wished the Michigan beauty was their girl. When Kellogg introduced Libbie to Schuyler Colfax, the speaker of the House, Colfax said, "I have been wishing to be presented to this lady, but am disappointed she is a Mrs.!" [11]

Libbie, used to the attentions of older men since she had been a teenager in Monroe, took the flirtations in stride. She went to dances, or "hops," with Michigan's congressional delegation. The congressmen enjoyed the company of the vivacious young officer's wife. Both Chandler and Kellogg got drunk at some of these events, and each tried to kiss Libbie. She was mature enough to be able to reject them in a way that preserved their friendships for her and Custer. Libbie in fact made a joke of it, writing to her father, "Mr. Ch. is an old goosey idiot. Now his wife is away he is drunk *all* the time. And O, so silly." [12]

Unlike his jealousy at the attention Libbie received from the West Point cadets on their honeymoon, Custer was not troubled by her dancing with politicians. Connections, he had learned from his mentors, were vital to promotion in the army. In the same way that she was proud of his military success, he was proud that she cut such a swath through the capital, establishing herself as a popular figure among the country's leaders.

"When I think of the sacrifices you have made for me, the troubles and trials you have endured to make me happy, the debt of gratitude you have placed me under, my heart almost fails me to think I have only the devotion of my life to offer you in return," Custer wrote to Libbie. "I read your description of the President's levee with much gratification. You certainly were honored by his Highness—as you should be. You know how proud I am of my darling." [13]

The Custers had been married only a few months, yet they already performed as a team, as much in sync as two actors who had been in a long-running play. Custer had few worries about the attentions thrown to Libbie. Always aware he was the poor blacksmith's son, he wrote Libbie that he would be concerned that meeting such powerful men would make her regret her choice in a husband except that she had written him that she preferred to be his adored wife.[14]

"I am so glad you attended the Hop, and am so much obliged to Mr. Chandler for inviting you," Custer wrote Libbie of Senator Chandler's escorting her to an event. He didn't care about the gossip it might generate. "You did perfectly right in accepting, it is just what I urged you to do. Do not heed the idle opinions of those whose time is occupied with other people's business."[15]

Custer was right to be careful about cultivating important politicians. The army was again facing another shakeup as Lincoln promoted Grant to command all Union forces. Grant decided to operate his headquarters from the Army of the Potomac, although he left Meade in technical command of that specific army. Of immediate concern to Custer was Grant's replacement of his mentor, Pleasonton, with Philip Sheridan, who was one of Grant's trusted officers from the Western theater.

Sheridan, like Custer, was an Ohioan, but he was eight years older. Like Custer, Sheridan had a troubled career at West Point. He was suspended in his third year for fighting with a classmate he had threatened to run through with a bayonet over an insult on the parade ground. He managed to graduate and was wounded fighting Indians in the Pacific Northwest. In the Civil War, Sheridan had worked his way up the ranks through successful performances in a number of battles, including a key attack at Chattanooga that helped break the Confederate lines.

Custer and Sheridan hit it off right away. They had the same aggressive, fighting spirit and the same vision of using the cavalry as an attack force rather than as an auxiliary for scouting and supporting the infantry. Sheridan sent for Custer to hold a get-acquainted meeting, and they spent the night talking until the early hours of the morning. Custer wrote Libbie that Sheridan "impresses me very favorably."[16]

Custer got an immediate chance to impress Sheridan at the battle of Yellow Tavern. As the Army of the Potomac moved south to battle Lee, Sheridan convinced Grant to let him operate the cavalry independently. He would swing loose of the army, threaten Richmond and Lee's supply lines, and, most importantly, bring Stuart to battle and defeat him. Stuart, the beau sabreur of the Confederacy, had long been a thorn in the side of the Union army. Sheridan took ten thousand troopers, the largest cavalry force ever assembled in the Eastern theater, and headed for Richmond. Stuart put his forty-five hundred troopers between Sheridan and Richmond and the two forces collided near an abandoned inn called Yellow Tavern less than ten miles north of the city. After several hours of indecisive fighting, Custer studied the Confederate lines and spotted a weakness. He told his band to strike up "Yankee Doodle," took his customary place at the head of his troops, and charged. The ferocious attack captured two cannon and scattered the rebels. Stuart led a counterattack and was shot in the abdomen by one of Custer's Michigan troopers. He died the next day. Custer's action had won the day and eliminated one of the South's most famous generals.[17]

Sheridan noticed. "Genl. Sheridan told Col. [Russell A.] Alger 'Custer is the ablest man in the Cavalry Corps,'" Custer wrote Libbie. "(This is for you only, my little one. I would not write this to anyone but you. You may repeat it to our own people in Monroe, but not to anyone in Washington.)"[18] Custer might have worried he would be revealing a confidence, but it also fit his characteristic worry that people would think he was bragging.

The press, too, noticed Custer. The *Herald* reported Sheridan's raid under the first bold headline "Sheridan!" followed with several decks of descriptive headlines culminating with "Gallantry of General Custer and His Command." The story incorrectly stated that Sheridan ordered Custer to carry the position when in fact the charge was Custer's idea. But the description of the charge made up for that error. "Gen. Custer placed himself at the head of his command, and with drawn sabres and deafening cheers charged directly in the face of a withering fire, captured two pieces of artillery, upwards of a hundred prisoners, together with caissons, ammunition and horses, which he brought off in safety. It was, without exception, the most gallant charge of the raid, and when it became known among the corps cheer after cheer rent the air."[19]

Custer wrote Libbie that he was receiving compliments almost daily. "Did you observe that in the headings in the *Herald* no cavalry General's name was mentioned besides that of Sheridan and your boy?

Some of the Richmond papers also speak highly of me," Custer wrote. But the recognition was only important because it would make Libbie proud. "That is all the reward I ask."[20]

Another story called Custer the "young 'General of the golden locks'" although the writer admitted that Custer had cut his hair short for the present campaign. "He has a sharp blue eye, a very slight impediment in his speech, and dresses in somewhat of the old cavalier style—black velvet jacket, with a blue shirt collar turned over the same, his Brigadier's star being worked in each corner. He wears a slouched hat with a star in the front, and a red scarf cravat around his neck. Whenever he orders a charge, he always leads in person, and bursts upon the enemy with a yell equal to that of any of the Rocky Mountain aborigines."[21]

Custer would need all of that fighting spirit as Grant ordered the cavalry to conduct another raid on June 5, this one toward Charlottesville to draw Confederate cavalry away from the main body of the Army of the Potomac. Rebel cavalry under Wade Hampton were waiting to block Sheridan's forces at Trevilian Station. Sheridan sent Custer on the right of the advance. After a march on a path so overgrown that the men could not ride in the standard column of fours, they stumbled upon Hampton's lightly guarded baggage train. Custer, eager for the prize, ordered a charge. He had ordered the men not to go beyond the depot, but in the excitement the troopers went much farther, alerting the rebels there were Yankees in the rear. Custer tried to pull out with his prize but was quickly surrounded by rebels pressing from all sides. He was determined to hold out until reinforcements arrived.

"The enemy made repeated and desperate efforts to break our lines at different points, and in doing so compelled us to change the positions of our batteries," Custer wrote in his official report. "The smallness of my force compelled me to adopt very contracted lines. From the nature of the ground and the character of the attacks that were made upon me our lines resembled very nearly a circle. The space over which we fought was so limited that there was actually no place which could be called under cover, or in other words the entire ground was in range of the enemy's guns."[22]

Custer's report left out the feeling of confusion in the battle. Another soldier remembered that Custer was asked if the Union baggage train should be moved to the rear for safety. "Yes, by all means," Custer said, and the officer rode off. Then Custer looked around and yelled, "Where in hell is the rear?"[23]

There was no safe place for the wagons, and a number of both the Union train and the rebel ones they had just taken were captured as the Confederates advanced. When Custer learned of the capture of the wagons, he was enraged, and the air was blue with profanity. Custer, like his mentor Kearney, was a colorful and creative curser, and his real quote was likely stronger than the one that Victorian-era journalists and historians passed down.

"The 'Boy General' now began to rave some and look around for reprisals, when Artillery officer Alexander Pennington rode up to him and said,

'General they have taken one of my guns!'

'No! Damned if they have; come on,' and off he dashed, followed by Pennington and a few men. They charged the enemy with the utmost fury and retook the piece."[24]

Staff officers from headquarters repeatedly tried to break through to Custer but were driven back. Finally, Capt. Amasa G. Dana made it to Custer. "[H]e found the inevitable fighting Custer, with his inevitable bugler sounding the advance," the *New York Herald* reported. "Dana's description of Custer's line of battle at this moment is most amusing. The first portion he came to was facing in one direction, and their seven shooters were going crack, crack, crack in the most lively manner. Reaching the centre he found that, facing in an exactly opposite course, the same weapons discoursing the same music there. Again the other wing was facing in a third front and just as fiercely engaged as the rest."[25]

Writing a week after the battle, it might have been amusing to the reporter, but at the time it was deadly serious to the trapped soldiers. Custer appeared to his men to be everywhere, directing troop positions and fighting beside them. His outlandish uniform dramatically served its purpose, giving the men comfort that he was with them, leading.[26]

He was hit in the arm and shoulder by spent balls but was only bruised. He was lucky. One of his men was hit and fell exposed to rebel fire. The man was obviously dying, but Custer couldn't stand to see the man hit again and dashed forward to carry him back to Union lines.

Custer's flag bearer, Sgt. Mitchell Beloir, was hit in the chest while riding beside Custer. "General, they have killed me," he said. "Take the flag!"

Custer tore it from the staff and tucked it in his shirt.[27]

The fight went on for three hours before Sheridan's other units forced the Confederates back, freeing Custer and his men. It was a costly battle, with 1,007 Union casualties; 416 came from Custer's brigade. Beloir lingered until the next morning.[28]

"With unfeigned sorrow I am called upon to record the death of one of the 'bravest of the brave,'" Custer wrote in his official report, noting Beloir had been with him since the brigade was organized. "Sergt. Beloir received his death-wound while nobly discharging his duty to his flag and to his country. He was killed in the advance while gallantly cheering the men forward to victory." With the sparseness of Hemingway, Custer concluded, "The men remained on the line all night."[29]

Custer and his men then got a brief break from the constant raiding, but the war was moving to a decisive phase. Grant had pushed Lee's army to the brink and had started a siege of Petersburg, the vital rail hub that provided the connection for supplies to Richmond. Lee sent Lt. Gen. Jubal A. Early with a small force through the Shenandoah Valley to threaten Washington and relieve pressure on his lines. The latest raid panicked the capital just as the presidential election campaign of 1864 was starting up. The valley had long been a source of supplies for the Confederate armies and a raiding path to Washington and points north. Early's venture was a sign that the rebels were not yet beaten after three years of war, and voters might think it was time to change presidential administrations and elect Democrat George B. McClellan.

On orders from Lincoln, Grant determined to whip Early and clear out the valley once and for all. Grant told Gen. Henry Halleck he wanted the Union army to "eat out Virginia clear and clean as far as they go, so that crows flying over it for the balance of the season will have to carry their provender with them." Grant wanted the valley made "a desert" as much as possible. All provisions, horses, and cattle would be removed, and people told to get out. He put Sheridan in charge of a newly created army, including Custer's cavalry brigade, to do the clearing.[30]

For Custer, this time was a turning point in his military career and his political philosophy. Like his beloved country, Custer was torn by conflicting emotions. His best friends were fighting for the Confederacy, and as a man of his times, he did not believe in full equality for African Americans. Yet he had seen slavery firsthand, and Eliza Brown, an escaped slave who served loyally as his cook, was cherished by him and his inner circle, including Libbie. Custer believed slavery was a scourge that had to be uprooted. The war had become more bitter every day, and it now seemed to the leaders that a "Hard War" strategy against civilians was the only way to bring the South to its knees.

Yet Custer was also a passionate Democrat who admired McClellan as the epitome of an officer and gentleman. Custer believed in McClellan with the blind eye of a boy's permanent loyalty to his first hero. McClellan, however, was the nominee of the political party that wanted to make peace with the rebels at any price. McClellan himself during the Peninsula Campaign two years earlier had insisted that his army treat Southern civilians with the utmost respect and not take any property, including slaves.

The Republican Lincoln, a Midwesterner from a modest background like Custer's, was more in line with Custer's current views of what the country needed. Furthermore, Lincoln had praised Custer to Libbie, who was leaning toward supporting the president. She couldn't vote, of course, but Libbie and Custer were so in tune that her opinion would greatly influence him.

Above all, Custer believed in the Union cause and the duty of a soldier. He participated in Sheridan's valley campaign with his typical drive. He played a key role in the battle of Winchester, which shattered Early's army, by leading a charge that routed an infantry unit. And in what had become a routine event, Custer rescued one of his soldiers. His new color bearer was hit and knocked from his horse. As rebel troopers closed in, Custer jumped from his horse. He grabbed the man by his collar and pulled him up with him on his horse. Custer galloped away fighting off the rebels with his saber until he was back in the Union lines.[31]

Custer had to carry out a duty that for someone who had many Southern friends had to be particularly distasteful. He ordered his men to burn barns and destroy crops. Col. John S. Mosby, the Confederate partisan ranger of the valley, ambushed some of Custer's men and executed several prisoners. Custer ordered houses burned in the immediate area for retaliation. Sheridan also ordered some of Mosby's men hanged, and Mosby retaliated in kind, hanging some Union prisoners and attaching a note to one saying it was in retaliation for Custer's executions. Mosby was in error; the executions were not ordered by Custer. Nevertheless, Custer was involved deeply in the Hard War strategy to make Southern civilians suffer so much they would demand peace.[32]

Incredibly, the connection to Democratic politics and McClellan, who was officially nominated for the presidency on August 31, 1864, continued to dog Custer even though his actions showed his devotion to the Union cause. Custer, unlike McClellan, would not negotiate or wage a piecemeal war. But those on the home front, away from the battle, worried and gossiped about Custer's politics. His politics didn't matter when he knocked aside rebel bayonet thrusts with his saber or led his men in a wild charge against canons firing grapeshot, but it was clear they would affect his promotions and postwar future.

Custer's brother-in-law, David Reed, his political patrons, and, of course, his father all worried about the election's impact on his career. Libbie worried about his safety more than his career, and she was just as conflicted as he was about the election. She wrote her parents in September that there was "great excitement" over the campaign in Washington, where she was staying. Banners for McClellan and Lincoln hung from the buildings. She could hear the soldiers groan or cheer for their candidates as they marched past. She wrote that she didn't know how Custer felt about the election, but that their friend Chandler was making fiery speeches against Copperheads.[33]

At about the same time she wrote Custer about her own confused thoughts. Libbie thought McClellan would be elected, and that might mean a dishonorable peace. "Autie it is treasonable and unwomanly but way down in my heart I want peace on any terms, for much as I love my country I love you more." Later in the same letter she described a conversation with an army major who was adamantly for McClellan and wanted to know Custer's politics. She said she didn't know, but she personally was for Lincoln. "It is generally thought now that Lincoln will be elected," she wrote, changing her earlier prediction.

"But I never say so, for fear people will think I am repeating your sentiments—and I dont even know them."[34]

Custer's reply reflected feelings torn between his love for his Southern friends and the United States, and his duty as a soldier. "I believe that if the two parties, North and South, could come together the result would be a union closer than the old union ever was," he wrote Libbie. "But my doctrine has ever been that a soldier should not meddle in politics."[35]

In a civil war with a home front roiled by politics, it was impossible for a charismatic general who was becoming a media star to avoid being sucked into the election. Christiancy was constantly writing about politics to Custer and warned him that although McClellan might personally want to put down the rebellion, his party would force him to accept peace on any terms. "If they [the Democrats] succeed it will be in effect, a triumph of the Southern confederacy, and will place the whole North under the control of the same spirit which [created] the Confederacy, and all the blood spilled in this war will have been shed in vain," he wrote. "They, the democrats, hate the military, they oppose enlistments they threaten resistance to the draft." No Democrats would join the army. "But I tell you the time will come when this war is over and the soldiers get home, that those who have served their country as [they] in the field will be found to be the popular men and will hold the offices."[36]

Christiancy, like most politicians, was always thinking a few elections ahead, and he seemed to dangle postwar office before his young friend. Custer's reply reflected his hardening feeling about ending the war. He denounced a peace commission and thought that it was cowardly and treasonous even to suggest one. Ever dramatic, Custer wrote "The Peace Commissioners I am in favor of are those sent from the cannon's mouth. The only armistice I would yield to would be that forced by the points of our bayonets, whose object would be to afford the opportunity for an unconditional recognition of the supremacy of the Federal Government. This appeal must come from the rebels; otherwise it will be a practical admission on our part that we are the vanquished party."[37]

Christiancy wanted to publish Custer's letter denouncing negotiations because it would make Custer look patriotic and show he was against the Copperheads.[38] Christiancy told Custer he had seen no other letter "of any kind breathing a more patriotic spirit or which shows so well in a nutshell the gross impropriety of proposing an armistice or sending peace commissioners." Christiancy read the letter to Emanuel Custer when he paid him a visit, with predictable results.[39]

Emanuel had been regularly devoting half of his letters to his son on the election and McClellan's chances in the Midwest. In one letter he wanted to know Custer's opinion of McClellan's prospects with the soldier vote. Sometimes he would close his letters with "three cheers for McClellan."[40]

Emanuel wrote Custer with "feelings of sorrow" when Christiancy read him the letter because his son appeared to have turned against McClellan. "I can't see how you could be again Mc when he has done so much for you I should have thought that if evry body els had turned against him that you would have remained his friend I know you thought more of him than any other man living. . . ." But what he was most worried about was Custer's political future. "I would not had you wroat that letter for five horses because I think if [sic] might be an eye sore some day against you my son the reputation that you have made for yourself is vary flattering and your prospect for the white [house] some day as a dimacrat if you should live is as good to day as may that has occupied it but if you identify your self with the Republican Party your chance is blasted for that party never can never live they may succeed this time but that will for ever sink them fore years more of Republican Rule and country will be about used up and that Party with it." He thought it was corrupt that officers were campaigning for Lincoln.[41]

David Reed worried about a rumor that Custer would make all his men vote for McClellan. "Don't you do or say any thing that rash," he wrote. Unlike his father-in-law, Reed could focus on other things besides the election. But as with most of the letters Custer got from home, the topics were rarely cheerful. Reed asked Custer to send at least part of the $200 (about $3,300 in 2020)[42] that Reed had paid on the mortgage on Emanuel's home. He said he wished Tom Custer was with his older brother and could save some money to help out Emanuel. "If it was not for you I do not see how they would get along." Reed, too, said the family tracked Custer in the papers. He reminisced about Custer as a small boy and how he now was so important and was fortunate to have been saved from his many brushes with death. Reed described how Ann prayed for him: "A My father if it is constant with thy will spare my Brother. May not the arm of the foe over come Him But will though protect & keep him in the hallow of thy hand."[43]

Ann's prayers for her little brother were answered as he continued to cheat death, even though he had close calls that would have made a more timid general lead his troops from the rear. At the battle of Guard Hill, his troopers saw him riding to the front when he slapped his hand to his head as if he had been hit. The bullet had flown by him, neatly cutting a lock of hair. Custer waved his hat at his men, signaling them forward.[44]

To Libbie, Custer wrote that he "had a severe engagement, and a very trying one." It was noteworthy, Custer wrote, because he was able to control his swearing, which he had promised her he would try to curtail. "During the whole time I never used a single oath," he wrote. "My staff spoke of it afterwards. This is the first time I have not been remarkably profane during a battle." Still the romantic, Custer wrote Libbie that he asked a musician to play their favorite song, "Then You'll Remember Me," outside of his tent on a moonlit night.[45]

The risk and the sacrifice were paying off. Because of his dedication to duty and high level of performance, Custer deserved promotion, and when Grant requested one of Sheridan's division commanders for assignment to Georgia, an opening was created. Sheridan transferred James Wilson and made Custer commander of the Third Division on September 30, 1864.[46]

Custer's first time leading the division in action was, like much of his life, a stage set for a star performance. Sheridan had ordered his men to destroy the command of Brig. Gen. Thomas L. Rosser, whose cavalry had been harassing the federals as they were applying the torch to the valley in carrying out Grant's orders. Custer encountered Rosser at Tom's Brook near Woodstock. Rosser was an old friend from West Point, but he had helped humiliate Custer at Trevilian Station, where his baggage was captured, including a photograph of Libbie, Custer's underwear, and Libbie's letters.[47] The letters were printed in Southern newspapers, where readers were titillated by her double entendres. Now Custer had a chance for payback. For Custer the performer, it called for more than a charge.

Custer rode out alone in between the lines. He reined his horse to a halt. He took off his rakish sombrero and bowed low toward his old friend in the rebel lines.

In words echoing the instructions he had given at the academy fist-fight that nearly cost him his commission, Custer shouted, "Let's have a fair fight, boys, no malice!"

Rosser immediately recognized Custer and pointed him out to his staff. "You see that officer down there. That's General Custer, the Yanks are so proud of, and I intend to give him the best whipping to-day that he ever got. See if I don't."[48]

For much of the day, the battle was back and forth. Rosser had cho-sen a good defensive position, but a Custer-led charge proved decisive. "Everything worked admirably, and the movements of the brigades were well timed," Custer wrote in his official report:

> The whole line moved forward at the charge. Before this irre-sistible advance the enemy found it impossible to stand. Once more he was compelled to trust his safety to the fleetness of his steed rather than the metal of his saber. His retreat soon became a demoralized rout. Vainly did the most gallant of this affrighted herd endeavor to rally a few supports around their standards and stay the advance of their eager and exult-ing pursuers, who, in one overwhelming current, were bear-ing down everything before them. Never since the opening of this war had there been witnessed such a complete and decisive overthrow of the enemy's cavalry. The pursuit was kept up vigorously for nearly twenty miles, and the dispersion of our panic-stricken enemies.[49]

Custer had learned from McClellan and Pleasonton to use the offi-cial reports to gain credit. He used his writing skill to not just describe the victory but to do so with a mocking tone that made the defeat seem all the more real. His joy was evident at getting revenge for the seizure of his baggage at Trevilian Station. His men had recaptured a stolen photograph of Libbie and seized Rosser's personal baggage.

Custer gleefully wrote Libbie that he put on a show for his men wearing Rosser's coat, which was much too big for him, around camp.

He later wrote Rosser a note thanking him for the "gifts" but asking him to get the tailor to shorten his coat so it would fit Custer better next time.[50]

"Next time" came in shocking fashion for the Yankees, who had assumed that the rebel army in the valley was beaten for good. Early's troops snuck up on the federals and a dawn surprise attack routed them at the beginning of what became known as the battle of Cedar Creek. Sheridan had been at a meeting in Washington but returned in time to see his army dissolving.

Custer dramatically greeted Sheridan by giving him a hug. In a rarity for Custer, he felt beaten. "Looks as though we are gone up today," he said.

Sheridan steadied him. "The right will prevail."

Custer then vowed to take back the federal camps by that night. "Or I will sacrifice every man in my division, and I will go with them."[51]

Sheridan took charge of the situation and organized his army for a counterattack. During the course of the battle, he noticed a gap in the Confederate lines and ordered Custer to attack. Custer once again rode in front of his troops repeatedly yelling "Charge!" The ferocity of the attack broke the exhausted rebels. Custer's troopers pursued them excitedly; their blood up, they captured scores of prisoners and cannon.

Custer wrote his report as if adding a chapter to *The Irish Dragoon*, one of his favorite cavalry novels when he was a boy.

"Hearing the charge sounded through our bugles the enemy stood long enough to deliver one volley; then, casting away his arms, attempted to escape under cover of darkness," Custer wrote. "This was the last attempt the enemy made to offer organized resistance. That which hitherto, on our part, had been a pursuit after a broken and routed army now resolved itself into an exciting chase after a panic-stricken, uncontrollable mob. It was no longer a question of speed between pursuers and pursued, prisoners were taken by hundreds, entire companies threw down their arms, and appeared glad when summoned to surrender."[52]

When Custer rode into Sheridan's camp that night, Sheridan pulled him off his horse, gave him a hug, and said, "You have done it for me this time, Custer!"

Custer was equally excited and literally picked the little general off the ground and twirled him around. Custer said with a laugh, "By God, Phil! We've cleaned them out of their guns and got ours back!"

Sheridan then tried to calm Custer: "There, there, old fellow; don't capture me!"[53]

One of the captured rebels was Gen. Stephen D. Ramseur, a West Point classmate of Custer's who had shared hijinks and drinking with him at Benny Havens. Custer, Merritt, and Pennington, also classmates, visited Ramseur, who had been shot through both lungs and lay dying. Ramseur had just learned his first child had been born and had worn a flower in his uniform in its honor. They talked of old times, but Ramseur was in excruciating pain despite being given laudanum. He died the next day, slipping in and out of consciousness and talking of his wife and child.[54]

The Union classmates then argued over credit for the victory. Who captured what became a bone of contention between Custer and Wesley Merritt, who commanded the First Cavalry Division and claimed his unit took some of the rebel guns Custer had captured. Merritt and Custer were rivals for promotion. Other officers also had resented the press coverage Custer received, particularly in the *New York Times*. Col. Charles Russell Lowell, who served under Merritt and was mortally wounded at Cedar Creek, had written a letter calling the *Times* reporter E. A. Paul, Custer's "absurd newspaper reporter."[55]

Merritt was enraged when Custer issued a general order to his troops after Cedar Creek praising them for their actions. "[Y]our conduct throughout was sublimely heroic, and without parallel in the annals of warfare," Custer wrote. "In the early part of the day, when disaster and defeat seemed to threaten our noble army on all sides, your calm and determined bravery while exposed to a terrible fire from the enemy's guns, added not a little to restore confidence to that part of our army already broken and driven back on the right."[56] The order was published in the press, and Merritt filed an official protest, asserting his outfit had captured twenty-two of the forty-five cannon Custer claimed. Custer in turn wrote in his official report that since "another command" wanted to share the honors, he would explain in detail how the guns were captured. He wrote that he personally took part in the charge that broke up the rebel lines, and thus was a direct witness.[57]

When Merritt filed his complaint, Custer countered by requesting the chief of cavalry in Sheridan's army, Alfred Torbert, to appoint a board of officers to investigate the case. As evidence, Custer included an article from the *New York Times*. Torbert examined both sides and did not believe an inquiry was necessary, letting Custer claim the guns.[58]

As he had learned from his mentors Pleasonton and McClellan, Custer assiduously worked the press. The *New York Times* and the *New York Herald* both quoted him as a major source of the battle. Custer even gave an extensive interview to the *Newark Advertiser* when he went to New Jersey to visit Libbie for a few hours during a trip to Washington. "General Custer represents that the victory of Wednesday was the most complete and decisive which has yet been achieved in the Shenandoah," the writer reported breathlessly in a story that was widely reprinted around the country. "Before the charges of our cavalry the rebel forces were scattered in utter confusion, throwing off everything that could impede their flight. Custer's division pursued the enemy from three o'clock in the afternoon until nine in the evening, driving them into the fields and mountains, capturing whole companies at a time, and putting hundreds of the fugitives *hors de combat*. Our men fought as they had never fought before, feeling that the annihilation of the enemy depended upon their blows."

Custer obligingly provided a list of captured items, including the number of the controversial cannon, which he personally counted at Sheridan's headquarters. Custer gave the reporter some drama, too, relating the story of Ramseur's capture. "Before his death Ramseur sent for [Custer], and the two, thus strangely brought together, reviewed in the presence of death, the reminiscences of their cadet life."

A local connection is always important for a newspaper story, and Custer provided one for the Newark paper. "He speaks in the highest terms of our New Jersey soldiers in the valley, and especially commends the Third cavalry, which he says have achieved a better reputation, considering the time they have been in service, than any regiment in that department." No wonder the reporter described the youthful Custer, who he noted was only twenty-four, as "a splendid specimen of the finished soldier."[59]

Reporters, after all, are human, and they respond to those who understand their job and treat them well. During the Civil War, reporters were under tremendous pressure to get copy. One journalist described the life of a war correspondent as riding all day to get news, then writing the story by the smoky light of a campfire, rushing off to get it to a telegraph, and then the next day reading how the editor had butchered the copy.[60]

Some newspapers saw their circulation quadruple as the public clamored for news about the battles their relatives were fighting in. Fortunes were made in journalism during the war, and it was high-stakes competition to get the best story first. Wilbur F. Storey, publisher of the *Chicago Times*, famously told his reporters, "Telegraph fully all the news you can, and when there is no news, send rumors."[61]

Public relations had not been invented yet, so there was no formal, steady source of news from the military. Generals, in effect, were their own press officers. Savvy ones knew how to use the system; the ones who didn't suffered and careers were made or broken. Meade, for example, had political aspirations for after the war. But he had a reporter humiliated for a minor offense, having him paraded through the camp wearing a sign labeled "Liar" while thousands of soldiers jeered at him. The reporter's colleagues agreed to boycott Meade from their copy, promoting other officers in his stead. The boycott might well have ruined his political career. Others, such as Merritt and Lowell, ignored the press and mocked officers like Custer who cultivated those relationships.[62]

Custer didn't necessarily love the press—he had been furious at criticism of McClellan and in some letters home he wrote about lies in the newspapers. But he had learned from McClellan and Pleasonton the importance of getting your story in the press. McClellan's failures had been defended by friendly newspapers to the extent that he nearly was elected president. Pleasonton parlayed a mediocre career into head of the cavalry of the Army of the Potomac. Custer was not unusual in cooperating with the press. He just did it better than most officers because he had an innate sense for how the press worked. He knew they needed stories, and he knew what kind they needed. An amateur writer himself who loved to read and see the theater, he knew the sort of details that made a good story.

Of course, press relations will only take you so far. Whether a politician, a general, or a performer, you need to produce results as well as manage the press. Custer did it all. He was fearless and successful on the battlefield, he wrote dramatic accounts in his official reports, and he gave exciting stories to reporters who needed them. The attitude of Merritt, Lowell, and others was the classic definition of sour grapes. To show how far their bitterness went, one person, apparently an officer at Cedar Creek, wrote a letter to the *Times* complaining that E. A. Paul had slighted Brig. Gen. Thomas Devin by attributing captured cannon to the credit of Custer. The writer claimed both Custer and the reporter knew Devin's unit had captured them. Paul published a reply, denying he would injure Devin, and that his source was official documents.[63]

It must have been particularly galling for Merritt and his supporters to see the official record and Sheridan vindicate Custer. Sheridan sent Custer, who was now indisputably his right-hand man and mentee, to Washington to present the captured battle flags to Secretary of War Edwin Stanton. The destruction of Early's army had made the end of the war seem closer and the reelection of Lincoln more certain. Everyone at the ceremony was in good spirits as Stanton joked with the enlisted men who accompanied Custer.

James Sweeney, who was not yet eighteen, told Stanton he and another cavalryman rode up to a rebel ambulance and ordered it to stop. Everyone was amused that the ambulance driver thought Sweeney was on his side. The driver told Sweeney that the general had ordered him to go on. Sweeney said, "What general?" The driver said, "General Ramseur." Sweeney said, "That is the very man I am looking for." They then captured the general, the driver, and the horses.

Custer interrupted the comedic scene to explain to Stanton that Sweeney had been wearing a gray jacket, which misled the rebels.

Stanton handed out medals to the troopers and then said, "To show you how good Generals and good men work together, I have already appointed your commanding General [Custer] a major general." Stanton shook Custer's hand and said, "General Custer, a gallant officer always makes gallant soldiers."

The crowd cheered tremendously, while an embarrassed Custer bowed. A reporter who witnessed the scene wrote that it showed Custer's "modesty was equal to his courage."[64] For Custer, it must have been a difficult ceremony as he thought about Ramseur's death. Custer and Libbie hoped to have children one day, and Ramseur had been killed just after his child was born. Custer's promotion and glory had come in part because of Ramseur's defeat and death. A similar scene could have played out in Richmond with Ramseur, Rosser, or some other rebel presenting Custer's flag to Jefferson Davis. After all, Custer had come close to being killed or captured at least a half-dozen times himself.

On the other hand, it would difficult to be humble after such praise from the secretary of war and the newspapers. In addition to an article about the flag ceremony, the *Times* published four stories that featured Custer, including the *Newark Advertiser* interview and an extract from Custer's letter to Christiancy arguing against peace negotiations. The *Times* noted that the letter from "the well-known cavalry leader" had "the ring of true metal."[65]

On the front page the *Times* published a detailed story about Cedar Creek that praised Custer for having displayed judgment worthy of Napoleon when he handled a threat from Rosser:

> It was a critical moment. Our infantry was advancing, and Merritt had driven the enemy on the left; a rebel battery near where army headquarters were located in the morning, was a tempting prize; Custer considered a moment, as if in doubt, whether to force through Rosser's command and attempt to capture prisoners and artillery across the creek in their retreat, or to capture the battery near headquarters, or effect a cross-ing between Rosser and the main column. The question was partially solved by the battery referred to falling back. Custer, quick as thought, withdrew all of his force from Cupp's Ford, except the First Connecticut, and ordered his whole command to move toward the creek as rapidly as possible, and at the same time the First Connecticut received orders to make a formi-dable demonstration to hold Rosser, in which the regiment was entirely unsuccessful. Custer, with his practical eye, saw at a glance that the important moment for a dash had arrived.[66]

Custer seized the moment and led the Union army to what the *Times* called "a glorious victory" and "one of the most remarkable" of the war. Custer had played a key role in clearing the Shenandoah of rebels, something the North had been unable to do in the previous three years of fighting. One of the most important papers acknowledged his importance and devoted significant space to his exploits. As noted, the secretary of war personally promoted him.

Custer celebrated in his typical fashion—he saw a comedy before going back to duty. A number of papers reported that he was spotted at Grover's Theatre for the first time wearing his major general's stars. The performance was Charles Dickens's *Dombey and Son*, featuring one of the famous comedians of the day, Dan Setchell, as Captain Cuttle. According to the story, Custer watched the play "with much approbation."[67]

Custer's every move was worthy of the personal columns. Custer was no longer in the shadow of Kilpatrick, Pleasonton, and others. He was a star in his own right.

The legend of Custer began when he waded across the Chickahominy River to determine its depth, looking for a suitable crossing place for the Army of the Potomac in the 1862 drive on Richmond. The scene was captured by combat artist Alfred Waud, who would find Custer a dramatic subject throughout the war. Library of Congress, Prints and Photographs Division, LC-DIG-ppmsca-21081.

Custer's ambition is captured in this famous Alexander Gardner photograph of Abraham Lincoln, George McClellan (*sixth from left*), and other officers in 1862. Custer, a young aide, is to the extreme right but appears to be trying to move toward the group being photographed. A closer look reveals a ghosted Custer, caught in movement by the slower exposure time of a nineteenth-century camera. Library of Congress, Prints and Photographs Division, LC–B8184–3287.

Custer's dramatic costuming is illustrated in this photograph of him, seated on the extreme right, with Maj. Gen. Alfred Pleasonton seated to Custer's right. Custer's self-styled uniform with the gold braid on the sleeves and his long hair make him stand out from all of the other officers, including his mentor Pleasonton, who had a reputation for being a fancy dresser himself. National Park Service, Little Bighorn Battlefield National Monument.

Custer during the Washita campaign had so adapted the frontier dress that Satanta, the famed Kiowa chief, mistook him for a scout when he first met him. National Park Service, Little Bighorn Battlefield National Monument.

Custer created a persona of a great hunter while stationed in Kansas, often taking famous guests on buffalo hunts. When the Grand Duke Alexis of Russia toured the United States in 1872, Sheridan assigned Custer to be his host. It was a sign of Custer's ability to relate to people of all levels of society and his knowledge of public relations. National Park Service, Little Bighorn Battlefield National Monument.

At Fort Abraham Lincoln, Custer and Libbie regularly entertained in their home. Here Custer holds the sheet music. Custer loved music, and he and Libbie had a favorite song they cherished, "Then You'll Remember Me." National Park Service, Little Bighorn Battlefield National Monument.

Custer loved performing, and he often was able to do so at Fort Lincoln. Here he is dressed as a Quaker peace commissioner with his younger sister Maggie, who was married to First Lt. James Calhoun. Custer must have used a pillow or some other kind of stuffing to give him the portly look, evidence of how deeply he got into tableau. National Park Service, Little Bighorn Battlefield National Monument.

Custer's office at Fort Lincoln was a space he had long dreamed of having after years of writing in hotels, on trains, or in temporary army camps. Note the piles of newspapers and books by his desk, a sign of a writer's office. He liked having Libbie sit with him while he wrote. She sometimes would purposely misremember an anecdote to get him to correct her and to jump-start his thinking whenever he had writer's block. National Park Service, Little Bighorn Battlefield National Monument.

Custer the man-about-town. Custer enjoyed dressing in fine clothes and was as comfortable in them as in buckskins or a uniform. When he was stationed in Kentucky after the war, the locals were amazed at the different outfits he would wear. Library of Congress, Prints and Photographs Division, LC-BH832–29187.

Custer's last fight is one of the most haunting battlefields in the world, with markers placed where the bodies were found. On Last Stand Hill, Custer's marker, center, stands out with black marking on the front. The view looks toward the Little Bighorn River and the site of the vast Indian village Custer tried to capture. Photograph by Catherine Mueller.

Libbie unveils the statue of Custer in Monroe, Michigan, in 1910, while President William Howard Taft stands behind her. Libbie became a successful writer, assuming the career that Custer likely would have continued had he lived. Her skill at writing and public relations contributed greatly to his place in American memory. National Park Service, Little Bighorn Battlefield National Monument.

Custer stands watch in Monroe, Michigan. The statue depicts Custer in a moment of concentration, surveying the enemy at Gettysburg before he led the charge that blunted the rebel attack. It's a fitting pose because Custer, although he could have had many other careers, devoted his life to guarding his country. Photograph by Catherine Mueller.

CHAPTER SIX

A Heart Too Full for Utterance

Winning the War

By early 1865 Custer had fulfilled the dreams of his youth—he had earned fame and glory fighting in a righteous cause. He had a beautiful wife who adored him. Yet he felt something was missing. On a leave in February he formally proclaimed his Christian faith at Libbie's church in Monroe. "Years of reflexion and study had convinced me that I was not fulfilling the end of my creator if I lived for this world alone," Custer wrote to a minister when discussing his conversion. "Life is at all times uncertain, but to one in my profession it is particularly so."[1]

Custer's decision pleased his once-skeptical father-in-law, who now unabashedly admitted Custer was right for his daughter. Daniel Bacon wrote Custer on February 8, 1865, that he was thankful Libbie had married him. The knowledge that she was happy allowed Bacon to accept the sadness he felt at her moving away. Bacon told Custer that he was "all I could desire or wish, and I am not without pride, at your well earned, and fully appreciated reputation." Most of all, Bacon was thankful that Custer was a confessed Christian. "How consoling to relatives and friends, if in the [providence] of God, you should in defence of the best government in the world, fall on the battlefield."[2]

Custer's own father echoed these sentiments in a letter the same month. Emanuel wrote how happy he was that Custer had made something of his life. "I am proud that I am the father of such a noble boy. I think it a great honor to any man to have such a son and I doant feal

123

under any obligation to any one for your success you have clum up the ladder of fame and honor your self what a great satisfaction it is to me when I look at you and then compair my situation with thousands of others who has welth and all they could ask for in this world and have sons that is perfect rakes."

Yet Emanuel, like Bacon, was proudest of all that Custer had professed his Christianity. His relief was tremendous that his son, who was in constant danger, was saved. He urged Custer, over and over, to be a Christian man and to look to a home in heaven when the sorrows of this world were finished. Emanuel warned his son that serving in the army would surround him with temptations, but he needed to keep his faith strong. "My dear son be sted fast allways abouding in the work of the lord that is the greatest and best act you ever done to bow in homble submission to the lord of lords that is all that you were wanting to make you one of the greatest of men. . . . I hope we will all meet in that good world live for it son."[3]

The risk of death was ever-present for Custer. Lincoln had been reelected and the Confederacy was gasping its last breaths, yet the ferocious combat went on. Custer never slowed down. Other men, sensing the end was near, might have been more cautious, but Custer fought all the more fiercely, as if the victory of the Union depended upon him alone. On March 2, Sheridan dispatched Custer to find Early's battered troops, who he had heard were ready for a last fight in the valley. E. A. Paul, who accompanied the column, wrote that they marched in the worst weather he had ever seen. "The rain fell in torrents and froze on men's whiskers as fast as it fell, and formed icicles on the limbs of trees. The column was compelled to move at a very slow walk through the deep mud and slush, and men as well as horses were chilled through, boots were filled with water and every rag of clothing was saturated with this element." Custer pushed the column on steadily if slowly, pausing only for an hour so stragglers could catch up. Paul and a few others went into the American House hotel in Staunton, Virginia, to warm themselves and found Early's name on the guestbook from the day before.[4]

Custer caught up with Early about 1 P.M. near Waynesboro, but he found the rebels entrenched with a clear field of fire for their infantry and artillery. It was a position usually considered too strong for cavalry to take. Furthermore, Custer's men were soaked and numb from the cold, and the horses were struggling over soft, sodden ground. Reiforcements from Sheridan and Merritt would be too far behind to be of any help. It was, Paul wrote, a situation "to test the skill, capacity and courage of any man."[5]

Custer rode along the front of the lines, studying Early's position. He noticed a weakness. "I think we can flank them on the enemy's left," he said excitedly.[6]

Thinking quickly, he seized the opportunity rather than wait for the rest of Sheridan's army. He ordered one brigade to feint an attack on the front of the line. When someone objected that it would draw heavy artillery fire, Custer said, "It must be done, shell or no shell."[7]

Custer led the charge himself, stampeding the rebels and dissolving what was left of Early's army. "So sudden was our attack and so great was the enemy's surprise that but little time was offered for resistance," he wrote in his official report, adding with a novelist's eye a telling detail that showed the reader what happened instead of just reciting facts. "The artillery, however, continued to fire till the last moment and till our troops had almost reached the muzzles of their guns. One piece was captured with the sponge-staff still inserted in the bore and the charge rammed half way home."[8]

Paul wrote that the rebel soldiers had no stomach for close combat. They surrendered without a fight as soon as Custer's troops rode into their lines. If they hadn't, they would have been slaughtered.[9] "No set of prisoners were ever so happy before," Paul wrote. "They expressed their entire satisfaction at the result, and gave vent to their feelings in repeated cheers for Gen. Custer."[10]

In all, Custer's troopers captured about a dozen cannon and almost two thousand prisoners at the cost of only nine causalities—a feat worth bragging about. When the rest of the Union army arrived in Waynesboro, Custer, always the showman, led a mini-parade of his troopers carrying the seventeen battle flags they had just captured. Capt. George B. Sanford, one of Merritt's staff officers, recalled that "It was a great spectacle and the sort of thing which Custer thoroughly enjoyed."[11]

The spectacle continued when Custer's troopers later presented the flags they had captured to Stanton in a ceremony in the secretary of war's office. Custer was needed at the front, so he could not attend, but Libbie represented him. After telling the crowd about their exploits, each trooper was introduced to Libbie by Stanton. Michigan Senator Jacob M. Howard thanked the troopers for their service on behalf of the people of Michigan, who he noted were "the immediate fellow citizens of General Custer." Newspaper stories about the ceremony invariably described Libbie as "the beautiful young wife" of Custer.[12]

Libbie wrote Custer that she was so excited she could hardly keep from shouting out her praise of him. She tried to keep her composure but admitted she started crying when she saw New York Senator Ira Harris tearing up. Before she left the ceremony, she told Stanton she had been waiting for a letter from Custer for a long time, but this event made up for it. Stanton consoled her, saying "General Custer is writing lasting letters on the pages of his country's history."[13]

Libbie herself was becoming a celebrity by association, and like her husband, she enjoyed it. "I was so proud I walked on air," Libbie wrote Custer. "People in the hall stared and pointed me out to each other: 'Custer's wife . . . That's the wife of Custer!'"[14] On the other hand, she worried about him. "Don't expose yourself in battle," she wrote in another letter that month. "Just do your duty, and don't rush out so daringly. Oh, Autie, we must die together. Better the humblest life together than the loftiest, divided. My hopes and ambitions are more than a hundred times already realized in you."[15]

Custer also fervently wanted just to be with Libbie. At about the same time Libbie was reveling in the War Department ceremony, Custer wrote her how much he longed for the end of the war. Unlike when he was a young officer and single early in the war, he no longer wanted a battle every day for the rest of his life. "I look forward to our future with earnest hope," he wrote, although he was honest that the end of the war would be the end of the high life of a general. "Our state may be far below our present one. We may not have the means of enjoyment we now possess, but we shall have enough to spare. Above all, we shall have each other."[16]

He looked forward to such a mundane thing as playing chess with Libbie. He sent her a set he took from Early's captured headquarters wagon, telling her it was a beautiful game, like a battle. "If you will learn, it will be a great source of pleasure to us hereafter." She wrote back that she watched two of their friends play, one representing Custer and the other Early. The "Custer," of course, won the match.[17]

But he wasn't thinking only of fun and games. Custer was also praying every day since his public acceptance of Christ in Monroe. Raised in a Christian household, he had offered brief prayers before battles earlier in the war. Now he was praying formally and with intense devotion. He saw a miracle in his survival of a serious fall from his horse. During a battle at Ashland, Virginia, he was riding a new horse, Jack Rucker. The band was playing inspiring music, the men were moving into position, and Custer was dashing around giving orders when Jack Rucker stepped into a hole. The horse turned a somersault, landing on top of Custer. Instead of struggling, the horse lay still. Custer's staff rode up in a panic, expecting him to be crushed. They rolled the stupefied horse off Custer, who had also been momentarily stunned. To everyone's amazement, Custer called for a new horse and took his place back in command.[18]

"Had he struggled, I should have been crushed to death," Custer wrote Libbie about the mysterious behavior of Jack Rucker. "But the noble animal seemed to comprehend the situation, for he lay perfectly still, without motion."[19]

Custer had named Theodore J. Holmes, chaplain of the First Connecticut Cavalry, to his staff. When Holmes saw Custer get up, he yelled "Thank God," which struck Custer as more than an empty phrase. They read a chapter of the Bible and prayed in Custer's tent that night, thanking God for the Union victory.

That month Holmes's congregation called him to leave the service and come back to preach. In his letter of resignation, Holmes told Custer that he felt privileged to have served with him. The chaplain, who had been wounded himself, had witnessed Custer survive close calls in combat as well as the accident with Jack Rucker. He had also seen the work of God in what others called Custer's Luck. Holmes wrote that he would pray that Custer would continue to be protected "by the Power that has so strangely shielded you in the past." He praised the Almighty for giving such a general to the Union cause, and one who led by moral example. "But even more I rejoice in the position you have taken deliberately, and, I believe, finally, in regard to a moral and religious life. You cannot know what a great power you are exercising in this way upon your staff, your command and upon the whole army." Custer wrote Libbie, telling her to share the letter with his family and friends.[20]

Yet as ever, Custer was also focused on earthly matters. He intently followed the newspaper coverage of himself, writing Libbie to see E. A. Paul's story in the *New York Times* of the Shenandoah battles, including Waynesboro, and to be sure to send a copy to his father and her own father.[21] Paul's story was effusive, especially of Custer's direction of the fight at Waynesboro. "Gen. Custer deserves the credit of planning and executing one of the most brilliant and successful fights that ever occurred in this or any other war."[22]

Other newspapers were just as fawning. The *New York Herald* reporter spent a paragraph of his story just describing Custer's appearance. "The Third Division, General Custer, as it passed through town, was particularly remarked for their soldierly appearance. At the head was its gallant leader, who had won a proud name by his intrepid deeds. His appearance on this occasion was unusually striking. He looked more youthful than ever. His golden locks streamed over his shoulders, and his jaunty velvet suite of clothes, his sailor shirt, adjusted after the most approved man-of-war style, looked quite picturesque."[23]

Custer could even read about himself in Southern newspapers. He sent a detail of twenty-five men to get a copy of a recent Richmond newspaper. Rebel newspapers could be a source of intelligence, as reporters often filed stories about the movements of their own armies. The newspapers no doubt also provided amusement for both Custer and his men, as they could read a jaundiced account of their exploits. In one weird Escher-like moment, the *New York Herald* published a story about the raid from the *Richmond Enquirer,* which in turn included an excerpt from a one-sheet paper published by Custer's troopers in the captured offices of a Charlottesville newspaper when they had stopped in that town. According to the *Enquirer,* Custer's men had tried to print it at the Charlottesville *Chronicle,* but some of the paper's type was missing. They then moved to the *Jeffersonian* and used its press to compose *The Third Cavalry Division Chronicle,* including a list of all the property they had captured or destroyed in the raid, advertisements offering rewards for Early and Custer's West Point classmate Rosser— written as if they were runaway slaves—and a Personals ad hoping to start a correspondence with some lady in Charlottesville that would lead to marriage.[24]

The *Enquirer* wrote that a number of slaves followed Custer's command on stolen horses. "The Yankees did not like to be troubled with them, and, if the report be true, they will not be troubled with them for any great length of time, for they are sure to find an early grave. Some of the Yankees cursed the negroes, telling them that they had better stay where they were for they were better off and much better provided for with their masters than they would be with the army."[25]

Paul, however, told a different story in the *Times*. A freed slave who was a nursing mother was having trouble keeping up with the column. A Union soldier volunteered to carry the baby for her for a while. When he wanted to give the baby back, the mother had disappeared, and he ended up carrying the baby all the way to camp.[26]

Certainly, Custer and his troopers were sympathetic to both the escaped slaves and Southern civilians and felt regret for the damage they were inflicting on the area. They captured a rebel soldier who was on leave at his mother's house. She begged them not to take him away because he was her only support. The officers collected $165 (a little more than $2,600 in 2020) for her and assured her that she would be well treated.[27]

To keep the men from abusing the population, Custer gave strict orders against straggling and independent foraging. The former Ohio schoolteacher was also sympathetic to the city fathers of Charlottesville and the faculty of the University of Virginia, who met him with a white flag and asked for the protection of the town and the campus. He put guards at every street corner while the cavalry marched through town.[28]

His kindness didn't protect him from the enemy, though. After he marched through Monticello, rebel snipers fired three shots at Custer, nearly hitting him and adding to the list of miraculous escapes he made from death. Custer and his men camped in the shadow of Thomas Jefferson's home, an iconic symbol of the common heritage of the combatants.[29]

In Fredricks Hall, Virginia, Custer set up his headquarters in the home of a wealthy rebel sympathizer. His men displayed their captured battle flags along the man's fence, and Custer's headquarters flag flew over the gate. The owner of the house and his family seemed to take it in stride—he admitted to Paul that it seemed the war was lost. The ladies of the house asked to hear some music, and one of Custer's officers called the band to perform a lively song. The ladies and the staff officers were enjoying a conversation when one of the women shouted, "Father's tobacco factory is on fire!"

Everyone could see a dark plume of smoke rolling up from the factory, the fire destroying the last of the host's assets. "The ladies retired in tears to their private apartments; the officers, mortified at the untimely conflagration, sought other duties," Paul wrote. "[The host] was standing at a window in an adjoining apartment at the time, and the scene almost overpowered him."

Paul, like the officers, was filled with conflicting emotions. The man had hoped to save his property while hosting the Yankees, but he got what happened to traitors who tried to destroy the Union. Still, it was hard to watch the grief-stricken family cry as their business went up in smoke. "God grant that I may never be compelled to witness such a scene again," he wrote. Paul did not describe the reaction of Custer, who must have seen the blaze. Custer didn't mention it in his letters to Libbie, either, writing instead about the victory the army had won and the battle flags hanging on the fence.[30]

Custer was sympathetic, but there was still fighting left to do, and the South would have to endure more suffering if it would not give up. He and his men were ordered to rejoin the Army of the Potomac, which had itself been enduring months of grueling siege warfare in a grim struggle to destroy Lee's army and capture the rebel capital. On March 28, Grant ordered Sheridan to seize the crossroads of Dinwiddie Courthouse to extend the siege lines further in an attempt to break Lee's defenses.

Lee attacked but was beaten back, and Union soldiers seized the railroad crossing the next day. Custer, as always, was ubiquitous. At Five Forks, Paul wrote that "When Gen. Custer came to the front a scene of the wildest excitement prevailed." Custer ordered the band to play patriotic songs like "Hail Columbia," and his presence riding up and down the line encouraged his weary men.[31]

Lee then decided to break out of the siege. Sheridan, with Custer in the lead, pursued Lee's collapsing army as he headed west in an effort to link up with the other main Confederate army in the Carolinas under Gen. Joseph Johnston.

The frantic newspaper coverage captured the mood of the country as the four-year nightmare of war crashed to an end. The April 4 *New York Times* featured a four-column drawing of a screaming eagle holding a banner labeled "Richmond" and a headline deck topped by "Grant. Richmond and Victory!" The April 6 edition described the occupation of the capital by federal troops and reported that Jefferson Davis was fleeing to Mexico.

The next day the *Times* published a dispatch from Sheridan to Grant that included a captured letter from a rebel colonel to his mother, telling her their army was "ruined." Sheridan told Grant he wished he were with him to see the progress his troops were making. "I feel confident of capturing the Army of Northern Virginia if we exert ourselves," Sheridan wrote. "I see no escape for Lee. I will put all my cavalry out on our left flank, except McKenzie, who is now on the right."[32]

Custer, on the left, spearheaded the frenzied pursuit. The rebels and their pursuers, who were spurred on by the thought that they could end the war, clashed in a series of battles. Confusion, passion, and excitement mixed with fear and exhaustion among the Union troopers as they closed in on Lee's wretched army.

Instead of pursuing a last chance for glory, others were terrified they would be killed when the war was clearly won and there seemed no point to the sacrifice. As Custer's men caught up with the rebels at Appomattox Courthouse, one trooper shot himself in the foot rather than participate in a charge.[33]

The rebels, of course, were even more demoralized. Paul wrote in the *Times* that Custer was able to drive off rebel forces three times his number, and was taking prisoners easily, the Confederates fleeing in confusion at the slightest attack. "The road bore evidence of the haste the enemy were in," Paul wrote. "A number of caissons and wagons were overhauled, disabled, and arms, accoutrements, blankets, clothing and cartridges were to be seen on either hand." Paul himself got confused covering the story, admitting in one that he had left out details in the previous edition in his hurry to make deadline. He started another story describing his exhaustion but wrote that he would try to compose a story even as he was surrounded by the turmoil of the battlefield.

In another story he wrote of the army's hope of ending the war if Lee would stop running and fight. "If [Lee] waits a few weeks longer he will have no men to surrender. His men are leaving faster than ever, and those who remain have given up all hope of establishing a 'so-called' Confederacy."[34]

Custer was always in the middle of the fighting, snatching sleep when and where he could. Near Dinwiddie Courthouse, he slept in the rain on the side of the road, having had nothing to eat since breakfast. His only cover was a rubber poncho. "For a pillow I had a stick laid across two parallel rails," he wrote Libbie. "Before I got the rails I slept a little, then woke to find myself in a puddle about two inches deep. Later I slept soundly."[35]

Injustice toward civilians angered him. The defeated Southerners would soon be their countrymen again. On April 8, while on the road to Appomattox, two women ran toward Custer screaming their house was being robbed. Custer jumped off his horse and ran into the house. He grabbed one man, a Union soldier, and punched him in the face, knocking him to the ground. Custer saw another man running away. Custer grabbed an axe handle, threw it toward the man like Thor, and hit him on the head. He had the two arrested and placed a guard on the house.[36]

In addition to drama there was comedy. At Five Forks, Custer, as usual, had his band play music to inspire the troops. But the band disappeared during the fight. When Custer saw some of the musicians later, he asked them where they had gone. "General, we were playing 'Hail Columbia,' when suddenly turning round I saw that all except three of my men had left," the band leader said. "And accordingly we followed them." Custer and the staff had a laugh at the comment, remembering the musicians trying to play while bobbing their heads to try to avoid the musket balls.[37]

The end almost came at Sailor's Creek, where Custer attacked rebel infantry trying to protect Lee's wagon train. Custer's brother Tom, who had joined his staff, was a demon in combat, winning one of his two Medals of Honor in the battle. Tom jumped his horse over the Confederate breastworks and struggled with a rebel color-bearer for his flag. The rebel shot him in the face, but Tom kept his grip on the flag with one hand and shot the rebel with the pistol in his other hand.

He took the flag to his brother and was going back to the fight. But Custer, seeing the blood pouring from the powder-blackened wound, ordered Tom to the rear.[38]

Custer was in tremendous danger, too. The rebel general Joseph B. Kershaw had ordered his men to concentrate their fire on Custer's personal guidon in an attempt to knock him out of command. The rebels shot his horse from under him and hit his color-bearer in the face, but Custer kept fighting.[39] "This was one of the grandest and most exciting scenes ever witnessed," Paul wrote. "The column swept along up to the enemy's works, and at one bound repassed over—the enemy throwing down their arms much faster than they could be reached." Custer captured about a half dozen rebel generals, among them Richard S. Ewell, one of Lee's corps commanders. The high-strung Ewell, who had lost his right leg earlier in the war, told Custer any more fighting would be a waste of life, and if he sent in a white flag, the bulk of the army would surrender. But Custer already had more prisoners than men in his command. He didn't want the remaining rebels to discover his disadvantage and attack.[40]

Instead the rebels asked for terms three days later, when Custer had them cornered at Appomattox and was preparing to attack. Just as he was about to order the charge, two rebel officers emerged from the woods waving a towel as a flag of truce.

Custer demanded to know what they wanted.

"Gen. [John B.] Gordon desires a suspension of hostilities," one of the rebels said.

"There can be no suspension of hostilities except on immediate and unconditional surrender of the entire army," Custer said. Following military protocol, he told one of his staff officers to ride back to the rebel lines to give the message to Gordon. He also sent an immediate message to his superior, Sheridan.

Custer then decided to go himself to talk with the rebel generals, including James Longstreet, Lee's senior officer. It was the grandest stage of the war, and Custer surely wanted a role in it. But he also had reason to worry about a rebel trick. After all, rebel snipers had tried to kill him after he had ordered guards to protect Charlottesville a few weeks ago. And during the pursuit to Appomattox the rebels had booby-trapped abandoned caissons, setting fires near them in hopes they would explode as the Union cavalry rode up. Shooting was also continuing up and down the line. In fact, rebels fired at Sheridan as he rode toward the surrender negotiations.[41]

What Longstreet and Custer said to each other will never be known for sure. The various participants recalled it differently, and Custer didn't write any details. But he returned quickly to his own lines, shouting joyfully, "It's all right, boys. Lee has surrendered."[42]

Custer was not at the surrender ceremony, which was held at the home of a local businessman named Wilmer McLean. Sheridan, who attended the ceremony, bought the table the documents were signed on from McLean. He gave it to Custer as a gift for Libbie with a note explaining "there is scarce an individual in our service who has contributed more to bring this about than your very gallant husband."[43]

Custer gave the credit to his men. The day of the surrender he had penned a quick congratulatory order to his troops, listing their accomplishments and telling them how much he admired them. He closed with a message remarkable for its clarity given it was written while he was in state of high emotion and exhaustion. In fact, at one point before the surrender an observer saw him sitting on a log, holding a cup of coffee, sound asleep.[44]

"For our comrades who have fallen, let us ever cherish a grateful remembrance. To the wounded and to those who languish in Southern prisons, let our heartfelt sympathies be tendered.

And now, speaking for myself alone, when the war is ended and the task of the historian begins; when those deeds of daring which have rendered the name and fame of the Third Cavalry Division imperishable, are inscribed upon the bright pages of our country's history, I only ask that my name may be written as that of the commander of the Third Cavalry Division."[45]

When he had a moment, he dashed off a quick note to Libbie, written in a large scrawl on a notebook sheet. "My Darling. Only have time to write a word. My heart is too full for utterance. Thank God peace is at hand, and thank God the 3rd Div. has performed the most important duty of this campaign and has achieved almost all the glory that has been won."

He then listed some of their accomplishments. He wanted to write more but had no time. He had done his duty, and he knew the future held a reduction in rank, pay, and opportunity for glory. But it wouldn't matter because he would be with Libbie.

"Hurrah for peace and my little durl," using one of his pet nicknames for Libbie. "Can you consent to come down and be a captain's wife? All well."[46]

He might come down to a captain's rank, but he was still, as Paul wrote in a story published three days later, "the hero of the hour."[47] The same edition ran a front-page headline declaring "The Era of Peace."[48]

The next day the lead headline reflected a new era: "Awful Event. President Lincoln Shot by an Assassin."[49]

At the moment of their greatest triumph, the country and Custer were plunged into a turbulent and confusing future.

CHAPTER SEVEN

Reconstruction

Seeing the Political Elephant

For four years Custer had been playing the role of warrior. When Custer was a new brigadier general leading charges in the Gettysburg campaign, he relished being the star, being the central figure in the pageantry of conflict. He wrote to Nettie Humphrey, his conspirator in passing letters to Libbie, "Oh, could you but have seen some of the charges that were made! While thinking of them I cannot but exclaim, 'Glorious War!'"[1]

Two years later, he'd had enough. "I hope that the last shot has been fired in this war," he wrote his sister Ann about a week after the surrender and Lincoln's assassination. "At least, I hope I shall not hear another. I feel confident that the end of the war is near at hand, and that we shall soon be enjoying the rich blessings of peace. I never needed rest so much as now. However I feel more than repaid for risk and labor."[2]

Custer felt rage at the Confederate leadership for starting the war. The same day he wrote to Ann he also penned a letter to his friend Christiancy, the Michigan Supreme Court judge, in which he wrote that "The deepest gloom has prevailed throughout the entire army since learning of the President's death." Custer wrote that he fully agreed with President Andrew Johnson's speech saying, "treason is the blackest of crimes, and . . . traitors must be punished." No single leader of the rebellion should go unpunished—to do otherwise would be national suicide, he wrote, warming to his topic with his usual dramatic style.

"Let those who have occupied prominent positions in the rebel State Governments or the so-called Confederate Government—all the editors and others, who, by their traitorous harangues or speeches, have stirred up the people to revolt, be condemned as traitors and punished with unrelenting vigor, until every living traitor has been swept from our land, and our free government and free institutions shall be purged from every disloyal traitor."

Custer believed he expressed "the universal opinion" of his comrades. The *New York Times* agreed, printing his letter with an introduction explaining that it showed "how the men who have been most conspicuous in putting down the rebellion look upon the bloody leaders who have managed it."[3]

At the time Custer wrote the letter, he and his men still feared they might have to fight the remaining Confederate army under Joseph Johnston in North Carolina. After resting near Petersburg, the cavalry corps began marching southeast. On the fifth day of the march, Custer announced to the troops that Johnston had surrendered. An anonymous Vermont cavalryman wrote his hometown paper that the men had been expecting the news but were nevertheless filled with joy. "For the first time in four long years the men turned about their horses, and felt that there was no war, and that they were marching home."[4] He told the readers they would be marching home with their "brows bound with victorious wreaths" and wearing a recently adopted badge of honor, the scarlet necktie worn by Custer. "He has always worn one, and it has been seen many a time flying at the head of the column in headlong charge against the enemy."[5]

Custer's personal uniform, once thought eccentric if not crazy, had proved to be a brilliant stroke of leadership and promotion. What he had learned from Phil Kearny at the beginning of the war was true: the look of the officer is an important component of leadership. Custer's men wanted to be like him, and the press and the public recognized him instantly.

A crowd discovered him at the National Hotel the day before the parade of the Union armies in Washington and gave him an enthusiastic serenade, after which they demanded a speech. Custer responded by introducing his friend, Michigan Senator Zachariah Chandler, who gave a speech on the heroism of the Union troops.[6] The attention continued the next day during the parade. Newspaper accounts uniformly mentioned that people cheered excitedly for him as he rode down the parade route. The *Cadiz Sentinel,* for example, reported he "was literally covered with wreaths of flowers as he rode along amid the plaudits of thousands."[7]

Custer's horse was spooked by all the attention, and the final straw came when a woman threw a wreath at him. "The horse started, but Custer caught the wreath while his steed started to run," reported the *New York Herald.* "Holding on to the wreath, his horse running away, he gave the salute in passing the reviewing stand, his long, fair locks streaming out behind. Near Seventeenth street he succeeded in stopping the untamed steed, and, returning amid deafening applause, replaced his sword and cap and proceeded with the review."[8]

Custer would need his sword because although the volunteer soldiers expected to be mustered out soon, professionals like Custer were bound for occupation duty. The cavalry, in particular, was needed in patrolling the defeated South, fighting any rebel holdouts in Texas, and guarding the Southern border with Mexico against any incursions from the French puppet regime ruling that country. The *New York Times* urged the government to keep a large cavalry force for such purposes and pointed out it already had great cavalry generals like Custer. After dealing with rebel holdouts, such a force would be needed to fight warring Indians.[9]

The day after the parade, the *Times'* suggestion was reality. It reported that Custer would be heading west under Sheridan's command.[10] Grant had ordered Sheridan to New Orleans to set up a headquarters from which he could protect the border and "scour" Texas for rebels—a force under Gen. Kirby Smith that had not yet surrendered.[11]

The orders had come so suddenly that Custer and Libbie barely had time to pack their few bags before they were on a crowded train headed west. At every stop Libbie enviously noticed the boisterous celebrations for soldiers returning home.[12]

The trip improved substantially in her mind at Louisville, where the Custers boarded the steamboat *Ruth* to sail south. "The decorations were sumptuous," Libbie recalled years later, remembering the chandeliers, paintings, and glass doors. Dinner was served by white-coated waiters to the sounds of pleasant music, and the menu featured new desserts every day.[13]

At one stop, John Bell Hood, the Confederate general who had lost the use of his left arm at Gettysburg and had his right leg amputated at Chickamauga, boarded the *Ruth*. Custer immediately introduced himself. Libbie was amazed that the former enemies greeted each other like old friends. Custer peppered Hood with questions about the Southern tactics in the great battles of the war. "At that time nothing had been written for Northern papers and magazines by the South," Libbie recalled. "All we knew was from the brief accounts in the Southern newspapers that our pickets exchanged, and from papers captured or received from Europe by way of blockade-runners."

Hood was a charming character, joking that he had tried five types of artificial legs but to his chagrin the best model was made by the Yankees. When Hood had to leave the boat, Custer was sorry to see him go and helped his fellow veteran down the gangplank.[14]

Custer had always gotten on well with Southerners dating to his academy days, and like most veterans he respected the courage and passion of his opponents. But for the first time Custer was able to witness the harsh cruelty of slavery in the deep South. Of course, he had seen discrimination before. Earlier in the trip, during a dinner stop in Ohio, a restaurant owner had refused to let the Custers' beloved servant Eliza eat with them because she was black. Custer refused to let her leave the restaurant, and after a tense confrontation, the owner backed down, although Libbie recalled wryly that the restaurateur made $1.50 pure profit by charging for herself and Eliza, who were both too frightened to eat anything.[15]

Custer, who had enjoyed seeing the play *Uncle Tom's Cabin* during the war, saw the story come to life in Louisiana. Every plantation had its own villainous Simon Legree and humble Uncle Tom, Custer wrote in a letter to his father-in-law. "In the mansion where I now write is a young negro woman whose back bears the scars of five hundred lashes given at one time, for going beyond the limits of her master's plantation. If the War has attained nothing else it has placed America under a debt of gratitude for all time, for removal of this evil."[16]

Regardless of his hatred of slavery, Custer treated the conquered citizens of Louisiana and Texas with respect. When the command began its overland march to Austin, Custer issued a general order greatly restricting his troops from foraging for supplies among the general population. "The command being about to march through a section of the country which has been beyond the control of the Government for four years, and it being desirable to cultivate the most friendly feelings with the inhabitants thereof, all belonging to this command will be required to exercise the most scrupulous regard for the rights and property of those with whom they may be brought in contact."[17]

The order must have appeared strange to his troops, who were veterans of the Hard War strategy that had devastated vast sections of the South in order to bring the population to its knees. Now they were expected to be kind to a rebellious population that had started the war—a population whose disloyalty was forcing them to serve occupation duty when the war was over. But Custer was under pressure to achieve three distinct goals: reintroduce the conquered people to the federal government, protect Union men and former slaves from reprisals, and keep his command combat-ready in case of trouble with the French regime in Mexico.

The men and Custer were separated by a sense of purpose, duty, habits, and, ultimately, class. For although Custer's Midwestern upbringing in small towns as the son of a blacksmith was similar to that of many of his soldiers, his lifestyle had changed drastically over the last eight years. Custer had left his rural background to attend college at West Point. After graduation, he had served with a number of spit-and-polish generals like McClellan and Kearny in an army that reflected that sense of military style. The troops he commanded now were from the Western theater, where the soldiers tended to be less disciplined and who prided themselves on their casual uniforms and swagger. Observers had noted the obvious difference in the attitude of the armies during the grand parade in Washington.

An even greater gulf existed in the sense of purpose of Custer and his men. Custer's career was the army, unless he decided to resign to pursue other interests. His soldiers believed they had done their duty and were ready to go home. Custer's sworn duty was the next mission, and it was one not without hazards. He was leading men into a hostile, violent region with some pockets of resistance still holding out. A potential belligerent foreign country was nearby. A complicating factor was that the civilian population was officially no longer the enemy, even if the people themselves might still feel separated from the government. Custer was still living in a state of war. His men were living in a state of peace.

The artistic Custer was also still living as Charles O'Malley, the fictional Irish dragoon he had read about in school. Like O'Malley in the Napoleonic wars and Custer himself in the Civil War, he interspersed his campaigning with fun, food, and romance. He and his officers went hunting, he socialized with wealthy planters, and he brought his love, Libbie, along with a wagon set up for her convenience. It was all too much for his soldiers, who chafed under his emphasis on training, discipline, and restrictions against foraging on the property of their very recent enemies.

They pushed, and Custer pushed back.

They stole food and harassed civilians. Custer had heads shaved and backs flogged, even though the latter punishment was one that had been abolished by Congress.[18] A number of men deserted, and when one lieutenant circulated a petition asking that an officer be relieved of command, which was mutinous, Custer ordered a court-martial, after which the lieutenant and a deserter were sentenced to death. In the days before the execution, rumors circulated that the troops would assassinate Custer rather than let their comrades die. "The threats, the ominous and quiet watching, the malignant, revengeful faces of the troops about us, told me plainly that another day might darken my life forever, and I was consumed by my own torturing suspense," Libbie recalled.[19]

Custer remained nonchalant and refused to arm himself or let his staff carry weapons to the execution. Custer, who would quote Hamlet in his letters, staged the event like the conclusion of a Shakespearean drama: The entire command of about five thousand formed a hollow square. Custer led the procession of the condemned and the firing squad in a slow ride around the square, close enough so that a soldier could strike him if he dared. The condemned men were blindfolded, and the charges against them were read. Just before the command "Fire!" was given, Custer had an aide pull the lieutenant aside. Custer had pardoned the man, who he had believed was "unduly influenced by others," but he wanted to prove to his men that he would not be intimidated.[20] The deserter was shot and killed.

The men complained in letters to their hometown newspapers. The *Ottumwa* (Iowa) *Courier* received several such letters and published an unsigned one as an example. The letter reported that Private Horace Cure had his head shaved and received twenty-five lashes without being tried by a court-martial. The story did not report what Cure had done, giving the impression that he was punished arbitrarily. Nevertheless, the *Courier* believed it had sufficient proof to demand punishment for the "inhuman" Custer. "We trust the Government will at once put him on his trial before a court martial, and if these charges are sustained, inflict upon him the full penalty due to such barbarities, more becoming a savage nation than the services of the most enlightened nation on earth."[21]

Another unidentified solider wrote to the *Rock Island* (Illinois) *Argus* that Custer favored freed slaves over the soldiers: "I don't think *they* [the freedmen] ever got their just deserts, for they were too lazy too [*sic*] work, and did nothing but lay around and steal, while General Custer upholds them and flogs volunteer soldiers." The man complained about Libbie riding in a wagon that should have been used for sick men, and that she ordered "one man tied up by his thumbs, to a tree, for going by headquarters without a coat on"—a dubious accusation, to say the least.[22] Custer admired his wife and took career and writing advice from her, but she left the military matters to him.

Doubtless Custer practiced harsh discipline, but it was likely less intense than that reported in some of the exaggerated newspaper accounts. Most of the negative stories were published in newspapers in small towns in the Midwest that were home to the disgruntled soldiers. The *New York Times,* however, carried a full-page report on conditions in Texas that included a half column devoted to the defense of Custer. The *Times* reporter in Texas, a veteran war correspondent named Ben Truman, wrote that the volunteer soldiers were urged to desert by friends and relatives in the North, who told them the war was over so there was no need to serve any longer. The troops were misbehaving badly in Texas, and Custer tried every humane way to keep his command intact.

He then tried a new way; and flogged several men and shaved their heads. This had the desired effect, but brought down the friends of these soldiers upon him, who charge him with being disloyal, inhuman, and everything that is bad. Now, I leave it to every one if Custer didn't do right. The volunteers are not acting in a good spirit here, while nearly half of them have deserted. This state of things operates badly in the two regular cavalry regiments which are stationed in this section, nearly one-third of whom have deserted. These deserters turn murderers and robbers and horse-thieves and are a terror to the traveling community. Scarcely a night passes but that some poor fellow is waylaid and killed.[23]

Despite the *Times'* defense, for the first time in his life, Custer was seen as a villain in letters from his own soldiers published in the press. Libbie recalled that Custer ignored the stories until one insulted his parents. A veteran of the command wrote years later that the letter had only detailed Custer's harsh treatment of the soldiers. Both accounts agreed that Custer threatened to horsewhip the author but backed down either because the author denied writing it or because he reached for his sword, daring Custer to fight. Maj. Jacob Greene stepped into Custer's office and the situation was defused.[24] In any case, it showed that Custer cared passionately about his reputation in the press.

It's possible the undisciplined, erratic, and in some cases violent behavior of Custer and his troops could be attributed to what is now called Post-Traumatic Stress Disorder. During the Civil War era, the effect of combat stress was called "Irritable Heart" or "Soldier's Heart" but was not treated or even discussed at the level it is today. Of course, it is impossible to diagnose cases more than a hundred years later, but it's reasonable to think that Custer and some of his men were seriously affected by the war. The conflict between Custer and his men in some ways sounds similar to the famous World War II incident in which Lt. Gen. George S. Patton slapped a soldier being treated for combat fatigue. The soldier who was slapped later said he thought Patton acted that way because he, too, was suffering from combat stress. One writer noted that "the difference between the *slapper* and the *slappee* was only a matter of rank."[25]

On the other hand, Custer's relations with civilians in Texas made him a popular figure in the state. When his command arrived at the Groce Plantation near Hempstead, the family was startled from their dinner by the sound of hooves and the rattle of sabers. The energetic stomping of Custer's heavy cavalry boots on the front porch must have terrified a family that had not seen Yankees before. But Custer, determined to enforce his orders against foraging, announced only that his troops would camp in their fields and use the water from the creek. True to Custer's word, his command took nothing else.[26]

Area civilians paid Custer back by entertaining him with dinners and presenting him with hunting dogs, which he promptly attempted to train by blowing a horn, much to the annoyance of Libbie. The peaceful relationship with civilians continued when the command moved to Austin. The provisional governor, Andrew Hamilton, gave Custer a large brick state building as a headquarters. The citizens and the Custers shared dinners, parties, and horse races. The Custers climbed Mount Bonnell, which overlooked the Colorado River, for picnics. One time Custer took the regimental band on a climb and directed them to play the "Anvil Chorus" so that the notes echoed down the river valley.[27]

Ever interested in education, Custer made frequent trips to the School for the Deaf, where he learned sign language from the children. It was a skill that would serve him well in communicating with the Plains tribes a few years later.[28] Playing with the children was a break from Custer's serious responsibilities as the de facto military governor of a conquered territory. Union men and freed slaves made constant requests for protection, and Custer received many reports of murders and abuse. The planters complained that the freed men would not work, allowing crops to go to waste. Custer, expressing the sentiments of much of the North, wrote his in-laws that the country should do all in its power to elevate the freedmen, but that he doubted they were ready for the right to vote. He cautioned his in-laws not to believe newspaper reports that everything was working smoothly in the South. "I regard the solution of the negro problem as involving difficulty and requiring greater statesmanship than any political matter that has arisen for years."[29]

No statesman could please everyone. Northerners who wanted a harsh Reconstruction policy attacked Custer in the press. Several newspapers reported that Custer either gave a treasonous speech in San Antonio or endorsed one made by a former rebel officer. The stories were vague, implying that he had made "disloyal" comments. Ben Truman reported in the *Times* that Wesley Merritt, another cavalry general assigned to Texas, had made the speech, and that it actually was pro-Union. In the speech, Merritt, who had been drinking, said he might come back to run for office in Texas someday, and he would rather have the vote of a loyal Texan than ten abolitionists.[30] But the version critical of Custer became so widespread that Custer felt compelled to refute it with a letter to the *Army and Navy Journal* explaining that he had never been closer than eighty miles to San Antonio and had never made a public speech in Texas. "[I]f I had, my voice would not have been raised in support of, and in sympathy with, the statements and doctrines of ex-[?]Rebels, *whose hostility and opposition to the government is now as strongly and openly manifested as at any time during the rebellion!* [Custer's emphasis] I hope my course during the war will be accepted as bearing me out in this statement." In fact, the *National Republican,* a Washington, D.C., paper that had drawn Custer's ire, published his letter with the comment that their column had promptly reported the accusation false.[31]

The attacks on Custer damaged but did not destroy his reputation. When the volunteer regiments were finally mustered out and Custer was ordered home, he was popular enough in Texas to run for Congress, at least according to Libbie. And his military supervisors were not bothered by complaints about harsh discipline or treasonous speeches. Secretary of War Edwin Stanton, who admired Custer's leadership, turned over complaints he had received to Gen. Philip Sheridan, who then wrote to Custer, "Your acts are my acts on any question of discipline." Sheridan also defended Custer to Grant, insisting that if anything, Custer had been too lenient.[32]

Custer himself was in fine spirits on the return trip upriver. He passed the time by teasing his father, who had come on the trip as a government contractor. Custer studied political issues in the press and then argued the Republican side against his passionately Democratic father. Custer was so enthusiastic in his arguments that even Libbie was temporarily convinced he had switched party loyalties. Custer's father was more sad than angry that his son had strayed and would struggle for days to persuade him back to the true faith. "It served to pass many an hour of slow travel up the river," Libbie recalled.[33]

Those hours gave Custer some time to think about his own future now that he would return to his regular army rank of captain and an unknown assignment. He had served a successful political role in Texas — why not make that a career? It made sense, because everyone knew veterans would exert an outsized influence on the nation's political battlefields for a generation through their large voting bloc, which would favor comrades who ran for office. "Place for soldiers! Such is the order of the day," asserted *Frank Leslie's Illustrated Newspaper*, one of the most prominent journals of the time. "Soldiers for policemen; soldiers for Judges; soldiers for Congress; soldiers for Governor, and double stars for Presidents!"[34]

On the other hand, many veterans, especially famous generals like Custer, were getting rich by working for railroads, insurance companies, and other businesses. Custer had many interests and talents, but his only extensive experience was leading men in combat. He enjoyed the excitement, the pageantry, and the sense of mission in the military. He had many options, but at only twenty-five years of age, no clear certainty about what he should do with his young life.

While Libbie went home to Monroe, Custer went to Washington to testify before the Congressional Joint Committee on Reconstruction. The Radical Republicans, who favored a harsh Reconstruction policy, controlled Congress. In detailed answers to about forty questions, Custer gave them plenty of ammunition for their view that the South needed a firm military occupation as opposed to the president's plan to return self-government to the former Confederate states as soon as possible.

Custer told the committee that while there were some loyal people in Texas and Louisiana, the majority were hostile to the federal government, and the government's lenient policy toward them was hurting Union men. If the government withdrew federal troops, former rebels would take over the state government, and it wouldn't be safe for Union men or freedmen. Union men were afraid to express their opinions in public, and freedmen were murdered weekly, if not daily.[35]

"Their bodies are found in different parts of the country, and sometimes it is not known who the perpetrators are; but when that is known no action is taken against them," Custer said. "I believe a white man has never been hung for murder in Texas, although it is the law. Cases have occurred of white men meeting freedmen they never saw before, and murdering them merely from this feeling of hostility to them as a class."[36]

Custer's testimony had once more made him a celebrity in Washington, just as he had been during the last year of the war. At first he was lonely without Libbie, writing her two days after his appearance before Congress that although he loved the theater and the opera, he had no desire to go without her. Yet his creative side reveled in the attention, especially from artists. A few days later he wrote Libbie excitedly that his hotel room table was covered with cards from people who wanted to see him, including artists, photographers, and the sculptor Vinnie Ream, who was working on a bust of Lincoln. [37]

Ream, only eighteen, had much in common with Custer. She was a self-made Midwesterner with good looks and an intense charisma that led jealous critics to claim that publicity and not skill was the reason for her success. Her family had moved from Kansas to Washington during the war so her father could find work. She got a job in the post office but also managed to study with the sculptor Clark Mills, an unusual feat for a young woman in the 1860s. Fearless like Custer, she went to the White House every time Lincoln met with the public until he finally agreed to let her sculpt him while he worked.[38]

Custer was only the second visitor to her studio when she had just started her career. She wasn't home when he called, so he decided to have a bit of fun with her. He left a note that said he had put his card on the ceiling of her studio, and she would need to find a ladder to get it down. It read "Through trials to triumph." Ream appreciated the encouraging note from the famous general and treasured it as an inspiration to work toward her goals.[39]

Hanging out with artists and celebrities was too much to resist. Custer was in his element, at home every bit as much as he was when on the campaign trail with his soldiers. Within a week of writing Libbie that he couldn't attend shows without her, Custer was sending her a list of shows and exhibits he was attending with other famous generals, politicians, and assorted movers and shakers.[40]

Politics, his old passion, was intriguing. He met with Michigan Senator Zachariah Chandler and other notables. "I never knew political excitement to run so high," Custer wrote Libbie. "Even the ladies are excited and engaged in these matters."[41]

Despite his testimony that favored the Radicals' position, Custer was starting to admire Andrew Johnson. His speeches were not flashy, Custer thought, and he didn't go back on his words like some politicians. "He is a very strong Union man," Custer wrote Libbie. "Union now and forever, one and inseparable."[42]

On leave from Washington, Custer headed to New York to explore business opportunities. He attended many plays and even went to a masquerade ball that was covered by *Harper's Weekly*. He wrote Libbie to check out the issue but assured her that his costume, which was the devil, was not as "horrid" as it would appear in print. Custer adored his wife and assured her in one letter that all his efforts at success were for her. But his artistic ego, his need to be the center of attention and part of the creative community, kept him obsessed with his own image. He wrote to his wife, who was unable to participate in his exciting trip, an excruciatingly detailed description of his costume, sounding like an actor describing his appearance on stage. The colors were like the uniform he created when he became a brigadier general: "Cape and coat black velvet with gold lace. Pants the same, reaching only to the thighs. Red silk tights with not even drawers underneath. Red Velvet cap with two upright red feathers, for horns. Black shoes with pointed toes upturned. Handsome belt. Mask, black silk."[43]

Libbie, meanwhile, wrote her aunt that Custer "was too necessary to my happiness for me not to miss him every hour he is away."[44] She occupied her time sewing and caring for her father. Daniel Bacon died on May 18, so Custer headed back to Monroe, still without a clear plan for his future, but certain of his own celebrity.

Politicians from both parties in Michigan wanted Custer to run for Congress. He declined in a letter to the *Detroit Free Press*, saying he did not think it was important to provide a reason for his decision. Certainly Libbie, who did not want him to enter politics, held a large influence.[45] But Custer nevertheless stuck his toe in the water by accepting an appointment to serve as a delegate from Michigan to the National Union Party convention, to be held in August 1866.[46] The party was a coalition of conservative Republicans and Democrats who supported Johnson's lenient Reconstruction policies and that was working to elect Johnson supporters to Congress in the fall midterms and Johnson himself in 1868.[47]

Custer seemed an odd choice for the convention because of his earlier congressional testimony, but he insisted that he supported Johnson. In early August Custer wrote letters to Johnson and then called on him at the White House to request an appointment as colonel in one of the new infantry regiments being organized. Custer even sent Johnson a letter with an enclosed news clipping that quoted him saying, "Andrew Johnson is my commander-in-chief and he speaks for me."[48]

Custer didn't get many clippings about himself from the National Union Convention. Most of the news coverage focused on speeches by convention leaders and the resolutions that the delegates adopted, which essentially endorsed Johnson's agenda. Custer began to attract more press attention when he was among the handful of officers who issued a call for a national Soldiers and Sailors Convention to meet in September. The group blamed the Radical Republicans for keeping the country divided and keeping Southerners in a state of "vassalage."[49]

By helping to organize the new convention, Custer had entered the thick of the political debate in the press. The wartime press had been united in promoting heroes like Custer, but in the heat of a political campaign, journalists at Radical Republican newspapers accused him of being a rebel sympathizer.[50] The *Cleveland Daily Leader*, like many Radical papers, attacked Custer for moving away from the position he had taken in his congressional testimony. The difference, the *Leader* wrote, was "Custer sober and Custer drunk; Custer himself and Custer the obedient servant of his Commander-in-Chief."[51]

There were too many critics to handle with the threat of a horse-whipping. As he had done with the rumors about giving a treasonous speech in San Antonio, Custer selected an important publication to air his response. He wrote an open letter to J. W. Forney, secretary of the U.S. Senate and the publisher of the *Chronicle*, a prominent Washington paper. Forney, a real power in the capital, had run an editorial called "Custer vs. Custer" detailing the discrepancy between Custer's congressional testimony and the National Union Party platform.

Custer's reply was a combination of righteous fury at the attack on his loyalty to the Union and a point-by-point refutation of the editorial's claims. Forney, Custer wrote, was trying to stir up violence with his criticism of the soldiers at the convention. "What have you done or accomplished to justify you in maligning and traducing those whose patriotism has undergone the test of battle and is beyond impeachment?"[52]

Regarding his views on Reconstruction, Custer explained that he had testified mainly about Texas, not the whole South. Texas was a special case because it was a lawless and dangerous state before the war, so its character was distinct from the rest of the South. It was true that conditions would be more dangerous if federal troops were withdrawn from the state, but that danger would apply to everyone, not just Union men. The most "prominent and intelligent men" in Texas had accepted defeat and were ready to obey the federal government. He was proud of his role in the convention and its platform, which was designed to secure the peace and reunite the country. "Duty, as well as interest, demands that this Government shall be national; this cannot be as long as twenty-four States legislate for thirty-six states, and 10 millions of our citizens are unrepresented."[53]

Johnson was impressed enough to invite Custer and Libbie to accompany him on his "Swing Around the Circle"—a speaking tour through the North from Washington to Chicago, where he would help dedicate a monument to Stephen Douglas. Johnson hoped to drum up support for his policies and candidates in the 1866 election. He invited Civil War heroes such as Custer, Ulysses S. Grant, and Admiral David Farragut to come on the tour and give it an air of patriotism and national unity. Custer accepted immediately, although he was in Michigan with Libbie and would not be able to join the presidential party until it reached New York.[54]

The presidential trip began on August 28 with high hopes for success. More than three dozen reporters covered the trip, ensuring a national audience.[55] Johnson gave speeches to enthusiastic crowds in

Baltimore, Philadelphia, and New York.[56] The military heroes were there for show and usually left the speechmaking to Johnson and Secretary of State William H. Seward, who introduced the dignitaries at most stops. With practice, Custer developed his own brief comments for the whistle-stop tour. At a typical appearance in Buffalo, Custer was introduced to the cheering crowd. "I do not intend to make a speech," Custer said. "If I did, I should speak as I fight; I have fought for the Union and Constitution for four or five years, and that is what I speak for." Custer then "retired to the ladies," according to a *New York Times* reporter, who failed to mention whether the ladies in question were Libbie and the other women in the party or women in the crowd. In either case, the reporter noticed that Custer was "an especial favorite with the fair sex." When Custer waved at one group of girls at an event near Niagara Falls, they sighed in response.[57]

Johnson, however, started to get hecklers when the tour moved into the more solidly Republican Midwest. In Cleveland the president argued with people who taunted him about a New Orleans race riot that symbolized the failure of his Reconstruction policies. Someone shouted "Traitor!" enraging Johnson: "I wish I could see that man. I bet you now that if the light fell on your face, cowardice and treachery would be seen on it." The crowd eventually cheered Johnson, but the interchange was widely reported as undignified. Even the pro-Johnson *New York Times* scolded the president that his behavior might have worked in Tennessee but was unworthy of the presidency.[58]

The tour made it through Detroit, St. Louis, and the dedication of the Douglas monument in Chicago without significant trouble, but in Indianapolis gangs of young men tried to block Johnson's carriage on the way from the depot to his hotel. The crowd shouted Johnson down when he tried to give his speech outside the hotel. Johnson gave up and went inside the hotel while outside Republican Radicals tore up the signs of Johnson supporters.[59] After supper, Custer witnessed a riot from his hotel window as gunfire erupted between the two factions. No one in the presidential party was hurt, but one bullet shattered a lantern outside Johnson's window and struck the wall of his room.[60]

Custer became fed up with the insults and threats of violence. When some in the crowd groaned during Johnson's speech in Louisville,

Custer yelled at the crowd, "Wait until next October and more groans than these will be heard," implying that Johnson's party would win the election.[61]

Custer's artistic side loved the cheers, the sighs from pretty girls, and the general attention generated by a political campaign. But like an inexperienced standup comedian, Custer had not learned how to handle hecklers. He started to argue with them, and his increasingly frequent confrontations with hecklers got his name in the headlines when the tour reached eastern Ohio, where he was born and spent the early part of his childhood. In Newark, Ohio, the crowd frequently applauded Johnson's speech, but a few people interrupted him by calling for Grant. Custer told the hecklers, "You cannot insult the president through General Grant," and then led the crowd in three cheers for the thirty-six states (meaning that the country was reunited). At New Market, Ohio, a crowd of about twenty-five men and boys showed up with a poster featuring the words "New Orleans; New Orleans" on it. They proposed three cheers for Radical congressman Thad Stevens, one of Johnson's main rivals. Gen. Daniel McCallum, a member of the Johnson party, told the crowd that the president would not speak if they were rude. They responded by offering three cheers for Grant and called for Custer to speak. Instead of his standard remarks, Custer told the crowd, "I was born two miles and a half from here, but I am ashamed of you."[62]

In Cadiz, near Custer's hometown of New Rumley, the townspeople put on an elegant meal. Afterward, Custer told the crowd that he was glad the president was able to meet some respectable men from Harrison County. In New Market, Custer said, he had seen the worst people on the whole trip. Someone in the crowd said, "We don't insult the president here."

Custer replied, "I repeat, I have not seen a worse class of people."

A person interrupted Custer by saying "Except the rebels."

"No, I don't except them," Custer said. "The rebels have repented. Do you know New Market is the home of every 'ism,' and that there is more infidelity in New Market than in all the country together?"

People in the crowd shouted that Custer was right. Johnson then made a brief speech calling for reconciliation and peace.

But in Steubenville there was no peace for Johnson as the crowd taunted him with groans. Custer repeated his line from Louisville that they would hear more groans in October, but Johnson tried to calm the younger man. "Let them alone," he told Custer. "They know not what they do."[63]

Custer left the tour after Steubenville to go to Cleveland to help lead the Soldiers and Sailors convention. The convention was front-page news around the country. Custer was not one of the main speakers, so he was rarely quoted. But as always, reporters noticed his mere presence. Radical newspapers mocked him. A *New York Tribune* reporter, looking over the hall for famous war heroes, wrote that Custer was the "most prominent and conspicuous" delegate. "His caliber is explained by the remark of an Ohio delegate, who said 'Custar [sic] is a man with a good deal of hair but very little brains.'"[64] The *New York Tribune* mocked the debate over who would be president of the convention, and claimed Custer was angry when John E. Wool was given the position. "[Custer] felt that he was the chief spirit of the Convention, and the one who first originated the scheme, but . . . the quarrel was compromised by putting Custer on the Committee to present the proceedings of the Convention to his Excellency [Johnson]. This will give Georgie a chance to apply for the vacant Brigadier Generalship in the Regular Army."[65]

Custer was even the subject of a column by Petroleum Vesuvius Nasby, the illiterate Copperhead alter ego of humorist David Ross Locke. "[T]here wuz Custer uv Michigan, with his hair freshly oiled and curled, and bustlin about ez though he hed cheated hisself into the beeleef that he reely amounted to suthin."[66]

Democratic papers, however, thought Custer and the convention did accomplish something. The *National Intelligencer* praised "the unaffected dignity of the proceedings, the elated patriotism of the motives, and the intrinsic truth of the resolutions and address of the Cleveland Convention," which it said had left the Radical press with nothing to do but personally attack soldiers like Custer.[67]

The conventioneers called for Custer to make a speech, but as he did on the Johnson trip, he declined while still making a point. "It has been said in certain circles that a soldier who is in the army has no right to interfere in political questions," Custer said. "I think, however, that the real objection is that we do not coincide with the particular views of those people. I intend to think and do as I please, but I do not intend to make a speech just now."[68]

Custer had the sort of charisma that could move a crowd without a speech. A reporter for the Republican *Boston Advertiser* wrote that Custer was the focus of attention, even when he was just sitting on the platform. "His boyish figure is full of springs and electricity. He seems fitful and nervous—sitting now half an hour in perfect silence and abstraction, and then turning uneasily in his chair or beating up and down the platform like a young leopard. . . . Whether the little cavalry-man has much intellectual ability is a question not yet settled. He has will that never fears, and is in himself a magnetic battery of wonderful power. He throws himself wholly into whatever he undertakes—for the instant, or the moment, or the hour, he is the thing he does."[69]

Toward the end of the convention, the crowd again called for Custer, who was on the platform, to make a speech. He shook his head slowly and walked behind a group of other generals and politicians on the stage. The crowd continued cheering, raucously demanding a speech from Custer. Gen. Gordon Granger told the crowd Custer would not make a speech. No one could hear Granger amid the tumult. Custer suddenly turned around and ran toward the front of the stage, pushing his way through the platform party while the crowd chanted his name. He called for three cheers for the old flag. The cheers, the reporter wrote, were magnificent and united the fractious convention. "How he did it I never shall know; but henceforth I can understand why the rebels so feared his cavalry; can understand how he got such splendid service out of his horsemen."[70]

He is the thing he does. In that phrase, the reporter captured Custer's essence better than anyone before or since. It is something that the most successful people in any field—but especially the arts—can do. Willem Dafoe, an actor who starred as Jesus in *The Last Temptation of Christ*, told an interviewer that the devil could tempt him with the offer to be able to completely disappear in a state of action. "It's the sensation that I seek over and over again," Dafoe said. "When you're in motion and doing something and the world drops away and you become that thing.

I would take that if I could do it forever."[71] For Custer, that ability had served him well throughout the war, as he was able to lose himself completely in his role as combat commander. At the convention, he showed he could take that same ability to other fields.

After the convention Custer went to the White House with other delegates to present its resolutions of support to Johnson. The next day it was announced that Custer had received a commission as lieutenant colonel of the Seventh Cavalry and was ordered to Fort Hays, Kansas. Critics claimed it was a political reward from Johnson. Appointments in the military almost always included a measure of political consid- erations, and no doubt Johnson appreciated Custer's support. But a skilled combat leader like Custer would have gotten an assignment in any case.

Custer's immediate future was decided. He would pursue his mili- tary career. But he could not quite let go of the family passion. About a week later Custer wrote a letter to a fellow Michigan veteran who had asked whether Custer would endorse a certain Johnson candidate for Congress. Custer wrote that he had heard the man had not supported the war effort, and that anyone elected to Congress should be "above suspicion." Radical papers gloated over what appeared to be Custer's abandonment of Johnson while Democratic papers called him a traitor to the party. The Radical *Chicago Tribune* wrote that Custer had turned on Johnson because he was mad about being banished to Kansas when he thought he had earned something more glamorous.[72] The *Detroit Free Press*, previously a strong supporter of Custer, accused him of being ungrateful and inconsistent in his politics.[73]

Custer never saw inconsistency between his support for Johnson's easy Reconstruction policy and his own personal loathing of slavery and Copperheads. As a veteran of hand-to-hand combat in some of the bloodiest battles in American history, Custer's motivation above all was to prevent a rekindling of the war while preserving the Union. He knew troops would be needed to preserve an ideal peace, but he had the intuitive sense that the American public then—just like it does now—will not support endless warfare. After all, he had seen his own troops rebel to the point of mutiny against their occupation duty. Johnson's policy was not perfect, but in Custer's mind it was the only one that would unite the country and finally end the war. With the compromising pragmatism of a true politician, Custer saw Johnson's policy as the best that could be accomplished at the time.

Custer was satisfied with his position. His quick and passionate answers to press criticism of his actions showed he cared about his reputation, but he wouldn't let the critics influence him. As Custer wrote to J. W. Forney, "If I satisfy my God, my conscience and my country, I achieved my highest aim."[74]

Custer didn't achieve his goal of helping Johnson's party control Congress. The Radicals decisively won the 1866 elections, giving them enough of a majority to impeach the president. Johnson was not convicted, but he served out his term as a lame duck. Custer's first active participation in a political campaign had failed. But he learned some valuable lessons. He had personally experienced what he had seen happen to his hero McClellan when he entered politics. McClellan, however, had also been criticized by the press while he was in the military because his campaigns were not successful. Custer learned that even a man like himself, who had rarely known defeat as a soldier, would be vilified when he entered political debates.

It was obvious that some stories about Custer in Texas were published simply to keep him out of politics. One Ohio newspaper, writing of the charges of Custer's cruelty to his troops, argued that this was a reason not to vote for men like him. "It shows the petty malice and tyranny that sometimes actuate officers of the army. And these are the very men, who, when they come home ask that their power may be perpetuated over the men they abused in the army, by electing them to office. We think the soldiers will say pretty unanimously 'not much.'"[75]

The fact that Custer was a target for abuse meant he was feared as a potential candidate. He had to be taken down before he ran for office. Interested in politics since he had claimed he and his father could whip all the Whigs in Ohio, Custer always knew it was a blood sport. Now he knew what it felt like to be the hunted. But that didn't mean he was through with politics. Defeats, whether in an election or a battle, did not mean you lost the whole campaign. There would be another opportunity later if he wanted it.

For now he would stay in the army, although the days of the glorious charges of the Civil War were over. But as Custer had written to his sister Ann early in the war, he had discovered that he was a naturally happy person who could be satisfied in any circumstance. Now he had the excitement of a new assignment in a part of the country he had never seen: The Great West. It was a chance for Custer the performer to take on a new persona.

CHAPTER EIGHT

The Hancock Expedition

Learning from Failure

Custer would have to rely on his natural happiness to enjoy the frontier. He had always admired the style and sophistication of wealthy men like McClellan and Kearny, two of his earliest mentors. When he had lived in New York to help McClellan prepare his final report during the war, Custer had written his family excitedly about his hero's house and his important friends.

Now Custer was a heroic figure himself, and a trip to New York reinforced what he would be missing in his new assignment. On his last leave to the city, he had visited the New York Broker's Board on Wall Street with friends and received not just the traditional three cheers, but three cheers and a tiger, as he wrote Libbie excitedly. When he visited the studio of the painter Ole Balling, he could see himself in a work called "Heroes of the Republic," where he was occupying canvas space with Sherman, Grant, and Sheridan.[1]

"Oh, these New York people are so kind to me," Custer wrote Libbie. "I would like to become wealthy in order to make my permanent home here. They say I must not leave the army until I am ready to settle here."[2]

But Custer was not yet wealthy and not yet ready to leave the army. He had participated in politics briefly with Johnson's Swing Around the Circle and the soldiers' convention, but that was not enough to persuade him on a new career. Still, in September of 1866, as Custer headed toward his new duty assignment, he and Libbie squeezed every last drop of high life out of civilization before they headed to Kansas— a state so remote that people in the army casually referred to living there as being "outside the states."[3]

They stopped in St. Louis, the traditional "Gateway to the West," to enjoy some entertainment. They visited a fair to look at prize livestock and other exhibitions. Custer was particularly taken by a riding contest in which some of the participants, former rebel cavalrymen, dressed like medieval knights. Custer, who always wanted to be performing, was so excited that he told Libbie he wished he could run down to the arena floor, jump on a horse, and try to catch the rings with one of the lances.[4]

They also saw the play *Rosedale* featuring Lawrence Barrett, a fellow Michigander who had given up a promising stage career to serve in the Civil War. *Rosedale* was a light comedy with a scene in which the hero plays up his wound to get more attention from the heroine, convincing her to repeatedly redo his bandages. Barrett also sang a song that became a favorite Custer whistled for years afterwards. Custer enjoyed the performance so much that he went backstage to meet Barrett.[5]

Although Custer was a celebrity himself, he was hesitant in approaching a star from another profession, and he apologized for the intrusion. Custer wasn't wearing his dress uniform, and he introduced himself to the actor, assuming Barrett wouldn't know who he was. But Barrett recognized him instantly from pictures he had seen in the press.[6]

Custer asked Barrett to come to his hotel so Libbie and the rest of their traveling party could meet him before they were sent to the wilds of the frontier. Barrett protested briefly that he had other obligations. He told Custer his rough gray traveling suit wasn't fit attire for a drawing room party. But Custer wouldn't take no for an answer.[7]

"The old lady told me I must seize you," Custer said, "and go you must, for I don't propose to return without fulfilling orders."[8]

In the end, the appeal of the fellow veteran, who was obviously on his way to a dangerous and uncertain future, convinced Barrett to come along.[9]

Barrett didn't regret being dragged to Custer's party. Barrett was a reserved man off the stage, but he had a good time and formed an immediate bond with the fun-loving Custer. He was fascinated by the two sides of Custer's character. Barrett found him to be a mix of a soldier and a scholar. Custer had a nervous personality but was able to control it at will. He also had an infectious laugh that seemed to come up from deep within his soul. Barrett compared Custer's laugh to that of Artemus Ward, a humor writer whose "lectures" were so popular and funny that he has been called America's first stand-up comic.[10]

"His voice was earnest, soft, tender and appealing, with a quickness of the utterance which became at times choked by the rapid flow of ideas, and a nervous hesitancy of speech, betraying intensity of thought," Barrett wrote of his first meeting with Custer. "There was a searching expression of the eye, which riveted the speaker, as if each word was being measured mercilessly by the listener."[11]

Custer was at home in the realm of ideas and art, which he loved, but duty quickly sent him to another world. Libbie wrote that Kansas was "about as different from the glitter and show of a gay city in a holiday week as can be imagined." Their journey by train from St. Louis took them gradually through ever-more-remote areas. Kansas City was a small town that seemed to have no future because of the roughness of the terrain. At Fort Leavenworth, an officer told them to buy a cookstove, because they would need it. After they left the fort, the towns got farther apart, and they realized they were now pioneers. When they reached Topeka, about seventy miles west of Kansas City, Libbie was surprised it did not look at all like a capital—the only thing that designated it as such was the stars surrounding its name in her atlas. The train tracks ended ten miles from their destination, Fort Riley. The last part of the trip was by wagon, of which Libbie wrote drily, "as a traveling conveyance, I would not call it a success."[12]

Like most arrivals on the frontier, Libbie was stunned by her first view of a plains fort. She had imagined it would be like the huge, solidly built coastal fortifications she had seen during the war, like Fort Monroe in Virginia. Her worry over Indians had been assuaged by this vision of an impregnable military post. "I could scarcely believe that the buildings, a story and a half high, placed around a parade-ground, were all there was of Fort Riley," she wrote. "The sutler's store, the quartermaster and commissary storehouses, and the stables for the cavalry horses, were outside the square, near the post, and that was all. No trees, and hardly any signs of vegetation, except the buffalo-grass that curled its sweet blades close to the ground, as if to protect the nourishment it held from the blazing sun."[13]

The plains surrounded the fort, the waving grass resembling the movement of the ocean. Haze covered the land in purple. Custer found it beautiful, telling Libbie that now he understood what Albert Bierstadt was doing with light in his landscapes of the West.[14]

Custer, now a lieutenant colonel in the downsized regular army, was assigned second in command of the Seventh Cavalry, a new regiment being organized under the command of Col. Andrew Jackson Smith, a fifty-one-year-old veteran with a record dating back to frontier service before the Mexican War. Smith let Custer handle day-to-day management of the new regiment. Many of the lower-ranking officers were Civil War veterans like Custer who had been reduced from heady volunteer ranks and were used to commanding larger units of troops.[15]

In the spring of 1867 the Seventh Cavalry was assigned to Gen. Winfield Scott Hancock's campaign to "show the flag" to the southern Plains tribes—including the Southern Cheyenne, Arapaho, and Kiowa. Sherman, commander of the army, ordered Hancock to "confer with [the Indians] to ascertain if they want to fight, in which case he will indulge them."[16]

Hancock, who Custer admired for his actions at Williamsburg, was ready to indulge them. But Custer, despite his reputation as a hell-for-leather cavalryman, was more cautious. He entered frontier service with plenty of combat experience but little knowledge of Indians other than what he had read in books like James Fenimore Cooper's *Leatherstocking Tales*, which portrayed Indians romantically as the "noble savage." As he had written in his West Point essay, Custer viewed the Indians with sympathy, realizing that if the roles were reversed, he, too, would fight rather than go to a reservation. In other words, he approached fighting Indians the same way he fought Southerners—he sympathized with them, but duty called him to battle.

Hancock initially tried to avoid battle by meeting with the representatives of a large village of various tribes that had camped about thirty-five miles from Fort Larned, a post in western Kansas about 300 miles from Kansas City. But the Indians, who were well aware of the 1864 Sand Creek Massacre in Colorado, in which militia had killed a number of women and children, were leery of letting any large body of troops near their camp. When Hancock marched toward the village, his column was met by warriors lining a ridge in their path. Custer, always appreciative of military costume, marveled at their display, which he wrote was one of the most impressive military shows he had ever seen: "It was nothing more nor less than an Indian line of battle drawn directly across our line of march; as if to say, Thus far and no further. Most of the Indians were mounted; all were bedecked in their brightest colors, their heads crowned with the brilliant war bonnet, their lances bearing the crimson pennant, bows strung, and quivers full of barbed arrows."[17]

The two sides negotiated, and the Indians agreed to let Hancock camp near their village with more talks to come. After dark a scout told Hancock, however, that the Indians were planning to leave. Hancock ordered Custer to surround the village.

This he did successfully. The moon was hidden behind the clouds, covering their movements. Custer approached the camp to open negotiations, hoping the Indians would not fire on them. The clouds parted, revealing the scene of silent mounted troopers circled around a dense village of tepees on the banks of a little stream. To Custer, it looked like a beautiful work of art. Duty intruded on his reverie, and he and three men crawled on hands and knees toward the encampment. The only sound from the village was barking dogs. When they got close enough, the interpreter, Edmund Guerrier, called out a greeting in Cheyenne. The only response was more barking.

Guerrier thought the presence of so many dogs meant the Indians were in the village. They must have ignored his greetings because they were waiting to jump the soldiers when they got closer. For Custer, it was as nerve-wracking as his first Civil War action at Bull Run, when he couldn't decide whether to use a pistol or a sword as he awaited the order to charge. Here, he decided to enter the village with his small party rather than order a general assault. "Each one grasped his revolver, resolved to do his best, whether it was running or fighting," Custer wrote. "I think most of us would have preferred to take our own chances at running." Only pride kept them from rushing back to jump on their horses and ride away.[18]

When they entered the village, they found it deserted. The Indians had fled in such a hurry they left their possessions and even some food cooking in a camp kettle. The only human inhabitants were an old man and a mixed-blood girl who Custer claimed had been the victim of "outrages, the details of which were too sickening to write about."[19]

Hancock believed the Indians had betrayed his trust, and he ordered Custer to pursue them. Custer, with the sensitivity of the artist, was better able to understand their motives than Hancock, and he tried to explain what had happened. "The hasty flight of the Indians, and their abandonment of, to them, valuable property, convinces me that they are influenced by fear alone, and it is my impression that no council can be held with them in the presence of a large military force," he wrote in a message to Hancock.[20]

Even though he disagreed with Hancock, Custer did his duty and went after the fleeing Indians. But he also indulged his passion for hunting. Imagining himself a skilled plainsman, even though he had never hunted buffalo before, he took off from the column, letting his English greyhounds chase a buffalo across the plains as if he were Charles O'Malley chasing the foxes in Ireland. Caught up in the moment as he usually did when he was excited, Custer rode out of sight of the column. When he finally decided to shoot the buffalo, it turned to gore his horse. The horse veered, and Custer lost control of the reins. He grabbed them with his gun hand and accidently fired right into his horse's head, killing him instantly.[21]

Custer looked around. He was lost in enemy territory with nothing but the oceans of waving grass on every side. He started walking in the direction he thought would take him to his command. Eventually some soldiers rescued him. But Custer's ability to "be the thing he does"—like an actor losing himself in a part—had nearly gotten him killed in his first Indian campaign. For Custer, it was part of the adventure, and he would write about it later in a self-mocking tone.

Meanwhile, Hancock made a blunder that was far costlier. He burned the abandoned Indian village Custer had captured, and then what had been occasional raiding by the Indians turned into a full-fledged war as infuriated Indians started regularly attacking railroad crews, hunters, stagecoach stations, and isolated farmhouses.

Still on the march Custer, came across deserted stage stations and occasionally one where groups of frightened employees had gathered for defense. They told hair-curling tales of atrocities. At Lookout Station, fifteen miles from Fort Hays, Kansas, Custer got his first glimpse of real Indian fighting. As usual, he was in the lead, and he was the first to reach the station. The stage and station buildings were burned to ashes. Custer had seen much violent death during the Civil War, but this was different. "Near by I discovered the bodies of the three station-keepers, so mangled and burned as to be scarcely recognizable as human beings," he wrote. "The Indians had evidently tortured them before putting an end to their sufferings. They were scalped and horribly disfigured."[22]

Custer pushed on to Fort Hays, where he planned to get supplies so he could continue the campaign. But when he arrived he found no forage for his animals and no orders for what he was to do next. For an active officer like Custer, the delay waiting for supplies was excruciating. And he missed Libbie, the one person in the world who could make miserable conditions tolerable for him. He wrote a series of letters urging her to come to Fort Hays as soon as she was able. She would be safe there because it would be a base of operations. "Come as soon as you can. 'Whom God hath joined . . . '," he wrote, quoting the Biblical passage used in the wedding ceremony. "I did not marry you for you to live in one house, me in another. One bed shall accommodate us both."[23]

He hated the primitive conditions. The fort was not completed, and the men slept in tents. In the cold, soggy spring, the ground never dried out, creating a goo that veterans said was worse than what they saw during the Army of the Potomac's infamous mud march in the Civil War, when artillery sank so deep only the muzzles were exposed to the air, and wagons sank to their wheel hubs.

One evening Theodore Davis, the combat artist for *Harper's Weekly*, was whistling while he sketched by candlelight. Davis had covered Union troops during the Shenandoah Valley campaign in 1864, so Custer was familiar with him. But any past association didn't protect him from Custer's temper. He burst into Davis's tent. "Stop this cheerfulness in purgatory," Custer said, "or I'll have you out here in the flood walking post."[24]

In Kansas Custer had found a circumstance that challenged his naturally sunny disposition. He started reading Robert Burton's *The Anatomy of Melancholy* to pass the time. This unusual book, first published in 1621, was written as a medical textbook of the study of what is now called clinical depression, but it was written in both satirical and serious tones and touches on a vast breadth of topics, including geography, poetry, and history. When a new paperback edition was released in 2001, reviewer Nicholas Lezard called it the "best book ever written."[25]

Still, reading Burton is only undertaken by the serious bibliophile. The massive volume can be a thousand pages or more depending upon the publisher, and the seventeenth-century writing style is difficult for readers who aren't used to it. Custer's book was about seven hundred pages[26]—certainly a useful length on a frontier post that saw irregular shipments of reading materials. Few people read it cover-to-cover but rather browse it as the mood strikes. Custer, who had the time, probably read it from beginning to end. One reviewer wrote that Burton fans are a distinct type of reader. "They are melancholic. They are erudite. They revel in learning. They know that the world is their book. They can step out of their 21st century vanity and return to a 17th century text and feel at home."[27]

Like many Civil War cavalry officers, Custer felt at home in the era of knights and ladies fair, or the grand European armies of the Napoleonic Wars, like those fought by his fictional hero, Charles O'Malley. The former schoolteacher was also erudite, reveling in learning, whether it was studying Indian customs, the habits of buffalo, or the geography of the Great Plains. He collected a menagerie of animals, including a young beaver, which he fed out of his hand at the table and let cuddle him in bed while he read. Custer wrote Libbie that the beaver's cry sounded so much like a baby that someone walking outside his tent would think he was keeping a nursery.[28]

But most of all, Custer missed his own lady fair. In a letter to Libbie he quoted some lines from a poem that he explained captured his own feelings about her "so truly":

By all kind words and gestures that I might,
I call her my dear heart, my sole beloved
My joyful comfort and my sweet delight,
My mistress, goddess, and such names
As loving knights apply to lovely dames.

Whate'er is pretty, pleasant, facile, well,
Whate'er Pandora had she doth excel.
Thou art my Vesta, thou my goddess art,
Thy hallowed temple only is my heart.[29]

Custer wrote that the lines came from a "most interesting" book he was reading—Burton. Then in the teasing style of the era, Custer alluded to its sexual content. "Written at so early a date there is less restraint than now obtains. It goes beyond 'Don Juan' in rich and racy terms, yet without a single immoral sentiment."[30]

Custer's reading was often interrupted by panicked alarms about Indians. He routinely sent soldiers to investigate the claims, but nothing ever turned up. Finally, when one breathless rider reported that five hundred Cheyenne warriors were chasing a wagon near Lookout Station, Custer ordered a forced march that eventually totaled fifty miles to try to catch them. When the soldiers arrived at the station, none of the guards on duty there had seen any Indians.[31]

Theodore Davis, who had tagged along on the scout, watched Custer interview the stage employees in a cave they were staying in while the station was being rebuilt. They were absorbed in a poker game.

"Have you seen any Indians near this place?" Custer asked.

"What's that stranger? I raise that blind," one of the players answered.

"Indian? I chip two better," another player said. "Dang me ef I know. I'm a rar hos ef I kere."

Custer realized he wouldn't get any useful information and walked off. Davis stayed and heard one of the players say, "Fellers, did yer ever see 'Wild Bill'? That was the chap; purty boy, wasn't he? Looked as ef he wanted a hand in, didn't he though?"[32]

Custer and Wild Bill Hickok, who was one of his scouts, did have a passing resemblance physically. But more than the whiskers and long hair, Custer was already starting to look like a frontiersman, adapting the costume and manners as if he were an actor taking on another role. The drawings of him by Davis in *Harper's Weekly* show a different man than the Civil War cavalier. Custer admired Hickok, whom he described as the quintessential plainsman: athletic, an excellent shot, and courageous without bluster. Custer thought he was the type of character a novelist would create.[33]

Custer and his scouts investigated the area further and examined the ground where the Indians had been seen. The "Indians" turned out to be a herd of buffalo. An infuriated Custer issued a general order explaining that the false reports were wasting the energy of the troops, and that anyone who issued a false report would be considered a "stampeder" and punished accordingly. "It is the duty of officers as well as men, who see objects resembling Indians, to ascertain positively before reporting," he wrote.[34]

The miserable and frustrating conditions were compounded by steady desertions. Davis wrote that in the summer of 1867 the Seventh Cavalry was losing fifty men a month and had lost almost eight hundred in less than a year, this loss about equaling the entire size of the regiment. Davis wrote that many of the deserters had enlisted with the intent to go West and see the country, and many left to make more money than they could earn in the service by looking for gold, working for the railroad, or doing other jobs. Custer himself thought most of the men left because of the poor food, and that contractors cheated the government by supplying the army with inadequate or spoiled rations.[35]

Whatever the reason, desertion was a serious problem because Custer and his men were in an active war. The Indians were still raiding throughout the Plains, and Hancock ordered Custer to patrol the region of the Platte River. They departed Fort Hays on June 1, 1867, but they always seemed to be just behind the Indians, discovering funeral scaffolds or old campsites but no actual warriors. In other places they found evidence of Indian raids, including burned ranches and the crudely marked graves of unfortunate settlers. One was marked with a board inscribed "Unknown man killed by Indians."[36]

It was a particularly brutal and frustrating type of warfare. The soldiers were exposed to constant dangers while never being able to give a hard blow to the enemy. Custer had not seen this type of fighting except against John Mosby, the rebel guerilla who led hit-and-run raids against Union troopers in the Shenandoah Valley in 1864.

Theodore Davis, as he did during the Civil War, brought the conflict home to *Harper's* readers with exciting sketches. His work in Hancock's War featured skirmishes and graphic depictions of soldiers' corpses scalped and mutilated by Indian warriors. Word pictures were provided by the evocative writing of a young reporter named Henry Morton Stanley, who was covering the war for the *Missouri Democrat*, which was based in St. Louis but which sent Stanley's dispatches all over the country.

Stanley was raised in an orphan's home in Wales as John Rowlands but changed his name to create a new life when he emigrated to the United States just before the Civil War. He enlisted in the Confederate army, was captured at Shiloh, and switched sides to gain his freedom from a disease-ridden Union POW camp. He was discharged from the Union army for illness, but later enlisted in the U.S. Navy and participated in the battle of Fort Fisher, North Carolina. The adventurous Stanley saw journalism as his ticket to travel and fame. His writing style was as unique as his life. Stanley, like Custer, was sympathetic to the Indians' plight while recognizing the impossibility of their resistance to the westward expansion of the United States. He practiced an early type of literary journalism, making himself part of the story, writing about his emotions while describing everything he witnessed in clinical detail, whether it was a flogging on an army post or a profile of a recovering scalped railroad worker who had feigned death to survive an Indian raid. Stanley's stories, such as an account of Indians threatening a stagecoach he was riding in, gave the idea that death could occur at any time on the frontier.[37]

Stanley explained that the army couldn't catch the Indians because they traveled light and fast on their ponies, unlike the soldiers bogged down by camp equipment. "The Indians are here and everywhere. Our cavalry might as well pursue that phantom ship called the 'Flying Dutchman' as pursue the ubiquitous hawks of the prairie."[38] Infantry struggled even more than the cavalry, marching with heavy packs under a broiling sun in hopeless pursuit of mounted Indians. "Many of them [the soldiers] were mere boys from fifteen to nineteen, and others were aged men. They desert at the first opportunity offered. Can you wonder at it?"[39]

The army had a difficult job. "It is a thankless life fighting Indians, and we, for one, side with the military," Stanley wrote. "They fight while fat citizens sleep, they are constantly on the alert, listening for the stealthy tread of the red assassin, dreading to hear the terrible war whoop sounding in the dead of night, by savages superior in numbers, and bent on massacre, while the patriotic loud mouthed and over-wise citizens are lolling on their beds of down."[40]

Stanley thought Custer had the right temperament for fighting Indians; he just needed the proper horses and supplies to chase them down. "A certain impetuosity and undoubted courage are his principal characteristics. From all we hear from persons qualified to judge, he must be a first-rate cavalry officer, and will no doubt perform any task allotted to him to the entire satisfaction of the western people."[41]

Although Custer missed Libbie and the excitement of the East, he approached his new duty assignment with the curiosity of the scholar. He had his chief scout, William "Medicine Bill" Comstock, eat with him every night so he could absorb his knowledge about the Plains and its people. Comstock explained to the neophyte frontiersman about Indian culture from fighting tactics to funeral practices.[42] Custer, also a passionate animal lover, captured wild animals and turned them into pets, including a young antelope.[43]

Many other officers couldn't handle frontier service and took to drinking to cope with the loneliness and primitive living. One such officer was Custer's second in command, Maj. Wickliffe Cooper, a Civil War veteran brevetted for bravery. The farther they went away from the post, the more he drank, and it worried Custer. One night, Custer noticed Cooper had not shown up for dinner, and he asked Davis to check on him. Before the reporter left the tent, they heard a gunshot. Cooper had killed himself. They found his body still warm and his revolver in his hand. All of the officers came to look at their comrade.

Custer gathered them outside of his tent and warned them about the perils of drinking. "Gentlemen, this is not the death of a soldier," Custer told them. "It is unnecessary, standing as we do in the presence of such an example, that I should say more."

When they arrived at Fort McPherson two days later, Custer arranged for a quiet burial, believing an officer who committed suicide was not entitled to military honors.

"Another of rum's victims," Custer wrote in a notebook. "But for intemperance Col. Cooper would have been a useful and accomplished officer, a brilliant and most companionable gentleman. He leaves a young wife, shortly to become a mother.

"I thank God my darling wife will never know anxiety through intemperance on my part. Would I could fly to her now . . . but a wise Providence decrees all."[44]

Duty also required he persuade the tribes to stop the fighting. While Custer was camped on the Platte River near Fort McPherson, the Sioux chief Pawnee Killer and some warriors approached Custer's command for a council. Custer gave them coffee, sugar, and other goods as an inducement to move their camp to the area of the fort and give up the warpath. The council was friendly, with "Little Bill," a pet antelope, sniffing the beadwork on Pawnee Killer's clothing. When a camp dog sniffed the antelope's hooves, Little Bill attacked it viciously, prompting the astonished warriors to admire his ferocity. Pawnee Killer asked Custer a number of leading questions about his plans, but Custer was wary enough not to give him any details. Nevertheless, the warriors left the meeting assuring Custer they would move near the fort and live in peace with their "white brothers."[45]

Custer always preferred peace and saw his opponent as a temporary enemy. After all, during the Civil War he had attended a rebel officer's wedding and taken special care of wounded prisoners.

Custer excitedly wrote Libbie about his first council meeting. He told her that he and Pawnee Killer recognized each other from the earlier meeting when Hancock had begun the campaign. "I feel much more hopeful than I did a few hours ago. . . . I encouraged peace propositions and have sturdy hopes of a successful and satisfactory settlement with the Sioux which will leave us only the Cheyennes to deal with. I am telegraphing the result of my peace talk with the Sioux to General Sherman and hope as another result to follow that I will see my little girl much sooner thereby."[46]

Sherman, however, had not made his military career through negotiations but rather a Hard War strategy that was based on his oft-quoted statement "War is cruelty. There is no use trying to reform it." Indians could not be trusted, Sherman told Custer, and ordered him to continue searching the area for Indians and pursue them in any direction as needed.[47]

Custer dutifully set off, but the pursuit proved as fruitless as before. Instead of finding the Indians, the Indians found the cavalry, harassing small detachments sent for messages or supplies and even attacking the main camp. One evening at dusk, Custer was lying in bed when he heard someone cry, "They are here!" He grabbed his rifle and ran out of his tent without getting dressed. The soldiers repelled the Indian attack, and Custer sent one of his scouts to ask the Indians for a parley.[48]

They agreed to meet on the banks of a river about equal distance between the camp and the Indians. Custer was surprised to see that one of the Indian negotiators was Pawnee Killer, who extended his hand in friendship as if they had not just attacked the camp. While they were talking, individual warriors slowly started joining the parley until Custer's detachment was getting nervously outnumbered. Pawnee Killer said the young men just wanted to say hello. Custer replied that if any more came to the parley he would tell his bugler to call his entire command forward.

The rest of the negotiations achieved nothing. Custer wanted to keep track of the Indians because he had small detachments on missions from the main body of troops and was worried for their safety. Pawnee Killer refused to stay near Custer's camp or let him follow the Indians to their village. But Custer, having learned the duplicity of his opponent, this time refused Pawnee Killer's request for coffee and sugar.

Custer proceeded on his mission and continued to hear troubling news of Indian attacks on garrisons and supply trains—one supply train had been attacked by about three hundred warriors. A detachment under Lt. Lyman Kidder had been sent with orders to find Custer but was missing. And, most worrying for Custer, he had written Libbie to meet him at Fort Wallace, but he had no idea where she was.[49]

Custer received orders to march to Fort Wallace, and he pushed the men hard, marching relentlessly in the hot summer weather. Some of the men reacted by deserting. At first the men started disappearing in twos and threes, but then on July 7 Custer received a report that between thirty and forty had deserted before reveille that morning.

Custer, who had fantasized in letters to Libbie about deserting himself, was not unsympathetic to the soldiers' condition. He knew their rations were poor, and the temptations to leave were many. But Custer had held to his sworn duty, and he expected his men to do the same. He couldn't afford the time and resources to go after the ones who had deserted, but he was determined to stop the problem. They were surrounded by roving bands of warriors. Another such mass desertion and the mission—even the survival of the remaining command—would be in question.

At a noon halt the next day, thirteen soldiers left the camp in full view of the command. Officers shouted orders at them and the bugler sounded recall. They ignored it. Here was mutiny. "The boldness of this attempt at desertion took everyone by surprise," Custer wrote later. "Such an occurrence as enlisted men deserting in broad daylight and under the immediate eyes of their officers had never been heard of. . . . This, unfortunately, was an emergency which involved the safety of the entire command, and required treatment of the most summary character."[50]

Several officers and troopers, including his brother Tom, were already mounted and volunteered to catch them. Custer agreed, and then called to First Lt. Henry Jackson, the officer of the day. Custer shouted loud enough for everyone around him to hear, "Stop those men. Shoot them where you find them. Don't bring in any alive." Most of the deserters got away, but the volunteers were able to corner a group of about five. When they were told to surrender, one of the deserters fired at Maj. Joel Elliott. The detachment returned fire, wounding three of them. Another deserter was injured when a horse trampled him.

The detachment brought the deserters back to camp, but when the regimental doctor, I. T. Coates, attempted to examine the wounded men, Custer said again at an exaggerated volume, "Doctor, don't go near those men. I have no sympathy for them." But privately he told the doctor to treat them.[51]

Custer's handling of the situation was forceful with a strong element of show. He didn't intend for the officers to summarily shoot all the deserters, nor did he want to deny them medical care. But he wanted anyone contemplating desertion to seriously wonder how far he would go. The theatrical Custer was playing the role of the merciless tyrant—this one necessary for the survival of his command.

At the next night's halt he ordered every enlisted man to get in his tent at taps and told them that the officers, fully armed, would patrol the camp. Any man stepping outside his tent would do so at the risk of being shot. Custer's measures worked, and the desertions stopped.[52]

It was a good thing, too, as evidence would soon show small parties of soldiers had no chance on the Plains. Four days later, they began to see signs of the missing Kidder detachment, which had been a constant topic of worry and speculation. They found a dead cavalry horse. Then irregular horse tracks. Then another dead horse. It was obvious that Kidder's command had engaged in a running fight for their lives. Custer's vivid imagination led him to speculate on what had happened.

"How painfully, almost despairingly exciting must have been this ride for life!" Custer wrote. "A mere handful of brave men struggling to escape the bloody clutches of the hundreds of red-visaged demons, who, mounted on their well-trained war ponies, were straining every muscle to reek their hands in the life-blood of their victims. They rode, and doubtless prayed as they rode, that they might escape the savage tortures, the worse than death which threatened them. Would that their prayers had been granted!"[53]

Custer found their prayers had been denied when he saw buzzards circling off the trail and smelled the horrible stench of the battlefield that he had encountered so often during the Civil War. But this site was unlike anything Custer had seen while fighting the rebels.

The bodies of Kidder and his eleven men were stripped and scalped, and their skulls were crushed. They were mutilated beyond recognition by hacking and slashing, and each body had more than twenty arrows in it. At least one man had been taken alive, and his charred corpse showed he had been burned to death. The bodies were lying in a sort of circle; no man had tried to run off. Custer took comfort that they had died heroically. Their death had meaning. They had done their duty.

"While the details of that fearful struggle will probably never be known, telling how long and gallantly this ill-fated little band contended for their lives, yet the surrounding circumstances of ground, empty cartridge shells, and distance from where the attack began, satisfied us that Kidder and his men fought as only brave men fight when the watchword is victory or death," Custer wrote.[54]

Custer thought that since they had shared their final dangers together, it was fitting they should be buried together, including their Indian scout. "A single trench was dug near the spot where they had rendered up their lives upon the altar of duty," Custer wrote. "Silently, mourn-fully, their comrades of a brother regiment consigned their mangled remains to mother earth, there to rest undisturbed, as we supposed, until the great day of final review."[55]

Custer pushed his command on to Fort Wallace, arriving there two days later on July 13. In all, his command had marched about seven hundred miles since June 1. They were exhausted and hoped to find relief at the fort. Instead, they found a post beset by cholera, poor sup-plies, and frequent Indian attacks. "No dispatches or mail had been received at the fort for a considerable period, so that the occupants might well have been considered as undergoing a state of siege," Custer wrote.[56]

Here was a situation tailor-made for a man who lived life as if he were a hero from a novel. Custer decided to lead a rescue operation, both for the fort and then to see his wife. He believed his orders were vague enough to permit him to go where he wanted. At the beginning of the campaign, Sherman had told Custer that he could go to Den-ver or to hell in pursuit of the Indians.[57] Custer decided to go to Fort Harker for supplies, which, while not a journey to the underworld, was a perilous trip through enemy territory. He picked a hundred men and the best horses available and set out as fast as they could ride.

They followed the Smoky Hill stage route, which included twelve stations between Fort Wallace and Fort Hays. At every stage stop they heard reports of roving bands of Indians. Sometimes their first greet-ing from the nervous stage employees was a gunshot from the fortified dugout. The stagehands were taking no chances when they saw an approaching group of riders. The Indian activity led Custer to believe he was being followed. At Downer's Station he was proven right. War-riors attacked a small party of stragglers about five miles to the rear. Two men were shot and presumed dead as the survivors raced breath-less to the main column.[58]

Custer ordered the men buried by a detachment of infantrymen at the station. His mission could not be delayed. They pushed on to Fort Hays, arriving at about 2 in the morning after marching some one hundred and fifty miles in fifty-five hours. Custer left Capt. Louis Hamilton in charge of the command with orders to rest while he, his brother Tom, Lt. William Cooke, and two troopers rode on to Fort

Harker, which had a telegraph station and the headquarters of the commander of the military district, A. J. Smith.[59]

Custer went straight to Smith's quarters, where a light was on, but the general was asleep. Custer woke him up, sat down beside him, and told him every detail he could think of about his marches. He then made recommendations for the rest of the campaign. Smith took notes and said he would telegraph Hancock in the morning. He told Custer to get some sleep. [60]

Satisfied that he had fulfilled his military duty, Custer wanted to start immediately on the second part of his rescue mission—finding his wife safe. He told Smith he wanted to take the train to Fort Riley, where Libbie was staying.

"How long can you give me?" Custer asked.

"Hurry back, we shall want you," Smith said. Smith woke up his adjutant, Capt. Thomas B. Weir, who Smith said would take Custer to the train station.[61]

When Weir entered the room Custer scarcely shook his hand before telling him they had to leave immediately, or they would miss the train. As they left headquarters, Smith told Custer to give his respects to the ladies at Fort Riley.[62]

Custer was at Fort Riley in a matter of hours. Libbie had been hearing constant reports about Indian raids and cholera, but she had gotten no recent letter from her husband. Day after day she would sit on the porch watching for the trooper who would bring mail. Day after day he would salute and say the same thing: "I have the honor to report there are no letters for Mrs. Major-General George Armstrong Custer."[63]

On the morning of July 19, she heard a saber clank on the porch while she was pacing restlessly inside. The door opened, and her hero appeared. He was a vision she thought more brilliant than the Kansas sun.

"In an instant, every moment of the preceding months was obliterated," Libbie wrote later. "What had I to ask more? What did earth hold for us greater than what we had?"

When Custer was excited, he spoke so fast that he was hard to understand. But Libbie was able to piece together from his jumble of words the message that she longed to hear: She was to return immediately with him. [64]

Custer had created a romantic story. He had rescued the besieged fort, leading his picked command on a desperate mission through countless hazards. The final scene was the reunion between the hero and his love, who was now safe in his arms. In his eyes, it was perfect.

The world disagreed. Smith had gone back to bed after Custer left Fort Harker, but when he woke up and thought about what had happened, he wired Custer to return immediately. When Custer returned, Smith had him placed under arrest for leaving his command without permission. On August 27, Grant, who was commander of the army, ordered a court-martial to try Custer on not only leaving his command without permission but several other charges, including ordering deserters shot without trial and misusing government property. The court-martial was to be held at Fort Leavenworth.

Custer chose Capt. Charles C. Parsons, an artilleryman with a good record as a military lawyer, to represent him. They were classmates at West Point, where Parsons had first seen Custer pranking another cadet in the pew in front of him in the chapel, sticking his fingers in the cadet's red hair and pulling them back as if he had been burned. Custer helped his friend with the defense through an activity he always enjoyed—writing. He composed detailed notes of the events in question as he remembered them.[65]

Custer was confident he had done his duty and was in the right. During the Civil War, hard rides were normal. Desertions were not tolerated. His old hero, McClellan, had ordered troops severely punished during the Peninsula campaign, reasoning that they must learn they "have a strict master." McClellan had even sent some mutineers to the Dry Tortugas. And Hancock and Sheridan had also ordered deserters shot without trial during the Indian campaign. Custer wrote one army friend from the Civil War that he would not hesitate to go to court based on the evidence.[66]

Custer's friends remained loyal. Letters of support came from many, including Thomas Weir, a fellow Michigander who had been a Confederate POW for seven months during the war. After his release, he served on Custer's staff. "I am anxious in the affair to go on your side," Weir wrote.[67]

Another member of Custer's staff during the Civil War, S. W. Barnhart, who was in Washington, told Custer that most men in the army thought the charges were due to jealousy somewhere along the chain of command. "As far as I have heard, nothing but the utmost astonishment and unbelief has been expressed," Barnhart wrote.[68]

Weir and several other men of the Seventh Cavalry were called to testify for both the prosecution and the defense, describing the events related to the charges. It didn't really matter to Custer's defense because he didn't dispute the facts. Instead, he based his defense on what he saw as the rightness of his actions. He wrote a final summation, which was read to the court by his lawyer and which wove a story justifying what he had done. Custer argued that different men might use different methods to achieve the same honorable goals, but that didn't mean they were wrong. "By the degree of good faith and sincere desire to discharge well and faithfully the responsible duties devolving upon me, which I hope to be able to make evident to your mind, I claim to be judged," Custer wrote in his summation.[69]

Custer wrote that after the campaign he had expected to be praised, not punished for his actions. "Here in the same view as before, I claim to be judged not entirely by what is now known but in the light of that information which was afforded me when the events contemplated in the first set of these charges transpired."[70]

Custer argued that his orders, particularly those from Sherman, gave him wide discretion. How could he be guilty of absence without leave when he reported to his commanding officer at Fort Harker, a post from which he could pursue Indians? With a typical evocative flourish that marked his writing, he argued, "Here, gentlemen, if the theory of the Prosecution be adopted, it is an absurdity that must be ridden bareback to arrive at any conclusion unfavorable to myself."[71]

It was evident that he enjoyed his writing and was confident in the story he told. He described the dire circumstances of the desertions that forced him to use harsh measures. His command had lost so many men, and he had heard from a trusted enlisted man of a plot for so many more that he faced losing a third of the unit. "Nothing more insubordinate could have been imagined than the disposition of those men who left the noon camp before the eyes of everyone and undertook to escape," Custer wrote in his summary. "Deeply conscious of what I was taking upon myself and, on the other hand, of what I owed to the service and to the men who were well disposed, I did that which under the circumstances it seemed to me an officer in my position was expected to do. What, it is becoming of me to inquire, would have been the result had I not taken those summary steps?" He would do it over again if he had the chance.[72]

Custer tried to explain the difference between reality and theatrics done for effect. When he told Henry Jackson not to bring anyone back alive, Jackson understood what he meant. That's why he brought back the prisoners unharmed. "And again, if I had intended that order to be obeyed literally, or if I had meant more than to have a desirable and necessary effect upon the command, I would have had those men shot when they were brought in and I would have held Lt. Jackson responsible for disobeying my order," Custer wrote.[73]

In similar fashion, Custer had told the doctor not to treat the wounded but in fact made sure they were cared for. One prosecution witness had testified about the quality of water available to treat the wounded and how Coates cared for them. "I do not know anything about this," Custer wrote sarcastically. "I am not on trial for malpractice, nor am I to be held responsible for Dr. Coates' professional views, although I will aver that from long observation I have the highest confidence in them. Hence it is sufficient to know that I did not stand in the way of the dressing of those wounds."[74]

Custer concluded by denying the charges in this case and by standing on his record of service. He would not appeal for mercy like he was a "forlorn object of compassion." On the contrary, he had done his duty as he saw it in Kansas and as he ever did during his career.

"I have never turned away from our enemy, as here charged, or failed to relieve an imperiled friend, as here charged, or left unburied or without having provided burial, of a single fallen man under my command," he wrote as he worked up to his peroration. "Or took it upon myself the responsibility of a single summary action that did not seem to be demanded by the occasion, as here charged. Or finally, ever saw a man in any strait suffer when by my authority I could relieve him, as here charged. So if I felt guilty of all or one of the Charges or Specifications, it is an era of my life of which I am not conscious."[75]

Capt. Robert Chandler, in summing up the case for the prosecution, wrote that he would not reply to Custer's address but would rather review the evidence. Like a good trial lawyer, he presented the facts and let the court decide. Where Custer was a storyteller, seeking to place the court members on the Plains, facing the Indians, Chandler was pedantic, explaining what was proved. Custer had claimed Sherman gave him orders to go in any direction, but he had not produced a copy of those orders. Officers had testified that Custer ordered them to shoot deserters. Officers had testified that the horses of the command were worn out. The only defense offered in the case of shooting the deserters was a justification for shooting them because of the dire circumstances in which Custer found himself.[76]

The court agreed with Chandler. It found Custer guilty of all charges and sentenced him to be suspended from rank and command for one year without pay. A subsequent proforma review by the adjutant general in Washington upheld the findings. As head of the army, Grant also approved the findings and the sentence. Both noted the leniency of the punishment considering the severity of the offenses.[77] In the ultimate humiliation for a soldier, particularly one such as Custer, who valued the pomp and ceremony of the military, his charge and sentence were read aloud in front of the regiment on dress parade.[78]

Libbie was outraged. Before the review of the sentence, she had written to her cousin Rebecca Richmond that the trial was "nothing but a plan of persecution." When the findings were upheld, she added that "the sentence is unjust as possible."[79]

Custer, too, believed the verdict was unjust. He thought the trial was fixed against him from the beginning because three of the members of the court were on Hancock's staff, and they had never commanded troops. He didn't object to their sitting on the court because his counsel told them they might not be removed from the court and then his objection would only make his situation worse.[80]

Concerned about his image, Custer wrote Judge Christiancy in Monroe to find out what the press was saying about him. Christiancy told Custer that the coverage he had read was favorable. "I never believed that you had been guilty of any offense serious enough to justify a court martial, but knew nothing of the facts except by public rumor." Custer had also discussed presidential politics with Christiancy, indicating he favored the Reconstruction views of Grant and Sheridan, which pleased the judge. Christiancy spent more of his letter discussing the presidential race than Custer's trial, and predicted Grant rather than Sheridan would get the Republican nomination.[81]

Politics swirled around the case and had to have figured in the charges and the outcome. Hancock's campaign had been an abject failure, and Congress was getting restless. In July, one senator claimed the war was costing $150,000 a day but achieving nothing.[82]

Both Grant and Hancock had presidential ambitions, and Grant was already being mentioned as a Republican presidential candidate for the following year. A scapegoat would be helpful so that the top officers were not blamed. Although privately Custer sympathized with Grant and Sheridan, publicly he was known as a Democrat and had been a supporter of Andrew Johnson, who was that year in mortal combat for his political life with the Republican Congress.

Whether the army brass intended to shift the blame for the failed war or not, to some journalists it appeared that they did. Custer, whose dramatic personality always made good copy, was an easy focal point for partisans to rally around or denigrate depending upon their politics. Republicans recalled Custer's association with Johnson and praised Grant. For example, the Adrian, Michigan, *Times and Expositor* editorialized that Custer owed his command to Johnson and that he shouldn't be able to use his Civil War record to cover for his current failures. Grant's word was supreme, according to the paper: "When General Grant deems Custer guilty, there must be good and sufficient reasons for such a conclusion."[83]

On the other hand, Democrats justified Custer's actions. "General Custar [sic] heard, last summer, that the cholera was raging violently at the place where his young wife was staying," argued the *Urbana* (Ohio) *Union*. "Without waiting for red tape formalities of a leave of absence, he went at once to attend to his wife's removal, and for that he had been court-martialed. The sentence has not yet been made known, the papers being yet under consideration by the War Department. The gallant service rendered by Custar, when the country needed it, should have shielded him from so petty a prosecution, and will doubtless secure prompt remission of the sentence, whatever it may be."[84]

Overall, the press coverage was not very intense. Many newspapers just reported the results. The press was more interested in Reconstruction and the battles between the president and Congress over how it should be administered. Unlike the Civil War, the Indian wars were far away from the main population centers and just not that interesting to the press. The exception would be a dramatic battle like the Fetterman massacre of the year before, where eighty soldiers under the command of Capt. William J. Fetterman were killed to a man by the Indians in Wyoming Territory.

A few deserters shot and an internal squabble over when a general needed permission to go from one fort to another was not going to generate much passion from a public that had just endured more than a million casualties and a devasted countryside in a civil war and was now trying to reorder its government. The wonder for most readers likely was why the army would go to such lengths to punish a hero of the last war. The *New York Times* reported from Fort Leavenworth that "there is considerable astonishment expressed at the result of the trial." The reporter reminded readers of Custer's Civil War record.[85]

"Gen. Custer is, to those who know him intimately, the very *beau ideal* of an American cavalry officer. He is a magnificent rider, fearlessly brave, a capital revolver shot, and without a single objectionable habit. He neither drinks, swears, nor uses tobacco in any form. His weakness, if he has one, is a fast horse, to get all the speed out of which there is no better man than the long-haired hero of the Shenandoah."[86]

Four years of war and two years of unpleasant and unrewarding service in Texas and Kansas had worn Custer out. The *Times* reported that Custer was looking forward to his suspension. "It gives him a respite that he has desired for a long time, not perhaps in this precise way, but he seems to be satisfied to take his blessings as they come. He proposes to remain in Leavenworth during the Winter and visit Europe in the Spring. It may be, too, that some of this wished-for leisure time will be devoted to the proportion of a work that will be decidedly interesting to those who have followed the fortunes of the General through his many campaigns."[87]

Custer didn't have the money to go to Europe, but he and Libbie were together, and that was enough for them. During the trial, Libbie had written her cousin that Custer knew the risks to his career when he left Fort Wallace to go to her. "We are quite determined not to live apart again, even if he leaves the army otherwise so delightful to us," she wrote. She was glad Custer would miss the next Indian campaign.[88]

Custer was determined live the life he wanted. He had a vision of how it would be, and like a great artist, he would not compromise. He had done his duty as he saw it; then he had flown to his wife when he thought she was in danger. His sense of duty led him to have deserters shot. His sense of the theatrical led him on his dash across Kansas to rescue his wife. It was no surprise the deskbound officers didn't understand; they lived on the sidelines, not in the arena. He would never grovel to them.

Custer's mentor, Sheridan, was concerned about him, and he wrote Custer encouraging letters. He also let Libbie and Custer live in his roomy headquarters in Fort Leavenworth while he was away. Custer wrote Sheridan that he did not want him to try to overturn his sentence; he would not accept it if he did. Sheridan was shocked at the sentence and told Custer he would look into his case, whether he wanted him to or not.[89]

Custer had already achieved everything he wanted in the army. He had led men in desperate battle to ultimate victory. He had met presidents and artists and actors. He had helped free a people from bondage and preserve the life of his country. Now the army had asked him to serve on a barren frontier that risked the life of his true love. What was the thanks he got? A court-martial and public humiliation.

He and Libbie enjoyed the winter at Fort Leavenworth, socializing with their many friends. Custer's pay was suspended, but he still got his living allowance, which kept him and Libbie comfortable. He subscribed to a number of newspapers and ordered a book called *The Lover's Dictionary: A Poetical Treasury of Lover's Thoughts, Fancies, Etc.*[90] Like Custer's favorite *Anatomy of Melancholy*, this dictionary was a massive tome of almost a thousand pages. It was filled with a mix of humor and serious stories about the ups and downs of love. Custer was focusing his time off on Libbie and literature, not thoughts of the army.

When June came, and the command prepared for the upcoming campaign, Custer and Libbie moved back to Monroe. He spent his time hunting, fishing, boating, and visiting boyhood friends. Meanwhile, he began charting a new path.[91]

As he often did, Custer used a literary reference—this time Dickens—to describe his situation. He was his naturally optimistic self: "I am like Macawber, waiting for something to 'turn up,'" he wrote a friend. "Meanwhile I am preparing to execute a long projected plan—to write a memoir of my experiences from West Point to Appomattox. Arrangements for this are concluded with Messrs Harper & Brothers. I have fifty pages of the script completed."[92]

CHAPTER NINE

Washita

As he always did, Custer put on a show for the outside world in what he called his "forced retirement," acting like it was a well-earned vacation.

In his memoir of the campaign, he made a weak joke about his comrades fighting while he was on inactive duty. "While they . . . were attempting to kill Indians, I was studying the problem of how to kill time in the most agreeable manner. My campaign was a decided success, I established my base of operations in the most beautiful little town on the western shores of Lake Erie, from which I projected various hunting, fishing and boating expeditions."[1]

Inside, Custer was torn between his sense of duty and longing for something more, a new kind of life of the mind, and with his artistic sensibility, he wanted an appreciation for what he had achieved. Custer felt betrayed by the army. In his memoir, he explained his actions and then commented that "it had apparently been deemed necessary that my connection with certain events and transactions, every one of which has been fully referred to heretofore, should be submitted to an official examination in order to determine if each and every one of my acts had been performed with due regard to the customs of war in like cases." He didn't write about the court-martial in any detail but concluded sarcastically that the "result seemed satisfactory to those parties most intimately concerned in the matter."[2]

The army was all he had known since college, but the court-martial was a harsh lesson that—no matter what his success in the field or his previous record—he could be sacrificed for politics. He always had craved more chances to express himself, whether on the battlefield or in his writing. From the time he had first left home to study to be a teacher, he had written lengthy, vibrant letters describing his activities. As he matured, his letters contained more analysis of the world around him and things he studied, like his description of *The Anatomy of Melancholy* to Libbie. The judgment of the court-martial was the ultimate restriction on his need to create. He would never be completely free to be the author of his own story as long as he was in an army so influenced by politics.

Nevertheless, the adventure of the campaign and the comradery of his fellow soldiers pulled him back to the army, which was given the job of protecting American citizens and businesses on the frontier. Custer felt an ache when he saw his comrades march off and knew he was not to be a part of the excitement. "With abundance of friends and companions, and ample success, time passed pleasantly enough," Custer wrote of his suspension in Monroe. "Yet withal there was a constant longing to be with my comrades in arms in the far West, even while aware of the fact that their campaign was not resulting in any material advantage."[3]

Custer was too kind in assessing the military's efforts on the Plains while he was absent. Indeed, the army, and especially Sheridan, needed Custer more than he needed them as the attempts to end attacks on railroads, settlers, and stagecoaches met with abject failure.

After the debacle of Hancock's campaign, the army tried an experiment with a group of fifty veteran soldiers and frontiersmen designed to travel fast and hit hard. The unit, self-styled the Solomon Avengers because they would pay back the Cheyenne for murders on the Solomon River, was led by Maj. Sandy Forsyth, a Civil War cavalryman who had served with distinction with Custer and Sheridan in the Shenandoah and Appomattox campaigns. But instead of paying anyone back, Forsyth and his Avengers were ambushed by as many as a thousand warriors on a fork of the Republican River on the eastern border of Colorado Territory. The embattled scouts made it to an island and held out against repeated attacks until a cavalry unit rescued them on

the ninth day of the fight. Their survival was an amazing feat of heroism and fortitude, but the Avengers were lucky they lived to tell the
tale. Strategically, it had little impact on the war other than to demonstrate that a small group of raiders was not the answer.[4]

At about the same time, Sheridan tried a standard military operation.
Maj. Alfred Sully led a combined force of the Seventh Cavalry and
the Third Infantry out of Fort Dodge in early September 1868. Sully
had led a successful campaign against the Sioux after their uprising in
Minnesota during the Civil War, so he had some experience. His 1868
expedition was handicapped by its bulk, which included slow-moving
baggage wagons, and the command was harassed by hit-and-run raids.
In one attack warriors grabbed two stragglers, threw them over their
ponies and rode off with them in sight of the command, the terror-
stricken soldiers screaming as they were carried to a torturous fate.
Sully never captured an Indian village and he ended that campaign
after only a week, claiming to have killed thirty Indians, a figure that
likely was exaggerated. The main result of the campaign was to show
the Indians that they could defeat the army.[5]

Sheridan had seen enough. He decided the only way to defeat the
Indians was to mount a winter campaign that would catch them when
they were hunkered down against the harsh Plains weather. But he
needed someone he could trust implicitly, someone he knew could do
the job. He cabled Custer in Monroe: "Generals Sherman, Sully, and
myself, and nearly all the officers of your regiment, have asked for you,
and I hope the application will be successful. Can you come at once?
Eleven companies of your regiment will move about the 1st of October
against the hostile Indians, from Medicine Lodge Creek toward the
Wichita mountains."[6]

Custer was still a young man—just twenty-eight—and he was not
quite ready to give up on the army. He was grateful for the opportunity
Sheridan had given him and the trust the commander and most of his
fellow officers had placed in him. He got on the next train available
from Monroe, not waiting for official confirmation of the end of his
suspension.[7]

When he joined the Seventh Cavalry in early October at its encampment about thirty miles from Fort Dodge, Custer found a regiment

that was somewhat disorganized and besieged by almost daily raids. It wasn't safe for anyone to walk outside the camp at any hour. Custer experienced the war personally when he sat down to his dinner, hungry after a long ride. Indians fired shots into the camp. "This was getting into active service quite rapidly," Custer wrote drily in his memoir. A few warriors rode by, hoping to tempt the cavalry to pursue them into an ambush. When no one left the camp, the rest of the warriors emerged from their hiding place, outside of rifle range, and taunted the soldiers before riding off.[8]

Custer immediately set to work on improving the morale and readiness of the regiment so it would be ready for the upcoming winter campaign. He ordered four detachments of about one hundred men each to leave on a scout that night in four different directions. Custer reasoned that one group might find the warriors if four quadrants were covered, and the troopers could sneak up on them under cover of darkness. They found no Indians, but the mission accomplished Custer's purpose of letting both his own soldiers and the enemy know that the army was no longer on the defensive.[9]

Custer's energetic presence created an instant change among the troops. "We had unconsciously fallen into a state of inertia, and appeared to be leading an aimless sort of existence, but with his coming, action, purpose, energy and general strengthening of the loose joints was the order of the day," said one officer.[10]

Custer also organized his scouts—the plainsmen like Wild Bill Hickok who were essential to Indian fighting. Custer had always been impressed and sought to learn from other men who had charisma and experience—men like McClellan and Kearny. He particularly admired scouts, whom he saw as courageous, adventurous men with special common sense and cunning. They were often mysterious, working under aliases with pasts that could not be nailed down.[11]

Upon arriving at the camp, Custer was taken with a rugged scout named Joe E. Milner, whom Custer knew only by his poetic nickname of California Joe. Custer thought California Joe stood out even among the typically unusual appearance of the scouts who served the army. His long, curling hair and beard disguised his age, which Custer thought was forty, but could well have been older. He was inseparable from his long Springfield musket and also carried a knife and pistol in his belt. Instead of a horse, he rode a mule, which could endure long marches without forage.

After a brief interview, Custer appointed him head of scouts because he wanted the various scouts attached to the different units to be under one leader. But California Joe wanted to interview Custer first.

"Are you an ambulance man ur a hoss man?" he asked Custer, wanting to know whether he would ride horseback and give active chase to the Indians or ride in a wagon like some older generals.

After some good-natured teasing, Custer satisfied California Joe that he would ride horseback because that was the only way to catch Indians.

"You've hit the nail squar on the hed," California Joe said. Custer had a found a scout he could trust, although as it turned out, not one suitable for leadership. On the first night mission, Joe got drunk celebrating his promotion and wandered off on his mule. He returned howling and screaming, thinking he was attacking an Indian camp. After the soldiers subdued him—with a dramatic struggle—he lost his promotion but not his job. Custer valued the man's knowledge too much to dismiss him.[12]

After organizing the scouts, Custer worked on training the troops. He had noticed that the Indians would ride within easy range of the camp, but the soldiers could not hit such fast-moving targets. Occasionally a trooper would hit a pony, but the dismounted Indian would be easily rescued by a friend who would come by and scoop him up like a circus rider. "It was interesting to witness their marvelous horsemanship," he wrote, "At the same time one could not but admire the courage they displayed."[13]

Although he admired their courage as much as he did those of the rebels, Custer was determined to do his duty and get his own troops ready to fight on even terms. He ordered two shooting drills every day with the targets set up at varying distances. As he had when he was a schoolteacher, he set up a competition with incentives to encourage the men to take their work seriously. The forty best marksmen out of the eight hundred troopers would be put into an elite sharpshooter detachment that would be relieved of guard duty and other onerous work, and they would get the plum assignments in battle. The soldiers took to the spirit of the competition, and in the end, Custer believed he had found a unit that would be able to bring down a warrior who dared to ride close to the command. "They were a superb body of men, and felt the greatest pride in their distinction," he wrote.[14]

Custer thought he had several young officers who could have served well as the leader of the elite unit. He chose William Winer Cooke, a Canadian who had been attending school in Buffalo, New York, when the Civil War began. Cooke enlisted in the Union army when he graduated at the age of sixteen and rose to the rank of brevet lieutenant colonel while serving with Custer and Sheridan in the Appomattox campaign. Cooke was one of Custer's trusted friends. He had chased after the deserters for Custer and had testified favorably during the court-martial. In addition, Cooke fit the Custer image of a cavalry-man. He was athletic—the fastest man in the regiment—an excellent shot, and he looked the part of the dragoon, sporting lavish Dundreary whiskers on his cheeks. Cooke, Custer wrote, not only was an out-standing officer who knew how to command men, but he could also "feel that *esprit de corps* which is so necessary to both officers and sol-diers when success is to be achieved."[15]

Custer hoped that another reorganization would increase the esprit de corps of the entire regiment: he "colored" the horses—sorting the horses by color and then distributing them to the individual squad-rons. It was a practice that was also used in Europe and had proven its utility for allowing commanders to instantly identify their units in the confusion of the battlefield.[16] Custer attended to the coloring with the same attention to detail he spent in organizing the target-shooting competition. He had his men spend an entire afternoon sorting the horses into groups of grays, bays, blacks, sorrels, chestnuts, browns, and "brindles"—mixed colors. Once the horses were assigned to squadrons, the noncommissioned officers got first choice, then the best soldiers got their pick, and the rest were distributed randomly. The distribution wasn't popular among the men because troopers usually became quite fond of their animals. After all, they entrusted their very lives to their horses when in combat. Capt. Albert Barnitz was incensed because all of the horses in his unit had been carefully trained. Two days after the project was completed, he wrote his wife how much he hated the way Custer dictated the arrangement of the horses. "Have felt very indignant and provoked all evening in consequence of General Custer's *foolish, unwarranted, unjustifiable* order.[17]

Custer knew the process seemed to be mere decoration, but to his artistic instincts, it was a useful exercise in making the regiment look good. And if the troopers looked good, they were more likely to have the confidence to do good work. He knew the feelings of upset would be temporary. The men would, as he wrote, become "fast friends" with their new horses. "It was surprising to witness what a great improvement in the handsome appearance of the command was effected by this measure," he wrote.[18]

Finally, Custer knew he would need Indian allies to act as scouts to find the warring tribes. An officer was sent to the Osage reservation and enlisted Little Beaver and Hard Rope—two tribal leaders—and eleven warriors. The reservation Indians were often the victims of attacks from the more powerful independent tribes, and the army had little trouble getting them to participate in a campaign against their enemies.[19]

In his free time Custer kept up with his own interests. He hunted, catching a pelican that he sent to the Audubon Society in Detroit.[20] He wrote a stream of passionate letters to Libbie. His work during the day kept him busy, but at night he missed her to the point of distraction. "There is nothing in this world that can at all compensate me for the loss of you," he wrote, adding he would rather have her than any woman in the world. "You are everything to me, both food and raiment, yes and sleep, for even yet I am restless at night and often wake to find myself feeling for you."[21]

He pondered their future together. The Custers, like most couples in the nineteenth century, expected to have children. Custer was raised in a large, close family and would have liked to play the patriarch over his own household just as his beloved father, Emanuel, had done. When they had been married scarcely half a year, Libbie had prayed for a child during a church service and wrote Custer excitedly: "If God gives me children I shall say to them: 'Emulate your Father! I can give you no higher earthly example.'"[22]

About five years later it was becoming obvious they probably would not have children.[23] Custer proposed in a carefully worded letter that they adopt his ten-year-old namesake nephew, Autie Reed. Custer was fond of the boy, as he was of all of his nieces and nephews. He would frequently close his letters to his sister Ann by telling her to give his love to "Emma and Aut," her children.[24] He explained to Libbie that young Autie was beyond the most troublesome age of children because he was ten, and that he felt it was his family obligation to help raise him. Nevertheless, he emphasized he was not pressuring Libbie to do it. He didn't want anything to interfere with their marriage.

"If you answer it with favor of it, well and good; if you from any cause or reason are not inclined to the idea, be frank enough to tell me, and you disapproving of the proposition shall not in the slightest way ruffle any feelings or cause me to think one jot less of you," he wrote. "Your wishes shall be law and I hope you will tell me your views with your usual candor."[25]

Libbie must have candidly told him no. The reasons are lost to history, as no letter from her about the topic has surfaced. At the time, she was staying in Grosse Ile, Michigan, with the family of Kirkland C. Barker, the former mayor of Detroit and a close friend of the Custers. The Barkers had young children, which might have annoyed Libbie during her visit. In one of his next letters to Libbie, Custer wrote that he was glad that she saw how much children would be a bother. The letter reads as if he were trying to convince himself as well as his wife of the joys of a childless marriage.

"Our pleasure would be continually marred and circumscribed," he wrote. "You will not find in all our travels a married couple possessing and enjoying so many means of pleasure and mutual happiness as you and your boy. Our married life to me has been one unbroken sea of pleasure."[26]

Politics, Custer's other passion, did not provide the usual pleasure at this time. Johnson, whom he admired, did not run for president after barely escaping conviction in his impeachment trial. The war hero Grant beat former New York Governor Horatio Seymour, who had not been a strong supporter of the Union. Custer wrote Libbie that hardly anyone on the post remembered that it was an election year, so little did they care about the political campaign.[27] The troops, and Custer, were more concerned about the upcoming campaign against the Indians. "I do not long for glory or fame," he wrote Libbie when describing his own feelings. "My reward is centered on ending this trying separation."[28]

Since the end of the Civil War and his postings in the West, Custer had grown increasingly impatient with any absence from his wife. During the war, he had service so active that it usually kept him too busy to dwell on missing her. The service in the great cause of his time was extraordinarily fulfilling. He knew he was doing his duty on the frontier, but he had learned that the hard riding and sacrifice did not earn the same rewards as they did during the Rebellion. The very nature of Indian warfare meant civilians would be killed. The army would have to attack villages in order to capture the Indians, and sometimes women and boys would fight, so it would be impossible in the heat of battle to distinguish noncombatants from warriors.

Then, too, anything the army did would be compared to the notorious Sand Creek Massacre of 1864, when Colorado militiamen had snuck up on a peaceful village of Cheyenne under chief Black Kettle. The village had been flying the American flag as a sign they were friends of the whites, but the militia indiscriminately killed women and children, then horrifically mutilated the corpses, later displaying their grisly trophies in Denver. The massacre was initially reported as a victory, and humanitarians raised a public outcry when more facts came to light. Two official investigations were conducted. The commander, John Chivington, had resigned his commission, so he escaped punishment from the army, but his reputation and political career were ruined.

Custer did not intend to kill civilians as Chivington had done, but he knew some women and children might well die in an attempt to capture a village. Before setting out on the campaign Custer told his officers to reconcile themselves to the fact that they would be criticized no matter what they did. If they didn't find the Indians, the Westerners they were charged with protecting would say they were incompetent or reluctant to fight. But if they found the Indians and defeated them, "a wail would rise up from the horrified humanitarians throughout the country, and we would be accused of attacking and killing friendly and defenseless Indians."[29]

Despite missing Libbie, and despite knowing he was risking his life for an indifferent public and an ungrateful government, Custer could not help but be somewhat excited about the campaign. Part of it was his nature. He was almost always excited about what he was doing as long as he was active. As the reporter had noted during the soldiers' convention in 1866, *He is the thing he does.* When he was on the campaign, he was completely in the role of the cavalryman.

Sheridan's plan for a winter campaign also excited Custer's creative nature. During the Civil War, the great armies usually holed up in camp in winter and engaged in mostly desultory raiding, preferring instead to lick their wounds and plan the next spring offensive. Sheridan proposed hunting the Indians deep in their own territory—areas where few white men had traveled—at a time when sudden blizzards could kill anyone caught in the open. The Indians, who knew the Plains, stayed in their camps.

Conventional wisdom said it couldn't be done. The great frontiersman Jim Bridger personally told Sheridan not to try it. "You can't hunt Indians on the plains in winter for blizzards don't respect man or beast," Bridger said while visiting Sheridan in St. Louis. The whole thing was crazy.[30]

But Sheridan knew he had someone crazy enough to carry out the plan. He told Custer he trusted him completely. "Custer, I rely on you in everything, and shall send you on this expedition without orders, leaving you to act entirely on your own judgment," he said at a breakfast meeting at Fort Hays.[31]

For someone like Custer, who thought artistically, the daring winter campaign was the perfect solution to the Indian war. It was a difficult challenge, to be sure, but the man who met the challenge would make history. Custer saw only opportunity. He knew the Indian ponies would be weak from lack of forage during the winter. The initiative would finally belong to the army. "To decide upon making a winter campaign against the Indians was certainly in accordance with that maxim in the art of war which directs one to do that which the enemy neither expects nor desires to be done," Custer wrote in his memoir. "At the same time it would dispel the old-fogy idea which was not without supporters in the army, and which was confidently relied on by the Indians themselves, that the winter season was an insurmount-able barrier to the prosecution of a successful campaign."[32]

Custer wrote Libbie excitedly: "Some of the officers think this may be a campaign on paper. But I know Genl. Sheridan better. We are going to the heart of the Indian country where white troops have never been before."[33]

In another letter he explained why he thought the plan would work if he could get one decisive battle. "The Indians have the belief that no white troops dare follow them into this country where no whites have been before. All the tribes committing depredations the past season are in the vicinity of the Wichita Mts. [Sheridan] expects, once they learn of his entry into their country, that they will combine against them. This is exactly what I desire. I only ask for one good opportunity to fight them, or better still to strike a village."[34]

At 4 A.M. on November 23, 1868, Custer and about eight hundred cavalrymen awoke to leave Camp Supply, a depot in northwestern Indian Territory, in search of a village to strike. A blizzard had hit dur-ing the night, covering everything in twelve inches of snow, and it was still blowing as the troopers ate their breakfast.

The regimental adjutant struggled through snow halfway up to his cavalry boots to report to Custer and asked, "How will this do for a winter campaign?"[35]

"Just what we want," Custer said.

As the troopers readied to march, Custer rode across the camp to Sheridan's tent to say goodbye. Sheridan's greeting to Custer was also a worried query about the storm's impact on the campaign. Custer again said, "Nothing could be more to our purpose."

He assured Sheridan that everything would be all right; the cavalry could move, but the Indians could not. As Custer left, Sheridan called out, "Goodbye, old fellow; take care of yourself!"

Custer rode back to the head of the column and gave the orders to march. The regimental band led the way, playing "The Girl I Left Behind Me," as the troopers disappeared into the swirling snowstorm.[36]

As they marched, the snow was falling so thickly the Indian scouts couldn't recognize the landmarks they normally used to find their way. Custer instead used his compass to guide the column toward Wolf

Creek, the planned first stop, about fifteen miles from Camp Supply. Struggling through the deep snow made the march seem like thirty miles. The troops started huge fires and slept in relative comfort; Custer had his dogs wrapped up with him in buffalo robes. The storm continued through the night, but Custer consoled himself with the idea that it would turn out to be an even worse enemy for the Indians.[37]

The next morning the snow stopped, but it had left eighteen inches on the ground. It was so dark when they got up that Capt. Barnitz had trouble telling the horses apart. One horse already had to be abandoned, and some of the mules were getting played out. The soldiers struggled through the snow for another day. When they camped, the troopers had the hard work of digging out snow for a place to spread grain for the horses, and then clear spots for their tents.[38]

The next day's march brought them past herds of game huddled together for warmth. Some of the men tried to hunt buffalo for fresh meat, but the deep snow kept both the buffalo and their hunters from getting much speed. The scene struck Custer as comical: "Occasionally an unseen hole or ditch or ravine covered up by snow would be encountered, when the buffalo or his pursuer or all three—horse, rider, and buffalo—would disappear in one grand tumble in the depths of the snowdrifts, and when seen to emerge therefrom it was difficult to determine which of the three was more badly frightened."[39]

Custer decided to get in on the fun and chased one yearling bull that his dogs had cut from the herd. They brought the buffalo to bay and got into a life-or-death struggle, too close for Custer to shoot without fear of hitting one of his dogs. He jumped off his horse and cut the bull's hamstrings with his knife. The bull tumbled over, and Custer shot him.[40]

The next day the column was approaching the area of the Canadian River, where the scouts thought roving bands of war parties would cross. Custer ordered Maj. Joel Elliott and three troops of cavalry, able to move faster than the main column because they would not have wagons, up the bank of the river to see if they could find a trail. It was hard going for Elliott's command.

"The morning was excessively cold, and a dense fog prevailed," Barnitz wrote in his journal. "It was necessary to dismount very often, and walk in order to prevent our feet from freezing." The soldiers' feet would break through the crust and sink into the deep snow. But they were rewarded by finding a trail. They sent word to Custer.[41]

Back at the main column, a jumble of worried images sped through Custer's mind when he saw a lone rider heading toward his command. But one decisive thought stood out: "If a trail has been discovered, then woe unto the luckless Indians whose footprints are discoverable in the snow; for so long as that remains and the endurance of men and horses hold out, just so long will we follow that trail, until the pursuer and pursued are brought face to face, or one or the other succumbs to the fatigues and exhaustion of the race."[42]

It was scout Jack Corbin, who breathlessly reported that Elliott had found the fresh trail of a large war party and was in hot pursuit. Custer asked him if he could get back to Elliott with orders if he were given a fresh horse. Corbin thought he could. Custer ordered him to find Elliott as soon as possible and tell him to chase the Indians as hard as he could. Custer would follow with reinforcements. Elliott was to let him know if the trail changed directions.

Custer gathered his officers and told them they would chase the Indians with only the supplies they could carry. The wagons would follow with an eighty-man guard. He looked at his watch and gave them twenty minutes to get their troops ready. Once they hit the trail, they would not stop till they found the enemy.[43]

They had already suffered for several days with the cold and snow. Now everyone knew they would be marching without their tents and baggage. They would not light fires so they could keep the element of surprise. "Yet these thoughts scarcely found a place in the minds of any members of the command," Custer wrote later. "All felt that a great opportunity was before us, and to improve it only required determination and firmness on our part."[44]

The reaction of Capt. Louis Hamilton confirmed Custer's opinion of the general excitement. Hamilton, the grandson of Founding Father Alexander Hamilton, happened to be assigned to guard the pack train—a duty that was rotated among the officers. When Hamilton realized he would be left behind, he immediately galloped to Custer and asked to be relieved of the guard duty so he could participate in the fight.

Hamilton was widely admired in the regiment, and other officers pressured Custer to make the switch. "We ought to have Hamilton with us," one implored. Custer agreed that Hamilton's experience was needed. He, too, wanted him charging into battle. But for Custer, something more was at stake—Honor. It was Hamilton's turn to guard the train. Changing the assignments would unfairly force another officer to give up his opportunity to be onstage.

Custer instead offered Hamilton a compromise. If he could find an officer who wanted to trade places, Custer would issue the order. Hamilton quickly dashed off and returned saying 2nd Lt. E. G. Mathey would trade places because he was suffering snow blindness. "It was exceedingly proper for him under the circumstances to agree to the proposed change," Custer wrote.[45]

With the pack train issue settled, the regiment headed out in pursuit of the Indians, planning to hit the trail Elliott had discovered. The horses became fatigued by the struggle through the thick snow. But Custer would not stop for food or rest. He knew they were getting closer to the enemy. He became worried, however, as there was no sign of Elliott or the Indians. Finally, near evening, one of the Osage scouts found the trail. It was a war party, he said. Custer increased the pace. The snow had started to thaw during the day, and he feared the Indians would be able to escape if it melted.[46]

At 9 o'clock that night they found Elliott's command by a stream. Custer and his men had not eaten since 4 A.M. that morning. He let the men unsaddle their horses for an hour's rest and eat a quick meal of coffee and hardtack. Little Beaver, the spokesman for the Osage scouts, told Custer they could easily overtake the village if they kept going, but to Custer's surprise he recommended they wait until daylight to continue the chase. Custer pressed him to explain his reasoning, but he couldn't give a good answer. Custer ascribed it to the Indians' reluctance to attack at night. He decided to move on.

The command rode for miles silently, the men ordered not to talk or even light a match to smoke. Finally, the two Osage scouts in the lead halted.

"What is the matter?" Custer asked.

"Me don't know, but me smell smoke," one of the scouts said.[47]

Several of the officers rode up. They all sniffed the air. None could smell smoke. The Osage must be scared, they thought.

Custer trusted his scouts. He ordered the two Indians to advance, but even more cautiously. Within a half mile they could see the glow of a fire. Everyone was breathless with excitement. They were convinced the Indians had made the fire. But where were they? How many?

The scouts dismounted and crept forward, guns at the ready. Custer and the others waited anxiously. They knew they would be good targets silhouetted in the moonlight if the Indians were aroused.

The scouts found the fire deserted. Here Custer appreciated the savvy of his Osage guides. When he rode up, he assumed the fire was made by the war party they were chasing. But the Osages explained to him that Indian boys attending the pony herd of a village had made the fire to keep warm. The war party had led him to a village, probably at most three miles away.

They continued their cautious pursuit. This time Custer rode with the Osages. When they got to the crest of a hill one of the scouts dismounted and crawled forward. After studying something, he crawled back to Custer.

"What is it?" Custer said.

"Heaps Injuns down there," the Osage replied. Custer crept back with him to the crest but couldn't see anything.

What made the Osage think there were Indians? Custer wanted to know. The scout said he had heard a dog bark.

Custer trusted the scouts, but he wanted to be sure before he attacked. He strained his ears. Finally, he heard a dog bark, and the tinkle of a bell, which could only be the kind that Indians put on their ponies. Then, as he started for his horse, he heard something that gave him pause. A baby cried.[48]

"Savages though they were, and justly outlawed by the number and atrocity of their recent murders and depredations on the helpless settlers of the frontier, I could not but regret that in a war such as we were forced to engage in, the mode and circumstances of battle would possibly prevent discrimination," he wrote later.[49]

Custer gathered his officers together to study the layout from the top of a ridge overlooking the village. Barnitz thought that wrapped up in their furs, the officers would look like a pack of wolves to the Indians.

But he worried that the loud crunching of the command through the snow would alert the village. Custer, however, was focused on the attack. He divided the regiment into four units, each to attack from a different direction. He would hit the village from all sides at dawn. In order to maintain surprise, he prohibited the men from lighting fires or even stamping their feet to keep warm.[50]

The men, although exhausted from the march, were too cold and keyed up to get much sleep. Custer wrapped his cape around his head and slept for about an hour. He then walked around the unit he would personally lead in the assault, checking on the men. They were huddled in groups of three or four, trying to stay warm. One group of officers was scrunched together, using one of their group as a pillow for the others. Few were talking. Custer knew from experience they were thinking about what might happen to them in the battle.

"Occasionally I would find a small group engaged in conversation, the muttered tones and voices strangely reminding me of those heard in the death-chamber," Custer wrote.[51]

He noticed the Osages were sitting up wrapped in their blankets. It looked like they had not tried to sleep, and Custer left them alone. He stopped to chat with the white scouts. The voluble California Joe, unlike everyone else, was eager to talk. He predicted a fierce fight, but he was worried which way it would go. He compared it to poker. The cavalry held the cards. So long as they kept the element of surprise, they would win. But if the Indians were ready, they would beat the Seventh badly.

"That's the very pint that's been botherin' me ever since we planted ourselves down here, and the only conclusion I kin come at is that it's purty apt to be one thing or t'other," he told Custer.[52]

After Custer left the scouts, the rest of the night passed quietly. The moon disappeared, leaving them in darkness about two hours before dawn. Custer knew he was only a few hundred yards from his attack point. In the valley below was the village. Were the Indians asleep? Or were they preparing an ambush? He had no idea how fierce the fight would be. But he knew full well what a battlefield was like, and he would be in the middle of one again.[53]

He gathered the officers in his unit together as dawn approached. As they prepared for the attack, they were astonished to see a bright light that looked to them like a signal rocket rising slowly on the horizon. Transfixed by the flaming globe of light, their only guess was that it was some sort of signal from the Indians. Perhaps one of the other units had stumbled into another village while getting into position. Certainly they had been discovered.

"How long it hangs fire!" one officer said. "Why don't it explode?"

Unable in the moment to appreciate its beauty, they were relieved when its ascension revealed it to be the brightest morning star they had ever seen.[54]

Custer ordered the men to shed their overcoats and haversacks so they could move freely in the fight. No one was to fire until he gave the signal. The band rode at the front so they could play "Garry Owen," the rollicking Irish drinking ballad that was a favorite of Charles O'Malley, the fictional dragoon Custer had read about when he was a boy dreaming of such moments.[54] In his own life, he continued to turn fiction into reality.

The distance to the village was longer than it looked from the hill. The horses' hooves loudly cracked through the snow. But they rode by the large Indian pony herd, which covered the noise. The village was so quiet Custer wondered if the Indians had slipped away as they had done at the opening of Hancock's War. And he worried about the other elements of the attack. Were they in position?

A single rifle shot sounded from the far end of the village. Indian or soldier, who could say? But the battle was on. Custer signaled the band to play and the buglers to sound the charge.[56]

The troopers charged excitedly into the village from four directions, just as Custer planned. The Indians were taken by surprise, but they rushed out of their tepees with their weapons and sought cover.

Custer, riding in the lead, held his pistol at the ready as he had done so many times in the Civil War. A warrior took aim at Custer with his rifle, but Custer killed him with a shot to the head.[57]

Although they didn't know it at the time, the cavalry was attacking the village of Black Kettle, the chief whose people had flown an American flag at Sand Creek, only to be massacred by the Colorado volunteers. A war party made up of some young men from Black Kettle's camp, along with warriors from other villages, had been raiding and had led the Osage scouts right to the village. Black Kettle got on a horse with his wife Ar-no-ho-wok and tried to escape. But the horse was frightened and hard to manage. Soldiers killed them as they tried to cross the river.[58]

Within moments, the cavalry took control of the village, which consisted of about fifty lodges totaling about two hundred and fifty people.[59] But the Indians hid behind trees on the riverbank and started pouring a hot fire into the troopers. The crack of gunfire, the shouts of the troopers and the warriors, and the screams and cries of the women and children created a maelstrom of noise and confusion. From where Custer was, in the center of the village, you could hear gunfire from every direction. Some of the fighting was hand-to-hand, and the Indian women and boys joined in.[60]

Capt. Frederick Benteen was charged by a boy of about fourteen. Benteen made signs for the boy to surrender, but he responded by shooting at Benteen three times, the last hitting his horse in the neck. Benteen tried one more time to get the boy to surrender, but when he aimed again at the captain, Benteen had no choice but to shoot him. He would regret it ever after.[61]

Francis M. Gibson, second lieutenant, remembered that the situation at one point was reversed, with the cavalry holding the village and the Indians firing from the outside. "As we were at very close quarters, and had exchanged places with them, the soldiers were in constant danger from hostile bullets fired from all directions," Gibson remembered. "Every man was kept busy as a bee, and every one knew he was fighting for his life. . . . The desperation displayed by both sides in this bloody conflict beggars description, and the marked bravery of both friend and foe was beyond need of praise."[62]

One group of about twenty warriors was so well protected that the cavalry could not dislodge them with a charge. Custer's creative idea of a sharpshooter company paid dividends when he ordered William Cooke's men to attack them. They sniped the Indians whenever they showed themselves, and eventually cleared them out.

Directing the battle from a small hill in the middle of the village, Custer could not see everything happening around him. He began to get casualty reports and other disturbing news. Hamilton, who in the initial charge had ridden near Custer, was shot in the chest, dying instantly. Barnitz had been shot through the body, the bullet hitting just below the heart, and was not expected to live. Elliott, Custer's second in command, had disappeared.[63]

The village was in Custer's hands, along with about sixty women and children prisoners. But at about 10 A.M. he first noticed some warriors on horses gathering on the hills around the village. He was not immediately concerned, and he ordered California Joe to round up the Indian pony herd. When the scout returned with the captured ponies, Custer noticed the number of warriors had increased to a worrisome horde. He had his interpreter interrogate the captured Indian women, and he learned that the village they captured was just one of a series of large camps stretching out over ten miles. They included camps of Arapaho, Kiowa and Kiowa-Apaches, as well as Cheyenne. They would have more than enough warriors to overwhelm his command.[64]

"What was to be done?" Custer asked himself. He knew he would be attacked by superior numbers as soon as the Indians were ready. His command had suffered serious causalities, key officers were incapacitated, and he was encumbered by prisoners and the Indian pony herd, which had close to a thousand horses. His soldiers were tired after a day of fighting, and they were without their overcoats and haversacks. Soon they would be cold and hungry. The supply wagons were lightly guarded and separated from the main command. If the Indians found them, he would be deep in enemy territory with no resources.[65]

As he pondered what to do, Custer could look in almost every direction and see warriors gathering in ever-greater numbers, waiting for his next move. "To guide my command safely out of the difficulties which seemed just then to beset them, I again had recourse to the maxim in war which teaches a commander to do that which his enemy neither expects nor desires him to do," he wrote.[66] Instead of following the cavalrymen's instinct to charge, and fight his way out with his spoils, the artist Custer came up with a creative strategy.

He had to find a way out to preserve his command, but first he had to complete his mission, which was to damage the enemy's ability to wage war. Following what he had learned in the Shenandoah Valley from Sheridan during the Civil War, he had already ordered his men to burn civilian material—this time the Indian lodges and their contents instead of the barns of rebel sympathizers. The action enraged the Cheyenne warriors, who renewed their attacks with added ferocity.

But what to do with the pony herd? He couldn't abandon the horses to the Indians. They were the main wealth of the tribe, and the resource that not only allowed them to roam and hunt free of the reservation but also to make war on the settlers. On the other hand, he couldn't easily take the ponies with him and fight his way out of the encirclement. If he tried, the Indians would think the raid was for plunder because that was one of the main reasons they raided—to steal horses. He instead wanted to impress on them the fact that attacking the settlers, stagecoaches, and railroads would lead to intense retaliation.

Custer made a decision that repulsed his men and shocked his enemy. He ordered the Indian prisoners to pick horses for themselves out of the herd, so they could ride back to the army camp. He also let the officers pick out any they wanted to keep as prizes of war. Then he had his men shoot the rest. For an animal lover like Custer, it was a hard choice. But it was the same logic used to convince the South to give up. He concluded that like most measures taken to win a war, it was cruel but necessary.[67]

Although he had done the distasteful necessity, Custer was still faced with extricating his troops. Again, he did what was unexpected. He marched toward the other Indian camps that the women had indicated lay in the distance.

"For a few moments after our march began, the Indians on the hills remained silent spectators, evidently at a loss at first to comprehend our intentions in thus setting out at that hour of the evening, and directing our course as if another night march was contemplated; and more than all, in the direction of their villages, where all that they possessed was supposed to be."[68]

Custer's surprise strategy did exactly what he had hoped. It broke the siege as most of the warriors fled to protect their own villages. Custer kept marching until well after dark, several miles beyond Black Kettle's village. As soon as he was sure the darkness could cover his maneuvers, he turned the regiment and marched as fast as he could back to the supply train. They reached it at 10 the next morning, overjoyed to find it safe and in one piece.

After resting the command, he continued the march to Camp Supply. With the instincts of a reporter wanting to get the news out as fast as possible, Custer dispensed with the normal process of getting official written reports from his subordinates and instead interviewed them and wrote the entire report himself in an hour or two. He wanted California Joe to leave as soon as it was dark to get the news of the battle to Sheridan. The scout took Jack Corbin with him on their dangerous trip through enemy country, but both seemed less worried than Custer, who was still trying to shepherd his exhausted command back to its base.

After marching for two more days, Custer was rewarded with an answer from Sheridan sent back with the scouts. Sheridan issued a special field order announcing the victory and thanking the Seventh, offering special congratulations to its "distinguished commander, Brevet Major-General George A. Custer, for the efficient and gallant services rendered, which have characterized the opening of the campaign against hostile Indians south of the Arkansas." The order regretted the loss of Hamilton, Elliott, and the other casualties, but it was complete vindication for Custer's conduct of the raid.[69]

Custer was so excited that he dashed off another message, letting Sheridan know his command would march in review when they rode the final leg into Camp Supply. For Custer, such an outstanding achievement called for a show. Both officers and enlisted men prepared their uniforms and horses to make the best impression. Custer was pleased that considering the hard campaign, they would still look sharp.

When the command set out, he arranged their order of march for the most dramatic visual impact. He wanted them to look striking when they reached the hills that descended into Sheridan's camp, which he knew would provide a beautiful backdrop for the pageant. When they reached the camp, the band struck up "Garry Owen," which was not only a war cry but a song to herald a triumph, just as it had been used by the Irish dragoons in *Charles O'Malley*.[70]

It certainly impressed the *New York Herald*'s De B. Randolph Keim, the only reporter to accompany Sheridan's campaign. Keim, twenty-seven, was a veteran correspondent of the Civil War, but he chose to cover Custer's battle from the safety of Camp Supply, sticking by the side of the man he considered the most important news source, Sheridan. The bitter cold weather had moderated, helped along by a bright sunny day. Keim, Sheridan, and the others marveled as they watched Custer's command enter the valley, appearing at first as small dark objects on the crest of a hill a mile from camp. Shouts and the celebratory fire of guns from Custer's column startled the camp's horse herd into stampeding toward the fort.[71]

Custer then paused the column at the crest of the hill. Sheridan and his staff readied for the review of troops. Everyone else not on duty gathered in excitement to watch the parade. The first thing they saw was the whooping Osage scouts. "Their faces were painted in the most fantastic and hideous designs," Keim wrote. "About their persons were dangling the trophies which they had captured in battle. Spears, upon which were fastened the scalps of their fallen foe, were slung upon their shoulders; from their own plaited scalp locks were suspended long trails of silver ornaments and feathers: over their shoulders hung shields and bows and quivers full of arrows, while in one hand they held their trusty rifle and with the other grasped the reins. Even the animals which the Osages bestrode were decorated with scalps and strips of red and blue blanket."[72]

Little Beaver rode at the head. He was sixty, but still a muscular six-foot-tall fighting warrior. He maintained a serious look befitting the leader of the column. But hearing the constant wild war whoops and rifle shots of his warriors, he couldn't contain his own excitement.[73]

"They call us Americans," he yelled. "We are Osages!" The warriors responded with another shout of celebration.

Next came the frontier scouts, led by California Joe, looking to Keim as wild as the Osages. His red matt of whiskers and knotty hair—covered with dust, and sticks, grass, and leaves poking out of the tangled mess—hid most of his face. "Joe was a suitable figurehead for this motley band of curiously clad, brave, adventurous and rugged men," Keim wrote.[74]

Custer followed the scouts, riding alone on a beautiful black stallion. He was dressed in a blue army coat trimmed with the yellow of the cavalry service but also featuring a fur collar and cuffs. Instead of an army hat, he wore a cap of otter fur.[75] Always particular in his uniform ever since he designed his own rig when he was first promoted to general, Custer had chosen something that bespoke his new self-created role, which was also symbolized by his place in the column, bridging the scouts and the Indian prisoners that followed him. Custer was the link between the civilized East and the Wild West. He was an army officer, the representative of the government and its civilization, but he had adapted to the ways of the frontiersman and the Indian. He had conquered the savage foe, as illustrated by the captured women and children, wrapped in their blankets and animal hides, looking straight ahead, riding the few survivors of the pony herd the Seventh Cavalry had not destroyed.

The troopers marched behind the prisoners, led in formation by the sharpshooters, Custer's innovation that had helped finish the battle. As Custer rode to within fifty yards of Sheridan, he left the column to ride up to his commander, who greeted him warmly.

Custer then returned to the column, and as his officers marched by Sheridan, they smartly saluted the senior officer with their sabers, following military protocol. Sheridan returned the salute by raising his cap. The end of Custer's pageant had concluded with a return to civilization. He had staged the perfect show for Sheridan and the press and the sole war correspondent on hand. Sheridan told Custer afterward that the combination of the military march of the troops and the wild display of the scouts made it one of the most beautiful and interesting scenes he had ever witnessed.[76]

CHAPTER TEN

A Hero and a Villain

Indian Fighting Brings No Glory

While Custer and his comrades on the frontier thought they had won a great victory, his prediction about the reaction back East came true. The show he had staged for Sheridan and Keim did not play well all over the country.

The Washita was also not as big a story as Custer was used to when he was earning headlines during the Civil War. Keim's *New York Herald* was the only newspaper that covered the Washita in any detail. For most other newspapers, the coverage consisted largely of edited copies of official U.S. Army reports or brief summaries of the *Herald*'s stories. Even the *New York Times* carried only a half dozen or so stories about the Washita in the three months after the battle.[1]

Most of the nation's press was much more concerned with the war over Reconstruction than the war with the Plains tribes, which was being fought in a remote area far away from the concerns of their readers. In Chicago, which was home to the military division's headquarters, a huge reunion of Civil War veterans took place in mid-December. The Chicago papers devoted dramatically more space to the veterans of the last war than the soldiers fighting the current one. The *Chicago Tribune*, for example, published more than two and a half pages about the reunion on December 16 and a page and a half the next day, including biographies of lesser-known generals like Alfred Terry, who was most famous for leading Union troops to victory at Fort Fisher in North Carolina, a relative backwater compared to the Army of the Potomac's campaigns. The *Tribune*'s rival, the *Chicago Times*, devoted the first four and a half pages on December 16 to the reunion, including such details as menus for the various meals, and coverage was continued on page 10 with even more details. It was an astounding amount of coverage in an age when newspapers were often less than ten pages long. The only news of the Indian war in the *Times* was a half column of wire updates from Kansas and the territories.[2]

Editorials about the grand reunion showed why it was such a big story—it could be used to argue about Reconstruction. The *Times*, a Democratic newspaper that favored quick readmission of the former Confederate states, editorialized that the next reunion should include Confederate veterans. The paper envisioned the most famous generals from both sides seated together on the stage. "It would be the best possible exemplification of Grant's motto: 'Let us have peace.'"[3]

It was the same unresolved debate from the 1866 midterms, when Custer had campaigned with Johnson in favor of an easy Reconstruction policy. Custer had also helped organize a soldiers' convention that included veterans from both sides. At that time, Custer had been so severely criticized for being sympathetic to former rebels that Libbie had urged him not to run for office, something he was sorely tempted to do.

Now, after the Washita, Custer was a political target, but this time the target of Democrats who accused him of treating Indians the same brutal way he had treated Southern civilians during the war. It was a new and unpleasant experience for him to be criticized for winning a battle. During the Civil War, most of the Northern press supported the war effort, at least to varying degrees. Generals were evaluated harshly, but the judgment was in most cases based on their performance. Custer, who was usually attacking and winning, got favorable press. Now he was viewed as a hero or a villain depending upon the newspaper's politics.

The villain story was generated largely by the opinion of E. W. Wynkoop, the federal Indian agent for the Cheyenne, who resigned in protest over the government's treatment of the tribe. Wynkoop gave a highly publicized lecture at the famous Cooper Union in New York

City, blaming the army, the government, and white civilians for violating treaties with the Indians and provoking them. A friend of the deceased Black Kettle, Wynkoop said the village at the Washita should not have been attacked to punish a few guilty Indians.[4]

In a twist for the Democrat Custer, the Republican newspapers tended to defend him. The *Missouri Democrat*, which despite its name was a Republican newspaper, plainly stated that Black Kettle deserved his fate. "Enough of this stuff about friendly Indians. Black Kettle and his band were the very men by whom recent devilish outrages were perpetrated on the border. They were pursued from that point to the very encampment in which they were slaughtered."[5] In another editorial, the *Democrat* argued that the Washita showed why Indian policy should be turned over to the War Department from the Indian Bureau. "All that is needed to give our Indian policy some sort of consistency, honesty and sense, is to put it under the control of a man like Sherman, with men like Sheridan and Custer to obey orders. A single year of such management—sharp shot for those who want to fight and good honest treatment for those who submit—will do more to settle the Indian troubles than fifty millions expended through agents."[6]

The reference to the three famous generals must have reminded readers of how they won the Civil War, and it was a theme picked up by many other Republican newspapers. The *Fremont* (Ohio) *Journal* wrote, "General Custer has not lost the dash and gallantry that characterized his leadership during the war of the rebellion. With his regiment he has struck the red-skins the first serious blow they have received during the present hostilities, and a few more of the same sort will put an end to our costly Indian war."[7] The *Green Mountain Freeman* of Montpelier, Vermont, wrote similarly that "Gen. Custer, with 600 men of the Seventh Cavalry, sallied out in one of the terrible snow storms of the plains, penetrated nearly to the Texas border, and accomplished results which do not compare unfavorably with his brilliant war record."[8]

Other Republican papers supported the army but emphasized what they saw as the barbarity of the Indians. The *Chicago Tribune*, for example, reprinted a piece from a Kansas City paper that said "Black Kettle knew that he was going to be killed as soon as he heard the first gun fired from the white man's rifle. He had many scalps dangling from his belt, of white women and men."[9]

The *New York Times* admitted the battle looked like "a murderous affair" because no warriors were captured, which indicated no quarter was given. However, the paper reasoned that the army punished the right bands, even if some innocents were killed, and a blow had to be struck. "It was a 'salty dose,' as Sheridan would say, that Custer administered to the Cheyennes, Arapahoes and Kiowas."[10]

It was just the right medicine, according to the *Santa Fe Weekly Gazette*. "All right. Mr. Indian wanted war. He could not live without it. Gen. Custer has shown him that one hundred and fifty could not live with it. We have always been indulgent to him. He has been accommodated in all ways. We have given him provisions, clothing, arms and ammunition, gew gaws and peace. This was not enough. He must needs have war. Well we are now giving him *that*. Real, good, genuine killing war. Such as will have a wholesome effect on the red gentleman in the future."[11]

But Democratic newspapers saw the killing as murder, not war, and the *Chicago Times* called for the ultimate punishment. "[T]he Indians surrounded, massacred, and scalped by Custar's [*sic*] command, were friendly Indians. This thing is almost too atrocious for belief; and yet evidence is accumulating that seems to substantiate this assertion of Colonel Wynkoop. The report demands investigation. If it proves true, Sheridan, who ordered the attack, ought to be court-martialed and hung."[12] The *Times* wondered in another editorial why Republican newspapers that complained about the ill treatment of freedmen in the South were not sympathetic to the Indians. "Where now are those people who weep over the laceration of a negro's back . . . . Come, gentlemen, let us hear your familiar howl."[13] In another editorial the *Times* blamed Republicans for both the Civil War and the Indian wars. "It was the same party that has given us an everlasting frontier war with the Indians of the plains, and that has afforded history the pleasant duty of writing up those two delectable performances—the Sand Creek massacre of friendly Indians by Chivington, and the surprise and slaughter of some more friendly Indians in the Ouachita region. In fact, this same party in power has given the country war to its heart's content. When it has not been driving the people to killing each other, it has engaged them in the occupation of killing off peaceful Indians."[14]

Democratic papers throughout the country echoed the *Times'* opinion. In Woodsfield, Ohio—only about seventy-five miles from Custer's hometown—the *Spirit of Democracy* in a headline accused Custer of murder, and in the body of the story reported a claim that Clara Blinn and her son—white captives in the village—were killed by friendly fire from Seventh Cavalry troopers. "That ought to quiet the murderer of women and children, also his superiors, Sherman and Sheridan, who approved the dastardly act. Verily, the Indian War, about which we have heard so much, is nothing more than rapine and murder for the benefit of land sharks, and thieving Indian agents, and the everlasting disgrace and infamy of such shoulder-strap squaw fighters as Custer and his gang."[15]

Throughout the South, editors condemned the attacks in the harshest terms. In Tennessee, the *Sweetwater Forerunner* was particularly venomous: "Sherman and Sheridan are just the men for the murderous work projected on the Plains. The people of South Carolina and Georgia can testify to their proficiency as plunderers and incendiaries. They are now distinguishing themselves as deliberate murderers, and earning a reputation that should damn them to eternal infamy."[16] The *Athens* (Tenn.) *Post* wrote sarcastically of Sheridan's role in the battle "The Barn-burner of the Shenandoah Valley don't seem to be adding much to his military reputation."[17] The *Charleston* (S.C.) *Daily News* wrote that it didn't know if reports of a massacre were accurate, but that the Indians should be treated fairly, and it looked like the army had provoked them: "If Sheridan and Custer be allowed to carry out their policy, and the old system of bad faith and treachery be persevered in, we shall have a general Indian war on our hands."[18]

The military was aware of the press coverage. Sheridan was furious. Like Custer, he was used to positive stories after a victory. It was shocking to him to be the villain, and it embittered him toward the press and the general public. Sheridan blamed the "Indian Ring," for stirring up the humanitarian outcry. Sheridan biographer Paul Hutton described the ring as "a nebulous combination of crooked politicians, conniving federal bureaucrats, profiteering businessmen, and thieving Indian agents, who, while never specifically identified, operated in the collective military mind as a grand conspiracy to defraud the Indians and the government." Sheridan saw the army as the defender of helpless civilians, and he wrote graphically in his annual report to the War department that the humanitarian critics were "the aiders and abettors of savages who murdered, without mercy, men, women and children; in all cases ravishing the women sometimes as often as forty and fifty times in succession, and while insensible from brutality and exhaustion forced sticks up their person."[19]

Sherman agreed with Sheridan about the brutality of Indian warfare, but he had also been accused by journalists of being insane during the Civil War, and he was more philosophical about bad press coverage. He told Sheridan that he had faith in him and Custer and would do what he could to counteract the bad press. He tried to calm Sheridan down and wrote to him, "This you know is a free country, and the people have the lawful right to misrepresent as much as they please, and to print them, but the great mass of our people cannot be humbugged into the belief that Black Kettle's camp was friendly."[20]

Custer understood the press like Sherman did, and he accepted the criticism except for an anonymous letter published in the *Missouri Democrat* that accused him of coldheartedly abandoning Elliot and his men and reveling in the slaughter of the pony herd, which he used to show off his target shooting. The letter described Elliott and his men fighting desperately while the "murderous redskins" closed in. The writer charged that the rest of the Seventh forgot Elliott and made no search for him.[21]

It was obvious the letter came from someone in the Seventh Cavalry. This, to Custer, was much worse than a news story written by a journalist who didn't know what he was talking about. This was a traitorous breach of the brotherhood of the regiment. Custer created a theatrical event to demonstrate his anger. He ordered the officers to his tent, and slapping his whip on the top of his boot, said that if he ever found out the identity of the author he would horsewhip him.

Benteen put his hand on his holstered pistol, ready to pull it. He stepped forward and said, "All right, General, start your horsewhipping now. I wrote it."

Both soldiers were veterans of the Civil War and had killed men in close combat, including just recently at the Washita. Neither was afraid of physical confrontation. Both were on edge from the hard campaign. Benteen, thirty-five, was about five years older than Custer and had been toughened by the brutal guerilla fighting in Missouri during the Rebellion. Custer had survived leading numerous charges on the massed killing fields of the Eastern theater. Someone would die if they kept going.

Custer hesitated while everyone waited to see what he would do. "Colonel, I'll see you again on this matter," Custer said finally. He dismissed the officers.

Benteen would gloat about the episode later to friends, bragging he had gotten Custer to back down.

But Custer, a practiced killer who had a temper when angered, demonstrated extraordinary self-control. His theatrics had backfired. He knew his duty was to retreat, even though his instincts were always to attack, from the time when he was a boy and had punched a taunting classmate through a window to his career as a cavalry officer who always led the charge. He had to put the regiment above his own desire for personal justice.

Benteen, too, was shown for what he was—a griper and troublemaker whose hatreds were more important than the health of the unit. He had betrayed his brother officers and the regiment.[22]

Custer could not spend time worrying about Benteen and the press. Despite the victory at the Washita, Sheridan wanted all the warring Indians brought to the reservation. On December 7, Custer and his regiment plus about seventeen hundred men of the Nineteenth Kansas Cavalry, a militia unit organized to help subdue the tribes, marched out of Camp Supply. Custer brought along as guides three of his captives including Mah-wis-sa, Black Kettle's sister, and Mo-nah-see-tah, the beautiful teenage daughter of Little Rock, a relationship which Custer thought made her Indian royalty.[23] Little Rock himself was a Cheyenne leader who was killed along with all the other Indian men.

They went to the Washita battlefield, and after a search of the area, found Elliott and his men about two miles from where they were last seen. Their naked bodies, frozen stiff, had been horribly mutilated. They were lying in a circle about twenty yards in diameter. Custer could easily imagine what had happened. To him, it was terrible yet heroic.

"No words were needed to tell how desperate had been the struggle before they were finally overpowered," he wrote in his memoir. "At a short distance from where the bodies lay, could be seen the carcasses of some of the horses of the party, which had probably been killed early in the fight. Seeing the hopelessness of breaking through the line which surrounded them, and which undoubtedly numbered more than one hundred to one, Elliott dismounted his men, tied their horses together, and prepared to sell their lives as dearly as possible."[24]

They examined the remnants of the encampment, which Custer now discovered had stretched from the battlefield for twelve miles along the river. He estimated it had contained over six hundred lodges, which explained the source of the masses of warriors that had menaced his command after they had captured Black Kettle's village. In writing about it later, Custer described the size matter-of-factly; he didn't second-guess his decision to attack without making a reconnaissance along the river.[25]

In Custer's experience, the element of surprise was more important than sheer numbers. He had caught them napping, and he had made them pay with the ferocity of his attack. It also showed the superiority of U.S. Army troops when they could catch the Indians in an open battle. Discipline and modern fighting techniques could make up for lack of numbers. It certainly worked at the Washita. Custer had succeeded where Hancock, Sandy Forsyth, and others had failed. He had captured an Indian village.[26]

And in the view of Custer and the army, the village was an appropriate target. There was no doubt that some members of Black Kettle's village had been engaged in warfare on the settlements. Custer's men also found the bodies of Clara Blinn and her son, Willie, who was only two years old. Blinn, twenty-three, was found with a piece of cornbread in her hands. She had apparently been eating when she was killed execution style, shot in the forehead and then her skull crushed. Her son looked like he had been starving. His only injury was a bruise, suggesting he had been picked up by his feet and dashed against a tree. Custer wrote, "They . . . had not long been in captivity, as the woman still retained several articles of her wardrobe about her person—among others a pair of cloth gaiters but little worn, everything indicating that she had been but recently captured, and upon our attacking and routing Black Kettle's camp her captors, fearing she might be recaptured by us and her testimony used against them, had deliberately murdered her and her child in cold blood."[27] Mah–wis–sa, a Cheyenne, helpfully explained to Custer that the bodies were lying in what had been the village campsite of the Kiowa Chief Satanta.[28]

The command followed an Indian trail from the battlefield in search of the murderers. The trail led to Fort Cobb, where Custer assumed the Indians had headed in order to receive protection from the fort, where they would pretend to be peaceful. As they approached the fort, a courier from Col. William Hazen, the officer at Fort Cobb in charge of distributing supplies to all peaceful Indians in the area, said the Kiowas had not been on the warpath that season. Shortly afterward, Indians approached under a white flag from Satanta and Lone Wolf (one of the principal chiefs of the Kiowa), wanting to parley. They held a white courier as a hostage.

Sheridan had hated Hazen since 1863, when they had both claimed credit for commanding the troops that reached the crest of Missionary Ridge during the Battle of Chattanooga and captured eleven rebel cannon. Custer's grudge went back even further. Hazen was the officer who had nearly gotten him kicked out of the army for not stopping the fistfight at West Point. No wonder the romantic Custer believed his Indian captives, whom he thought of as Indian royalty because they were members of a chief's family. Mah–wis–sa had flattered Custer, calling him the "big chief" and offering one of the young Cheyenne girls to be his wife. Custer demurred but came to rely on her for information. In contrast Hazen fit the villainous role of a government bureaucrat duped by the enemy. The troops had found government rations in Black Kettle's camp. It seemed Hazen was not only protecting warring Indians but was also feeding them. The truth was that Mah–wis–sa, who wanted to blame the Kiowas for the Blinns' deaths, had deceived Custer. Santanta was guilty of raiding in Texas, but he was nowhere near the Washita during the battle.[29]

Both Sheridan and Custer wanted to attack, but Sheridan acceded to Hazen's request and ordered Custer to negotiate. Custer, De B. Randolph Keim, Sheridan's aide-de-camp, Lt. Schuyler Crosby, some other officers, and about fifty scouts rode toward a valley where two Indians waited. Hundreds of warriors on the surrounding hills rode back and forth, brandishing their weapons and yelling their war cries. The two Indians on the valley floor were Satanta and Lone Wolf. They said they wanted to see the Big Chief, so Custer rode ahead with Crosby and Keim.[30]

"It was not certain whether the Indians meant war or peace," Keim wrote, "and every man of our party had his pistol and rifle ready, and kept mounted, prepared for emergency, should any hostile demonstrations be made."[31]

Satanta was one of the most intimidating warriors on the Plains, yet he could laugh with the happiness of a child. The reporter Henry Morton Stanley wrote during the Medicine Lodge Peace negotiations to end Hancock's War that Satanta had recognized him from an earlier meeting and greeted him with a bear hug. It shocked the witnesses, who knew of him as the warrior credited with killing the most white men on the Plains.[32]

In greeting Custer, Satanta was ready to be friends, too, although he mistook Lt. Crosby for Custer, who had gone so deep into his frontiersman role that he was unrecognizable as a soldier in his worn buckskins and long hair and beard. The Kiowa chief offered his hand to Crosby with a hearty "How!" Crosby refused to shake it.

Satanta angrily pounded his chest and said "Me, Kiowa!"

Keim thought Satanta was so furious that he looked like he was going to signal his warriors to attack. But the chief hesitated, seeing Custer's troopers moving forward. Satanta, realizing the buckskin-clad scout was really the big chief, approached Custer for a handshake. Custer, too, refused to shake hands but explained through an interpreter, "I never shake hands with any one unless I know him to be a friend."[33]

Satanta accepted this reasoning and said he was a friend of the white man. Custer said he should release the courier for proof, and Satanta agreed, and added that he and the other chiefs would ride with Custer to Fort Cobb and that their village would follow.[34]

They did ride with Custer, but the chiefs left one by one, pretending to send word to the village to hasten the group along. Custer gradually realized it was a strategy to distract him while the village escaped. By the time they got to Fort Cobb, only Satanta and Lone Wolf were left. Custer, under orders from Sheridan, made them prisoners with their release dependent upon their village surrendering.[35]

Despite promises, the village never appeared. Custer filled part of the time with shooting contests with Santata's son, Tsa'lante, a young warrior who acted as a courier between Satanta and the village. Satanta told Custer that his son was the best shot in the tribe, and the regular shooting matches turned into a symbolic contest comparing the manhood of the white man with that of the Indian. Satanta watched the matches from the lodge, and said Custer only won because his rifle was better than Tsa'lante's. Custer agreed to switch rifles out of fairness but he was anxious that if he lost he would lose face with the Kiowa.

Intent on learning Indian culture, Custer was relieved when he was able to beat Tsa'lante using the Indian's rifle. "I attached no little importance to these frequent and friendly meetings between Satanta's son and myself," he wrote. "Any superiority in the handling or use of weapons, in horseback exercises, or in any of the recognized manly sports, is a sure steppingstone in obtaining for the possessor the highest regard of the red man."[36]

In war, the friendship between enemies is short-lived. Sheridan grew impatient with delays and ordered Custer to tell the Indians he would hang them if their villagers were not at Fort Cobb by sundown the next day. Tsa'lante then rushed off, and Satanta's people began showing up before the deadline expired.

The next step was to bring in the other roaming tribes—the Cheyenne and Arapaho. Iron Shirt, a Kiowa-Apache chief, and Mah-wis-sa were dispatched as emissaries. As they prepared to ride off, Custer felt anxious for the success of their mission, which would mean the difference between peace and the barbarities of frontier war. Mah-wis-sa reached for her belt to tighten her blanket around her and noticed that her mutch-ka, or hunting knife, was missing.[37] Custer knew it was considered the essential tool on the frontier, used for everything from preparing game to doing leather work. He pulled his own knife out of its holster and gave it to her, telling her to bring it back before the change of the moon. For the next three weeks Custer and his men settled down to the dull routine of camp life.[38]

Iron Shirt returned with a message that the Cheyenne chief Little Robe and the Arapaho chief Yellow Bear would soon come to visit. (Mah-wis-sa had not been permitted by her people to leave.) Little Robe and Yellow Bear came to the fort, but their tribesmen did not follow. Custer decided there was only one way left to try to end the war: He would take a small force to negotiate with the Indians rather than the whole regiment, which would intimidate the Indians and induce them to flee. He suggested the idea to Sheridan, who agreed only because Custer volunteered; he would not order men to go on such a risky mission.[39]

Custer thought a select group of forty soldiers would be the right size—big enough to protect itself yet not so big as to threaten the Indians. His picked team included sharpshooters and trusted officers such as his brother Tom. His favorite interpreter from the Washita, Raphael Romero, whom the soldiers nicknamed "Romeo," came along, as well as the two diplomat chiefs, Little Robe and Yellow Bear. In a nod to emotion rather than practicality, after an initial hesitation he allowed Daniel Brewster to join the expedition. Brewster, twenty, was an immigrant from New Jersey who had lost his father and brother in the Civil War. After his mother died, he and his sister moved to Kansas to stake a claim on the Solomon River. His sister, Anna, subsequently married a carpenter and moved to a nearby homestead. Only a month later she was captured during one of the frequent Indian raids on the Solomon.[40] The boy hoped to find his sister in one of the Indian camps.

Many of the other officers of the Seventh thought Custer was crazy to go on such a mission, or as he wrote later, "closely bordering on imprudent, to qualify it in no stronger term."

One officer, as he told Custer good-bye, gave him a small pocket derringer, loaded and ready.

"You better take it, General; it may prove useful to you," he said.

As was his usual habit Custer was already armed to the teeth with pistols and a rifle. But everyone on the frontier knew what the derringer was for.

"That little pistol was given me in order that at the last moment I might become my own executioner—an office I was not seeking, nor did I share my friend's opinion," Custer wrote.[41]

For Custer, it was a dramatic element that only made the upcoming story more thrilling. He had no intention of failing.

The momentous nature of the trip didn't stop Custer from indulging his curiosity in the world around him. He watched with fascination how the chiefs created smoke signals—the same ones he had seen from a distance so many times before. "I was glad, therefore, to have the opportunity to stand behind the scenes, as it were, and not only witness the *modus operandi*, but understand the purpose of the actors," he wrote.[42]

One time he was awakened in the middle of the night by Indian singing. He wasn't worried because the camp was well guarded. It was like so many other camp scenes during the Rebellion. He couldn't help but make his way over to the sound of the lighthearted Indian melody, which was a cross between a song and a chant. Neva, the Blackfoot guide, was building up the fire with some twigs. Romeo and Yellow Bear were enjoying some broiled ribs. Little Robe, reclining by the fire, was doing the singing. Custer asked through the interpreter why he was singing so wildly at night. "[He] replied that he had been away from his lodge for a long time, and the thought of soon returning, and of being with his people once more, had filled his heart with a gladness that could only find utterance in song."[43]

Brewster, too, had joined the group. As they all shared the comradery of the campfire, Little Robe admitted that the Cheyenne had two white women as prisoners. The description of one matched Brewster's sister. Custer cautioned Brewster privately not to let the Indians know his relationship to the captive or else they might quit revealing information.[44]

After a few more days of riding, they reached Yellow Bear's Arapaho village, and Custer opened negotiations with the head chief, Little Raven. Unlike Hancock and other officers, Custer was able to persuade them to let his troops camp right next to the Indian village. Custer had learned much about the Indian way of fighting, and he knew the main motive of the warriors was to protect their families. He reasoned that if his force was camped close by, the warriors would be less likely to attack, for a skirmish would involve casualties among the women and children in the village.

Custer had grown to admire Little Robe and Yellow Bear while traveling with them. But he still maintained the general uneasiness of a commander for the safety of his troops. He enjoyed sleeping outdoors, with his saddle for a pillow and the night sky for a view. But he would wake up several times in the night, sit up with his rifle across his lap, and study the sleeping forms of his men and the horses nibbling at the grass. Only after he called out to the sentry and got a reply that all was well could he go back to sleep.[45]

It turned out Custer need not have worried. Little Raven liked the way Little Robe and Yellow Bear had been treated, and he agreed to move his village near Fort Sill, a post about one hundred and fifty miles southeast of the Washita battlefield. But Custer couldn't find out the location of the Cheyenne village, which he suspected held the missing white women. Running out of supplies, he marched the regiment back to camp.[46]

Sheridan was called away to Washington, but he ordered Custer to take the Seventh and the Kansas troops on a westward march to find the Cheyenne and finish the war. They soon found a trail, lost it, then picked up another trail. After days of marching, Custer's Osage scout, Hard Rope, led him to an Indian pony herd. As Custer studied it, he noticed about fifty Indians watching his movements.

He suspected he had found the Cheyenne village. He knew if he attacked, the Indians would kill the white captives, just like they had done to Clara Blinn and her son at the Washita. Therefore Custer began riding in a circle, occasionally moving toward the Indians in a zigzag—the symbol on the Plains to request a parley.

Three Indians galloped toward Custer. He signed for only one to approach and held his right hand up and carried his revolver in his left, indicating that he was friendly. After greetings, he learned that Little Robe's village was nearby, and that the chief, Medicine Arrow, was among the Indians watching him. After some negotiations, Custer agreed to go with Medicine Arrow to his village to assure them his troopers meant no harm. Custer rode into the village with only William Cooke and the regimental doctor, but he believed he was safe because the Cheyenne did not want the soldiers to attack the village.[47]

Medicine Arrow took Custer to his lodge, where they smoked a ritual pipe—a torture for the nonsmoking lieutenant colonel. Custer told them his mission was peace negotiations; he didn't want to press the matter of the missing women yet. Medicine Arrow showed Custer where he could camp near his village.[48]

As his troops set up camp, Custer learned from his Indian guides that the white captives were in the village. Medicine Arrow visited Custer's headquarters and told him that some of the young men from the village would visit and entertain Custer with music. "This idea was a novel one to me, and I awaited the arrival of the serenaders with no little curiosity," he wrote.[49]

Custer, ever appreciative of a show, was fascinated by the dozen riders who rode to his camp and galloped in circles as they played music for the cavalry officers. "The musicians were feathered and painted in the most horrible as well as fantastic manner. Their instruments consisted of reeds, the sounds from which more nearly resembled those of the fife than any other, although there was a total lack of harmony between the various pieces," he wrote.[50]

Custer became alarmed when he received reports that the village was packing up. The Indians would escape before he had a chance to rescue the women. He dared not order his troops to attack for fear the Indians would kill the captives. Instead, Custer ordered his officers to leave the performance one by one and then have a hundred soldiers slowly wander over and mix with the Indian guests, who numbered about forty. He surreptitiously pointed out the Indians he wanted seized as hostages at his signal.

When all was ready, Custer told Romeo to ask for silence. Custer then stood up, unbuckled his pistol belt, and let it drop to the crowd, signaling he wanted no bloodshed.[51]

Here was drama worthy of the Irish dragoon Charles O'Malley on a daring mission behind French lines. Custer had no certainty the Indians would not shoot him and a number of other soldiers as they fought their way to freedom. The captive women could have been killed as soon as the first shots were fired in the cavalry camp. But Custer's scene played the way he wanted.

Through Romeo, Custer told the Indians to look around and realize there was no escape. He had reasonable demands, and if they were met, he would let them go. The Indians did not surrender immediately. They gestured and argued wildly among themselves. For a few moments Custer was sure a fight would break out.

For George Armstrong Custer, it was the most exciting moment he had ever had with Indians, including the fight at the Washita. Near him stood a chief brandishing a cocked revolver, even though he was counseling his people to be calm. Another warrior standing near him drew the attention of Custer and the other officers as he coolly prepared for a fight. "He stood apparently unaffected by the excitement about him, but not unmindful of the surrounding danger," Custer wrote. "Holding his bow in one hand, with the other he continued to draw from his quiver arrow after arrow. Each one he would examine coolly as if he expected to engage in target practice. First he would cast his eye along the shaft of the arrow, to see if it was perfectly straight and true. Then he would with thumb and finger gently feel the point and edge of the barbed head, returning to the quiver each one whose condition did not satisfy him."[52]

Finally, the Indians made a rush to escape. Custer signaled his men to let them go except for four chiefs he kept as hostages. Several days of negotiations followed. Little Robe visited Custer and admitted the Cheyenne had the women. He wanted to release them and had tried to buy their freedom but could not persuade his people to give them up. Custer was in a difficult situation. He couldn't keep his troops at the village indefinitely; the Kansas militiamen, in particular, were getting restless and wanted revenge. They were starting to run out of rations. Custer turned his own supply wagon over to the troops, telling them he could live without eating as long as the men could.[53]

Custer forced the issue by threatening to execute his three hostages (one chief had been sent back to the Indians as a courier).[54]

Custer orchestrated the event for maximum dramatic impact on the Indians. He called for a delegation of chiefs from the village and held a meeting at his headquarters that included the three captives. He told them he was determined to get the white women released. If the women were not produced unharmed by sunset, he would execute his three prisoners and resume active warfare. To add to the implied threat of another Washita-style attack, Custer pointed out that the Indian ponies were underfed, and the Indians could not hope to escape his troops once the fighting started.

"The delegation, after a brief interview with their captive comrades, took a hasty departure, and set out upon their return to the village, deeply impressed, apparently, with the importance of promptness in communicating to the chiefs at the village the decision which had been arrived at regarding the captives," Custer wrote.[55]

The prisoners, too, were deeply impressed with Custer's resolve. They asked to see Custer and wanted to know if he really meant to execute them. Custer assured them he would carry out the threat. One chief then told Custer he was an important chief with a lot of influence. If Custer released him, he would hurry to the village and bring back the women in time to save his comrades.

Custer told him that his prestige made him the most important prisoner, because the Indians would be sure to release the captive women to prevent his death.

As he did when handling the mutiny among his troops in Texas, Custer staged the execution. He took the Indian prisoners to a large tree and showed them the limb that would be used to hang them. He ordered nooses put on the limb to emphasize the point. On the day of the deadline, the troops were lined up on alert ready to fight. They hoped the Indians would bring in the captives, but they didn't know which direction the Indians would come from. The prisoners muttered to themselves and occasionally looked at the nooses swaying from the branch.[56]

Around 3 o'clock Custer could see about twenty mounted figures approaching. He scanned the horizon with his field glasses. His officers stood by, anxiously wondering if the Indians had brought the captives. As they got closer, he noticed two figures mounted on one pony. Could those be the women?

Someone from the Kansas troops yelled, "Hurrah! They're coming!"

Custer, always sensitive to the protocols of a military pageant, ordered the Kansas officers to accept the prisoners since the women had been taken from their state. The officers, embarrassed that the women's ragged clothing barely covered them, wrapped their coats around them. Col. Horace L. Moore, one of the militia officers, asked the older woman if she was Mrs. Morgan.

She said she was and introduced the other captive, eighteen-year-old Sarah White.

"Are we free now?" Mrs. Morgan asked. (Mrs. Morgan was Anna Morgan, Daniel Brewster's sister.)

Moore said they were.

"Where is my husband?" she asked.

Moore said he was at Fort Hays, recovering from his wounds.

"Where is my brother?" she asked.

Moore told her he was in camp. He didn't tell her that he had placed Brewster under guard that day to keep him from shooting the Indians in revenge.

Moore recalled later that Sarah White didn't ask about her family. She had seen the Indians kill them.[57]

When the captives were safely within army lines, many of the men were overcome with emotion.

"Men whom I have seen face death without quailing found their eyes filled with tears, unable to restrain the deep emotion produced by this joyful event," Custer wrote. "The appearance of the two girls was sufficient to excite our deepest sympathy."[58]

The women were dressed like Indians with leather leggings and moccasins, but their dresses were made out of flour sacks with the brand names plainly visible. It was an irritating sign to Custer, who knew it meant their abusers had gotten their supplies from the government. The Indians had also given them jewelry such as bracelets made of copper wire and bead necklaces to make them look better upon their return.

Daniel Brewster, who was standing by Custer, said, "Sister, do take those hateful things off."

Daniel Spotts, a Kansas militiaman, wrote in his diary that the girls look pitiful, especially Anna, who looked like she was fifty years old even though she was less than twenty-five. "She was stooped, pale and haggard, looking as if she had been compelled to do more than she was able," Spotts wrote.[59]

The stories the women told of their captivity horrified Custer, a man of the Victorian era, in which women were to be protected and cherished. In marrying Libbie, Custer had promised his father–in–law that she would never have to work in the kitchen. The white captives, in contrast, were treated like slaves.

"Besides indignities and insults far more terrible than death itself, the physical suffering to which the two girls were submitted was too great almost to be believed," Custer wrote. "They were required to transport huge burdens on their backs, large enough to have made a load for a beast of burden. They were limited to barely enough food to sustain life; sometimes a small morsel of mule meat, not more than an inch square, was their allowance of food for twenty-four hours. The squaws beat them unmercifully with clubs whenever the men were not present."[60]

Given the women's brutal treatment, it was likely the women would have been murdered if Custer had attacked the village. Seeing them released, he felt his decision not to attack the village had been the correct one, even though the Kansas troops were eager for revenge. He was gratified when several officers admitted he was right, and that the release of the girls was a far better feeling than a victory over the warriors.

They marched back to Fort Hays, where the Morgans were reunited. James Morgan was still lame from the Indian bullet he had gotten in the raid that stole his wife. He had thought she was dead or would never return. Sarah White moved to Cloud County, Kansas, became a school teacher, remarried, and raised seven children with her husband, H. C. Brooks.[61]

"They could not find language to express their gratitude to the troops for their efforts in restoring them to each other," Custer wrote. "As the Indians had robbed them of everything at the time of the attack, a collection was taken up among the troops for their benefit, which resulted in the accumulation of several hundred dollars, to be divided between the two captives."[62]

The Indians, of course, also wanted *their* captives to be released. But Custer held them, explaining that releasing white prisoners was only half of the deal—the Indians were also to move to their reservation before he would release his prisoners.

Although both Custer and Sheridan believed this point marked the end of the campaign, Custer took the Indian captives to Fort Hays, where they were placed in a stockade with the prisoners from the Washita while the officers waited for the roaming tribes to return to the reservation.

Custer, reunited with his Libbie after a hard campaign, wanted to show her the evidence of his victory. He took Libbie on a tour of the stockade, where his terrified wife marveled at how he walked freely unarmed and unafraid among the prisoners. When he introduced Libbie as his wife, some of the Indian women asked if she was his only one. They looked at him with pity when he said yes.[63]

Libbie also was finally able to get a look at the Indian princess, Mo-nah-see-tah, who Custer had written about in such detail in his letters.

Libbie thought she had the ordinary beauty of youth but that when she smiled her face was transformed, covering up some of her harsh features. Libbie wanted to see Mo-nah-see-tah's baby, who was born in the camp.

"It was a cunning little bundle of brown velvet, with the same bright, bead-like eyes as the rest," Libbie wrote. "The mother saw a difference, doubtless. She was full of maternal pride, and ran into the tent again to bring a ferrotype of this young chieftain that had been taken by a travelling photographer who stopped at the post."

Mo-nah-see-tah asked Custer why the baby was on her left arm in the picture when she had held him in her right while the photo was taken. Despite his knowledge of sign language, he couldn't explain the photographic process that produces a mirror image, and Mo-nah-see-tah looked skeptically at him. She believed the Great Spirit had moved the baby in the image.[64]

Other communication problems were more serious. An infantry unit was in charge of the stockade and did not have an interpreter on duty when the commander decided for security reasons to move the three hostages to a different guardhouse. The three chiefs thought they were going to be executed because of their rough treatment by the guards and they fought back. One was shot to death and another died from a bayonet wound. The visits to the stockade ended because of the violence, and all of the prisoners were soon ordered released.

Custer took Libbie to see them march away. She marveled that they had been captured with almost no possessions but had accumulated so much property that they needed wagons to take it with them. The Indians, glad to be going back to their people, laughed and chatted as they rode away, and the troopers sent them off with a loud cheer.

The sole remaining guard, who walked a beat on an elevated platform, came down and seemed relieved that his duty was over. The stockade was quickly torn down.

"And with it departed all trace of the Indian captives, save the circles made by their tents in the soil," Libbie wrote.[65]

Custer had mastered a new role: Indian Fighter. But there was as much criticism as glory in it, and the attention won might be as ephemeral as the prisoners' stockade. Once again, the restless Custer faced an uncertain future.

CHAPTER ELEVEN

Exploring New Paths

Writer, Teacher, or Businessman?

There were still some sporadic Indian raids over the next few years while Custer was stationed in Kansas, but no major campaigns. The pause gave Custer an opportunity to enjoy garrison life in Fort Hays with Libbie and his friends and to reinvent himself as a celebrity hunting guide to the Wild West.

The Civil War had made Custer famous as a dashing cavalryman— the young general with the long golden curls and the beautiful wife who charmed the capital. The Washita campaign made Custer's reputation as an Indian fighter. True, the attack on Black Kettle's village was controversial, but there was no denying that Custer had succeeded in capturing a village where other famous generals had failed. His rescue of Sarah White and Anna Brewster Morgan was the stuff of novels—a feat worthy of Charles O'Malley, the fictional Irish Dragoon.

Custer's feats of hunting were popularized by the start of his writing career. He had begun writing for publication in 1867 when he submitted articles for the magazine *Turf, Field and Farm* during the downtime brought on by his court-martial and subsequent suspension from the service. His first series of articles published, between September and December in 1867, dealt with some buffalo hunting but also included his version of Hancock's Expedition—a version in which he blamed Hancock for starting the Indian war.[1]

Custer put professional writing aside during the Washita campaign. But when he returned, he found a letter from his friend, the former mayor of Detroit, Kirkland C. Barker, who was a big fan of *Turf, Field and Farm*. Barker urged him to start writing more hunting stories for the magazine.[2] The young publication, which was founded in 1865 by a Civil War veteran named Sanders Dewees Bruce, was an excellent vehicle for increasing Custer's fame and giving him a platform to present himself as one of the premier Western hunters. Bruce was a Kentuckian who used his expert knowledge of the state's horse-breeding industry to launch a writing and publishing career in New York City. He started *Turf, Field and Farm* with the assets of a struggling magazine called *Spirit of the Times* and turned it into one of the top sports magazines in the country. Bruce made his magazine appealing to sophisticated readers, and it advertised itself as denouncing "pugilism, and all low, disgusting sports." In addition to covering what it considered sophisticated sports, it included articles on the military, the theater, and general news.[3]

Custer's work for *Turf, Field and Farm* took advantage of an increase in interest in sports, leisure, and tourism that followed the Civil War. The media of the time encouraged Americans to turn West in their imagination even if they were not among the hardy pioneers daring to make the move physically. Dime novels told the tales of outlaws, frontiersmen, and Indians to people bored with their own lives working on farms or in factories. Painters such as Albert Bierstadt and Thomas Moran brought home the wild beauty of the plains and mountains to people trapped in crowded and smoky cities. Western newspaper editors boomed the prosperity of their towns. Entrepreneurs, politicians, and railroad companies promoted tourism.[4]

Custer's magazine articles fit nicely in that promotional media stew. Magazines are unique among media because loyal readers have an affinity for their favorite publication that goes much deeper than that for newspapers or books. Every magazine has a distinct personality, a certain style of writing and design that sets it off even from others in its own genre. The loyal readers see their favorite magazine as an older brother or sister, or good friend, someone who has traveled, is experienced and a little more sophisticated than the reader—someone to emulate.[5]

Custer's writing style was perfect for a sporting magazine. His nom de plume—a common convention in nineteenth-century journalism—was "Nomad," a great byline to convey a sense of adventure and a devil-may-care attitude. Most readers knew Nomad was Custer, but the pen name added a certain frisson, like James Bond being called "007." What hunting fan in 1870 would not want to be a nomad—a dashing cavalryman, wandering over the Great Plains shooting buffalo and other dangerous game and fighting Indians? Custer addressed these fans directly, writing in the first person with a self-deprecating humor that showed he was the kind of man you would want to hunt with. Yet he told of remarkable feats of riding and shooting and frontier skills that let you know you'd be safe on his expedition. His knowledge of dogs, horses, guns, and Indians was something the Eastern reader could aspire to in his fantasies.

"It is utterly useless to attempt the description of a buffalo hunt—the enjoyable part must be seen, not read," Custer teased the reader, then of course described the dangers of the hunt. "One must find himself astride a good horse, with a trusty pistol or carbine in his hand, then after a hard gallop in pursuit of his buffalo, to get near enough to the latter to plant one or more well-directed shots just behind the fore-shoulder, then see the immense animal come to bay and offer battle. This is when it behooves the hunter to have his wits about him; if not, he will find himself and horse suddenly caught upon a pair of powerful horns and lifted into the air."[6]

Custer then told the reader that three hunters in his party, including himself, had ridden horses that had been gored. Custer's horse had been injured in the hindquarters and the side. Only its thick saddle-cloth had protected it from a serious wound. "Let no one imagine a tameness about buffalo hunting," Custer wrote. "On the contrary, I believe it is the most exciting of all American sports."[7]

No wonder so many people wanted to hunt with Custer. He received about two hundred requests—from politicians, celebrities, rich people—even British royalty. P. T. Barnum, the legendary showman and circus owner, took his friend John Fish, an English industrialist, to Kansas for a buffalo hunt when he wanted to give him a tour of the United States. Custer, as was his practice, provided an escort of fifty cavalrymen and took them on an excursion to find a herd. Barnum killed a couple of buffalo, but Fish only got saddle sore and nearly shot a trooper. They left shortly afterward with adventures Barnum put in his autobiography.[8]

Barker, who had urged Custer to write more hunting stories, got a firsthand taste of the hunt that nearly proved fatal. After he chased a buffalo and emptied his revolver into its sides, the buffalo turned and gored Barker's horse. Barker lost his seat and struggled to stay on the horse while a horrified Custer and the other hunters watched helplessly. Barker finally was thrown off the horse and knocked out. Custer and the others chased the buffalo away and brought Barker around with "restoratives."

Custer was impressed that Barker, instead of being intimidated, said his near brush with death was just what he wanted. No money, he told Custer, could buy the black eye and bruised cheek he had experienced in the hunt. Barker participated in the next hunt and brought down a buffalo after emptying four revolvers into him. He got off his horse and jumped on top of the buffalo, waving his hat and giving three cheers—a feat Custer thought meant Barker truly deserved his presidency of the Detroit Audubon Club.[9]

Custer's talent at arranging exciting hunts was also useful to the government as public relations. Sheridan sometimes asked Custer to host special visitors, like two members of the British nobility, Baron Waterpark (Henry Anson Cavendish), and Lord Berkley Paget. The nobles, according to Sheridan, were obsessed with buffalo hunting, and he asked Custer to satisfy them. Custer enjoyed hosting the nobility, much as he had relished working with McClellan in New York, where he was able to associate with the upper crust. Custer described the background of his celebrity guests for his readers, although he confused their titles, referring to Cavendish as Lord Waterpark, and not mentioning their first names.

More important for Custer was their backgrounds. He noted with admiration that Lord Paget's grandfather had fought with Wellington at Waterloo, and that his uncle was second in command to Lord Cardigan, who rode in the famous Charge of the Light Brigade. Custer, like most officers of his era, would have studied the hopeless attack in 1854 at the battle of Balaklava in the Crimean War. He would have been familiar with Tennyson's poem that immortalized the cavalrymen who did not question their foolish orders but knew "theirs was to do or die" as they rode into "the valley of death." The romantic Custer told his readers that one of Paget's sisters was married to the Marquis of Hastings, a dashing sportsman who had owned fifty racehorses before his tragic death, and whose story Custer wrote would be familiar to the readers of *Turf, Field and Farm*.[10]

Custer knew his readers would be impressed, as he was, that the nobles were world travelers, having "done" India, toured Canada, and spent "the season" in Newport, where Waterpark made a bet with a wealthy New York woman who teased him that he would not kill a single buffalo. "It was difficult to determine which my noble lord considered the greatest incentive, the actual killing of the buffalo or the winning of the wager," wrote Custer, who had come a long way from the carpenter's apprenticeship in Ohio.[11]

Custer made sure his baron would at least have a good time. In addition to the usual camp equipment and escort, Custer brought along the Seventh Cavalry band to entertain his guests in the evening after the hunt. They marched out of the fort playing "Garry Owen," giving the expedition what Custer thought was a martial feeling. But the tone soon changed when they picked up a group of about one hundred and fifty Ohio tourists—about half of them women—whom some regimental officers had arranged to meet at a train station near the fort.

Custer had to go back to Charles Lever's novel about the Irish dragoon to describe the rollicking look of the huge hunting party. It looked, Custer wrote, like election day in Ireland, when the politicians would gather their supporters and march raucously to the polls, ready for a fight or a frolic. "Perhaps our English friends were reminded of this resemblance as they cast their eyes back and surveyed the *hunters*," he wrote.[12]

The Englishman certainly took the hunt seriously. Waterpark killed not one but four buffalo, and Paget bagged five. "Our English cousins were jubilant with joy and enthusiasm," Custer wrote. "They could not find words to express their admiration for our greatest of all American sports. Such remarks as 'Today is the best spent in America,' 'I would gladly come all the way from England for such a day's sport,' 'It's not so tame as I imagined,' and 'Zounds, how that fellow of a bull charged me' were taken as indications of the appreciation of the hunt." Paget enjoyed it so much that he later sent Custer a cased Galand & Somerville revolver—a modern weapon prized for its unusual construction—as a gift.[13]

It was a good present for Custer, who appreciated firearms for both work and play and was proud of his marksmanship. He had unusually good eyesight that helped him spot game. Annie Gibson Roberts, who was twenty-one when she visited Fort Hays during the summer of 1870, described riding with Custer. He pointed out a white object in the distance. She told him that it looked like a handkerchief hanging on a bush.

"No, that is the white stripe on the side of an antelope and I am going to bring it down," Custer said.

He dropped to one knee and fired his rifle. Roberts saw a puff of dust and what she still imagined as a handkerchief fall to the ground. They walked to the white object and found an antelope, shot dead, the bullet hitting the prime place behind the shoulder. They measured the distance, which was 650 yards.[14]

Roberts was not easily impressed. She was the child of a prominent civil engineer from Pennsylvania. Her mother died when she was eight, and two years later her father took her and four of her five siblings with him when he went to Brazil to supervise a railroad construction project for the emperor, Dom Pedro II. She was ten years old at the time and had great fun growing up in Brazil, riding, swimming, and playing with her brothers and sisters. Their pets included an armadillo and a swamp rat, and their dinners sometimes included snake, monkey, or red ants.[15]

Her love of the outdoors and taste for adventure was something she never outgrew. In 1869, her father had accepted a job to work on a bridge being built across the Mississippi River at St. Louis and moved his family to the Southern Hotel in the city. The hotel was a hub of social life for young officers stationed at Jefferson Barracks, and a number of them courted Annie, but she accepted none of the marriage proposals that came her way. The bold young lady did, however, accept an invitation from her uncle, Maj. George Gibson of the Fifth Infantry and commander of Fort Hays, who invited her to spend the summer at the post. It was common for young female friends and relatives of the families stationed at frontier posts to make such trips. The posts were isolated, and the officers' wives were lonely for female friendship as much as the bachelor officers longed for women to escort and perhaps court.[16]

It was no surprise that Annie became warm friends with the Custers during her visit, as all three shared a zest for life and new experiences. Libbie had not been to Brazil, but she had followed her husband as close as she could to the front during the Civil War and then to the Wild West of Kansas and Texas. Annie particularly admired Libbie for disguising her fears, and the ladies often participated in the buffalo hunts. For Annie, who was such an enthusiastic horsewoman that she kept an exact list of the names of all the different horses she rode that summer, it was pure adventure. But one jolting nighttime ride up and down hills in a wagon to get to a buffalo herd was something Annie thought would make a brave man pale.

"All honor be to Mrs. Custer for the nobility with which she has always calmly endured such terrors, and repressed any verbal utterance of them in the unselfish desire never to mar the enjoyment for others," Annie wrote in her diary. "One who has looked below the surface knows the will power and strong repression she must have exerted, and yet this was only one of a hundred such instances in her [eventful] life."[17]

Libbie and the women visitors also had to endure the fear of Indian attack, although the plains were quiet enough that summer that Annie said to Custer during the buffalo hunt that it would be fun to see half a dozen "hostile" Indians.[18]

"If four or five Indians *allow* you to see them, they are either friendly or else there are many more behind them," Custer said.

Annie then noticed some movement on the horizon and said they looked like buffalo. Another person thought they were elk.

Custer scanned them with his binoculars but said nothing. The objects kept moving closer, and everyone could tell they were men on horseback.

Custer rode toward them with three other officers and an orderly. Wesley Merritt was left to guard the ladies. Merritt kept his hand on his pistol, his face red, pacing in front of the wagon the women were riding in.

Custer's group charged the riders. Shots were fired. A riderless horse galloped toward the wagon. Libbie fell to her knees and yelled, "Autie will be killed!"

Annie dived under the seat of the ambulance, grabbed the derringer kept there and, as she wrote, waited for "the coming horror."

Lt. Edward Mathey raced up, waving his arm and yelling, "Corral the ambulances, the Indians!" But Mary Reno, Maj. Marcus Reno's wife, smelled a rat and told him to quit making a fool of himself. She sat calmly in the wagon, holding her little boy.

"Yes, quit this damned nonsense," Merritt said. "Don't you see you are frightening the ladies?"

Mathey grinned and admitted that the Indians were scouts from another camp. Custer had arranged the joke. "How we all laughed when it was over," Annie wrote.

Custer's rough humor had frightened Libbie, but she gave no sign to Annie that she disapproved. It was part of his charm.

"General Custer possessed a happy nature," Annie wrote. "There was a great deal of the lighthearted good spirits of the boy about him. He was fond of a joke and was quick to see and appreciate wit and humor, but like all unusual and original men, he had moods of silence when he seemed too full of earnest, serious thought for words."[19]

Others noticed the same mix of juvenile humor and dark seriousness. Another visitor to Kansas, Libbie's cousin Rebecca Richmond, brought an autograph book that asked the signatories to respond to forty questions, a common pastime in the nineteenth century. Custer wrote funny answers to most of the questions. When asked his favorite occupation, he responded sarcastically, "Making my friends miserable." His favorite object in nature was Libbie's chignon used as a crow's nest. His favorite color was a spotted pup. Custer was daring when asked his favorite style of beauty. He wrote it was a blonde like Lydia Thompson, who was a part of a risqué dance troupe from Britain that toured the United States that year.

But some of the questions prompted him to be reflective. They seemed to make him think about the military life he had chosen—frequently leaving your loved ones with the possibility of never seeing them again. The sweetest words in the world, Custer wrote in response to a question, were "fare thee well and if forever still fare thee well."

His greatest fear was, simply, "The battle field." The historical character he would like to emulate was "Lazarus." The final question of the
survey asked about his aim in life. He wrote, "To avoid death."[20]

When Annie discussed death with him, he was fatalistic, knowing
it might be his destiny as a soldier. When drafting a newspaper story
about him years later, she recalled she had once warned Custer not
to stray from the others when on the march or a hunt. She told him
she'd dreamed that he was shot in the head by an Indian while he was
riding.

"I can not die before my time," Custer replied. "And if by a bullet
in the head—why not?"[21]

But Annie's main memory of Custer was not of a soldier, a silly
prankster, or a great hunter. Years later she recalled a pleasant afternoon that summer in Kansas when she saw Custer gently rocking Libbie as she reclined in a hammock. The sun made his golden hair shine
in contrast to his blue uniform. He looked like a warrior yet with a
gentle manner, occasionally whispering something in Libbie's ear that
would make her blush. Annie, then a young, romantic woman, wondered whether such a love would ever come to her.

Custer saw her staring at them and seemed to know what she was
thinking.

"Annie, I am the happiest man in the world!" he said enthusiastically. "I envy no one. With my dear little wife whom I adore and the
7th Cavalry, the proudest command in the world, I would not change
places with a king."[22]

The public thought Custer was a sort of western royalty—the king
of the Indian fighters. People traveling through Kansas wanted to see
him, and they had different impressions.

R. H. McKay, an army doctor stationed at Fort Leavenworth, studied Custer closely when he and Libbie attended a dance at the post:

> I watched him with a good deal of interest, for at that time he
> was a distinguished man in the service, and I must say I was
> rather disappointed in his appearance. He seemed to me under-
> sized and slender, and at first blush to be effeminate in appear-
> ance. Maybe his long hair, almost reaching to his shoulders,
> gave this impression, but the face was something of a study

and hard to describe. Something of boldness or maybe dash, a quick eye, and he was intensely energetic, giving the impression that he would be a veritable whirlwind in an engagement. He did not convey the idea of a great character. He was a very graceful dancer.[23]

Custer enjoyed the celebrity. He knew the tourists wanted to see the heroes of the frontier—the scouts, the lawmen, the gunfighters. By this time, Wild Bill Hickok was a deputy United States marshal in nearby Hays City. Tourists from the East wanted to see Wild Bill, who had been featured in dime novels and magazine articles. One time, Hickok, who was uncomfortable with his fame, hid in the back room of a saloon. Some of the tourists who were acquaintances of Custer persuaded him to find his old scout and introduce him to the group.

"Bill's face was confused at the words of praise with which General Custer introduced him, and his fearless eyes were cast down in chagrin at the torture of being gazed at by the crowd," Libbie recalled. "He went through the enforced introduction for General Custer's sake, but it was a relief when the engine whistle sounded."[24]

For the attention-loving Custer, the train whistle no doubt produced a longing for something bigger than Fort Hays. As he had during his suspension after Hancock's War, Custer began to think of something besides the military. When the position of commandant of cadets opened at West Point, he wrote a letter to Sherman, applying for the job and saying he was no longer needed with the Seventh Cavalry since Col. Samuel D. Sturgis had been named the commander of the regiment. (Custer had hoped the promotion, to colonel, would go to him.) [25] The appointment at West Point instead went to a Civil War veteran named Emory Upton, who had written a book on infantry tactics and was considered a military scholar and innovator. Upton had commanded artillery, infantry, and cavalry during the war. In this case, it seemed Custer's carefully crafted image of the dashing cavalryman and frontiersman had pigeonholed him as just a fighter in the minds of his superiors.

Custer saw himself in a different way. He had leave coming after all his arduous campaigning. Over the next few years he would take business trips to Chicago, Monroe, and Washington and one long leave to

New York. He usually went without Libbie, as the trips were ostensibly for business. Custer, in the middle of the Gilded Age, tried to make his fortune by selling stock in a Colorado silver mine he had become involved in with a Michigan friend. Custer's fame and connections secured some investors, but the project ultimately failed.[26]

He was always more of a romantic dreamer living life as a character in a novel rather than a businessman. Custer's artistic side consistently distracted him from business as he spent much of his time seeing shows, flirting with beautiful women, or socializing with entertainers, tycoons, and politicians—all of whom enjoyed the company of the gallant hero, letting them feel close to an adventurous life they would never have.

Custer analyzed the shows he attended like a theater critic, writing Libbie in detail about the emotions they stirred in him. One of his favorite actors was Joseph Jefferson, who he saw play his signature role, Rip Van Winkle, in Chicago. Custer wrote Libbie as if he were an expert on acting, claiming that the most gratifying sound to a dramatic actor is complete silence. Not a sound was heard from the spellbound crowd during the first act, Custer wrote, although the rest of the play was full of laughter and tears. "When the daughter, grown to a young lady, recognizes in the decrepit, tattered old man her lost father, there was not one person not affected by it. I never saw the play before, nor so deep an impression has it made on me, do I desire ever to see it again."[27] He enjoyed plays in which he could see some sort of satire that reflected an aspect of his own life. On a trip to New York he wrote Libbie and told her how much he enjoyed seeing *The Liar*, a French farce in which the main character, played by Lester Wallack, exaggerates his military service in order to impress women. "He wore a big wig of long light hair like mine," Custer wrote Libbie. "He was so funny in the part."[28]

Custer was equally enamored of musical shows—especially the opera. A friend of Custer's bought a box at the Academy of Music and invited the famous general to use it whenever he pleased. The novice opera devotee took full advantage, often squiring the famous soprano Clara Louise Kellogg, who was three years younger than Custer. They had become good friends, but apparently platonic ones as he wrote frequently and in great detail of his visits with her to Libbie.

Clara called Custer the "Golden Haired Laddie" and thrilled to his stories of Indian fights.

"He was a most vivid creature; one felt a sense of vigour and energy and eagerness about him," She wrote years later. "And he was so brave and zealous as to make one know that he would always come up to the mark. I never saw a more magnificent enthusiasm. He was not thirty at that time and when on horseback, riding hard, with his long yellow hair blowing back in the wind, he was a marvelously striking figure. He was not really a tall man, but looked so, being a soldier."[29]

Custer, lost in the world of the arts, did not see how his behavior would be perceived by a wife left alone on the frontier halfway across the country. He cluelessly wrote about waiting for Kellogg downstairs in her home while she dressed upstairs and sang his favorite songs for him, such as "She's Waiting, I'm Coming." The oblivious Custer described the moment for Libbie: "I could hear her moving about overhead, and it reminded me of you in Monroe days when I sat in the parlor below, waiting."[30]

The ever-indulgent Libbie knew flirtations were part of their relationship and she had accepted them. About six months earlier they had some sort of quarrel over his behavior toward women that prompted Custer to write a soul-searching, pleading letter to Libbie to restore her loving feelings to their marriage. No letter from Libbie about the incident has been found, and as they remained devoted to each other for the rest of their lives, it's evident they resolved their differences.[31]

Libbie knew that Custer had always sought to make himself more attractive to her by telling her how much other women were interested in him—a not uncommon if unwise tactic in relationships. And Custer, as he always did, interspersed such details with tidbits that indicated he was faithful. Regarding Kellogg, he told Libbie how particular she was as a lady; he assured her the opera singer was not someone who would violate social norms.[32]

Miss Kellogg, as Custer referred to her in his letters, was so careful of appearances that she had ridden alone with a gentleman in a carriage only twice while living in New York, and in one of those daring episodes had her coachman with her. "How many ladies in a private station say as much?" Custer wrote.

Custer liked the fact that Clara Kellogg hated affectation. In a bit of name-dropping to Libbie—another hallmark of Custer's traveling letters to his wife—he repeated her opinion of the famous painter of Western landscapes, Albert Bierstadt, whom she did not like very much. "Miss Kellogg is very dainty in regard to gentlemen," Custer explained. "She became disgusted with B because he appeared before her in brown stockings, and also because he mis-spelled a word in the first letter he wrote her."[33]

Despite fawning over the soprano, Custer made sure in the same letter to remind Libbie of the strength of their own marriage. He saw Shakespeare's *Winter's Tale*, a play about misplaced suspicion of adultery, writing that it aroused the same intense emotions in him that he felt when seeing *Othello*, which included similar themes. He was grateful, Custer wrote Libbie, that he had a wife he was sure was faithful.[34]

Custer was surely faithful physically to Libbie because he looked on women like Kellogg primarily as artists—what he admired and what he wanted to be. His sculptor friend Vinnie Ream invited him to visit her for the unveiling of a work she had done of Lincoln. Custer couldn't come to the show and wrote her a letter touching on his regret at not being an artist himself.

"You are young and have a fame far in advance of your years and to attain which others in your profession of acknowledged genius have been compelled to devote a lifetime," Custer wrote. "Go on dear friend conquering, and to conquer, your victories are lasting and unlike mine are not purchased at the expense of the lifeblood of fellow creatures leaving sorrow, suffering and desolation on their track."[35]

Of all the types of famous people Custer met, writers impressed him the most. "I was at a dinner party—one I can never forget, for the talented and distinguished men I met there," Custer wrote breathlessly to Libbie.

Custer sat next to Horace Greeley, the owner and editor of the *New York Tribune*, one of the most popular newspapers in the United States. Greeley had been a champion of the Union cause during the war and encouraged settlement of the West. Sitting nearby was Whitelaw Reid, one of the most famous battlefield correspondents of the war and one of Greeley's editors. Sitting opposite Reid was Charles Dana, who during the war had served as assistant secretary of war and worked closely with Grant. Now he was editor and part owner of the *New York Sun*. On Custer's other side was Bayard Taylor, the novelist, poet, and travel writer. Taylor regaled Custer with stories of his travels to central Africa.

Custer, who had always loved poetry, was particularly excited to meet Edmund Clarence Stedman, the author of a poem featuring cavalry fights called "Alice of Monmouth: An Idyll of the Great War" and other lyrical poems.

"Mr. Steadman [*sic*], who sought for an introduction to me, told me that during and since the war I had been to him, and, he believed, to most people, the beau ideal of the Chevalier Bayard, 'knight sans peur et sans reproche' and that I stood unrivaled as the 'young American hero,'" Custer wrote Libbie.[36]

All the socializing could not help but boost Custer's ego, although Custer, as he often did, told Libbie to keep the details to herself because he did not want to appear to be bragging. "I was so complimented and extolled that, had I not had some experience, I should have been overwhelmed," Custer wrote.[37]

Custer might not have been overwhelmed by the attention, which he had been experiencing for close to ten years. But he was changing. Just over thirty years old now, Custer had started to put on weight—enough that he had to buy suspenders to keep his pants up. He joked about it to Libbie, but it was an outward sign of the changes he was undergoing as he approached middle age.[38] He had gone from the Boy General to frontiersman, Indian fighter, and hunter. He had experienced some success as a writer for a sports journal. He relished the attention of writers in New York. Could he be one of them?

Francis P. Church, who had founded the *Army and Navy Journal* with his brother, William Conant Church, asked Custer to write a series of articles about his experiences in Kansas for *Galaxy*, a monthly literary magazine they had launched in 1866. The magazine was popular and paid well, and it attracted some of the greatest writers of the day, including Henry James, Walt Whitman, and Mark Twain.[39] Church offered Custer $100 (about $2,100 in 2020) per article, an amount that amazed the aspiring writer. Plus, Church took an option to publish the articles as a book.[40]

Custer was about to add a new role to his repertoire of characters: Man of Letters. It was one he had long aspired to but could scarcely believe was real now that it was happening. He told Libbie he was surprised someone would pay him so much for his writing. Still, it wasn't enough to completely change careers, even if he was ready to, and he was not. He accepted a new assignment to a duty station in Elizabethtown, Kentucky. He had hoped to be assigned again to the West, he wrote Libbie. "Duty in the South has somewhat of a political aspect, which I always seek to avoid," he wrote, meaning he would be on Reconstruction duty.[41]

Libbie found the town boring and old. She wrote her sister-in-law Maggie, who was now married to James Calhoun, an officer in the Seventh, that the only way to get a true idea of their boardinghouse was to imagine you were your grandmother. "The old standing corner clock has not been allowed to run down for forty-five years," Libbie wrote. "The dog is sweet sixteen and can scarcely walk. An old gentlemen boarder of the old school is equally unsteady on his legs. But, who, over seventy, wishes to marry again. . . . No, not the old landlady who was his sweetheart, but a young girl."[42]

Custer, as he usually did, found things to like. He enjoyed the applesauce and hot biscuits served with every meal, and the conversation of the other boarders, which included a retired congressman who was the veteran of many duels and had the scars to prove it. Custer bought Libbie a sewing machine, and she started making clothes for herself, Custer, and her brother-in-law Tom. "I can make it fly," she wrote excitedly to a friend.[43]

One of Custer's main duties, in addition to suppressing the Ku Klux Klan and breaking up illegal distilleries, was buying horses and mules for the army since he was located in the heart of horse country. Without the threat of combat, Custer had free time to concentrate on his writing, which he proceeded to do with characteristic vigor. He worked on articles about thoroughbreds in Kentucky for *Turf, Field and Farm*, and *Galaxy* articles about his service in Kansas.

Custer made a couple of trips from Kentucky that showcased his political skills. In June 1871 he attended a reunion of veterans of the River Raisin Massacre, which had been fought in Monroe during the War of 1812. The British and their Indian allies had defeated the American forces and taken more than five hundred prisoners. As many as one hundred of the prisoners were murdered by members of the allied tribes, which included the Delaware, who about fifty years later would provide scouts for the army during Hancock's War. As a boy growing up in Monroe, Custer was well-versed in the tragic yet heroic story of American soldiers fighting against the odds.

Custer's father served as chairman of the reunion and introduced the mayor after an open-air banquet. A patriotic song followed the mayor's speech, and Custer was introduced. He protested that he had not come prepared to give a speech. But like a politician on the stump Custer shook hands with the veterans and gave a spontaneous speech quoting the Gettysburg address and comparing the dedication of that national cemetery to the event honoring the River Raisin veterans.[44]

Going back to his leadership of a singing competition that took place at West Point between Southern and Northern cadets, Custer always seemed to know what to say to excite a crowd. At a reunion of Civil War veterans in Detroit, a college professor read a poem about Sheridan's ride during the battle of Winchester in 1864. The poem drew enthusiastic applause, but when Custer was introduced to give a brief speech, he said that Sheridan's horse Rienzi, who had carried him on the ride, was from Michigan. The Detroit crowd went wild.[45]

A more important bit of politics was Custer's participation in a buffalo hunt Sheridan organized for the Russian Grand Duke Alexis, the son of Czar Alexander II. The hunt was part of a much larger trip for Alexis, who was also an officer in the Russian navy, to develop his military and diplomatic skills. (The world trip might also have been designed to get him to forget a love affair with a commoner—a story that would have appealed to the romantic Custer.)

Russia had supported the Union during the Civil War, and relations were good between the two countries. Civil War hero Admiral David Farragut had led an American naval squadron to Russia as a goodwill gesture in 1867, and the duke's trip was part of a reciprocal move by Russia.[46]

Sheridan wanted the best experience for Alexis, so he arranged for Buffalo Bill Cody to act as guide and the Sioux chief Spotted Tail to bring a hundred warriors to provide native color. Custer was necessary as the premier Indian fighter and celebrity hunter. He was also used to dealing with important guests, and he didn't disappoint Sheridan when hosting the Russian duke. Alexis had so much fun that the group took a train to Denver for parties and another buffalo hunt in that area.

"All returned safe and well," Custer telegraphed Libbie, but he couldn't resist adding some self-deprecating humor. "Hunt a splendid success. Grand Duke killed three buffalo. I killed my horse. Gen. Sheridan & Staff & myself invited by Grand Duke to accompany him to Denver and the mountains returning via Kansas Pacific. We leave tonight at ten. Will telegraph from Denver."[47]

On the train ride across Kansas, Custer and Alexis practiced using their Spencer rifles shooting at buffalo from the train. They headed east to St. Louis, where Sheridan left Custer in charge of the foreign royalty. Custer arranged a tour of Mammoth Cave, and he and Libbie accompanied Alexis to New Orleans. The trip was naturally well-covered by the press and it further solidified Custer's reputation as a hunter and frontiersman.[48]

Custer's best friend, the actor Lawrence Barrett, wrote that Alexis liked Custer because he was genuine and not caught up in the flattery and ceremony of diplomacy. He and Custer maintained their friendship through correspondence after the duke returned to Russia—a friendship that Custer treasured.[49]

After the royal hunt, it was back to the routine of garrison duty and horse buying in Kentucky. In Elizabethtown, Custer amazed the locals with the variety of his outfits. Sometimes he would be in uniform, sometimes in his buckskins, and other times in civilian clothes, including a stylish dove-gray top hat he had bought in New York.[50] Custer was a soldier, but he was also part politician and part frontiersman. With his duty as a celebrity hunting guide for the army, and his contract with *Galaxy*, he was a writer and an intellectual. Like an actor, Custer was comfortable in any of those roles, and like a politician he was comfortable with everyone he met. Yet his actor friend Barrett noticed he was restless.

"Enjoying his vacation as keenly as a school-boy, General Custer was always apparently 'awaiting orders,'" Barrett wrote. "And when they came, his whole manner changed: he seemed to put on the soldier with the uniform."[51]

The orders came in February 1873. The Seventh Cavalry was going to the Dakota Territory to protect the construction of railroads, and Custer was to play the role of soldier again.

CHAPTER TWELVE

Warrior and Writer

For Custer, who always embraced completely the role he was playing at the time, the promise of active service in the West was exciting, and he put on a show of boyish excitement for Libbie and their servant Eliza.[1]

"As soon as the officer announcing the order to move had disappeared, all sorts of wild hilarity began," Libbie recalled. Custer teased Libbie, picked her up, whirled her around the room, and put her on the table. He threw a chair into the kitchen to let Eliza know they were changing stations again. In a moment of quiet, Libbie pulled out an atlas to look up the Dakota Territory. "When my finger traced our route from Kentucky almost up the border of the British Possessions, it seemed as if we were going to Lapland."

As a military family of modest means, they didn't have a lot of household possessions. The kitchen utensils were shoved in uncovered barrels, the bedding was rolled in waterproof cloth, the personal items such as books and pictures were boxed, and they were ready to go.[1] The Custers and the rest of the Seventh Cavalry went by steamboat from Kentucky to Cairo, Illinois, where they boarded trains that took them to the end of the track at Yankton, Dakota Territory (present-day South Dakota). They rode the last three hundred and fifty miles on horseback. It might not have been Lapland, but their new station was far away from the developed part of the United States.[2]

Custer reported for duty at Fort Rice on June 10, 1873, and ten days later he was off on an expedition to protect a Northern Pacific railroad survey project through Indian territory. Libbie and Maggie, now sisters-in-law, went back to Monroe. They would return when the expedition was over and Custer went to his permanent station at Fort Abraham Lincoln near Bismarck.

The commander of the expedition was Col. David S. Stanley, forty-five, who had won the Medal of Honor at the Battle of Franklin during the Civil War but suffered from alcoholism in his postwar service. Custer played his customary role of frontiersman and scout, roaming ahead of the command each day and relaying messages to Stanley. As always, Custer liked center stage, and he acted as if he were the commander rather than Stanley. At thirty-three Custer had started to mellow and to adapt to the frontier army. Although he still pushed his men, he didn't rely as much on the harsh discipline he had imposed on the recalcitrant volunteers in Reconstruction Texas or the frustrated regulars he molded into a fighting unit in Kansas.

Stanley had ordered August Baliran, the post sutler, banished from Fort Rice for selling alcohol to the troops. Custer, however, let him go along, reasoning the troops could have liquor in moderation and that it might help morale. When Stanley found out, he ordered Fred Grant (the president's oldest son, who was serving as aide-de-camp) to confiscate the liquor. Grant went straight to Custer, who warned Baliran. The sutler distributed his supply among Custer's officers. When Grant searched Baliran's wagons, he of course found no liquor, and Custer's handling of the affair was appreciated by both officers and men.[3]

But not by Stanley. "I have seen enough of him to convince me that he is a cold-blooded, untruthful and unprincipled man," Stanley wrote his wife. "He is universally despised by all the officers of his regiment excepting his relative and one or two sycophants. He brought a trader in the field without permission, carries an old Negro woman [Eliza], and cast-iron cooking stove, and delays the march often by his extensive packing up in the morning. As I said, I will try, but am not sure I can avoid trouble with him."[4]

Stanley issued orders that seemed designed more to assert his authority than to benefit the command. The colonel, perhaps because of his alcoholism, had forgotten he gave Custer permission to bring the stove on the march. But on the campaign, the stove irritated him, particularly because it took too much time to pack. The reason it took too much time to pack was the officers were playing cards late into the night and oversleeping. The stove, which they used for their late breakfast, had to cool off before it could be packed. Custer didn't tell Stanley because he wanted the men to have some pleasures while they were campaigning.[5]

The cook stove and Custer's ranging in front of the command angered Stanley, but the use of a government horse by Fred Calhoun, a railroad employee and James Calhoun's brother (and thus Maggie's brother-in-law), brought matters to a head. Stanley ordered Custer to his tent and demanded to know why he let Calhoun, a civilian employed by the railroad, use a government horse. Custer replied he authorized the use in the same way Stanley let Sam Barrows, a *New York Times* correspondent, use an army horse.

Furious, Stanley had Custer arrested and ordered him six times to abandon the cookstove. Thomas Rosser, Custer's West Point friend and rebel cavalry rival, was working for the railroad, and he tried to convince Custer to apologize. But Custer, who was cheerfully riding at the rear of the column in punishment, refused because he believed he was following army regulations.

Within two days, Stanley had sobered up and apologized to Custer, telling him he hoped he would forget the incident, and that he would turn over a new leaf in their relations. Both men wrote to their wives that they were satisfied with the outcome. Stanley told his wife that Custer was behaving much better.[6] Custer wrote Libbie that Stanley frequently asked for his advice since the incident. "With his subsequent faithful observance of his promise to begin anew in his intercourse with me, I banished the affair from my mind," Custer told Libbie. "Nor do I cherish any but the kindliest sentiments towards him, for Genl. Stanley, when not possessed by the fiend of intemperance, is one of the kindest, most agreeable and considerate officers I ever served under."[7]

Custer's tolerance of Stanley was yet another sign of his maturation. His reacquaintance with Rosser reminded him of the war and his past glories. Almost a decade had gone by since Custer had dramatically tipped his hat to the big Texan before their men fought at Tom's Brook in the Shenandoah Valley. At that time Custer had commanded thousands of men in a division in a war for the survival of the country. Now he was commanding about seven hundred men in a regiment guarding railroad surveyors.

Despite the intervening years, Custer had immediately recognized Rosser's voice when he heard him talking outside of his tent one day on the march. The two men stretched out on a buffalo robe in Custer's tent and traded stories about the war. Rosser said that at Tom's Brook he had seen Custer through binoculars and told another officer, "Do you see that long-haired man in the lead? Well, that's Custer, and we are going to bust him up." But the opposite happened, and Rosser admitted the fight was the "worst whipping he ever had." To Custer, it seemed like the days when they were cadets trading dreams of what they would accomplish.[8]

This expedition didn't promise glory like the Shenandoah campaign, but it was still dangerous. The Sioux were watching, angry that the railroad would go through their lands. On August 4, while Custer was scouting ahead with about a hundred troopers, the Arikara scout Bloody Knife, Custer's favorite, found an Indian trail of twenty warriors and warned Custer to expect a fight. It came while the column was halted at a grove of cottonwood trees by the Tongue River, trying to rest from the heat, which had been reaching over 100 in the afternoons. Someone yelled, "Indians! Indians!" A handful were trying to steal the horses.[9]

The troopers drove off the warriors. Custer jumped on his horse and took twenty troopers to give chase. After two miles it was apparent the warriors were decoys—the same tactic they had used to lure Fetterman and his command to their massacre outside of Fort Phil Kearney seven years earlier.

Suspicious, Custer halted the chase. He and his orderly rode forward in a circle to signal that they wanted a parley. The Sioux didn't. About three hundred warriors came screaming out of a nearby stand of trees. Tom Custer, who had stayed back with the bulk of the scouting unit, ordered the men to dismount and form a skirmish line to try to repel the attack. His older brother was on his own.

"Wheeling my horse suddenly around, and driving the spurs to his sides, I rode as only a man rides whose life is the prize, to reach Colonel

[Tom] Custer and his men, not only in advance of the Indians, but before any of them could cut me off," Custer wrote later.[10]

Custer reached the lines just ahead of the Sioux, and three volleys from the troopers broke their charge. Seeing that his small command was trapped in the open, Custer withdrew to a dry streambed. They used it as a breastwork for three hours, fighting off the Indians, who were sniping from the tall grass. One warrior regularly charged the line and rode away. Custer challenged Bloody Knife to see who could bring him down when he charged again. Custer and his scout fired at the same time, and the warrior went flying off his horse. Neither Custer nor Bloody Knife could tell who fired the fatal shot, and they argued for the credit.[11]

After three hours of fighting, the command was running out of ammunition. Custer ordered a charge, and the surprised warriors fled. Only one trooper had been killed. But on the way back to the command they found the bodies of August Baliran and John Honsinger, the regimental veterinarian. The two had left the main command to join Custer and had been ambushed by about thirty warriors. It was a warning to all about not leaving the main command in Indian country.[12]

A week later they learned it was not necessarily safe to be with the main command, either. On August 11 the troopers were attacked before reveille by warriors firing from across the Yellowstone River. Custer ordered his men to stop firing back until the Indians appeared in larger numbers. They soon did, and the firing was so heavy the horses had to be moved to keep them out of range.

Custer ordered his sharpshooters to fire from behind trees on the riverbank. Private John Tuttle, one of the regiment's best marksman, killed three warriors before he himself was shot dead. Custer, back in his role as soldier after his layoff from fighting in Kentucky, seemed to be everywhere at once on the battlefield. Wearing a brilliant red shirt, he rode around the field giving orders and drawing fire from the warriors.

"He seemed to bear a charmed life," wrote Barrows, the *Times*'s correspondent. "Fear was not an element in his nature. He exposed himself freely and recklessly." [13]

When Indians crossed the river in large numbers and threatened the command, Custer ordered a charge. Unlike so many fights in the

Civil War, Custer delegated the attack as he oversaw the entire battle. With the band playing "Garry Owen" to send them off, Tom Custer led a charge that drove the Indians from the field and chased them for eight miles.

They estimated the Sioux numbered from five hundred to 1,200 warriors; Custer had only about 450 troopers. Twice in a week Custer had been outnumbered but had won sharp skirmishes with the Sioux by using discipline and fire control—the main advantages American soldiers had against the Indian warriors, who individually were fearless and skilled fighters but didn't normally operate as a cohesive team. Custer had not grown soft in Kentucky. As a battlefield commander, he was still an excellent leader and tactician.[14]

Even on a wilderness campaign, Custer wanted a dramatic ceremony. He ordered that the regiment's one fatality, Tuttle, be buried with full honors witnessed by the entire command. After the funeral, a campfire was built over the grave to disguise it from the Indians because the soldiers feared they would dig up the corpse and mutilate it. Careful notes were made of the location, so it could be found later for a more permanent marker.[15]

The Indian fights, however, were a fairly small part of The Yellowstone Expedition of 1873, which lasted about three months. Custer spent more of his time scouting and hunting, and he learned taxidermy from one of the expedition's civilian scientists. He prepared several trophies, including a buck for Tom, who planned to send it to his girlfriend, and one for the Detroit Audubon Club. "You should see how devoted I am to this very pleasant and interesting pastime," he wrote Libbie. "Often, after marching all day, a light may be seen in my tent long after the entire camp is asleep, and a looker-on might see me with sleeves rolled above the elbow, busily engaged preparing the head of some animal killed in the chase. Assisting me might be seen the orderly and Hughes, both from their sleepy looks, seeming to say, 'How much longer are we to be kept out of our beds?'"[16]

The expedition was well-covered by the press, and Custer's hunting and fighting exploits added to his reputation. Rosser, the soldier-turned-engineer, remembered the Yellowstone River fight as the most dramatic event of the expedition. He had seen Custer have his horse shot from under him and then remount to continue to lead the fight, looking over the battlefield and suppressing his excitement so he could calmly calculate his next move. Custer's face, Rosser thought, showed a strong sense of purpose.

"I thought him then one of the finest specimens of a soldier I had ever seen," he wrote to Libbie years later.[17]

Custer, however, saw himself as more than a soldier. Increasingly he was focused on other interests, and not just stuffing trophy animals for museums and private collections. His articles for *Turf, Field and Farm* and *Galaxy* had whet his appetite for a writing career. He had always been an enthusiastic reader, and he enjoyed seeing his name in print. He proudly wrote Libbie that many newspapers referred to him in their coverage of the expedition, and he sent her a clip from a *Chicago Post* story that called him the "Glorious Boy." He wondered if she thought of him the same way the *Post* did. He answered his own question later in the letter.

"Writing to others seems difficult, but to you not so," Custer wrote. "When other themes fail, we still have the same old story which in ten years has not lost its freshness . . . indeed is newer than when, at the outset, we wondered if it would endure its first intensity."[18]

He was being disingenuous in complaining about writing letters. His output was prodigious, and his letters were long, detailed, dramatic, and often when writing to Libbie, poetic. Yet he was not sure he could be a professional writer. Libbie recalled that he was surprised when an editor approached him to write a series of articles about his experiences. Custer hesitated because he wasn't sure he could do it, and the editor upped his offer, not realizing Custer had considered the initial sum quite large.[19]

On the Yellowstone Expedition, Custer continued to knock out letters to Libbie, one of them forty-two pages long. "This would make an article for the 'Galaxy,'" Custer wrote. "It is for my Gal. Don't you think you should send me a check?"[20] He was joking, sort of. After being published regularly, Custer knew what the editors wanted, and he was storing away anecdotes and data for future articles. At the end of the expedition, he wrote Libbie excitedly about the different publishers who wanted him to write for them.

"The 'Galaxy' people are stirring me up for more articles," he wrote. "They will get [Theodore] Davis of Harper's 'Weekly' to illustrate them. A telegram from the N.Y. *Times* asked me to write up the trip. I enclose a slip from the 'Army and Navy Journal' with a complimentary reference to your Bo."[21]

The expedition a success, Custer was ordered to command Fort Abraham Lincoln, the new post being constructed south of Bismarck. Libbie joined him, and they became involved in an active social life at the fort since they were the senior couple. They had a large two-story house with plenty of fireplaces for the cold winters. But on February 9, 1874, a freezing night in Dakota Territory, Libbie was awakened by a roaring noise in the chimney. She woke up Custer to investigate, and he found the room above them on fire. Custer called for water, hoping he could put it out, but before Libbie could get the water, she heard an explosion. The chimney had burst, covering Custer in plaster. He narrowly escaped, but the house didn't, despite the efforts of a bucket brigade. They also lost most of their possessions. But both Custers were philosophical. Libbie said the only irreplaceable loss was her collection of newspaper clippings of Custer dating to the war. The bucket brigade and favorable wind had kept the fire from spreading to the other houses. "It is better that we should have been burned out than that the calamity should have fallen upon others here," Custer wrote his mother a few days after the fire. Custer secretly prepared temporary quarters in a building next to Tom's house and threw a surprise housewarming party for Libbie when it was ready. It was no use crying over spilled milk, he told her.[22]

In fact, Custer relished being able to design a bigger place with a larger library/office that would allow him to retreat from the rest of the activity in the house. When he had drawn up the plans for their first house at Fort Lincoln, he triple-underlined "MY ROOM" above the door of his library with the motto "Who enters here leaves hope behind." Libbie wrote that it was Custer's joking way to indicate he didn't want his studies or writing interrupted.[23]

In the new house, Libbie got the bay window she wanted plus a thirty-two-foot-long parlor designed for entertaining. Sliding doors opened into the kitchen. Upstairs there were plenty of rooms for guests—important for accommodating the visitors so important for the morale at an isolated frontier post. A large room for a billiard table upstairs provided more entertainment, which was an expected duty of the commanding officer.

Downstairs Custer had his long-dreamed-of office, bigger and better than the one that burned. He filled it with animal trophies he had stuffed himself, Indian artifacts, weapons, and reading material. On the wall were pictures of Sheridan, McClellan, and Barrett—the men he most admired. He also had two pictures reflecting what he was most proud of—his Civil War record and his marriage. One photo showed him in his Civil War uniform and the other showed Libbie in her bridal gown.

On his desk were two statuettes illustrating scenes from the war. One was called "Wounded to the Rear: One More Shot," by John Rogers, a popular sculptor at the time, and it showed two wounded Union soldiers, both appearing defiant in the face of their injuries. One soldier holds his rifle as if he were ready to fire once more at the enemy, the other is seated bandaging his wounded foot. The second statue was "Mail Call" and featured a soldier holding an inkstand and scratching his head with the pen as he contemplates what to write—a fitting piece to inspire Custer's literary work.

Libbie was amused that no matter how often the statues broke in moves, Custer would carefully repair them with glue and fill in the empty spaces with putty. The most recent repair on the neck made the soldier look like he had a goiter and prompted Libbie to laugh at Custer's amateur sculpting. He would not give up the statues, however, and said he would paint them and put them in a dark corner where no one would notice the repairs.[24]

"My husband was enchanted to have a room entirely for his own use," Libbie wrote. "Our quarters had heretofore been too small for him to have any privacy in his work. He was like a rook, in the sly manner in which he made raids on the furniture in the house."[25]

Libbie enjoyed his office, too. They would sit together in the room at dusk, the fireplace's flames reflecting in the eyes of the stuffed animals, creating a fantastic scene that would let the imagination run wild. She thought a stranger suddenly transported into the office would be scared. But she and Custer were so happy together that it seemed cozy to them.

"We loved the place dearly," she wrote. "The great difficulty was that the general would bury himself too much, in the delight of having a castle as securely barred as if the entrance were by a portcullis."[26]

It was in this room, where he felt so comfortable, that Custer became a professional writer. Since he was a boy, Custer had spent his life moving around, working as a carpenter's apprentice, shuffled to his sister's house, then going away to the normal college, then to West Point, and immediately after graduation living in countless army camps and forts from Virginia to Texas to the Great Plains. Sometimes he lived in tents, sometimes he lived in family homes requisitioned by the army, and sometimes he shared crude quarters in frontier forts with Libbie.

Finally, at Fort Lincoln, he had his own grand house, designed the way he and Libbie wanted it. A half dozen or so photographs exist of Custer's house at Fort Lincoln—officers, wives, and friends in group photos on the porch, wide shots of the whole house, and a couple of interior shots of the living room showing guests enjoying an evening of music listening to someone play the piano. Two photographs, widely reproduced in Custer biographies, show him in his office. In one close-up, Custer is studying a thick volume on his desk, papers in a couple of piles in front of him. In the second picture, the photographer set his camera further back to show the whole side of the room. Libbie sits at the desk opposite of Custer, reading a book. This time Custer is leaning over the desk, pen in his right hand, while he holds his head in his left hand deep in thought. Next to Custer is a small bookcase, about the height of the table. The top shelf is filled with books, the bottom shelf crammed with newspapers and magazines. To anyone who writes for a living, it is instantly recognizable as a writer's office. And it's evident that Custer, by arranging these photographs, saw himself as a writer.

When these pictures were taken, photography was still a relatively new technology—the first photograph had been taken in France less than fifteen years before Custer was born. Advancements were slow, and cameras were bulky. It took time to set them up, and the exposure time was so long that action shots were impossible without significant blurring. Still, Custer, who was always interested in new things, was a fan of the art. And the camera loved him. His looks, dress, and charisma made him a popular topic. He was one of the most photographed men of his time. There are only about 122 known photographs of Lincoln but 158 of Custer.[27] It's a sign of Custer's artistic side that when he chose to present himself to be photographed at Fort Lincoln, it was not as a soldier, it was not as a hunter, it was as a writer.

Custer was not playacting for the camera. He was a naturally prodigious writer, working not just in his office, but on trains, in hotel
rooms, and during military campaigns.[28] A near lifetime of writing fast
at night—first craftily drafting letters under the covers at West Point
after curfew, and later composing them in spare moments in the field—
had trained him to write fast and with little editing, much as a reporter
learns to write stories swiftly and clearly for deadline. Custer thought
it was funny when an editor told him his writing showed the result of
careful, painstaking effort. Libbie, who at Custer's insistence, would
often sit with him in his office while he wrote, recalled that he would
write page after page without the aid of notes, only his memory.[29]

John Barry, Custer's boyhood friend from Stebbins Academy, thought
Custer was a good, clear writer, and that his letters always were fun to
read. Barry recalled that once when visiting with Kirkland C. Barker
in Detroit, Custer got a letter from his publishers requesting an install-
ment for a story. Libbie was not on the trip, and Custer laughed and
said, "This is pretty short notice, when my authorship is done by my
wife, who is far away; however I will just write a chapter or two, if you
will excuse me."

Custer left his friends and after a half hour produced a manuscript.
"Well, you fellows know I wrote this, anyhow," Custer said with a
laugh.[30]

Custer was making light of the teasing he was getting from some of
his West Point classmates who never imagined, based on his academics, that he would be a writer one day. They thought his educated and
cultivated wife must be his ghost writer. One classmate, J. M. Wright,
thought "[The] greatest surprise in Custer's whole career in life was
that he should turn out to be a literary man."[31]

Libbie supported his writing career just as she did all of his efforts.
She hated to be a nagging wife, but she gave in to his demands to scold
him about deadlines and keep him working. When he was in a writing
fervor, she would protect him from the many visitors that would drop
by the house.

"When he was in the mood for writing, we used laughingly to refer
to it as 'genius burning,'" she wrote. "At such times we printed on a
card, 'this is my busy day,' and hung it on the door. It was my part to go
out and propitiate those who objected to the general's shutting himself

up to work." If he got writer's block, Libbie would start telling a story of their past, but purposefully bungle it. He would take the story over and finish it with a succession of well-constructed scenes. "Afterward he was commended for writing as he talked, and making his descriptions of plains life 'pen pictures,'" she recalled.[32]

Custer's ability to take readers through his words to the Great Plains to hunt buffalo and fight Indians made him part of an extraordinary change in journalism in the latter half of the nineteenth century. The telegraph, invented in 1844, was ever more rapidly making the United States—and even the world—a smaller place in the public mind. Because of exploration, only a few places in the world remained uncharted and mysterious: central Africa and the polar regions. In the Unites States, the growth of railroads allowed people to traverse the country if they had the money and time, but there were still parts of the West unreachable by locomotive or telegraph, and few white people had visited them. Many Americans were struggling in humdrum, ten-hour-a-day, six-day workweeks and needed mental escape from the disruption of industrialization.[33]

Newspapers and magazines responded with a new model of journalism that featured entertaining stories rather than the dull repetition of political news. This new type of journalism was the forerunner of the literary journalism or narrative nonfiction that burgeoned in the 1960s in the United States with writers like Tom Wolfe, Joan Didion, and Hunter S. Thompson. In its simplest definition, literary journalism uses the techniques of fiction such as dialogue, scene-by-scene construction of stories, and "thick description"—deep detail of people and scenes—to tell an engaging story that has news value, although it is usually not about breaking news. In many cases, the writer narrates the story or even becomes the main protagonist. For others, like Thompson, the line between fact and fiction becomes blurred as the writer, in the words of Thompson, is pursuing truth "on a higher level than nickels and dimes."[34]

A number of nineteenth-century journalists—particularly humorists—practiced this new style although few other than Mark Twain would be familiar to modern readers. Twain, like Thompson, exaggerated stories to make an entertaining point. Custer, who was only a year younger than Twain and a fellow Midwesterner, also tried to make his writing funny as was evident in his self-mocking tale of shooting his horse while hunting buffalo. But Custer's writing was perhaps more like that of Henry Morton Stanley, the young Civil War veteran who Custer had met while he was covering Hancock's War for the St. Louis *Missouri Democrat*. Custer, who devoured newspapers, especially those that covered his adventures, would have read Stanley's stories because they were syndicated around the country—including in the *New York Herald*—and were the main news source of the campaign. By the time Custer was writing in his office at Fort Abraham Lincoln, the ambitious Stanley had become James Gordon Bennett Jr.'s star reporter. In 1872, Stanley had led a *Herald* expedition to the heart of unexplored central Africa to find a missing missionary. Stanley's first-person account of finding the missionary and his self-reported greeting—"Dr. Livingstone, I presume?"—had won him everlasting fame and a career that other writers aspired to.

Custer and Stanley wrote about some of the same events and characters of Hancock's War, and their descriptions of Wild Bill Hickok, who was a scout, were very similar. Writing in 1867, Stanley described Hickok as surprisingly cultivated, with his speech sounding like he had attended college. He was, Stanley wrote, "as handsome a specimen of a man as could be found. . . . Tall, straight, broad, compact shoulders, herculean chest, narrow waist, and well-formed muscular limbs. A fine, handsome face, free from any blemish or blotch, a light moustache, a thin pointed nose, bluish-gray eyes, with a calm, quiet, benignant look, yet, seemingly possessing some mysterious latent power, a magnificent forehead, hair parted from the center of the forehead, and hanging down behind the ears in wavy, silky curls."[35]

Writing about a half dozen years later, Custer described Hickok's speech as unexpectedly free from vulgar expressions. Custer thought Hickok "was one of the most perfect types of physical manhood I ever saw." Custer's description was like Stanley's, touching on the same points. "In person he was about six feet one in height, straight as the straightest of the warriors whose implacable foe he was; broad shoulders, well-formed chest and limbs, and a face strikingly handsome; a sharp, clear, blue eye, which stared you straight in the face when in conversation; a finely shaped nose, inclined to be aquiline; a well-turned mouth, with lips only partially concealed by a handsome moustache. His hair and complexion were those of the perfect blond. The former was worn in uncut ringlets falling carelessly over his powerfully formed shoulders."[36]

Did Custer refer to Stanley's story when writing his own description of Hickok? Libbie said Custer wrote without notes. The only evidence is the similarity of the copy. Certainly, though, writers consciously and unconsciously mimic the style of those they read. And Custer wrote in a style that was like Stanley's: thick description of people, animals, and places, a self-deprecating tone, thrilling narrative, and politics interspersed with the adventures. Stanley's adventures were about battling the harsh terrain and warring Africans, while Custer wrote about doing the same things on the Great Plains, with Indians substituting for Africans. Stanley wrote about the evils of the slave trade. Custer railed about the evils of the government policy that cheated Indians of their promised annuities and forced them into war.

At any rate, Custer's writing for *Galaxy* and other publications had the hallmarks of literary journalism. His articles were filled with descriptions and scenes that brought the reader to the plains with him. When discussing the differences between the Indian ponies and the cavalry horses, Custer noted that the Indian ponies could survive without grass during the winter. "It was somewhat amusing to observe an Indian pony feeding on the cottonwood bark," he wrote. "The limb being usually cut into pieces accustomed to his kind of 'long forage,' would place one fore foot on the limb in the same manner as a dog secures a bone, and gnaw the bark from it."[37] He described step-by-step how Indians created a signal fire and compared it to a painting called "The Smoke Signal" by the popular Western artist John Mix Stanley, a ready reference for his readers.[38]

When Custer introduced characters or sketched scenes, he would sometimes recreate dialogue, and in the case of the scout California Joe, he would try to capture the frontiersman's dialect. Before the Washita attack, Custer asked California Joe about the prospects of a fight, and their chances of winning it.

"Fight!" responded California Joe, "I havn't nary doubt concernin' that part uv the business; what I've been tryin' to get through my topknot all night is whether we'll run aginst any more than we bargain fur."

"Then you do not think the Indians will run away, Joe?"

"Run away! How in creation can Injuns or anybody else run away when we have 'em clean surrounded afore daylight?"

"Well, suppose then that we succeed in surrounding the village, do you think we can hold our own against the Indians?"

"That's the very pint that's been botherin' me ever since we planted ourselves down here, and the only conclusion I kin come at is that it's purty apt to be one thing or t'other; if we pump these Injuns at daylight, we're either goin' to make spoon or spile a horn, an' that's my candid judgement, sure. . . ."[39]

To the twenty-first century reader, the dialogue might sound forced and tedious. But in the 1870s such dialect recreation was common, particularly in humor pieces like those of Mark Twain, and Custer was trying to entertain as well as inform. He had a natural ability to alternate humorous scenes such as California Joe's antics with serious descriptions of fighting. Custer could also draw out a scene, such as sneaking up on an Indian village, to give the reader the sense of fear the soldiers felt at going into battle. He did this with an honesty that was disarming and human. Rather than portray himself as the fearless cavalryman, Custer freely admitted his own fears and sometimes made himself the butt of his own jokes. When he approached the Indian village at the beginning of Hancock's War, he confessed he was as anxious as the rest of his advance party. When he wrote about shooting his own horse while chasing a buffalo, Custer let the reader inside his head as he flew end-over-end of his collapsing horse.

"My only thought, as I was describing this trajectory, and my first thought on reaching *terra firma*, was 'What will the buffalo do with me?'" Custer wrote. "Although at first inclined to rush upon me, my strange procedure seemed to astonish him. Either that or pity for the utter helplessness of my condition inclined him to alter his course and leave me alone to my own bitter reflections."[40]

Custer might have exaggerated some of the details for dramatic effect. He was raised in the brag culture of frontier Ohio, where exaggerations were an accepted part of storytelling. Libbie admitted that in the frontier posts, where entertainments were few, stories were retold often and occasionally embellished to make them fresh.[41] If Custer did that in his published stories, he was following the tradition of American tall tales, and also in good company with his peers. Both Twain and Stanley were known to have spiced up their stories as well, as did some twentieth-century literary journalists like Hunter S. Thompson. Custer knew his audience. His *Galaxy* articles were so popular that they were published as the book *My Life on the Plains* in 1874.

Like all writers, Custer had to deal with criticism. The Seventh Cavalry's Capt. Frederick Benteen famously called Custer's book "My Lie on the Plains,"[42] and Col. William B. Hazen, who Custer had criticized in the book, privately published a rejoinder pamphlet called "Some Corrections of 'My Life on the Plains.'"[43] But Custer also received high praise from Sherman, who told him that he and everyone in his family had read the book with "deep interest." Sherman thought Custer's articles about the Plains were the best he had ever read on the topic. Critics had given Sherman some "hard knocks" when he wrote his own memoir of the Civil War, but he urged Custer to write one because it would be a valuable contribution to history.[44]

Custer had matured as a writer and he had developed a distinct voice. He thought his contribution was telling the cavalryman's side of the story. He portrayed the conflicted state of mind of professional soldiers tasked with protecting their countrymen and following the orders of their leaders in a thankless job. Custer was determined to do his duty as a soldier, yet as a writer he could understand the viewpoints of the various people he wrote about, including the people he was fighting. Like Stanley, he admired many Indians, including Satanta, who he thought was a remarkable man for his skilled oratory and his courageous fight against the inroads of civilization.

"If I were an Indian," Custer wrote, "I often think I would greatly prefer to cast my lot among those of my people adhered to the free open plains rather than submit to the confined limits of a reservation, there to be the recipient of the blessed benefits of civilization, with its vices thrown in without stint or measure."[45]

Sometimes critics of the army accused soldiers of wanting a war for glory, Custer wrote. "I have yet to meet the officer or man belonging to the army who, when the question of war or peace with the Indians was being agitated, did not cast the weight of his influence, the prayers of his heart in behalf of peace."[46] In the concluding chapter of *My Life on the Plains*, Custer told the reader that he was preparing for another campaign. "Bidding adieu to civilization for the next few months, I also now take leave of my readers, who I trust, in accompanying me through my retrospect, have been enabled to gain a true insight into a cavalryman's 'Life on the Plains.'"⁴⁷

Custer's next campaign was to be an exploration of the Black Hills to find a site for a new fort. The Black Hills were sacred to the Sioux, and the Fort Laramie treaty of 1868 forbid whites from entering them. But an exception was made for government officers, and Sheridan believed a fort in the heart of Sioux country was needed to discourage raiding on railroads, trails, and white settlements. As in previous expeditions, scientists went along with the military to study the region. Looking for gold was not a stated purpose of the expedition, but rumors had long circulated that the region was one of great mineral wealth. The press and public expected the expedition would confirm the rumors.⁴⁸

Unlike during the Yellowstone survey, Custer was the sole commander of the expedition. He thought it would be a grand trip, and he invited his best friend, Barrett, to accompany him, telling the actor "You would return a new man and feel as though you had really been drinking the true elixir of life."⁴⁹

Custer intended to keep enjoying that elixir, at least for Libbie's sake. After the close calls on the Yellowstone survey, he took what for him were painful precautions. He assured her that he only rode a few miles in advance of the column to scout the trail, and he took seventy or eighty men with him. He never rode out of the lines to hunt. "I feel like a young lady fond of dancing who is only allowed to sit and look on at some elegant party," he wrote Libbie. "But I try to render strict obedience to the orders of my Commanding Officer, issued when I started."⁵⁰ Reporters accompanied the expedition, and Custer urged Libbie to clip stories about it. "They will be interesting, and of value, later," he wrote.⁵¹

The big news from the expedition was the discovery of gold on July 30, 1874. The newspaper stories played up the amounts found and stirred public clamor to open the Black Hills to white settlement and exploration. Miners were already entering the area illegally, so the government organized another expedition in the spring of 1875 to confirm the results and find out how much the Black Hills were really worth. Custer expected to lead the expedition, and James Gordon Bennett Jr. asked him to write stories for the *New York Herald* during the campaign.

But the expedition was put under the purview of the Department of the Interior, so it would not be seen as a military campaign, and a less famous officer, Col. Richard Dodge, led a less conspicuous escort. At the same time, a federal commission led by Iowa Senator William B. Allison opened negotiations with the Sioux to buy the Black Hills.[52]

In the meantime, Custer had gone back to duty at Fort Lincoln. In December 1874 he had sent a detail to the Standing Rock Agency to arrest the Sioux warrior Rain-in-the-Face after he was overheard bragging about killing Baliran and Honsinger. Tom Custer personally tackled Rain-in-the-Face and took him prisoner. But Rain-in-the-Face escaped from custody a few months later when friends of some of his fellow inmates cut a hole in the jail wall, allowing the warrior to get away unpunished.[53]

A presidential election was coming up in a year, and Custer's thoughts turned to politics when he heard of the election of Andrew Johnson to the Senate from Tennessee. Most political observers thought Johnson's career was over after he finished his presidential term in disgrace. But he continued to pursue office and was finally vindicated in 1875.

One of the letters of congratulation Johnson received was from Custer, who had no reason to curry favor with him, as the Radical press had accused Custer of doing in 1866. "I have watched the successive steps which preceded your election with the warmest interest," Custer wrote, "and when the final result was reached, by which the nation was again to have the benefit of your voice and your experience in its highest legislative body I felt that the constitution, the Union— and a pure government by the people were again to have your powerful and patriotic influences exerted in their defense."[54]

As he often did after a campaign, Custer was thinking about other careers. He enjoyed the military and living in the West, but his artistic sensibility craved the excitement and culture of the East. He and Libbie thus traveled back to the "States" to see family and friends and to explore their options.

Gilded Age Crusader

At the end of 1875, Libbie and Custer went to New York for their long-awaited leave. The city was the perfect place to visit for Custer because it was the center of his main interests—the arts and politics. Here he could hang out with celebrities, take in shows, and meet with publishers and civic leaders.

The trip was a whirlwind of typical Custer activities. Libbie, who enjoyed the celebrity lifestyle as much as Custer, wrote excitedly to her brother-in-law Tom that they had so many invitations it was hard to accept them all. They ate with various British earls and knights as well as their actor friend Lawrence Barrett and his wife. But Libbie's favorite treat was a luncheon at the studio of the famous Western artist Albert Bierstadt.[1]

They loved Barrett's performance in *Julius Caesar*, which featured a closing scene of Brutus being burned on a funeral pyre. "Why Tom, it makes you want to scream to see the funeral pile blazing, and Mr. Brutus raising above it."[2] Custer saw the play forty times by Libbie's count, sitting in Barrett's dressing room chatting with him before he went on stage. Custer was spellbound every time he saw the acting of his friend.[3]

One play Libbie didn't like was *Ours*, a drama about the Crimean War by T. W. Robertson, a writer considered revolutionary at the time for his "problem plays"—so called because they dealt with serious issues.[4] Custer and Tom, who was visiting briefly along with another officer from the Seventh Cavalry, insisted that Libbie see it with them, although they were afraid it would make her cry.

"It ended my going [to the theater]," she wrote. "When we reached the part in the play where the farewell comes, and the sword is buckled on the warrior by the trembling hands of the wife, I could not endure it. Too often had the reality of such suffering been my own. The three men were crying like children, and only too willing to take me out into the fresh air."[5]

But for Custer the trip wasn't all fun. Brother Tom had gone back to Bismarck, and Custer wrote him what he had learned from his contacts about the House of Representatives' plan for reducing the army. The House planned to cut five regiments of infantry and one of artillery, but the cavalry would not be touched—crucial news for the Custers. Frozen at lieutenant colonel since the end of the war, Custer was also concerned about promotion, just like most of his fellow officers. He was still addressed as "general" as a military courtesy because of his Civil War rank in the volunteers, but that honorific did not pay the bills of the life he and Libbie wanted to live. He had thought he had earned a promotion through his successful campaigns in the West. But promotions were extremely rare because of the small size of the army and the plethora of young, talented officers from the war. Men had to wait a long time—like vultures, Sherman thought—for older officers to die or retire voluntarily. (There was no mandatory retirement.) George Crook was the most recent of Custer's peers to get a general's star in the regular army, in 1873. Since presidents appointed generals, it also helped to have some political pull.[6]

Custer wrote Tom that he did not think he would be promoted in 1876. Left unsaid was that with Grant, a Republican, in the White House, his chances would be more difficult than if a Democrat were elected in the fall. Prospects were good for a Democrat, as the public was tired of fifteen years of Republican rule and a costly reconstruction of the South. Custer could also read the tea leaves about the coming Indian troubles over the Black Hills. "I expect to be in the field, in the summer, with the 7th, and think there will be lively work before us," he wrote. "I think the 7th Cavalry may have its greatest campaign ahead."[7]

Exciting and potentially more life-changing news was an offer Custer had received from James Pond of the Redpath Lyceum Bureau, who wanted him to go on a nationwide speaking tour. The Redpath, founded by abolitionist James Redpath, was the premier speaker's bureau in the country, with clients including humorist David Ross Locke, reformer Wendell Phillips, preacher Henry Ward Beecher, and Custer's fellow *Galaxy* correspondent, Mark Twain. Speaking fees ranged from $50 a night to the record $1,000 a night for Beecher. Nathaniel Banks, a Union general in the war and former Massachusetts governor, earned $100 a night, and he had nowhere near the success Custer had in the war. The speakers worked hard, often giving talks five nights a week, but they made a lot of money. Locke, who had mocked Custer for his foray into politics in 1866, made more than $30,000 in one tour.[8]

"When I tell you the terms, you will open your eyes," Custer wrote Tom. "Five nights a week for four to five months, I to receive $200 a night." It was, simply put, a fortune. He would be earning as much as Locke, one of the top writers of the day. The fee in 2020 dollars would be about $4,800, or $480,000 for the contract. Any way you measured it, the contract would set Custer on a new career, not only more lucrative than the army but the kind of lifestyle he and Libbie had always dreamed of.[9]

Custer didn't feel ready yet, however. As a former schoolteacher, he knew the importance of mastering your material before addressing a group. "They urged me to commence this spring, but I declined, needing more time for preparation," he told Tom.[10] Custer wanted that final promotion and to leave the military stage with one last success. Practically, for his future plans, he wanted to finish his Civil War memoir, which would give him more content for his lectures, and he wanted to practice. He'd always been drawn to the stage, and he liked performing in amateur tableaus at Fort Lincoln. It was a common entertainment of the Victorian era, in which people would put on costumes and stage scenes from popular plays or books. The audience would try to guess what scene they were reenacting. Custer was photographed playing various roles, including a Quaker peace commissioner, a Sioux chief, and Buffalo Bill. One photograph of Custer as a peace commissioner shows him in a costume with a prominent belly that must have been created with the aid of a pillow or some other stuffing. In that picture as in several other theatricals from the period, Custer looks comfortable pretending to be someone else. Like Barrett, who was photographed in costume from *Julius Caesar* and other plays, Custer wanted a record of himself as a performer.[11]

Custer, of course, had also given speeches, such as his brief comments in Andrew Johnson's Swing Around the Circle, and events like the River Raisin veterans reunion. But this tour would be a regular job. Custer knew frontiersmen were already in demand for shows. His friend Buffalo Bill had organized an acting troupe and invited Wild Bill Hickok to tour. Wild Bill hated every minute of it and quit. Custer planned to practice with Barrett so he could succeed.[12]

Barrett thought Custer's leave was the happiest time the two had together in their long friendship. He remembered best an evening they spent together at the Century Club, one of New York's most exclusive private clubs, dedicated to promoting interest in literature and the fine arts. Although not as educated as many of the other club members, Custer was the center of attention. "With that rare facility given but to few, he drew from the artist and the historian the best fruits of their labors, and as warmly listened as he could warmly speak," Barrett remembered. "His love for art was not affected dilettantism. Appreciating the glories of nature with an enthusiast's soul, he learned to trace her likeness in the works of her copyists."[13]

Custer got his leave extended so that he was gone about five months before he was ordered back to his post. It was a difficult trip to make in winter to Bismarck, and the train got stuck in a snowdrift. Tom Custer met the train with a sled and took Libbie and his brother to the fort through a storm.[14]

Back in the nation's capital, a storm was brewing, too—a political one that would engulf Custer in its periphery as a celebrity who could be of use in the battle between the Democratic House of Representatives and Grant, the Republican president. America in the 1870s was experiencing the beginnings of the Gilded Age, an era satirized in the 1873 book *The Gilded Age: A Tale of Today*, by Mark Twain and his writing partner Charles Warner. Historians would later use the book's title to name the era, but Custer and his fellow Americans knew only that they were living in an age of rapid and unsettling change. The Gilded Age was marked by industrialization, fast economic growth, and an increasing gap between abject poverty and ostentatious wealth. Politically, the era featured government corruption, scandal, and intense partisanship, with high voter turnout and nerve-wrackingly close elections.

The corruption and unrest generated demands for reform. Unions fought for better working conditions, reformers campaigned for the rights of women, Indians, and former slaves, and the House investigated the various scandals of the Grant administration. Reform become one of the main issues of the 1876 presidential election as the two parties fought over who would be the best at implementing change.

Custer was on the front lines of these Gilded Age battles between corruption and reform, and the dueling facets of his personality made him a player on each side. On the one hand, Custer was a man of his times, seeking a share of the wealth being created as the country's economy exploded after the war. Ever since he was a boy, Custer had dreamed of fame and fortune, something beyond sweating as a tradesman in a small Midwestern town. His ticket out had been West Point, and his brilliant military career had fulfilled his dreams of fame. Custer was a household name. His friends were actors, politicians, and publishers. But his military career did not provide the money to live the high life on his own. He was always a guest in the big city, never the host.

Custer schemed to make his fortune, and some of those schemes came close to crossing the ethical line—if they didn't actually cross it—in the freewheeling Gilded Age. He used his name to raise money for a speculative mine in Colorado. It failed, and his partners lost the thousands they had invested on his sales pitch. He speculated in railroad stocks, remarkably trading almost $400,000 in short-selling transactions that might have been illegal, although not at all uncommon in that era. For Custer, it was a form of gambling, a vice he wrestled with all his life and tried to stop because of Libbie. He ultimately lost $8,500 that he had to cover with a promissory note cosigned by Ben Holladay, a stagecoach and steamboat entrepreneur with a reputation for loose business standards.[15]

But Custer's sense of duty as an army officer and his romantic notion of his role as a hero led him to fight corruption. He was disgusted by the way the government treated Indians and soldiers on the frontier. Custer saw firsthand how government contractors cheated Indians of the rations that had been promised them as part of deals to open their ancestral lands to white settlement. The army was left the distasteful duty of fighting against people they knew had some justified grievances while their own government provided the Indians with modern weapons—intended for hunting but often used against settlers and soldiers.

Perhaps the biggest affront to Custer was the selling of post traderships by government officials, who would award the contracts to those who paid them a premium kickback. It occurred in plain sight of Custer, and his crusading nature, his thirst for being in the thick of things drew him into the political reforms that were stirring. His connections and affinity for politics and journalism were the pathway.

Custer's own writings, now in book form, made plain his opinion that Indian affairs should be managed by the military, which had as an incentive the prevention of war, rather than the civilian Indian Bureau, whose contractors thrived on graft. So much dirty money was floating around, Custer wrote, that the Indian lobby was like a third branch of Congress in its influence on public policy, which purported to help the Indian but in fact was a way for agents to make money and for Congress to distribute lucrative patronage.

"The salary of an agent is comparatively small," Custer wrote. "Men without means, however, eagerly accept the position; and in a few years, at furthest, they almost invariably retire in wealth. Who ever heard of a retired Indian agent or trader in limited circumstances? How do they realize fortunes upon so small a salary?"[16]

Indian agents would sometimes cheat their wards on their annuities, or sometimes they held back some goods, claiming the Indians had committed some violation of their treaty. The goods would then be given to a trader, who would sell the Indians their own government annuities at a tremendous markup. Custer wrote, "I have seen Indians dispose of buffalo robes to traders, which were worth from fifteen to twenty dollars each, and get in return only ten to twenty cups of brown sugar, the entire value of which did not exceed two or three dollars. I have known the head chief of a tribe to rise in council in the presence of other chiefs and officers of the army, and accuse his agent, then present, of these or similar dishonest practices."[17]

In addition to his own writing, Custer played the role of investigative reporter, gathering information and helping *New York Herald* journalist Ralph Meeker on his undercover work in Dakota Territory. Meeker investigated graft at posts throughout the territory under the fake name of J. D. Thompson. Custer went so far as to cash a draft for Meeker from the *Herald* so that he could preserve his anonymity.[18]

All the press coverage led to a House investigation of corruption at the traderships focusing on Secretary of War William W. Belknap, Grant's friend from the war. Belknap resigned one step ahead of impeachment. But the House continued the investigation anyway, and Heister Clymer, the Democrat chair of the investigating committee that bore his name, called Custer as a witness. Thus Custer would be heading back East almost immediately after he had returned to Fort Lincoln.

For Custer, the call came at an inconvenient time. Two years earlier, he had predicted the Indians would fight over the Black Hills when they thought the government was acting in bad faith, and that prediction was now coming true, although the government was instigating the fight. The Grant administration had tried to buy the Black Hills, but the Indians refused to sell. The country was still in a recession since the Panic of 1873, and the public demanded access to the resources of the area. The army couldn't keep out the miners who were flooding the region illegally. The Grant administration then decided to tell the Indians in the Black Hills to report to their reservations by January 31, 1876, or be declared hostile. The deadline effectively meant war since the Indians camping off their reservation couldn't return in the dead of winter even if they had wanted to. Custer expected to lead a force from Fort Abraham Lincoln, and he needed time to prepare.[19]

But Custer did as he was called to do and testified before Congress on March 29 and April 4.[20] As always, Custer became the thing he was. He played to the hilt the role of crusader against corruption. On March 29, he testified that contractors had systematically cheated the government and the Indians, in one instance by purchasing corn for the military that had already been paid for by the Indian Bureau. But the most shocking part of his testimony was that the Sioux reservation was enlarged in order to provide more profits for the traders. Clymer asked Custer directly if he thought this was done to increase the profits of Orvil Grant, the president's brother, who had Indian trading posts on the Missouri River. Custer said it would be improper for him to answer, which the *New York Sun* interpreted as meaning that he agreed with Clymer's implication. Custer claimed he had tried to report the scandals but Belknap and others would do nothing about them. It was surprising, Custer said, that the army had not become completely demoralized by the scandals. It was a credit to the officer corps that they had kept their honor and morale, he said.[21]

Anti-administration papers praised his testimony. The Washington *Evening Star* thought Custer confirmed what everyone knew—that the Indian Bureau was riddled with fraud. "General Custer has a refreshingly straightforward way of giving his testimony on the witness stand," the paper editorialized. "He makes no flank movements, but bears down directly upon facts as he understands them."[22] The *New York Sun* thought Custer's testimony was the climax of the scandal. "He gave his evidence frankly and fearlessly, and even when the truth bore hard on the President he did not waver."[23] The *New York Herald* called Custer's testimony "a sad commentary" on the Grant administration: "Custer's evidence shows how deeply corruption had penetrated the army circles in the West."[24]

In contrast, pro-administration papers, such as the *Washington National Republican*, dismissed Custer's testimony as hearsay because he did not have direct knowledge of the corruption but was rather repeating stories he had been told. "It is strange that Gen. Custer was so careless in his statements before the Committee on War Expenditures," the paper editorialized. "He did not state any fact as of his own knowledge. His testimony was of the severest kind, full of wholesale denunciations, and calculated to impress the listener with the belief that our entire Indian Bureau and other organized systems on the frontier are thoroughly corrupted." No Republicans on the committee were present to challenge Custer, the paper noted, and Custer had a motive to discredit Belknap because he did not get the assignment he wanted.[25]

Custer's dramatic presence was gold for the committee, and they asked him back again less than a week later. On April 4, the committee asked Custer why army officers had not disclosed the corruption on the frontier until now. Custer said Belknap had issued an order in 1873 that forbid them to complain to Congress. They feared that if they made any complaints, they would lose their commissions, he stated.[26]

Confident that he had done the right thing, Custer had no fear but instead reveled in his role. He enjoyed mingling with powerful congressman. He wrote Libbie about socializing with Clymer and other politicians such as Samuel S. Cox, who gave a speech sympathetic to Indians and mentioning the Washita. Cox told Custer, "I guess I have taken your scalp," and Custer replied, "Wait till I get you on the Plains! Then I will turn you over to those gentle friends of yours."[27] As was his habit, Custer followed the news coverage of himself, but criticism from reporters didn't bother him any more than criticism from politicians. He learned from Lawrence Gobright, Washington correspondent for the Associated Press, that Belknap's friends were passing around gossip to try to smear him, but Gobright said he had refused to print it. "The Cincinnati 'Enquirer' and St. Louis 'Republican' and other papers of that stamp commend me in highest degree," Custer wrote Libbie. "The two radical papers, controlled by the Belknap, Babcock, Shephard clique, vie with one another in abusing me. I do not let this bother me."[28]

He wrote one letter to Libbie after having lunch with Clymer in the House restaurant. Custer wrote while sitting at the table in the committee room that was the site of the Belknap hearing. He told Libbie he had recently dined with Congressman Henry B. Banning, who as chair of the House Committee on Military Affairs was preparing a speech about transferring the Indian Bureau to the War Department. "He took many arguments in favor of it from my book," Custer wrote, "but asked me not to mention this till afterwards, lest others also might use it."[29]

His duty done in Washington, Custer was ready to go back to lead the expedition against the Indians. "One reason I desire to leave is that I am called on to do more than I desire," he wrote Libbie. "The men in the Army Ring who of late had influence now are glad to hide their heads. I care not to abuse what influence I have."[30] Libbie was worried about his involvement in politics, but he tried to reassure her. "I believe I have done nothing rashly," he wrote. "And all honest straightforward men commend my course."[31]

His conscience clear, Custer turned to other thoughts. He wanted Libbie to tell Bloody Knife he had bought him a silver medal with his name engraved on it. His letters turned increasingly, as they usually did, to journalistic-type accounts of what he had seen, including descriptions of the scenery, ladies' fashion, and the theater. But he fought the temptation to have fun in order to focus on his writing. He shut himself up in his room and wrote all day to finish a *Galaxy* article. His burgeoning literary career was drawing a lot of attention, and he enjoyed receiving compliments for the work and passing them on to Libbie. Even the head of the army had noticed.

"Custer, you write so well, people think your wife does it, and you don't get credit," Sherman teased him.

"Well, General, then I ought to get the credit for my selection of a wife," Custer replied.

The committee finally released Custer, and he left for home, stopping in New York along the way, where he continued to write and to work on his publishing contacts. "I get more requests for articles from periodicals and dailies than ten writers could satisfy," he wrote Libbie. He persuaded Whitelaw Reid, publisher of the *New York Tribune*, to hire Annie Yates's brother Dick to work as a correspondent on the upcoming expedition. Yates had first met the Custers in 1870 when she was Annie Gibson and was visiting her uncle, Maj. George Gibson, the post commander. She had married Capt. George Yates, one of Custer's friends in the Seventh Cavalry.

A representative from Sheldon and Company, which was publishing *My Life on the Plains*, made a special trip to see Custer. "He is enthusiastic over my 'Galaxy' articles, and insists on my sending them in regularly," Custer told Libbie. "He will secure an English publication when the book appears here."[32]

Custer also took a side trip to see the Centennial Exposition in Philadelphia. The huge fair, which was attended by about ten million people—a fifth of the U.S. population—included a Smithsonian display of Indian artifacts. The exhibit included weapons, tipis, and canoes as well as life-size mannequins modeling Indian clothing, all to give modern Americans an idea of how their society had surpassed its aboriginal ancestors.[33] Custer told Libbie that the Smithsonian had shipped five boxcars of Indian artifacts for the exhibition, but that Spencer Baird, the museum official in charge of the display, had asked him to get a complete lodge when he returned to the West.[34]

When, or if, he would be able to go, however, was up in the air because the congressmen managing the Belknap hearings recalled

Custer. They planned to impeach Belknap, even though he had resigned to avoid an impeachment trial. The scandal was spinning out of control into partisan vindictiveness, and Custer was getting caught in it. Henry Banning called Custer to testify in front of his military affairs committee on April 18. Custer again provided hearsay testimony, criticizing Maj. Lewis Merrill for taking bribes while on Reconstruction duty with the Seventh Cavalry in South Carolina.[35] (The regiment was split at that time, and Custer was stationed in Kentucky, so he had no direct knowledge of the allegation.)

Once again, the press coverage split along partisan lines in criticizing or praising Custer. The *New York Times*, a Republican paper, hinted Custer was cooperating with the Democrats so that he could be promoted to brigadier general after the election.[36]

Although the great national drama was being fought ruthlessly by powerful journalists and politicians still bitter over the Civil War and Reconstruction, Custer thought he was in control of the part he was playing—that his strength of character and being in the right would pull him through. He was used to bad press coverage since his association with Johnson in 1866. It was expected that any public event would be viewed through the lens of politics, whether it was a battle like the Washita or a fight in the halls of Congress.

"The Radical papers continue to serve me up regularly," Custer admitted in a letter to Libbie. "Neither has said one word against Belknap." But he made a joke out of the experience. He described sitting in his assigned seat on the floor of the Senate dressed in his brother Tom's coat, pants, and vest—an outfit that the newspapers commented on. Custer joked to Libbie that he would charge Tom a fee for advertising his clothes. He bragged that Gen. John McDonald, also testifying, told him he liked his article on Bull Run. Custer asked Sherman and the new Secretary of War, Alphonso Taft, to get him released from the inquiry so he could return to his command.

Custer wrote Libbie not to worry about his actions. He knew that every move he made was watched by the press. "This only makes me more careful," he wrote.[37]

But his actions had put him on the wrong side of Grant, who in a fit of anger decided to punish Custer by removing him from command of the expedition, telling Sherman and Taft at a cabinet meeting to assign someone else.[38]

When Custer finally obtained his release from the Senate, he thought he was free to go back to Fort Abraham Lincoln. But Sherman told him he should call on Grant before he left Washington. Custer went to the White House twice, but both times Grant refused to see him, once making him wait five hours before sending word he would not see him. Custer knew he was in trouble at this time, and he sent Grant a note explaining that the president must have gotten the wrong impression. Confident in the rightness of his position and his ability to persuade through a dramatic message, he wrote, "I desired this opportunity simply as a matter of justice and I regret that the President has declined to give me an opportunity to submit to him a brief statement which justice to him as well as to me demanded."[39]

Custer's theatrics did not play to Grant, however. The men were two opposite types of soldiers that have been present throughout American history. One is the flamboyant, imaginative, and creative type, a soldier who often skirts or breaks the rules but gets things done. The other is more solid and conventional. One likes the show business side of the military, the uniforms, parades, and glory. The other provides the strategy and eschews the limelight. In this sense, Custer was to Grant as Patton was to Eisenhower—useful in combat but also a troublemaker who can become expendable. Furthermore, Grant was fiercely loyal to his family and friends, and Custer had betrayed both, and the military, by criticizing fellow officers and Grant's brother.[40]

Like a movie star who thinks a film cannot be made without him, Custer overestimated his value. He dropped off his self-righteous note and walked to the War Department, seeking Sherman. The general was not in Washington, but Randolph B. Marcy, the inspector general, gave him permission to rejoin his command. Digging his hole deeper, Custer at some point gave information to the *New York World*, a prominent anti-administration newspaper owned by his friend August Belmont, a player in Democratic politics. The story revealed details that only Custer and a few others would have known about his treatment by Grant at the White House. The story asserted Custer was removed from command for spite. The story, which was reprinted in newspapers around the country, said Sherman and Taft told Grant his decision was wrong. "Gen. Sherman went further and said Custer was not only the best man but the only man to lead the expedition now fitting against the Indians. To all their entreaties Grant turned a deaf ear and said that if they could not find a man to lead the expedition he would find one; that this man Custer had come here both as a witness and prosecutor in the Belknap matter to besmirch his reputation and he proposed to put a stop to it."[41]

The story flabbergasted both Taft and Sherman, who denied it in news stories. Sherman said the army had "hundreds" of officers who were just as qualified as Custer to lead the expedition.[42]

If the story was meant to pressure the man who defeated Robert E. Lee in the bloodiest campaign of the war, it was a spectacular failure, blowing up in Custer's face. He was stunned when his train stopped in Chicago and he received orders from Sherman (directed by Grant) that he should not have left Washington without seeing Grant and Sherman, and that the expedition would go without him. Custer telegraphed Sherman, who allowed him to proceed to department headquarters in St. Paul to await further orders.[43]

Custer's drama had created a conundrum for Sherman, Sheridan, and Alfred Terry, the commander of the Department of Dakota, whom the War Department had designated to lead the expedition after Custer's removal. All wanted Custer to participate, especially Terry, who was a lawyer by profession and had been appointed a colonel in the Union army when he raised an infantry regiment at the start of the Civil War. Terry served creditably and was promoted to brigadier general in the regular army after he had led the expedition to capture Fort Fisher in North Carolina in 1865. He stayed in the army after the war but he did not have extensive combat experience against Indians and was counting on Custer's expertise in the upcoming campaign.

Sheridan, too, had counted on Custer, his trusted, aggressive cavalry leader since the Civil War and the victor of the Battle of the Washita. Sheridan had devised a plan of three columns converging on the Indians from different directions. Brig. Gen. George Crook, forty-nine, another Sheridan Civil War protégé and a commander who had led successful Indian campaigns in the Southwest, would take about 800 men north from Fort Fetterman in Wyoming Territory. Terry would be in overall command of two columns, one of about 450 men under Col. John Gibbon, also forty-nine, heading east from Fort Ellis in western Montana Territory; the other column of almost 1,000 men to be commanded by Custer and heading west from Fort Abraham Lincoln. No one knew exactly where the villages were, but Sheridan had a solid plan with experienced commanders and plenty of troops who could trap the Indians and force them onto the reservations. Now that plan was in danger because Custer could not keep himself from creating a drama when the spotlight called.[44]

Custer the writer was effective at creating a scene and evoking emotion, but he needed a different type of writing to help him out of this jam. In tears, he asked Terry for help, and the lawyer and the cavalryman together crafted an appeal to Grant that was both humble and logical. It ended with a request that the president consider their common dedication to service: "I appeal to you as a soldier to spare me the humiliation of seeing my regiment march to meet the enemy and I not to share its dangers," said Custer.[45] They sent it to Sheridan's headquarters in Chicago, and Sheridan endorsed it and sent it to Grant, although he added that he wished Custer had avoided the controversy and that if permitted to go on the expedition he would learn to refrain from discrediting his profession and the service.[46]

Journalists also pressured Grant to restore Custer's command, accusing the president of rank partisanship and small-minded vindictiveness. Newspapers editorialized against Grant from coast to coast. The *Los Angeles Herald*, for example, wrote that Grant had a weak mind because he couldn't control his temper. Custer, on the other hand, had done his duty by testifying. "The careers of Generals Grant and Custer will bear comparison, and we have no doubt that he [Custer] fears no investigation, whether of a political or military character. The fact that any investigations into the career of the former are distasteful, to say the least, lies in the fact of this unwarranted indignation at the respectful response of General Custer to the summons of a Legislative Committee of investigation."[47]

A *New York Herald* story reported the incident with the screaming headline "Custer Sacrificed" and a subhead referring to Grant, "Caesar's Spleen."[48] In an editorial in the same issue, the *Herald* claimed that Grant's decision showed he was unfit to be president. "No formal charges are preferred against Custer, and he is disgraced simply because he did not 'crook the pregnant hinges of the knee' to this modern Caesar. At least such is the excuse, though the fact was that Custer danced attendance on the President for several hours and was refused audience. Being repulsed, he proceeded on his way to his command only to be overtaken by the telegraph like a common fugitive and humiliated by being ordered out of his train to 'await further orders.'" But history would vindicate Custer, the paper claimed. "While General Custer is to be pitied, he may console himself with the reflection that his implied disgrace cannot tarnish his reputation or injure his standing in the army, however much it may humiliate him personally for the time being. He will be considered a victim, and not a delinquent."[49]

Grant denied that he banned Custer from the expedition for partisan reasons, stating that he ordered Custer to stay in Washington only to complete his testimony. Republican newspapers generally sided with Grant and downplayed Custer's testimony as worthless. The *Hartford Courant* thought Grant did the right thing because Custer left his post when he should have been preparing for the expedition. "Had he been as anxious to attend to his duties as he was to play the gossip he would have superintended the outfit and taken command of the expedition. Being absent, the President has relieved him from duty and ordered him to report to the regiment of which he is lieutenant colonel, and will appoint some other officer to take charge of his command."[50]

With the growing public controversy and the knowledge that his commanders wanted Custer, Grant issued orders through Sherman to Terry that Custer could accompany the regiment but was not to command the expedition. Sherman told Terry, "Tell Custer to be prudent, not to take along any newspaper men, who always work mischief, and to abstain from any personalities in the future. Tell him I want him to confine his whole mind to his legitimate office, and trust to time. That newspaper paragraph in the *New York World* of May 2nd compromised his best friends here, and almost deprived us of the ability to serve him."[51]

But Custer was not like Sherman, who hated journalists ever since reporters had suggested he was insane during the Civil War. Custer knew that news coverage was as essential to a soldier as it was to an actor such as his friend Barrett. A man working in the profession of arms or the profession of the arts found purpose in doing his job as best he could, but he also needed others to witness it, to give it meaning beyond the act itself. Custer would no more go on a campaign without a journalist than he would without a horse. Both were needed to ride to glory.

As for Sherman's advice to focus exclusively on the task at hand—that was something the many-faceted Custer was able to do only when he was actively, intimately engaged in the task, whether locking himself in a room to write, leading a crowd at a convention, or attacking an enemy position. Thoughts of his myriad other interests—politics, writing, and a speaking tour such as Mark Twain's—would distract him until he was active. At that time his single-minded obsessiveness—the absorption of the artist at work—would take over.

Soon that whirlwind of focus would point tenaciously at the Sioux and Cheyenne, whom the government had decided to force onto reservations. Custer would not stop until he caught them. He expected success, as did Sheridan, Sherman, Terry, and the journalists who would report the victory. The *Dallas Herald* predicted, "Custer may be thrown into the shade during the remainder of Grant's term, but that officer's knowledge of Indians and Indian warfare will bring him to the front again."[52]

CHAPTER FOURTEEN

Custer's Last Stage

Grant had meant to put Custer in the shadows, but allowing him to go on the campaign was all the cavalryman needed. Custer, always ambitious, saw himself as the star, and certainly not a man to play second fiddle to an officer like Terry, who had no combat experience with Indians. When Custer got the news at headquarters in St. Paul, he walked down the street excitedly and ran into Capt. William Ludlow, who had served with him on the Yellowstone and Black Hills campaigns. Custer told Ludlow he had just found out he had been reinstated. Although Terry would be in overall command, Custer said, he would be able to "cut loose" and do what he wanted—just as he had while serving under David Stanley during the Yellowstone expedition.[1]

Custer became more somber when he actually had to start the campaign and leave Libbie once more. The Seventh Cavalry, numbering twelve companies, was supposed to march out of Fort Lincoln on May 14, 1876, but had been delayed by cold, wet nasty weather that made it too muddy to haul the supply wagons. They had camped in tents on the plains near the fort, waiting for the weather to cooperate, the tension building for the troops and their anxious families. On May 17 the day was overcast, but Terry ordered the command to march out with a parade to reassure the families that the regiment was strong enough to handle anything it faced. Libbie and Maggie had been camping with their husbands and rode beside them on the parade and the first day's journey from the fort. Maggie's husband, James Calhoun, was a lieutenant in the regiment through Custer's influence. Calhoun had promised Custer when he got his appointment that he would prove he could be relied on in a crisis. The wives knew this campaign could require such promises be kept.

The parade started well enough as the bandsmen played "Garry Owen" jauntily while the troopers passed in review. But the scene was darkened by the crying families of the enlisted men, who were not comforted by the martial display.[2]

"The wives and children of the soldiers lined the road," Libbie wrote. "Mothers, with streaming eyes, held their little ones out at arm's length for one last look at the departing fathers." The toddlers didn't understand why their mothers were sad, and some of them made a game out of imitating the military parade. They marched in their own ragtag column, beating on old tins for drums and using sticks with handkerchiefs tied to them for flags. The Indian scouts beat their own drums in a war song that to Libbie sounded like a funeral dirge, adding to the cacophony of melancholy lamentations.[3]

The band played the traditional "The Girl I Left Behind Me," as the regiment marched past the officers' quarters. The tune was cheerful, but the lyrics were too much for the officers' wives, who disappeared into their homes to pray and face their fears alone.

As the column marched out of the fort, Libbie noticed that the peculiar weather conditions of the sun finally breaking through the mist had created a mirage of a twin column that appeared to be marching in the heavens in tandem with the real men on the ground.[4]

Libbie, always worried about her husband when he went on campaign, felt more apprehensive that usual. "With my husband's departure my last happy days in garrison were ended, as a premonition of disaster that I had never known before weighed me down," she recalled. "I could not shake off the baleful influence of depressing thoughts." Her duty as the post commander's wife was to comfort the other families, but she found to her shame that she felt selfish and couldn't help anyone else. She could focus on nothing but her own worries.[5]

Custer, on the other, appeared to be joyous. "His buoyant spirits at the prospect of the activity and field life that he so loved made him like a boy," she wrote.[6] He told Libbie they would be reunited in a few weeks at the supply depot. A steamboat would bring supplies up the Yellowstone River, and Libbie could catch a ride and meet Custer.

If Custer had noticed the mirage, he said nothing about it to Libbie, instead commenting on how grand the soldiers looked. *Bismarck Tribune* reporter Mark Kellogg, the only full-time journalist on the campaign, noticed that Custer, looking dashing in his buckskins, seemed to be everywhere in the camp in the days before they left the fort. "Here, there, flitting to and fro, in his quick eager way, taking in everything connected with his command, as well as generally, with the keen, incisive manner for which he is so well known," Kellogg wrote. "The General is full of perfect readiness for a fray with the hostile red devils, and woe to the scalp-lifters that come within reach of himself and brave companions in arms."[7]

Kellogg, forty-three, was a telegrapher turned reporter who had never been to war. His boss, a wounded Civil War veteran named C. A. Lounsberry, had begged off going himself, claiming he had to take care of his sick wife. Lounsberry sent Kellogg, a widower with two children, in his place, giving him his Civil War pistol for protection. Kellogg's stories reflected the enthusiasm of the rookie who sees the assignment as a ticket to fame and fortune.[8]

Custer's performance for Kellogg, Libbie, and the men under his command was aimed at a specific audience. Privately, Custer was more subdued. His orderly noticed that as Custer watched Libbie ride away from the column for the last time his face was pale and he looked solemn. Custer said softly, "A good soldier has two mistresses. While he's loyal to one, the other must suffer."[9]

Custer also knew that this campaign, as he told his brother Tom, would be a tough one. He had fought the Sioux on the Yellowstone Expedition, and he predicted they would fight hard on this one.[10] Research into the mindset of soldiers reveals that virtually all experience some level of fear as they go on campaign, and the tension grows as battle approaches. When the Seventh Cavalry rode out of Fort Lincoln, everyone knew combat was not likely for days or even weeks, yet they did expect to see action at some point. For the new troopers, the feelings would have included the excitement of adventure, of the anticipation of the supreme test of manhood. They also were aware that as part of the Seventh Cavalry, they were members of the most famous Indian-fighting unit in the army and serving under its most celebrated officer. Pvt. Charles Windolph, a German immigrant, captured this feeling when he recalled that riding well-armed on a good horse made him feel proud and "ready for a fight or a frolic."[11]

A significant portion of the enlisted men in the regiment—about a quarter—had been in the service less than a year, and others were not much more experienced. About 40 percent were immigrants like Windolph, with varying levels of English comprehension. Typically, the main fears of inexperienced soldiers like these are not being able to handle combat and showing cowardice in front of their comrades.[12]

The old veterans, like Custer, would experience a different feeling as they rode toward action. The veterans had seen the wounded suffering in agony and the dead bodies of their comrades torn apart by gunfire. They went forward knowing all too well what might happen to them, and their fears more typically involved thoughts of crippling wounds. It's a mistake, a World War I veteran wrote in his memoir, to assume that a soldier becomes less fearful the longer he serves. In fact, some argue that courage is like a bank, and every man eventually draws his last draft if he is repeatedly exposed to hard combat.[13]

And the Seventh's officer corps had many combat veterans, who, like Custer, had survived a number of ferocious battles in the Civil War and against Indians. These men would know what to do in combat, but as old hands they would have their own anxieties as battle drew closer. Since his earliest days in the Civil War, Custer had mused over death in his letters home, and he admitted in the autograph book passed around at Fort Hays that his greatest fear was being killed in battle. Few men are completely fearless, but Custer, despite his reputation for physical courage and his relish for action, was not one of those. Lawrence Barrett, who knew Custer as well as anyone but Libbie, and whose acting profession would have led him to study human behavior, wrote that Custer's courage was not the "bulldog kind" that knew no fear. "His courage was purely mind over physical fear," Barrett said. Custer deliberately put himself in danger because he knew it was the way to be successful. Only from the front could he encourage his men. "He had counted the cost of success and was fully prepared to pay it," Barrett wrote. "He wanted honor or distinction among his fellow men, or death on the field."[14]

For Custer, there were many honors at stake in this campaign. He had told Tom he wanted to be promoted soon, and success in the field would be crucial in the fierce competition for the next brigadier's star awarded. He also was thinking of possible careers if this campaign was to be his last. He could write and go on the speaking tour, but he could also enter politics. His writing career was no secret, but his political ambitions, if any, were hidden. His association with Democrat politicians, journalists, and money men led to speculation later that he was angling for political office, perhaps even the presidential nomination that summer. An Arikara scout, speaking almost forty years after the battle, claimed Custer met with the scouts the night before the expedition left Fort Lincoln and told them he would become the Great White Father—president—if he won a battle. Custer, so the story goes, presented a medal to Bloody Knife and told him he would take him to the White House with him, and that he would always take care of the Arikaras.[15]

That spring Custer had bought a silver medal for Bloody Knife with his name inscribed on it,[16] but there's no known record of him discussing his political future other than the unconfirmed conversation with the scouts. That's not to say Custer did not muse about a political career. He did. His father had warned him during the Civil War about associating with Republicans as it would hurt his chances of being president one day. Custer might well have been dreaming about running for president someday, but probably not in 1876. The expedition would take him too far away from a telegraph to get news of a victory at the Democratic convention, which would be held in June. And the Democrats already had several solid possible nominees, including Samuel J. Tilden, whose reform record as New York governor was just what the public was seeking in an election with an anti-corruption theme. Still, any political career would be derailed by a military blunder. For Custer, thirty-six, and at a crossroads in his life, the campaign was indeed one of the most important of his military career.

Yet with all that was at stake, Custer kept writing professionally. The other officers, after their evening meal, would enjoy a pipe and the comfort of the fire, swapping tales or singing songs. Custer usually retired to his tent, working late into the night on articles for *Galaxy* and anonymous dispatches for the *New York Herald*.[17] The other officers took Custer's obsession in stride. Lt. Winfield Scott Edgerly, dining one night with Custer and Capt. Thomas Weir, asked him whether he wrote the article he had just finished from memory. "No, from notes I brought along," said Custer, who had planned to keep up his journalistic work on the campaign.[18] Kellogg, the full-time writer, also noticed Custer's habit. In one story he described Custer as always being in the saddle during the day, scouting, hunting, or looking for signs of Indians. The rest of the time, Custer was eating, sleeping, or writing.[19]

As he had done since West Point, Custer devoted time to composing long letters. He kept up a steady correspondence with Libbie, who in turn him apprised him of political news and coverage of the Indian wars while also evaluating his writing. She loved the *Galaxy* article that was part of the beginnings of his Civil War memoir, but she feared he had praised McClellan too much and took his side against the Republican administration. The article would cost him his friendship with Zachariah Chandler, the Republican senator from Michigan. Chandler could be a powerful enemy, she warned her husband. Nevertheless, she thought he was growing as a writer.

"You improve every time you write," she said. "There is nothing like the McClellan article for smoothness of style. I have this month's 'Galaxy' with the Yellowstone article. How fortunate you had left it with Mr. Sheldon. I am anxious about the one you sent by the Buford mail."[20]

She was also anxious about Indians. "I cannot but feel the greatest apprehension for you on this dangerous scout," she wrote to Custer. "Oh, Autie, if you return without bad news the worst of the summer will be over. The papers told last night of a small skirmish between General Crook's Cavalry and the Indians. They called it a *fight*. The Indians were very bold. They don't seem afraid of anything."[21]

The Indians had plenty of reasons to feel confident. Crook had started his column in early March, and one of his units surprised a Cheyenne village on March 17. They burned the village and captured the pony herd. But the Indians fought back, and the troopers withdrew. The Indians followed and recaptured most of their herd. Disappointed in the botched attack, and believing he had lost the element of surprise, Crook returned to Fort Fetterman to refit before heading out again at the end of May.[22]

After Crook's failed opening of the campaign, the various northern tribes began joining together for mutual defense. Their numbers swelled as agency Indians left their reservations to hunt with their roaming brethren in what was an annual migration. This confederation of bands, emboldened by their strong population and success against Crook, was further excited by a vision from Sitting Bull, a key spiritual leader of the Sioux.[23]

Sitting Bull had organized a Sun Dance for sacrifice and prayer. Jumping Bull, his adopted brother, cut fifty matchhead-size pieces of flesh from each of Sitting Bull's arms. The chief then danced for more than twenty-four hours, much of the time under a bright sun, and without taking foot or water. He eventually fainted, and when he revived, he announced that he had seen soldiers riding upside down into an Indian village. A voice proclaimed to him that the soldiers would die, but the Indians should take no spoils from them. The stirring forecast of a great victory added to the Indians' feeling of invincibility.[24]

Meanwhile, Crook had made it up to Rosebud Creek in Montana Territory. On June 17, hundreds of warriors, excited by the power of their numbers and Sitting Bull's vision, attacked Crook's column. The battle lasted most of the day before the Indians left, confident they had taught the soldiers a lesson. Crook claimed he won because he held the battlefield, but he also withdrew and then camped for the next few weeks with only feeble attempts to locate the Indian village. Crook also did not bother to send word to Terry or Custer. It would have been difficult but not impossible to send scouts to the other columns. Reporters with Crook managed to get stories back to their newspapers in the States by June 23. Information about the aggressiveness and size of the Indian force would have been helpful to Custer and the other officers, who were operating on the assumption that the Indians would not stand and fight a pitched battle.[25]

From the beginning, just about everyone involved in the campaign was confident of victory, from Sheridan down to the newest trooper, and including the reporter Kellogg, whose dispatches brimmed with praise of Custer and the army. All were focused on finding the Indians and capturing them before they could scatter. Terry had received reports that he could face as many as fifteen hundred Sioux lodges and told Sheridan that he might not have enough troops. Sheridan told him not to worry about Indian numbers but instead be concerned that they would stay together long enough to be caught. It was impossible, Sheridan told him, for any large gathering of Indians to stay together for even a week.[26] One young trooper had an equally nonchalant attitude. He was found asleep on the picket line, and his comrades told him Sitting Bull might catch him napping. The soldier hadn't even heard of the famous Sioux chief and wanted to know who was "sucking Bull"?[27]

Kellogg reported the troopers were cheerful and energized after leaving the boredom of the fort. He compared their readiness to that of their foe. "The troops are so thoroughly organized that if the Indians can be found, they will be taught a lesson that will be a lasting one to them. It is believed they intend to fight but they are no match for the force sent against them."[28]

Terry, Kellogg thought, was beloved by the officers and men because he was kind and concerned for their welfare. Whatever worries Terry had expressed to Sheridan, he impressed the reporter with his confidence, telling him he hoped the Indians would be brave enough to offer battle. Custer struck the admiring Kellogg as fearless. "His energy is unbounded," Kellogg wrote. "Fatigue leaves no traces on him, and whatever care possesses him is hidden within his inner self. His men respect him, and will dare to do brave things under his leadership."[29]

Terry admired Custer's frontier skills, especially his ability to find a trail. Lt. Edgerly recalled that Terry came up to the fire where Custer and some officers had lain down and exclaimed, "Nobody but General Custer could have brought us through such a country." Custer reveled in the praise and wrote Libbie about it. But he could also be disobedient. Terry was furious and chastised Custer when he, Tom, and his brother Boston, who had joined the command as a civilian forage master, had ridden off from the command without permission.[30] The brothers delighted in the rough teasing they had done all their lives. At one point Tom and Custer rode behind some hills, hiding from

Boston. They fired over his head to scare him. The prank was similar to the one Custer and some other officers had played on Libbie and Annie Yates years before at Fort Hays.[31]

As the command got closer to the Indians, Custer became more serious. On June 9, Terry learned from John Gibbon, who was leading troops east from Fort Ellis, that his scouts had spotted an Indian village on Rosebud Creek. The village could have moved since Gibbon found it, and Terry wanted to check the various creeks and rivers. He ordered Reno on a scout up the Powder and Tongue Rivers while Custer continued to march along the Yellowstone. In full warrior mode, Custer wanted to go straight to the area where the Indians had last been seen and he vented about it to Libbie and in a dispatch to the *Herald*.[32]

Reno angered Terry when he went beyond his orders and explored the Rosebud valley, a trip that everyone feared might alert the Indians and prompt them to scatter. Reno did discover a trail and old Indian campsites, but although he had already disobeyed his orders in going beyond his directions, he turned around instead of chasing the trail.

Custer in turn thought Reno had missed the opportunity of a lifetime. If Reno had pursued the Indians, he would have made a name for himself.[33] "I fear their failure to follow up the trails has imperiled our plans by giving the village an intimation of our presence," he wrote Libbie. "Think of the valuable time lost."[34] Custer's reaction showed both sides of his personality. He believed that when an opportunity occurs, you have to take center stage and shine. Yet he also analyzed it from the military viewpoint—speed is of the essence in pursuing Indians.

After hearing from Reno, Terry held a meeting with Custer and Gibbon on June 21 aboard the supply boat *Far West*, moored at the confluence of the Yellowstone and the Rosebud (Libbie had not been able to make the trip). The lawyer-turned-general drew up a plan that focused on catching the mobile village before the various bands could scatter. Following the lead of their division commander, Sheridan, none of the officers was worried about the number of warriors they might face. For Civil War veterans, it was like fighting rebel guerillas—the main problem was forcing them to stand and fight, where superior discipline and tactics would prevail over sheer numbers. Terry offered Custer the use of two Gatling guns—a nineteenth-century machine gun—and a battalion of the Second Cavalry. But the cumbersome Gatling guns would slow Custer, who intended to ride hard and strike fast, and he decided not to take them. The group also decided the Second Cavalry was not needed and in fact would weaken Gibbon's column. Custer, knowing from experience what was most useful in tracking Indians, did take six of Gibbon's Crow scouts, who were familiar with the region. The Crows were excited to be reassigned to Custer because they heard he would follow a trail to its end, and he was solicitous of them, often visiting their campfire to eat and talk with them.[35]

It was obvious from the composition of the columns and Terry's directives that Custer was leading the strike force that would capture the village or drive it toward the other units. Custer was in his most familiar role, one he had excelled at since the war: he would be the tip of the spear. The following morning, June 22, Terry gave Custer written orders summarizing the conversation from the previous day. The orders were based on the limited information they had about the location of the village, but everyone involved knew what they did *not* know—whether the Indians had moved the village, and if so, its new location. Terry gave Custer directions, but he included caveats because the cavalryman would need the freedom to make decisions based on what he learned. After all, Custer was the experienced Indian fighter, not Terry.

"It is, of course, impossible to give you any definite instructions in regard to this movement, and were it not impossible to do so, the Department Commander places too much confidence in your zeal, energy, and ability to wish to impose upon you precise orders which might hamper your action when nearly in contact with the enemy," Terry wrote. "He will, however, indicate to you his own views of what your action should be, and he desires that you should conform to them unless you should see sufficient reasons for departing from them."[36]

Custer was so proud of Terry's confidence in him that he quoted part of the paragraph above in a letter to Libbie, knowing she would appreciate the praise given to him. He apologized that he only had a few moments to write because he was consumed with the final preparation for the next day's march. "Do not be anxious about me," Custer wrote. "You would be surprised how closely I obey your instructions about keeping with the column. I hope to have a good report to send you by the next mail. A success will start us all toward Lincoln."[37]

Orders from Terry in hand, Custer focused on the mission. Sabers were boxed and tents stowed. The column would travel light and fast. Custer called his officers together, and he told them the pack mules would carry fifteen days' days rations so they could stay on the trail until they caught their quarry. He reorganized the Seventh by eliminating the battalion structure. Instead of the commanders of two battalions reporting to Custer, each of the twelve company commanders would report directly to him, giving him more control of the march. Two officers, Lt. Edward S. Godfrey and Capt. Myles Moylan, complained to Custer after the meeting that the mules were worn out from Reno's scout and might break down under such a heavy load.

"Well, gentlemen, you may carry what you please," Custer said, choosing not to argue or order them to do it. He had to worry about the overall mission. "You will be held responsible for your companies. The extra forage was only a suggestion, but bear this fact in mind, we will follow the trail for fifteen days unless we catch them before that time expires, no matter how far it may take us from our base of supplies. We may not see the supply steamer again."

Custer paused before leaving. "You had better carry along an extra supply of salt. We may have to live on horse meat before we get through."[38]

Here was Custer the artist becoming Custer the warrior. Like a writer or an actor, Custer spoke in dramatic terms with dramatic gestures. He created scenes and spoke in phrases that the people around him remembered clearly for years afterwards. That was his nature. Internally, his focus narrowed like a writer obsessed with finishing a story. He approached the coming battle like he did the *Galaxy* piece he finished on his most recent leave when he locked himself in his hotel room to get it done. As the political reporter noticed at the 1866 convention, *He is the thing he does.* His intensity of personality began to shift to one immediate goal—in this case capturing the Indian village.

That night he came out his tent to join Edgerly, Tom, First Lt. William W. Cooke, Boston, and his namesake nephew, Autie Reed, as they sat around the campfire smoking and telling stories. His beloved nephew, age eighteen, had come on the trip to experience the frontier. Custer had wanted to adopt him years ago and Libbie had declined, but now Custer could give him the ultimate experience of testing his manhood in battle but with the protection of his uncles. The group had apparently been discussing their prospects in the campaign.

"General, won't we step high if we do get those fellows!" Edgerly said.

"Won't we!" Custer replied. "It all depends on you young officers. We can't get those Indians without hard riding and plenty of it."[39]

The rookies, such as Boston Custer and Autie Reed, were excited. Both wrote letters home saying they expected to get some buffalo robes and Indian ponies. Boston told his mother he was confident they would catch the Indians with some hard riding. The scouts had said there were about eight hundred Indians ahead, and probably more. "But, be the number great or small, I hope I can truthfully say when I get back, that one or more were sent to the happy hunting-grounds," he wrote.[40]

The veterans had a different outlook. Custer's seriousness and the knowledge of what lay ahead affected the men and officers who knew what to expect from a battle. A number of them wrote what they thought might be their last letters home, made out their wills, or gave instructions to comrades on handling their possessions if they died. Cooke and Charley Reynolds, a veteran scout and one of Custer's favorites, both told other soldiers they thought they would be killed.[41]

Terry and Gibbon were also anxious. What better tonic than a review of the troops before they left? The event was arranged, and at noon on June 22 the Seventh Cavalry marched in front of Terry, Gibbon, and some other officers. Custer led the parade and then rode up to Terry to watch with his colleagues. The performance of military ceremonies, the showmanship, was something Custer always enjoyed. Everyone thought the regiment looked in fine shape, and Gibbon remarked on the high quality of the horses. After the last trooper rode past, Custer shook hands with the officers as he gave his farewells.

Gibbon, half-jokingly, said, "Now Custer, don't be greedy but wait for us."

"No, I will not," Custer said with a laugh, and rode off to lead his command, leaving Gibbon and the others to ponder whether he meant he would not be greedy, or whether he would not wait. Some thought Custer the practical joker was teasing. More likely, it was just a reflexive response he tossed off without thinking. He was focused on his duty—finding the village.[42]

Custer and the Seventh marched twelve miles that afternoon and halted about 4 P.M. At sunset Custer called his officers to a meeting. Godfrey remembered that everyone was in a serious mood. Custer's manner was unusually subdued. From this point forward, Custer said, bugle calls would only be permitted in an emergency. He would regulate only two things from his headquarters—when to move out (5 A.M. every morning) and when to halt for the day, which would depend on circumstances. He expected his commanders, who he acknowledged were experienced officers, to take care of the details of their commands and to keep them within supporting distance of each other.[43]

Custer told the officers they might face as many as fifteen hundred warriors. He explained that he had declined the offer of the Second Cavalry battalion because its presence would have created jealousy between the two regiments. He had declined the Gatling guns because the guns would slow them down. He warned the officers to husband their rations as they might be on the trail longer than expected. "He intended to follow the trail until we could get the Indians, even if it took us to the Indian agencies on the Missouri River or Nebraska," Godfrey recalled.

Custer, who had stressed the importance of the loyalty of the officers throughout the meeting, concluded by requesting them to make any suggestions to him at any time. The officers then synchronized their watches and went to attend to their duties. Custer's talk unsettled them.

"In it he showed a lack of self-confidence, a reliance on somebody else; there was an indefinable something that was not Custer," Godfrey remembered. "His manner and tone, usually brusque and aggressive, or somewhat rasping, was on this occasion conciliating and subdued. There was something akin to an appeal, as if depressed, that made a deep impression on all present."

Godfrey and two other young officers, Lt. George Wallace and Lt. Donald McIntosh, walked for some distance in silence, wondering what the meeting signified.

Wallace said finally, "Godfrey, I believe General Custer is going to be killed."

"Why, Wallace, what makes you think so," Godfrey asked.

"Because I have never heard Custer talk in that way before," Wallace said.

Godfrey went to check on the horse and mule herd and ran into the scouts, who were talking around their campfire. Half-Yellow-Face, the chief of the Crow scouts, told Mitch Bouyer, an interpreter who was half Sioux, to ask Godfrey a question.

"Have you ever fought against these Sioux?" Bouyer asked.

Godfrey, who had been on the Black Hills expedition, said he had.

When Bouyer asked him how many Indians he thought they would fight against, Godfrey repeated Custer's estimate.

"Well, do you think we can whip that many?" Bouyer asked.

"Oh yes, I guess so," Godfrey said.

Bouyer interpreted the conversation for the Crow and Ree scouts.

Turning to Godfrey, he said emphatically, "Well, I can tell you we are going to have a big fight."[44]

As promised, at 5 the next morning the regiment was on the move. In eight miles they found the remains of a large Indian campsite. It included many wickiups—small bushes with canvas covers thrown over them. Godfrey and the others assumed they were dog shelters. They were actually temporary lodges for warriors from the agencies who were joining their kinsmen. The column passed through two more of those sites before halting about 5 P.M. after a march of more than thirty miles.[45]

They had struck Reno's trail, and they followed it another thirty miles on June 24. They also found the Sioux Sun Dance site, which included signs of powerful medicine, such as a white man's scalp. Custer's scouts started to get nervous. The column passed through many successive Indian campsites. It looked like one village that was moving constantly. In reality, they were individual camps converging into one gigantic village. The trail now looked fresh, and the valley they marched through was scratched by lodge poles dragged by the Indian ponies.[46]

That night, the Crow scouts rode into camp with exciting news. The trail veered west, toward the Little Bighorn. Custer's quarry was hardly a day's ride away. He called his officers to a meeting at about 9:30, just after some of them had lain down to sleep. It was so dark they had to grope their way to Custer's tent. Fixated on the village, Custer told them to be ready to march at midnight. They would approach under cover of darkness and rest that day while scouts found the exact location of the village. They would then attack at dawn on the 26th and catch the Indians by surprise. Gibbon was supposed to be at the mouth of the Little Bighorn and would be near enough to provide support.[47]

After an exhausting night march, the troopers halted at 2 A.M. At dawn the camp stirred. They brewed coffee, but the water was so alkaline it was almost impossible to drink. Custer, riding around the camp bareback, stopped at the various companies to tell them to be ready to march at 8 A.M. Just before the march, Godfrey rode to Custer's camp. The general, Bloody Knife, some other scouts, and an interpreter were squatting in a circle. Custer was preoccupied and looked serious. Bloody Knife said something that caught Custer's attention. He asked the interpreter sharply, "What's that he says?"

The interpreter told him Bloody Knife said they would find enough Sioux to keep them fighting for two or three days.

Custer smiled and said, "I guess we'll get through them in one day."[48]

At about this time, Custer received a message from Lt. Charles Varnum, the officer in charge of the scouts, that they had spotted smoke and the Indian pony herd from a peak called the Crow's Nest. Custer rode off to check it out himself. When he arrived, he couldn't see the pony herd or any signs of the village. The scouts tried to point it out, but he couldn't see it.

"I've been on the prairie for many years," Custer said. "I've got mighty good eyes, and I can't see anything that looks like Indian ponies."[49]

Bouyer, the interpreter, was adamant that there was a huge village ahead.

"If you don't find more Indians in that valley than you ever saw together before, you can hang me," he said.

Custer laughed. "It would do a damn sight of good to hang you wouldn't it?" he said.

Custer, like many men, swore lustily in battle. But he had mellowed since the Civil War and usually kept his word to Libbie that he avoided such language. His use of the mild profanity stuck in Varnum's mind because the only other time he had heard Custer swear was during the fight with the Sioux on the Yellowstone.[50] Libbie always wanted him to minimize risks, in order to return home to her. A letter from her was on its way to him, telling him she had dreamed of him the night before. She closed by writing, "Your safety is ever in my mind. My thoughts, my dreams, my prayers are all for you. God bless and keep my darling."[51] But Libbie was four hundred hard miles of trail away. With the intense concentration of a writer on deadline, Custer was focused on finishing the project. Safety, home, Libbie—everything else was pushed aside.

And he was so close. He had the village almost in his grasp. The final act would be a surprise attack from different directions. Just like at the Washita, it would panic the Indians. If he didn't catch the whole village, he could take prisoners that would convince the rest to report to the agencies.

But he had one problem. The scouts told him they had seen three different groups of Sioux warriors. Some of them must have headed to the village to sound the alarm. Custer rode back to the camp, and Tom greeted him with more bad news. A sergeant and some troopers had gone back on the trail to recover a box of hardtack that had fallen off a mule. They found some Indians opening it and the two groups exchanged shots.[52]

It looked like the battle had already begun. If that was the case, the warriors would fight a delaying action while the village scattered into small, mobile bands. Instead of the end of the campaign, this fight would mark the beginning of a frustrating pursuit that would last all summer with no guarantee of ending the war. It would be Hancock's Expedition all over again.[53]

Custer was alone in command. His instinct had always been to hit hard, going back to the time he had rammed his fist through a school window to slug a boy who was taunting him. This instinct had been honed through years as a cavalryman: assess the situation quickly, and attack immediately if action is warranted. On June 25, all of his information showed that he had been spotted. The village would scatter as soon as it was alarmed. Custer thus ordered an immediate march toward the village. He would learn the exact location and then plan the assault.[54]

At about noon Custer called a halt to organize the command for the approach to the village, as he knew it was close. Custer assigned Capt. Fredrick Benteen three companies of about 125 men each (Companies D, H, and K) to scout the hills to the left. That would ensure there were no Indians to the rear of the command as they approached the village and would catch any who might even now be fleeing in that direction. Capt. Thomas McDougal was assigned about 135 men (Company B) to guard the pack train, which would follow. Custer and Reno took the remainder—three companies (A, G, and M) of about 140 men for Reno and five companies (C, E, F, I, and L) of about 225 for Custer, each marching on a side of a creek that they hoped would lead them to the village.[55]

One of the Crows, Half-Yellow-Face, told Custer through Bouyer that he should not divide the command.

"There are too many of the enemy for us, even if we stay together," Half-Yellow-Face said. "If you must fight, keep us all together."

"You do the scouting, and I will attend to the fighting," Custer said. Custer admired his scouts, but the fighting was his job. Dividing the command had worked for the great Southern general Robert E. Lee several times during the Rebellion, and for Custer at the Washita. It would work here. An artist controls his own creation, not his assistant.

The scout stripped and painted his face. Custer asked him why he did that.

"Because you and I are going home today, and by a trail that is strange to both of us," the scout said.[56]

Custer and Reno marched on for about ten miles. They stopped at an Indian campsite with a tipi containing the body of a warrior.[57] The interpreter Fred Gerard was on a small hill just to the north of the tipi. Gerard could see a group of Indians in the distance riding their horses and throwing up dust.

Gerard waved his hat to get attention. "Here are your Indians, General, running like devils," he shouted.[58]

Custer and Reno picked up the pace. They rode three miles till coming to a fork in the creek. Custer could see dust rising from behind the hills screening the Little Bighorn valley. He had found the village. He knew the Indians were running away. It was time to attack.[59]

Custer told his adjutant, Cooke, to order Reno to move forward rapidly and then charge the village. Cooke told Reno he would be supported by the rest of the outfit.

Reno moved forward, but he didn't charge the village. Mounted warriors came out of the village to meet the attack. The cavalry had taken them by surprise, but they weren't running. Today, flushed with the power of their numbers and Sitting Bull's vision, they would stand and fight.

Reno, fearful of his command being overwhelmed, dismounted his men in a skirmish line. Under growing pressure from the warriors, he moved the command into a grove of cottonwood trees. Reno was a veteran of hard combat during the Civil War. At Williamsport, his horse had been shot and fell on him. He had been breveted for gallantry and meritorious service. But at the Little Bighorn, with hundreds of Indians closing in on his small command, he became confused and indecisive. He ordered the troopers to mount up and get ready to break out. Bloody Knife, standing close to Reno, was hit in the head. The shot splattered blood and gore in Reno's face. The screaming Indians, the cries of the wounded and dying, the confusion, heat, and dust—it must have seemed as if he were at the gates of hell itself with howling demons trying to drag him in. Isolated from the rest of the command, feeling abandoned, Reno panicked. He ordered the troopers to dismount. Then he ordered them to mount again and he led a wild retreat to the hills beyond the Little Bighorn.[60]

Custer had no idea his friend and favorite scout and been killed and that his second-in-command had lost his senses to the stress of combat. Custer had stopped to water his horses while Reno had headed toward the village. While he was waiting, Gerard came up with news from Reno's command that the Indians were not running from Reno but were coming out to give battle. Daniel Kanipe, a first sergeant in Tom Custer's company, also reported they had seen some fifty mounted warriors on the bluffs to the right of the command.[61]

The news of the warriors on the bluffs accelerated the instincts of men already in attack mode. Custer ordered a fast trot up the slope.[62] He would hit the village from another angle, just like at the Washita.

After riding about a mile, they halted at the top of a hill. For the first time, Custer could see the full size of the village, and it was the biggest one he had ever seen in his ten years on the Great Plains. He could also see the beginning of Reno's engagement. Hundreds of warriors were rushing out to meet the dismounted skirmish line. It did not look like Reno would make the charge he had been ordered to do. The whole regiment had to get into the fight immediately. A few horses got excited and carried their riders ahead. Custer, always aware of the impact of his performance in front of the troops, made a joke.[63]

"Boys, hold your horses," Custer said. "There are plenty of them down there for us all."

Through Tom Custer he ordered Kanipe to hurry back and get Capt. McDougal to rush the pack train to the front. If any packs got loose, he was to cut them off rather than waste time fixing them. If he saw Benteen, he was to tell him come forward fast.[64]

Custer then ordered his command forward along the bluffs. The ride was difficult, so he called a halt. Custer and Cooke waved their hats at Reno's troops, who were engaged in the valley. Some hard fighting today and the campaign would be over. Custer knew he could go home to Libbie, and a new future. All his combat experience taught him that the moment called for drama. Turning toward his men, Custer shouted their reward, and his:

"Courage, boys, we've got them!" he yelled. "We'll finish them up and then go home to our station."

The men drew confidence from Custer, just as his soldiers did during the war. They cheered loudly.[65]

Custer turned the command down toward Medicine Tail Coulee, which led to the Little Bighorn river and would provide a way to attack the village. He halted to send a more explicit message to Benteen to ensure the command would work in concert. He had Cooke write a message for trumpeter Giovanni Martini to deliver: "Benteen. Come on. Big Village. Be Quick. Bring Packs. W. W. Cooke. P.S. bring pacs [sic]."

On his way to Benteen, Martini ran across Boston Custer, who was racing to join his brothers. From Boston, Custer would have learned that Benteen was following the trail to join the rest of the command. Custer's main attack would be much more powerful with Benteen's companies, and almost the whole regiment would be in action.

But the rest of the regiment was not acting as Custer expected. Reno's panicked retreat from the woods had turned into what the excited warriors later remembered as a buffalo hunt. The troopers, riding for their lives, had offered little resistance as they splashed across the river and up the steep hills. Warriors shot them and clubbed them from their horses. About forty of Reno's men were killed—including Bloody Knife and Charley Reynolds—and another thirteen were wounded.[66] When the remnants of the broken mob reached the relative safety of a hilltop, it was capable of little else other than to fight for its own survival.

Benteen's command had suffered nothing more than some up- and down-hill riding when he received Custer's pointed command to come quick to the battlefield. Benteen had been riding without a sense of urgency, believing his mission to scout the hills was senseless.[67]

Benteen picked up the pace only slightly after getting Martini's message. As the soldiers approached the battlefield, they began to hear gunfire and could see smoke and dust from grassfires and Indians riding around a few troopers in the valley—some of Reno's stragglers. A desperate Reno greeted Benteen when his command reached the hilltop where the survivors had gathered. Reno had lost his hat and had a handkerchief tied around his head.

"For God's sake, Benteen, halt your command and help me," Reno said. "I've lost half my men."[68]

Reno, the senior officer, was in command in name only. The unrattled Benteen took over, exerting leadership through the force of his personality. Neither man, however, made a move to follow Custer's orders to "come quick." Reno instead went on a fruitless attempt to recover the body of his friend and adjutant, Benjamin Hodgson, who had been killed crossing the river.

Many of the junior officers gathered on the edge of the bluff to study the valley, where they saw a number of Indian horsemen. Suddenly the Indians started heading in the direction that the soldiers had last seen Custer. Hardly a rider was left in the valley before them.[69]

Reno fired a revolver at the Indians as they rode off, but they were way out of range. The soldiers could see a few warriors on foot killing and scalping the wounded left in the valley. Old men and women came out of the village and went to work mutilating the corpses. A sergeant asked Reno to detail a rescue mission to save the wounded, and Reno told him to feel free to do it himself.[70]

They could hear gunfire coming from Custer's direction, and someone in the group of junior officers said the command should do something or Custer would be after Reno with a sharp stick.

They heard two distinct volleys of gunfire, much louder than the other sounds of battle. Could it be a signal? Or was Custer just hotly engaged?

"Custer is giving it to them for all he is worth," someone else said.[71]

A general military principle is to march to the sound of the guns. But the only help Custer would get from Reno was a potshot at the hordes of warriors rushing his way.[72]

Custer, at the top of the bluff looking toward Medicine Tail Coulee, assumed that his subordinates would follow his orders. He made his final plans. Custer sent Capt. George Yates with two companies—about seventy-five troopers—down Medicine Tail Coulee to find a ford for the crossing. Capt. Myles Keogh dismounted the remaining three companies—including Calhoun's Company L—on the ridgeline, where they could cover Yates's rear and await Benteen's reinforcements.[73]

Indians at the ford drove back Yates with sharp fire. As his command retreated back uphill, Yates kept the Indians at bay with fire from a dismounted skirmish line. When Yates's men arrived at the ridge, Custer took command of the two companies and led them along the ridge moving northwest toward the river. There was no sign of Benteen or Reno, and he was being pressed by increasing numbers of warriors. If he could find another river crossing at the end of the village, he could capture prisoners as he had at the Washita and gain the upper hand.

But the warriors swirled around the soldiers in increasing numbers, hiding in the ravines and coulees that covered the area. They would dart up to fire guns or shoot arrows at the troopers and then disappear. Warriors also fiercely attacked Keogh's command. The warriors drove off the soldiers' horses, leaving the dismounted cavalrymen fighting desperately for their lives. Sheer numbers overwhelmed them. Keogh was killed. Calhoun, too, died trying to hold the line for Custer, proving he could be counted on when the crisis came. The few survivors made their way on foot toward Custer and the other two companies.

They knew now it was a fight for survival. The warrior numbers had grown to the point that they outnumbered the soldiers by as much as ten to one. Custer's goal was to hold out for rescue from Benteen and Reno.

The general did not panic. He was not fearless, as his friend Barrett knew and as the balloonist Lowe saw when he took Custer up in the air when he was a young officer. But the fear Custer experienced was, as for all commanders in battle, mitigated by knowing he was responsible for the mission and for the lives of his men.[74] Chaos was all around him: screaming men, pounding horse hooves, gunfire so loud Reno's men could hear it three miles away. The dust was so thick on this hot June afternoon that he would have had trouble recognizing the men near him.

For Custer, it was a familiar maelstrom. The anxiety of planning the attack and the fear leading up to battle were gone as he became swept up in the mechanical aspects of fighting that he knew so well. He had been here before. At Trevilian Station, surrounded by rebels, he had wondered where in the hell the rear was. He had brought his command out of that; he could do it again. And like Kidder and Elliott, who had died fighting in their own last stands in Kansas and at the Washita, he would circle up and fight to the end. There was no surrender when fighting Indians, and in any case, Custer would not have given up. He learned watching Hancock at Williamsburg that he would rather die fighting than be dishonored.

There was no cover on the hill, so Custer ordered the men to shoot some of the horses to create a makeshift fort. He had been using a pistol while he was mounted, and he shot his own horse, pulled out his Remington sporting rifle, and lay behind the body. An experienced combat veteran, he made himself as low as possible as he fired deliberately but quickly at the enemy. He was a good shot, as he had shown the tourists who had visited him for buffalo hunts in Kansas. But the dust from the battle and smoke from the guns made it hard to see. With sweat running into his eyes, it would have been difficult to aim well enough to hit the warriors who hid in the tall grass and ravines. One warrior in an elaborate feather headdress popped up, making a clear target. Custer drilled him in the forehead. But one steady shot could not fight off thousands of warriors.[75]

Arrows flew into the little fort like modern-day mortars, killing and wounding the men, who instinctively huddled together, trying to draw courage from each other, especially from Custer and the other fierce leaders, Tom Custer and Cooke. Eventually Custer ran out of ammunition for the rifle, and the fire from the fort slackened as few troopers remained alive or strong enough to fire a gun.

The warriors sensed the fight was almost over and rushed the hill. A group of about ten troopers rushed downhill to try to escape. Custer stood alone. One warrior remembered he looked like a sheaf of corn with all the ears fallen around him. Custer drew his pistols and fired repeatedly at the charging warriors as the battle turned to close combat. He shot a warrior dead. He aimed at another warrior coming at him but felt the sickening click of the hammer hitting an empty chamber. He was out of bullets.[76]

It was a ridiculous situation, the kind played so expertly by the comedian Clarke, who had driven Libbie and Custer into fits of laughter when they went to the theater as newlyweds. Custer had been the hero of ferocious battles in the Civil War, with the country's very existence at stake and hundreds of thousands of men filling the air with shot and shell. He had been wounded slightly, hit by spent bullets, and survived hand-to-hand combat. Presidents, Russian royalty, and famous actors had wanted to be near him, the media had lionized him, and most importantly, his wife had adored him. Now he was going to die with empty pistols in a skirmish on an unnamed hill two day's ride from the nearest telegraph. It wasn't like dying in a charge at Gettysburg. Like all Indian army veterans, he knew the public would quickly forget this particular fight.

Always appreciative of a good practical joke, Custer laughed. Several warriors fired at Custer. One bullet struck his chest, knocking him down. It was a mortal wound, but Custer, refusing to give up, struggled to his hands and knees. With the automatic memory of so much combat, he pulled the trigger on the empty pistol. Then, as in Annie Roberts Yates's nightmare, one bullet struck him in the temple. He died fighting.[77]

Three miles away, on the bluff, a few junior officers began on their own initiative to move their commands toward the gunfire. They could see horsemen riding around and shooting at objects on the ground. The warriors spotted them and quickly chased them back to their shelter.

As the resistance ended on Custer's hill, the Indians begin the ritual mutilation of the dead and the robbing of the bodies of clothes and possessions. Indian women rushed to the hill to join the warriors in the slaughter, finishing off the wounded and sometimes scalping or mutilating the soldiers while they were still alive.

After a siege of Reno's command the next day, and sniping at the survivors of the Seventh Cavalry, the Indians packed up the village and moved on. Terry's command arrived and told the survivors the horrific news. Custer and all his men were dead. They went over the field, trying to figure out what had happened, as they buried the bodies.

Godfrey remembered that many of the corpses had a pained, terrified look on their faces. Not so Custer, whose body was stripped but not scalped or dismembered, as were many of the others. "He laid on his back, his upper arms on the ground, the hands folded or so placed as to cross the body above the stomach," Godfrey wrote. "His position was natural and one that we had seen hundreds of time while [he was] taking cat naps during halts on the march."[78]

Custer had died the way he wanted to, with honor. In death, Custer had fulfilled the prophecy he had scrawled in his notebook so many years ago when he was studying to be a teacher at the McNeely Normal School. Custer had copied the first two lines of the poem "Ambition" by Nathaniel Parker Willis.

The poem opened by describing ambition as a cheat that sneaked into a gifted boy's home. Because Custer was a student with big dreams, those lines had resonated with him. But there were many more lines to the poem than Custer had copied. Willis wrote that ambition, after entering the boy's room, suddenly expands the walls so the boy could see the stars, and then ambition's fingers clutched him. Soon, it is all he can think of. He pursues it his whole life. He finally attains the rewards of money or fame. But ambition eventually sends him "stripped and naked to the grave."[79]

CHAPTER FIFTEEN

Forgotten Honor

Custer's lifelong ambition for greatness, fueled by his artist's need to be recognized, had led him to craft a public character of such a distinct, charismatic image that his death is more famous than that of any American soldier killed in battle before or since.

Custer thought there was no glory in Indian fighting compared to what he had experienced in the Civil War. The fame he got for the Battle of the Washita was tempered in equal measure by his infamy for civilian casualties. He knew it would be the same for his last campaign even if he had won a great victory. But the news of his disastrous last battle, which stood in such contrast with his image of the invincible cavalryman, was so stunning that it seared a place into the nation's consciousness that remains to this day.

Custer's death and the near-destruction of the Seventh Cavalry was the kind of news event that happens once in a generation. The Little Bighorn was as unbelievable as the sinking of the *Titanic*, as thorough a defeat as Pearl Harbor, and as infuriating as 9/11.

There had been nothing like it in American history, nor is there likely to be again. At the Little Bighorn, a famous war hero who was also a popular celebrity and writer was killed with all his men in a desperate fight against overwhelming odds. The "last stand" narrative is a standard trope of Western culture dating back to the Spartans at Thermopylae, so the Little Bighorn had a built-in storyline that guaranteed some notoriety.[1] There had been other last stands in American history. The Little Bighorn is different because of Custer. No other last stands had the perfect mixture of celebrity, heroism, and myth that came together at the Little Bighorn.

Capt. William J. Fetterman and his command of eighty men were all killed near Fort Phil Kearny only ten years before. Fetterman, however, was not a celebrity, and the battle was quickly forgotten. The closest comparison to Custer's death is Davy Crockett's fate at the Alamo. Crockett was a famous congressman who, like Custer, had written a popular memoir of his frontier adventures. But Crockett was not a professional soldier leading the U.S. Army's elite unit. Crockett was a Tennessean who was a newcomer to the Texas Revolution. He shared top billing in the Alamo story with William B. Travis and Jim Bowie. The Alamo is not known as Crockett's Last Stand.

Not so the Little Bighorn, whose battlefield was later known as the Custer National Battlefield—the only one in the country named after an individual—until Congress renamed it in 1991. Yet "Last Stand" in the United States still means Custer's Last Stand. To this day, when soldiers and journalists look for some historical reference point for a fight against the odds, they use Custer. When an American convoy was overrun by Iraqi forces during the battle of Nasiriyah in a famous incident in 2003, one soldier said he felt like Custer.[2]

Why did the Little Bighorn take such a lasting place in American culture? It wasn't a particularly bloody or militarily significant battle. A little over three hundred troopers and civilian workers were killed at the Little Bighorn; the Union Army suffered more than twenty-three thousand casualties at Gettysburg. And in comparison to other shocking events such as Pearl Harbor and 9/11, the Little Bighorn had relatively little impact on U.S. history. Although the Sioux and their allies won a great victory, it hardly delayed their eventual subjugation to government authority. U.S. casualties were easily replaced, and the army continued its relentless pursuit of the allied tribes with the added incentive of revenge and a prudent caution born of hard experience. Within a year most of the bands had surrendered, and Sitting Bull led a remnant to exile in Canada. (He would surrender six years later and wind up performing for a time in Buffalo Bill's Wild West show.)

It's all the more remarkable that Custer's story became legendary because it had to survive an initial wave of cynical spinning by partisans in an election year and blame-shifting by army generals and the commander-in-chief, Grant.

The first news stories, delayed because of the distance of the battlefield from the nearest telegraph office, landed like a thunderbolt for most Americans on July 6, amid the height of year-long celebrations of the country's centennial. The contrast between how Americans saw themselves—as a young, vibrant military and industrial power—with the Little Bighorn's humbling of the U.S. Army by a shrinking, nomadic population still living in shelters made of animal skins—was almost too much to comprehend.

The centennial fair in Philadelphia, visited by thousands of Americans, had featured displays of tribal life and culture as if Indians had already been banished to historical study. A San Francisco newspaper, writing on June 26 about the history of the telegraph, captured the optimistic mood of the country by predicting that the technology would reduce the occurrence of war by promoting understanding among the peoples of the world. In such a modern age, how could Custer have been defeated?[3]

Many Americans, including Sherman and Sheridan, could not believe the initial reports, thinking they must have been exaggerated. The *New York Times* admitted in an editorial that the war was so far removed from everyday life for most Americans that they had forgotten it was going on until they heard the news of Custer. "Horrible!," "Butchered Boys," and "An Awful Slaughter" were typical headlines screaming across front pages around the country. The battle dominated American news pages for the next month.[4]

One of the first questions to be answered was "Who was to blame?" Since Custer was the commander on the scene, the ultimate responsibility was his, as he well understood from the time he had witnessed Hancock's risky decisions at the Battle of Williamsburg. Hancock's choice paid off; Custer's did not. Custer had solid reasons for his decisions, and he was operating under intense time pressure. There were mitigating circumstances to consider, and more facts to be gathered. But daily journalism can't wait for nuance, especially when covering such an explosive story.

Sherman defended Custer, saying he probably had good reasons for splitting his command. But other military leaders quickly threw Custer under the streetcar. Sheridan, who had told his officers not to worry about the numbers of Indians they would face, said the defeat was an unnecessary sacrifice caused by a misunderstanding coupled with too much courage. Terry, the lawyer who needed Custer's Indian-fighting expertise, had given him wide discretion in his final orders. But after the defeat, Terry wrote a report to Sheridan—quickly published by the press—that Custer was surprised and paid for his mistakes with his life. Grant, who had ordered thousands of men to their deaths in fruitless assaults during the war—especially at Cold Harbor—had the temerity to say Custer's actions were a waste of troops.[5]

Grant was no longer a soldier but a politician, and his comments reflected another key early part of the story—its value for politicians to attack the opposing party. American newspapers in 1876 were proudly partisan, identifying clearly—sometimes with a banner on the front page—with the Democratic or Republican parties. Because 1876 was a presidential election year, Custer and Grant became convenient symbols for their party's share of the blame for the Little Bighorn. Republican newspapers tended to emphasize Custer's foolishness in attacking such a large village. Democratic newspapers attacked Grant for sending Custer to battle without enough troops, which they claimed he had kept in the South to enforce Reconstruction and ensure that the Southern states voted Republican. In the sensational style of the day, journalists used evocative language to attack their political enemies. The Republican *Commonwealth* (Topeka), for example, said Custer was as arrogant as rebels who thought one Southerner could whip five Yankees, and the *Chicago Inter-Ocean* accused Custer of "madcap haste, rashness, and love of fame" that cost his life and those of his men.[6]

Democratic newspapers were even harsher toward Grant, frequently writing vicious copy like that of the *Dallas Daily Herald*, which screamed that the administration was "dripping with the blood of Custar [sic] and his men." A number of Democratic newspaper editorials darkly suggested that Grant had set Custer up to be killed so that he could no longer provide testimony about administration corruption. The typical argument went that not only did Custer have too few troops, but the administration had supplied the Indians with superior weapons as part of their reservation annuities. The *Louisville Courier-Journal*, edited by Custer's friend Henry Watterson, went so far as to suggest that a rifle Grant had presented at the White House to Sitting Bull might have been the weapon used to kill Custer. (It turned out that a completely separate Indian named Sitting Bull had visited the White House, so subsequent stories proved Grant was at least innocent on that score.)[7]

But after about a month of intense coverage, the country moved on to other topics such as Reconstruction, the economy, and the election. Although opinion differed on who was to blame for the Little Bighorn and how to treat the Indian population (suggestions ranged from extermination to full citizenship) the Indian war faded as a political issue. The public was united in the opinion that because American troops had been killed and the country humiliated, the war *had* to be won, regardless of whether the Indians were justified in their anger at treaty violations.

The election instead turned on Reconstruction. Republican Rutherford B. Hayes eked out a one-vote margin in the electoral college with enough political shenanigans that Southerners threatened to restart the Civil War. After much tense negotiation, the Democrats accepted Hayes, but the Republicans agreed to end military rule in the South. After ten years of fruitless violence, the country had caught up to the opinion of Custer, who had been mocked for his support of Johnson in 1866 and the return of the Southern states to the Union.[8]

Amid the rage, grief, shock, and debate over who to blame and how to move forward, it took an arts critic to fully understand why Custer's story would be remembered long after the other concerns of 1876 were forgotten. Andrew Wheeler, who wrote under the pen name Nym Crinkle, immediately recognized that the blend of art and real adventure in Custer's life ensured him a permanent place in American culture as the embodiment of the frontiersman and Indian fighter. Wheeler was known as a merciless critic. Custer's friend, soprano Clara Louise Kellogg, was once so upset with one of Wheeler's reviews that she confronted him in person about it.[9]

Wheeler, writing about *My Life on the Plains*, sniffed that Custer wrote only "good newspaper English" and sprinkled his memoir with dime novel clichés. But he admitted that the simple writing was part of the book's charm and made it authentic. Americans had always been interested in the frontier, Wheeler wrote, and that interest was stoked by fiction. Custer, however, was the fictional hero brought to life and popularized by his own memoir. With his long hair and buckskin suits, tearing across the plains on his thoroughbred horse accompanied by a pack of staghounds, Custer was an exciting character enlivening a boring age.

Wheeler wrote, "And when at last he fell in battle fighting against the odds and surrounded by his comrades he crowned the story of his life with so fit a death that it will be many years ere his name fades from its place in history and literature—if it ever fades and does not rather become enduring in popular tradition like that of [Kit] Carson or [Daniel] Boone."[10]

Wheeler had recognized what the political journalist had seen ten years earlier when Custer seized control of the crowd at the Soldiers and Sailors Convention: *He is the thing he does.* It was a truism for solders in the Indian-fighting army that they would never win glory, but Custer's dramatic death proved that idea false. Custer forever after was the symbol of the heroic frontier soldier—underpaid, underappreciated, and serving in hostile lands to help the country grow across the continent.

Others besides Wheeler saw the artistic possibilities in Custer's life. Walt Whitman wrote a poetic eulogy for the warrior "of the flowing hair in battle" who was most glorious in defeat because he sacrificed himself for the country. In fact, so much poetry was written after the battle that one newspaper joked that Custer was lucky he was killed so he wouldn't have to read all the bad poetry written about him. Humor, in fact is one way events are preserved in memory, and the flip side of Custer's tragedy provided opportunities for wisecracks about arrogance that resonate to this day. One newspaper wrote, less than two weeks after the news was first reported, that "Custer's death was Sioux-icide."[11]

What lingered was the general consensus that Custer was a hero despite his faults. The *New York Herald* started collecting money for a monument fund and editorialized that "the underlying thought in this massacre is duty and valor. General Custer sought this duty like a true man and performed it like a brave man. These are qualities we can never honor too much in this hard, mean, money-grubbing age. Even those who would criticise the judgment of Custer, or who would think if they had been there they would have done so much better, will not deny him the highest qualities of manhood and soldier-ship."[12]

Custer's Last Stand was indeed a grand story that took on a life of its own. The story was also undeniably advanced by Libbie, who in her widowhood continued the magical synergy she had enjoyed with Custer during their marriage. She promoted his image with the savvy and media skills she had used to encourage his writing and cultivate professional relationships for him.

Libbie reacted to Custer's death with the same type of forced courage he used when he entered battle. She faced her fear, focused on the task at hand, and plunged ahead. She had had a terrible feeling about the expedition since Custer left Fort Lincoln. The day of the battle, which was a Sunday, Libbie and some of the other women met to sing hymns, as was their habit. Although they had no knowledge of the battle, a gloomy feeling kept them from finding any comfort. One woman suggested they sing "Nearer My God to Thee." Another woman couldn't stand the thought and said, "No, not that one, dear."[13]

About a week later, on the Fourth of July, the wives sat together on a porch listening to music and trying to stay cool in the summer heat. An Indian scout came up and excitedly told them that Custer and his whole command had been killed. He had heard it from a scout who had just ridden to the fort. The women, as army wives, understood first reports were often exaggerated, and they dismissed it as probably a skirmish. Nevertheless, they expected something terrible had happened. They spent a restless night.[14]

Official word came to the interim post commander, Capt. William McCaskey, at 2 A.M., when he opened a message brought from the *Far West*, the supply ship that had carried the wounded downriver to Bismarck. Accompanied by the post surgeon and other officers, he went to Libbie's house first because she was the commander's wife. Libbie and Maggie and Custer's niece Emma Reed, who were staying at the house, wept as McCaskey read Terry's dispatch.

Libbie knew her duty as the post commander's wife was to inform the twenty-five other women that they were now widows. Even though it was summer, she put on a shawl and went outside with the officers. As they left, Maggie ran out and said, "Is there no message for me?"

The only message for the women was, "They had all died fighting."[15]

Libbie, thirty-four, would have to fight through her grief while in the public eye as the widow of Custer. Col. Nelson Miles, who had been friends with the Custers since their families were both quartered at Fort Hays in 1869, found her so depressed that he was worried about her mental and physical health. But she couldn't recover at the post since she was no longer married to an officer. Libbie packed up her belongings and on July 30—less than a month after she first heard the news of Custer's death—started the long train trip back to Monroe. Annie Yates and her three children, and Maggie Calhoun, both also now widows, and Custer's niece Emma Reed made the trip with her. At a stop in Fargo, people gathered to greet them, men and women crying at the site of the soldiers' families. The widows, dressed in deep mourning, walked slowly into the station, Libbie with her had bent down and Maggie with a vacant stare, her face like marble. When they stopped at the Palmer House in Chicago, they ate in a private parlor and retired to their rooms, declining to receive any visitors. The Rev. Erasmus Boyd, who had been the principal of Libbie's old school, greeted them in Monroe. Libbie gave a cry of anguished grief and fainted in his arms. But after a memorial service on August 13, Libbie had to figure out what to do with the rest of her life.[16]

Her main financial asset was an army pension of $30 a month—a little more than $720 in 2020. Most of Custer's estate had been used to pay off debts, so she had almost no savings.[17] Newspapers and veterans collected money for the widows, and the Grand Duke Alexis sent $500 (about $12,000 in 2020), but she had no home of her own and no job.[18]

She did, however, have a mission that became more clear as time passed, and that was to promote Custer's memory as a hero. Her first opportunity was to help a dime novel author named Frederik Whittaker write a laudable biography of her husband. Whittaker was a wounded cavalry veteran of the Army of the Potomac who had met Custer at the office of Custer's publisher in New York. Whittaker was the first in what would be a long line of "Custerphiles"—authors who are fascinated by the romantic aspects of Custer's life and tend to write favorably about him. In September, Whittaker wrote an article for Custer's old magazine, *Galaxy*, that faulted Terry and Reno for the

Little Bighorn disaster. Libbie, seeing what side of the blame debate he was on, agreed to give him access to Custer's letters for his book, *The Complete Life of General Custer.* Whittaker, used to cranking out quickie novels, incredibly finished the biography for delivery in bookstores by November, only five months after the Little Bighorn. Because he wrote so soon after Custer's death, while memories were still fresh, and he had the cooperation of the woman who knew Custer best, Whittaker's book is valued by historians and is still in print. Whittaker's bias drew some criticism, especially for his treatment of Grant and others. But his book was a thrilling read of a topic of general interest. The Republican *Chicago Tribune* admitted that the book, although appearing to be too enthusiastic about Custer in the beginning, would win readers to Custer's side by its finish. Custer "was a true hero, and will be regarded as such in the future history of his country," the *Tribune* concluded.[19]

Clement Lounsberry's *Bismarck Tribune*, whose Mark Kellogg had died with Custer, thought Whittaker's book was one of the best biographies ever published because it captured the drama of Custer's life. "Nothing more romantic and fascinating can be found in all history than Custer's life on the Plains for the past ten years. He was always cool and calculating, but never hesitated to make the most desperate attacks when the proper moment arrived. His life among the Indians was a succession of escapes from death, and he was no sooner out of one danger than into another. He was always fighting against superior forces, and always coming out triumphant." When Custer saw at the end that his command was doomed, he died fighting. "This he did grandly," the *Tribune* concluded.[20] Whittaker's book, written with Libbie's help, set the narrative tone for Custer's story for almost sixty years—that he was a hero of the republic. Authors, painters, and performers usually followed Whitaker's view.

Having set the literary pattern, Libbie also began to take firm control of Custer's image in public displays. The general, like the other causalities, had been buried in a hastily dug shallow grave on the battlefield. The next year the army was going to send a detail to the battlefield to properly bury the men and remove most of the officers for formal interment elsewhere. Libbie had requested a West Point burial for Custer. When she learned that the funeral, scheduled for summer, would occur when few cadets would be on campus, she took action like a press agent and arranged to have his remains stored in a vault in Poughkeepsie, New York, until a fall ceremony, when classes would be in session. As she expected, the funeral was dramatic, with crowds lining the Hudson River to watch a flag-draped ship carry the remains to West Point, where a service was held at the academy chapel. Custer was buried with full military honors at the college he so loved, a fitting resting place for the schoolteacher turned soldier.

The event was well covered by the press. *Harper's Weekly*, which had first made Custer famous with a cover illustration of him leading a charge in 1864, published illustrations of the funeral. One showed the caisson carrying Custer's coffin with a riderless horse and marching officers trailing behind. The other showed an honor guard firing a salute over the open grave.[21] The *New York Herald* wrote that the funeral showed the affection Americans held for Custer. "The day was beautiful and thousands of people assembled to witness the solemn event. The ceremonial was properly entirely military in its character, and was the more impressive because of its dignified simplicity. There was no oration, nor was there need of any, for the draped flags, the muffled drums, the imposing procession, the still multitude of specta-tors, and, more than all, the bier upon which laid the mortal remains of one of the bravest of American soldiers, had eloquence deeper than any words." The only thing left to do, the paper editorialized, was to put a monument over his grave that would be worthy of his service.[22]

The *New York Herald* had been leading a fundraising effort for a Custer monument that had drawn contributors from all walks of life. One anonymous schoolgirl sent ten cents, confessing that she cried after reading the *Herald* story about the Little Bighorn. "All the girls and women, I fancy must feel as I do, for such heroes as General Custer are what they most admire, and then you know, they are scarce," she wrote. "Leave it to the school girls and a monument will soon be raised to the gallant General Custer, for he was a man."[23]

The publicity for the funeral provided new impetus to the *Herald's* fundraising efforts. A wealthy young college student named Theodore Roosevelt gave $100. Custer's artist friend Albert Bierstadt donated $50, and the actress Clara Morris, famous for her portrayal of suffering women, performed for the first time in *Jane Eyre* in a special benefit for the monument. The show drew a packed house with hundreds more waiting in vain for standing room admission. Morris, who was a great admirer of Custer, noted in her diary that she got eight curtain calls that night. But she was even more proud of the $1,794.50—about $43,000 in 2020—collected at the box office. She sent it all to the *Herald*, paying the play's expenses out of her own pocket. "I wish it were five times as much—and if it were five one *thousand* times as much it could not express my devotion for and to the memory of our dead hero!" she wrote.[24]

All of the fundraising efforts netted enough money for a statue, but not for an equestrian one. The monument committee selected a self-taught sculptor named J. Wilson McDonald, who had done some busts of famous men, but his design for Custer was repulsive to Libbie. She thought the design's portrayal of Custer's uniform and weapons, as well as his pose, was horribly inaccurate. The face was too old and the hair too long. She refused to attend the unveiling at West Point and started a campaign to have the statue removed, writing to Sherman and Robert Lincoln, son of the former president and now secretary of war. The army moved the statue to storage, but it disappeared and to this day no one knows what happened to it. The episode removed any doubt that Libbie was in charge of the Custer story. In the Victorian era's sensitivity toward women—especially widows of heroes—few would now dare start a fight with Libbie Custer.[25]

At this time Libbie was living in New York. After a brief stay in Monroe, she had found the town as stifling as when she had been a young woman and had left for an adventurous life with Custer. She had considered various careers, including nursing, but she accepted a job as secretary for the Society of Decorative Art in New York. Her dream since her schoolgirl days in Monroe had been to be a writer or a journalist. She had served as Custer's editor and coach, and the standing joke in the army was that she had written Custer's books and articles. Perhaps she could be a writer, too. In the publishing center of the country, she would get her chance.[26]

Whittaker had encouraged her to tell the Custer story through her eyes. He thought it would help her get over her grief and also provide a glimpse into Custer's private life, which would add to the historical picture. "Remember that you are the centre of interest to a great proportion of our nation and that every one is anxious to hear what Custer's wife can tell them of the inner life of their pet and hero," he wrote her.[27]

Libbie, like many would-be writers, was worried that she could produce a book. Whittaker assured her she could do it and told her to write as if she were speaking to the reader. The general's publisher, I. E. Sheldon, suggested that she write down everything she could remember and then select the best pieces for a book. "I would advise you not to think at all of how it will read. Just write them out in the most natural way as if you were talking to friend . . . . I think little by little you are securing the material to make an interesting book."[28]

In 1882 Libbie started seriously thinking about writing a memoir of her last years with Custer. She finished *Boots and Saddles* three years later. The book, which started with a brief overview of their early life and ended when Libbie received the news of his death, did indeed give the public a view of Custer at home and of life in general on the isolated frontier posts. Her conversational, self-deprecating style was a hit with readers and critics. It arrived in bookstores in March 1885, and its first printing of two thousand sold out quickly. Near the end of the year it had sold fifteen thousand, and it is still in print today.[29]

The *New York Tribune* praised the book for its vivid portrayal of life in the frontier army and especially the sketch of Custer's personality. "Custer was a man of many splendid and fascinating qualities, and in this simple and affectionate account of his character and habits he appears more winning than ever before."[30]

The *Portland* (Maine) *Daily Press* agreed and called the book "delightful" in a typical review. "From the first page to the last the reader is en rapport with the author, and in laying down the volume the feeling is that one has become a personal friend, an intimate associate, through sympathy, admiration and affection, for the brilliant General Custer and his brave and loving wife. The narrative is full of vitality, and so keen a personality that one becomes absorbed as if it were one's own experience. Every page has in it a sort of vivid excitement which gets into the veins and makes the reader at one with the writer and a participator in the events of each day, the simplest of which is full of interest."[31]

Using her frontier experiences, Libbie had created an author's persona that complimented the one Custer had made for himself. Libbie, like Custer, could make fun of her fears and the rough living on the Plains. She overcame her trepidation and dutifully followed her husband from fort to fort, always striving to make the best of the situation. If Custer was the embodiment of the frontier soldier, Libbie was not only the symbol of the frontier woman, but the spokeswoman for the tight, closed society that she and others called affectionately "our little Army." It's hard to read the Custers' books and not feel empathy if not affection for them and the other families of that army.

Boots and Saddles launched an impressive career for the hardworking widow. She published *Tenting on the Plains*, a memoir of their life in Texas and Kansas, in 1887, and *Following the Guidon*, a Civil War memoir, in 1890. She also began writing essays on various topics that were published in newspapers around the country. She even covered the funeral of her husband's nemesis, Grant.[32] Her success as an author garnered an invitation from the Redpath Lyceum Bureau—the one that had negotiated with Custer before his death—to go on a speaking tour, which she accepted. The girl who had first gained local fame for her school graduation speech was, at forty-eight, a world traveler, author, and lecturer, all by telling the story of her husband and the frontier army.[33]

The increasing fame of George Armstrong Custer led to a 1907 Michigan campaign for a statue in his adopted home state. This one would have enough funding for a grand equestrian design. Theodore Roosevelt, now president, once again endorsed the project, telling the fundraising committee what everyone already knew more than a quarter century after the battle—that Custer had become "the typical representative of the American regular officer who fought for the extension of our frontier."[34]

This time the committee made sure to consult with Libbie on the artist, the design, and the location. Libbie chose Monroe over the state capital of Lansing, and she picked as sculptor Edward Clark Potter, who had won a gold medal at the St. Louis World's Fair in 1904 and was famous for equestrian statues of George Washington and Joseph Hooker. (He would complete his most famous works in 1911—the lions in front of the New York Public Library.)[35] Potter submitted five models. Libbie chose one that showed Custer having just spotted Jeb Stuart's cavalry approaching the Union lines at the critical moment of Gettysburg. Unlike many such statues, the monument conveys a moment of reflection rather than action, a pose that would rebut the critics who called him rash. Custer would be captured in bronze at age twenty-three, and at the height of his service. The Little Bighorn, where he achieved immortality, is mentioned only in the plaque detailing his service record.[36]

At a banquet on the night before the unveiling, Libbie was honored by the Civil War veterans of Custer's Michigan brigade. At one point the band played "Then You'll Remember Me," the first song music sheet Custer had given her so many years ago. It was an emotionally exhausting event for her, but she was comforted by the attitude of the veterans, many of whom told her that the statue and the preservation of Custer's memory was largely due to her efforts.[37]

The next day, June 4, 1910, Libbie pulled the ribbons, in cavalry colors of yellow and blue, that unveiled the statue, hidden behind two giant flags. President William Howard Taft, stopping in Monroe on a trip through the Midwest, gave an extemporaneous speech, declaring that Custer was among the greatest cavalry commanders in the history of the world. Custer was the "right arm" of the Army of the Potomac's cavalry throughout the war, Taft said, but his service in the Indian wars was the most interesting part of his career.

"He was one of the 25,000 men composing the regular army whose work we do not fully appreciate as much as I wish we did," Taft said. "The army then and the army of today is one of which the United States may well be proud. I say this merely to note the indebtedness of the country to the army during the opening of the west and to testify to the effectiveness and heroism of George Armstrong Custer in that great battle which continued for a decade, the great war for civilization, of which he was the most conspicuous and shining sacrifice."[38]

Libbie wrote that she appreciated Taft's speech because he spoke knowledgably about the thankless service in the difficult and often-criticized Indian campaigns. "He enumerated the trials of our officers on that bleak frontier. The cruelty, the dangers of protecting the settler, the perils they underwent in guarding the builders of the railroads, the driving out of the Indians. . . . I was so touched at this allusion to a few officers (McKenzie, Miles, Crook, and the General tho' he did not call them by name) who had come from the Civil War where they had commanded tens of thousands, to an unknown country where their armies numbered hundreds only. . . . I felt this so deeply on the frontier, and admired so the uncomplaining service of these distinguished Generals who had so little support from the Government and so much criticism from civilians."[39]

In 1910, at the time of the statue's unveiling, Custer had been dead for almost thirty-five years, and Libbie was approaching seventy. The country had changed in many ways. Only illustrated newspapers had published images of Custer when he was alive, woodcuts made from the drawings of sketch artists like Alfred Waud, who had captured Custer testing the depth of the Chickahominy in his first notable heroics. Now papers around the country could print actual photographs of his wife unveiling his statue. A new entertainment medium was just developing that would find Custer's story an irresistible tale that could be shaped to fit multiple views of history. The first American action film, shot just the year before, was a western—*The Great Train Robbery*—demonstrating the importance of the West to the nation's self-image. Libbie, who had shrewdly given former Custer scout Buffalo Bill Cody permission to incorporate the Last Stand in his Wild West Show, was interested in her husband's portrayal in entertainment media. She had even attended a Wild West show opening, despite the fact the performance included some Indians who had fought her husband at Little Bighorn. She was rewarded by the success of the show in promoting Custer's image throughout the United States and Europe. Now she was ready to cooperate with movie producers. She wrote a letter to Pathé films that she would consult on costumes and would let them examine some of the general's uniforms. She wouldn't lend them, however, for fear she would not get them back.[40]

But the carnage of World War I seemed pointless to many Americans, and interest in military heroes like Custer began to wane. Stories coming out of World War I often featured depressing antiwar themes like those in *A Farewell to Arms* and *All Quiet on the Western Front*. Libbie realized that the times and attitudes were changing. In 1929, when she was eighty-seven, Libbie told a newspaper reporter interviewing her on the anniversary of the Little Bighorn that she felt like an antique, although she enjoyed her life in New York with her friends and her work, which included writing another memoir of her Civil War experiences. She also kept up an active correspondence with veterans of her husband's units, but she insisted she didn't live in the past.

"I go to the theaters and the picture shows, but I am not keen on seeing war plays!" she said. "I have been greatly interested in the signing of the peace treaty and the gathering together of the representatives of all the nations."[41]

She died of a heart attack on April 4, 1933, at the age of ninety. Libbie had outlived most of those who survived the Little Bighorn, yet no one contributed more to its place in American culture than she did.

As Erich Maria Remarque wrote of the veterans of World War I, many of the Little Bighorn survivors were "men who, even though they may have escaped shells, were destroyed by the war."[42] Thomas Weir, thirty-eight, who had vainly tried to rescue Custer at the Little Bighorn, was the first to go. He was posted to New York city on recruiting duty, an assignment usually considered a reward, but he couldn't accept what had happened. He wrote plaintive letters to Libbie that he would tell her secrets about the battle, but he never did, drinking himself to death less than six months after the Little Bighorn.[43]

Reno, too, could not forget, and critics like Whittaker would not let him, blaming him for the defeat. Reno demanded a court of inquiry to clear his name, and he was exonerated of cowardice in 1879, although the court noted that some of his subordinates had exercised more leadership than he had. He drank heavily, got in trouble often, and was summarily dismissed from the service in 1880 after peeping through a window at the daughter of his commanding officer. He died of throat cancer in 1889. Found among his effects was an unfinished manuscript in which he wrote that he was haunted by "the harrowing sight of those mutilated and decomposing bodies crowning the heights where poor Custer fell."[44]

Benteen had a little more success in the army, participating heroically in the Nez Perce campaign, and he was promoted to major in 1882. But Benteen, like so many Indian war soldiers, drank heavily. He was almost kicked out of the army in 1887 for drunkenness and disorderly conduct, but President Grover Cleveland reduced his sentence to a one-year suspension, and Benteen retired in 1888 from disability. He died ten years later.[45]

Edward Godfrey had the most success of the Seventh's officers. He was severely wounded at Bear Paw Mountain fighting the Nez Perce but won the Medal of Honor. He went on to a distinguished career serving in the Spanish-American War and the Philippine Insurrection before retiring in 1907 with the rank of brigadier general—the star Custer had coveted. He lived long enough to celebrate the fiftieth anniversary of the Little Bighorn by shaking hands with White Bull, a Sioux veteran, at a ceremony on the battlefield. Godfrey died in 1932 at age eighty-eight and was buried at Arlington National Cemetery, like Libbie an antique in a modern age.[46]

The consensus opinion of Custer as a hero changed soon after the deaths of Godfrey and Libbie. A former newspaper reporter turned novelist named Frederick F. Van de Water was researching a new fiction book about the Old West when he got hooked on the Custer story. Van de Water's *Glory-Hunter*, published in 1934, became arguably the most influential biography of Custer aside from Whittaker's book. Van de Water turned Whittaker's heroic image of Custer upside down, portraying him as an arrogant, brutal commander who succeeded through luck or the advantages of overwhelming force. Van de Water claimed he wrote to find the truth about Custer, but his truth emphasized the negative surely as much as Whittaker had emphasized the positive. The book found a ready audience at a time when people were disillusioned by World War I and journalists cheered the "debunking" trend among historians eager to smash traditions. Custer had his defenders, then as now, but despite the subsequent publication of more balanced biographies, Van de Water's villainous image is the one that gradually became the dominant view in American culture in the twentieth century and continues to the present day.[47]

The Van de Water version of Custer became particularly evident in the powerful media of film and television. There were some exceptions, most notably a film called *They Died with Their Boots On*. This very loose biography of Custer was released in December 1941 with the explicit intent to boost American patriotism and sympathy for Great Britain in its fight against the Nazis. An English officer was added to the Seventh cavalry to show how the United States and Great Britain were longtime allies. The character even introduces Custer to

"Garry Owen," which provided a stirring theme song throughout the movie and a rousing, upbeat sendoff for the film's ending message—that heroes like Custer and his men would always be ready to sacrifice themselves for America. Warner Brothers shot the film when Americans were worried about Nazi aggression and figured they would be drawn into the war at some point. Its release in the same month as the attack on Pearl Harbor gave the film an undeniable resonance with current events. As undermanned American forces in Guam, Wake, and the Philippines were overwhelmed by exuberant Japanese forces, *They Died with Their Boots On* showed that Americans could lose a battle but would never be defeated. A film that was essentially a formulaic action vehicle for swashbuckling star Errol Flynn turned out to be the studio's third highest-grossing movie of the season.[48]

The Australian Flynn, who was one of the biggest action stars at the time, captured Custer's charisma better than any actor has ever done. Flynn, who was thirty-two when he made the movie (Custer was thirty-six at the Little Bighorn) had the combination of looks, style, and intellect that—as is said of the most successful male stars—made women love him and men want to be like him. Like Custer, Flynn was a natural athlete. He excelled at tennis, did some professional boxing, and was drawn to rugged outdoor activities, especially sailing. And like Custer, Flynn rebelled at the confines of school but aspired to be a writer, authoring several novels and memoirs and doing some newspaper reporting.[49]

But another striking parallel between actor and warrior was the destruction of their respective images. Less than a year after the release of *They Died with Their Boots On*, Flynn was charged with three counts of statutory rape by two teenage girls who had come to Hollywood to pursue movie careers but had no luck breaking into the business. Flynn was acquitted after a sensational trial, but his public image became that of a coarse, notorious ladies' man as more of his affairs became public. His name gave rise to the wartime expression "in like Flynn," which described any man who had made a sexual conquest, and later came to mean easy success at anything. Flynn continued to make movies, but he could never quite recapture the stardom he had won before the trial. Flynn had been a hard drinker for most of his life, and he had a brief comeback playing versions of what he had become—a charming, aging drunk—in the *The Sun Also Rises* and a few other films. But he died at fifty in 1959, his body worn out by his dissipating lifestyle.[50]

Flynn biographer Peter Valenti noted that the actor's downfall reflected in part an unattractive aspect of human nature, that is, gloating at the tarnishing of a successful man's image.[51] In journalism, this is the longtime practice of building someone up, tearing him down, and then sometimes writing a comeback story. Of course, Flynn's problems were of his own making. But there was an undeniable jealousy and cynicism that prompted the public to revel in the contrast between his heroic screen image and the sordid details of his personal life.

So too with Custer. The perfect image crafted by his wife was successful in the Victorian era but made Custer a perfect target for the hardboiled cynicism of the twentieth century, especially in the wake of the carnage of two world wars that made people question the merit of public institutions, including the military. The Custer created by Libbie showed only his good qualities, while the historical record left plenty of negatives to sift through for anyone who wanted to write a hatchet job like *Glory-Hunter.*

Occasionally biographies were published that sought a middle ground, but historical forces in the second half of the twentieth century and beyond have kept the pendulum of public opinion stuck on the negative Custer. The Civil Rights movement and the protests against the Vietnam War helped move journalists from a "we" mindset when covering the government and the military to an "us vs. them" stance. Scenes of police using fire hoses on peaceful protesters in the South made government seem like the enemy of minority rights rather than a protector of freedom as it was in World War II. Similarly, stories of atrocities by American troops in Vietnam and lies by American officials made the military seem like the villain instead of the hero.

Custer at the Washita became the perfect symbol for American arrogance and cruelty in Arthur Penn's blockbuster 1970 movie *Little Big Man.* The scenes of the battle were exaggerated to cast the Indians as victims with no explanation of the reasons for the attack or to show that the Indians fought back ferociously. Penn admitted he tried to draw comparisons between the Washita and the My Lai Massacre, in which American soldiers killed about three hundred and fifty civilians in Vietnam. The Last Stand scene of *Little Big Man* showed Custer as not just evil but insane, arguing with an imaginary Grant as warriors methodically killed his cowardly soldiers. Played for laughs was a soldier who throws a blanket over himself in a ridiculous attempt to hide in the middle of the battlefield. Few moviegoers likely knew that the reaction of such futile hiding and withdrawal into self is not uncommon among soldiers overcome mentally by the stress of combat. No matter. Laughs at the expense of the villain might be cruel but were readily accepted by the audience. And by 1970, less than a hundred years after the battle, it was plain that Custer and the military were seen as villains in popular culture.[52]

The American Indian Movement protested the centennial ceremony at the Custer Battlefield National Monument in 1976, claiming the museum and the monument glorified genocide. The government officially removed Custer's name from the battlefield in 1991, designating it as the Little Bighorn Battlefield National Monument. Markers where warriors were killed were added beginning in 1999 to parallel the unique feature of the battlefield—tombstones placed where soldiers' bodies were found. An Indian memorial, constructed near Last Stand Hill, where an obelisk honoring Custer's men stands, was dedicated in 2003. These changes were a necessary move to broaden the interpretation of the battle. A century after the battle, the descendants of all the participants in the Little Bighorn were citizens and could share the memory just as the descendants of Union and Confederate veterans could share Gettysburg as a sacred site dedicated to courage and honor.

Yet in bowing to the attitudes of the twenty-first century, the new memorial sacrifices historical accuracy to politics. The Indian memorial recognizes Crows and Rees—Custer's scouts—alongside their historical enemies the Sioux, thus for the casual observer reducing the battle to a modern interpretation of all Indians against Americans of European descent. An attentive visitor might notice that the scouts are also honored on the obelisk as part of the American military, which ironically, in modern terms was the more "diverse" force, as it included an African American interpreter, Indian scouts from at least two different tribes, and immigrants so recent that many, including Custer's trumpeter, Martini, barely spoke English.

Custer's name is off the battlefield, but his charisma and the magical symbolism of the Last Stand have kept him alive in the popular imagination and kept visitors coming to that remote section of Montana. However, the movement to remove unacceptable figures even from discussion in the public square threatens to erase Custer from national memory other than as a bogeyman whose name—devoid of any historical reality—is a powerful epithet to hurl in debate with political opponents.

In 2017 the fast-food chain Sonic tried to promote a new frozen dessert called the Custard Concrete with a commercial that featured one of its pair of comedic spokesmen dressed as Custer. The silly banter concerned whether Custer's name was actually "Custard." Despite the fact that the character was dressed in a facsimile of Custer's Civil War uniform, social media critics flamed the ad as insensitive for featuring a murderer of Indians. Sonic apologized and quickly withdrew the ad.[53]

As the second decade of the twenty-first century came to a close, agitation to remove from public view the names and images of historical figures deemed offensive gained momentum in the United States. Most of the effort has focused on figures who supported slavery or fought for the Confederacy, but those associated with the frontier are also under attack. As of this writing, Custer's monuments have survived, perhaps because they are in remote locations like Monroe, Michigan, and New Rumley, Ohio.

The true scope of Custer's life seems as remote from the public consciousness as his monuments are from the population centers of the country. Custer personally sacrificed many things in his life of service to the United States. He was killed in action at thirty-six, not yet in middle age, and with opportunities in several fields that engaged his passion. Had Custer stayed in the military, he would at least have gotten the star that went to his subordinate Godfrey and might have ended up in command of the army as did his friend Nelson Miles.

Like so many other generals in American history, Custer could have turned to his family passion—politics. Hancock ran for president on the Democratic ticket in 1880, coming within about ten thousand votes of James Garfield. Custer, who could fire up a crowd like he was leading a charge, might have been nominated instead with the help of his powerful New York political friends. It's entirely possible that Custer would have found the extra votes in key states necessary for victory that Hancock, with his stiff personality, could not get.

Or Custer could have left the army to pursue show business. Custer's old scout Buffalo Bill Cody made a fortune performing on stage a heroic version of his own life and Custer's Last Stand. Custer could have done at least as well, coached by best friend Lawrence Barrett. And certainly, Custer would have continued his writing career. With Libbie's talent for promotion, he probably would have been even more successful than she was.

Most of all, Custer sacrificed the best part of his life—living with Libbie. They would never grow old together, sitting at night in his office, talking pleasantly as they did at Fort Lincoln. Libbie reluctantly took on the writing and speaking career that would have been her husband's.

Custer's sacrifice is best captured by his statue in Monroe. Custer sits on his horse, watching. He is on guard for the country, ready as all soldiers are to give everything for their fellow citizens. He is at the corner of a bridge over the River Raisin, the namesake for a battle that claimed the lives of an earlier generation of American soldiers who Custer learned to revere when he was a boy.

Most tourists looking at the statue today associate Custer with the Indian wars. One woman told a National Park Service guide at the River Raisin battlefield that there should not be a statue in town honoring a murderer of Indians. She had no idea that the statue was of Custer in the Civil War, where he helped save the United States and leave a legacy of freedom that permits people to despise or venerate their ancestors as they choose.

Who knows how long the statue will stand? It is a grand remembrance of heroism, an American intent on doing his duty. In the second decade of the twenty-first century, such statues were out of vogue. More popular are makeshift memorials on roadsides to people killed in car accidents. Bronze statues erected today often celebrate musicians or athletes who have entertained us, usually while earning vast fortunes, rather than honoring men who have done great things in battle. Monuments to military heroes are removed if, like Custer, their life offends modern sensibilities of how people in past generations should have lived and thought.

For now, Custer still sits astride his horse high above drivers and pedestrians as they go about their business, oblivious to the dangers of the outside world that require men like Custer to stand on guard. The statue is so high above the crowd that passersby, if they choose to look up, can't really tell that Custer's eyes were those of an artist, not a soldier.

Notes

ABBREVIATIONS

CC   Custer Collection, Monroe County Historical and Museum Association Archives, Monroe, Michigan.

EBCP Elizabeth Bacon Custer Papers, Beinecke Rare Book & Manuscript Library, Yale University, New Haven, Conn.

FC   Dr. Lawrence A. Frost Collection of Custeriana, Monroe County Historical and Museum Association Archives, Monroe, Michigan.

GACC General George A. Custer Collection, Monroe County (Michigan) Library System.

PREFACE

1. Styple, *Generals in Bronze*, vii–viii. Kelly began doing these interviews after Custer's death.
2. Ibid., xii–xx, 254.
3. Ibid., 67.
4. Yu, et al., "Pantheon 1.0." Grant is ranked under political leaders.
5. Slotkin, *The Fatal Environment*, xvii, 11–12.
6. White, *"It's Your Misfortune and None of My Own,"* 625.
7. Barnett, *Touched by Fire*, 403; 410–12.
8. Philbrick, *The Last Stand*, xxi.
9. Stiles, *Custer's Trials*, xviii–xix.
10. Ibid., xix–xxi.
11. "A Pen Picture of Custer," *Daily* (Columbus) *Ohio Statesman*, October 2, 1866.
12. Slotkin, *The Fatal Environment*, 373–74.

CHAPTER 1: WHAT IS AMBITION?

1. Hopedale, Ohio, Teacher's Class Notebook, Box 3, Folder 22, Dr. Lawrence A. Frost Collection of Custeriana (hereinafter known as FC). To read the entire poem, see Willis, *Ambition*, in *The Oxford Book of Children's Verse in America*, 41–42.

2. Wallace, *Custer's Ohio Boyhood*, 8.

3. Ibid., 8, 11.

4. Merington, *The Custer Story*, 6; Monaghan, *Custer*, 5.

5. Monaghan, *Custer*, 3; E. B. Custer, *Tenting on the Plains*, 182. Emanuel repeated the anecdote often. In the version recounted by Libbie Custer, Emanuel told her that George said they would whip all the Whigs in Michigan. Father Custer misremembered, as they were living in Ohio when George was five.

6. "Hurrah for the Democratic Pyramid!" *Cadiz Sentinel*, September 11, 1844.

7. Ambrose, *Crazy Horse and Custer*, 88; Wert, 19; Frost, *Custer Legends*, 101. Nevin Custer recalled that his older brother had a wooden sword; other sources claim it was a toy musket. He likely had both. *Cadiz Sentinel*, September 11, 1844.

8. Whisker, *The Rise and Decline of the American Militia System*, 15, 16, 331, 333.

9. Mahon, *History of the Militia and the National Guard*, 83.

10. E. B. Custer, "A Tribute of Love," unidentified newspaper clipping, December 11, 1892, Box 1, Folder 2, FC.

11. "The Rumley Democratic Meeting, *Cadiz Sentinel*, August 27, 1856.

12. Monaghan, *Custer*, 4–5; "Emanuel Henry Custer," *Monroe Democrat*, Dec. 1, 1892.

13. Monaghan, *Custer*, 6; Wallace, *Custer's Ohio Boyhood*, 28–29; Hunter, *The Judge Rode a Sorrel Horse*, 16–17; Beemer, "The Unknown Custer," *Greasy Grass*, 10–11. This part of Custer's life is difficult to pin down, more so even than the childhood of most people because his family moved several times, and he moved away to live with his half-sister for a time. Wallace characterized the carpentry work as a job to "tide him over" between school terms rather than an apprenticeship. This seems unlikely.

14. Wallace, *Custer's Ohio Boyhood*, 23.

15. Frost, *Let's Have a Fair Fight!* Ambrose, *Crazy Horse and Custer*, 92.

16. Barry, "John M. Barry Remembers Custer," *Newsletter of the Little Big Horn Associates*, 8.

17. McClellan, introduction to *The Hoosier Schoolmaster* by Eggleston, 3.

18. U.S. Census Bureau, "Resident Population and Apportionment of the U.S. House of Representatives," https://www.census.gov/dmd/www/resapport/states/ohio .pdf; Cayton, *Ohio*, 2–3, 15.

19. Cayton., *Ohio*, 75–76.

20. Roberts, *Buckeye Schoolmaster*, 77.

21. Ibid. 3–4.

22. Ronsheim, *The Life of General Custer*, 3.

23. Cayton, *Ohio*, 58–59.

24. Wallace, *Custer's Ohio Boyhood*, 24.

25. Village of Hopedale, "Our History," http://www.hopedaleohio.com/our-history .html.

26. "McNeely Normal School," *Cadiz Sentinel*, August 10, 1859.

27. Wallace, *Custer's Ohio Boyhood*, 24–26.

28. Hopedale notebook.

29. Ibid.

30. "Education," *Cadiz Sentinel*, March 21, 1844.

31. Hopedale notebook.

32. Ronsheim, *The Life of General Custer*, 5.

33. Ibid.

34. Wallace, *Custer's Ohio Boyhood*, 25.

35. Monaghan, *Custer*, 8–9; Ronsheim, *The Life of General Custer*, 4. Ronsheim spelled the friend's name "Dickenson."

36. Wallace, *Custer's Ohio Boyhood*, 25.

37. Ronsheim, *The Life of General Custer*, 62; Wallace, *Custer's Ohio Boyhood*, 25, 28.

38. Roberts, *Buckeye Schoolmaster*, 12, 247; Wallace, *Custer's Ohio Boyhood*, 35–37.

39. Roberts, *Buckeye Schoolmaster*, 177, 187.

40. Hopedale notebook.

41. Wallace, *Custer's Ohio Boyhood*, 37; Ronsheim, *The Life of General Custer*, 4.

42. Roberts, *Buckeye Schoolmaster*, 7–8.

43. Wallace, *Custer's Ohio Boyhood*, 32; Monaghan, *Custer*, 10–11; Wallace, *Custer's Ohio Boyhood*, 32.

44. Monaghan, *Custer*, 10–11.

45. Ronsheim, *The Life of General Custer*, 5–6.

46. Ibid., 1.

47. Merington, *The Custer Story*, 7; Wallace, *Custer's Ohio Boyhood*, 34; Beemer, 3–4, 8.

48. Ambrose, *Crazy Horse and Custer*, 92; Cooper, "James Buchanan: Campaigns and Elections," University of Virginia Miller Center, https://millercenter.org/president/buchanan/campaigns-and-elections.

49. Ronsheim, *The Life of General Custer*, 5; Wallace, *Custer's Ohio Boyhood*, 32–33; Merington, *The Custer Story*, 7–8; Monaghan, *Custer*, 11–12.

50. "At West Point," *Cadiz Sentinel*, June 4, 1857.

51. Monaghan, *Custer*, 12.

52. E. H. Custer to George Armstrong Custer, February 20, 1865, Box 1, Folder 20, FC.

53. Ambrose, *Crazy Horse and Custer*, 100; Ronsheim, *The Life of General Custer*, 7; "Delinquency Record of Cadet George A. Custer, USMA Class of June 1861," Box 8, Folder 4, Custer Collection, Monroe County Historical and Museum Association Archives (hereinafter referred to as CC).

54. Farley, *West Point in the Early Sixties*, 75.

55. Michie, "Reminiscences of Cadet and Army Service," 194.

56. Monaghan, *Custer*, 34; Schaff, *The Spirit of Old West Point*, 66–67.

57. Schaff, *The Spirit of Old West Point*, 193–94.

58. Ibid., 28.

59. Ambrose, *Crazy Horse and Custer*, 108; Monaghan, *Custer*, 20; Frost, *Let's Have a Fair Fight!*

60. Schaff, *The Spirit of Old West Point*, 82.

61. Michie, "Reminiscences of Cadet and Army Service," 186.

62. Custer to brother and sister, January 27, 1858, Box 1, Folder 9, CC; Ambrose, *Duty, Honor, Country*, 129–33; Ambrose, *Crazy Horse and Custer*, 115; Merington, *The Custer Story*, 10.

63. Michie, "Reminiscences of Cadet and Army Service," 194; Merington, *The Custer Story*, 9.

64. Ambrose, *Crazy Horse and Custer*, 110–11.

65. Ibid., 110; Ambrose, *Duty, Honor, Country*, 147; Monaghan, *Custer*, 32; Manuscript, "The Red Man," Reel 1, Frame 0332–0334, General George A. Custer Collection, Monroe County (Michigan) Library System (hereinafter referred to as GACC).

66. "Angels of Mercy," *Cadiz Sentinel*, December 22, 1858; Schaff, *The Spirit of Old West Point*, 86; Frost, *Let's Have a Fair Fight!*

67. Schaff, *The Spirit of Old West Point*, 201–9.

68. Ibid., 84.

69. Ambrose, *Crazy Horse and Custer*, 114.

70. Michie, "Reminiscences of Cadet and Army Service," 194–95.

71. "Lieutenant G. A. Custer," *Cadiz Sentinel*, July 17, 1861.

72. Roberts, *Buckeye Schoolmaster*, 13.

73. Merington, *The Custer Story*, 10.

74. Frost, *Let's Have a Fair Fight!*

75. Ibid.

76. Ibid.

77. Ibid. The fight occurred on June 29, 1861,

78. Ambrose, *Crazy Horse and Custer*, 117.

CHAPTER 2: STAFF OFFICER

1. Warner, *Generals in Blue*, 20; Monaghan, *Custer*, 77–79; Merington, *The Custer Story*, 30–31.

2. Merington, *The Custer Story*, 30–31.

3. Ray, "Our Special Artist," 43, 94. It's unclear whether the sketch of Custer in the Chickahominy was published at the time. The author has only found the drawing in a collection of Waud's work. "Our Army Correspondence," *New York Herald*, May 27, 1862; "Bully for Custer!—A Harrison County Boy Promoted," *Cadiz Sentinel*, June 11, 1862; Stiles, *Custer's Trials*, 52.

4. Wilson, *Under the Old Flag*, 101–2.

5. Carroll, *Custer in the Civil War*, 89.

6. Schaff, 85–86; Monaghan, *Custer*, 18, 22; Carroll, *Custer in the Civil War*, 89–90. Coddington, "Custer and His Roommate Part Ways," *New York Times*, February 15, 2012, notes Parker was the son of a prominent Kentucky doctor and was first cousin of Mary Todd Lincoln.

7. Warner, *Generals in Blue*, 429–31.

8. This account is from Carroll, *Custer in the Civil War*, 90–92.

9. Ibid., 92–94.

10. Ibid., 96.

11. Keegan and Holmes, *Soldiers*, 259–62.

12. Carroll, *Custer in the Civil War*, 102.

13. Ibid., 103–4.

14. Ibid., 110.

15. Merington, *The Custer Story*, 13.

16. Catton, *Mr. Lincoln's Army*, 32–33.

17. Monaghan, *Custer*, 57; Warner, *Generals in Blue*, 58–59.

18. Carroll, *Custer in the Civil War*, 114–15.

19. Catton, *Mr. Lincoln's Army*, 65–66.

20. Ibid. 115, 185.

21. Ibid., 32–33; Carroll, *Custer in the Civil War*, 116.

22. Carroll, *Custer in the Civil War*, 116.

23. Ibid., 117.

24. Ibid., 115.

25. Wert, *Custer*, 45; Crary, *Dear Belle*, 107.

26. Frost, *Let's Have a Fair Fight!*

27. Custer to Ann Reed, March 28, 1862, Reel 1, Frame 0432-0435, GACC.

28. Carroll, *Custer in the Civil War*, 129–30; Monaghan, *Custer*, 64; "Our Army at Manassas," *New York Herald*, March 18, 1862. Many newspapers carried a version of the *Herald's* story.

29. Sears, *George B. McClellan*, 1–3;

30. Merington, *The Custer Story*, 27–28.

31. Warner, *Generals in Blue*, 462–64.

32. Haydon, *Military Ballooning during the Early Civil War*, 113–14; "The Siege of Yorktown," *New York Herald*, April 15, 1862; "General Porter's Balloon Reconnaissance of the Enemy," *New York Herald*, April 16, 1862.

33. Styple, *Generals in Bronze*, 163.

34. Carroll, *Custer in the Civil War*, 147.

35. Custer to Ann Reed, May 15, 1862, Box 1, Folder 21, FC.

36. Carroll, *Custer in the Civil War*, 147–50.

37. Warner, *Generals in Blue*, 202–3.

38. Jordan, 43–45; Carroll, *Custer in the Civil War*, 153–54.

39. Carroll, *Custer in the Civil War*, 155–56.

40. Ibid., 157–58. Jordan, 44, wrote that Hancock "bellowed" the order.

41. Custer to Ann Reed, May 15, 1862, Box 1, Folder 21, FC; Monaghan, *Custer*, 72, 75.

42. Merington, *The Custer Story*, 29–30.

43. Ibid.

44. Custer to sister, March 11, 1862, Box 1, Folder 21, FC.

45. Custer to sister, April 19, 1862, Box 1, Folder 21, FC.

46. Ibid.

47. Custer to brother and sister, July 13, 1862, Box 1, Folder 21, FC.

48. Ibid.

49. Ibid.

50. Ibid.

51. Ibid.

52. E. H. Custer to George Custer, April 18, 1862, Box 1, Folder 20, FC; E. H. Custer to George Custer, Feb. 2, 1862, Box 1, Folder 20, FC.

53. Roberts, 243.

54. E. H. Custer to George Custer, April 18, 1862, Box 1, Folder 20, FC.

55. Ann Reed to George Custer, April 18, 1862, Box 3, Folder 11, FC.

56. Whitaker, *A Complete Life*, 1:124.

57. Ibid., 1:122–24.

58. D. Grossman, *On Killing*, 114–19; Holmes, *Acts of War*, 376–93; Keegan and Holmes, *Soldiers*, 267–68.

59. Ann Reed to George Custer, August 13, 1862, April 18, 1862, Box 3, Folder 11, FC.

60. Whitaker, *A Complete Life*, 1:125–29.

61. Ibid., 129.

CHAPTER 3: GETTYSBURG

1. Custer to Cousin Augusta, October 3, 1862, in Stiles, *Custer's Trials*, 77.

2. Whitaker, *A Complete Life*, 1:135.

3. Merington, *The Custer Story*, 46–47.

4. Leckie, *Elizabeth Bacon Custer and the Making of a Myth*, 3–5.

5. Ibid., 5–8, 12, 16.

6. Ibid., 20–22.

7. Ibid., 8, 21–22.

8. Ibid., 8.

9. Ibid., 22.

10. Ibid., 25–26.

11. Monaghan, *Custer*, 112; Leckie, *Elizabeth Bacon Custer and the Making of a Myth*, 26.

12. Sears, *George B. McClellan*, 84.

13. Ibid., 124, 142–43.

14. Ibid., 345.

15. "General McClellan in Retirement," *New York Herald*, November 13, 1862.

16. Sears, *George B. McClellan*, 345.

17. "The Report on the Conduct of the War," *New York Herald*, April 6, 1863.

18. Monaghan, *Custer*, 113.

19. Carroll, *Custer in the Civil War*, 71, 73.

20. Ford, *A Cycle of Adams Letters*, 8. Adams was the grandson of President John Quincy Adams.

21. Styple, *Generals in Bronze*, 120.

22. Warner, *Generals in Blue*, 373; Monaghan, *Custer*, 115–16.

23. Monaghan, *Custer*, 93.

24. Ibid., 116–17, 131.

25. Whitaker, *A Complete Life*, 1:149–51; Merington, *The Custer Story*, 53–54.

26. Urwin, *Custer Victorious*, 51; Monaghan, *Custer*, 121.

27. Whitaker, *A Complete Life*, 1:163; Monaghan, *Custer*, 123.

28. Monaghan, *Custer*, 123; Stiles, *Custer's Trials*, 80, 88–89.

29. Monaghan, *Custer*, 124–28; Hatch, *Clashes of Cavalry*, 75–78, 81; Wert, *Custer*, 78.

30. "The War in Virginia," *Chicago Times*, 11 June 1863; Ripton, "From the Army of the Potomac," *Chicago Times*, 17 June 1863.

31. Merington, *The Custer Story*, 55–56.

32. "The Latest by Telegraph," *Detroit Free Press*, June 20, 1863; "The Latest by Telegraph," *Detroit Free Press*, June 23, 1863; "The Latest by Telegraph," *Chicago Times*, June 20, 1863; "Particulars of the Desperate Fight at Aldie," *Baltimore American & Commercial Advertiser*, June 20, 1863; "Army of the Potomac," *Baltimore American & Commercial Advertiser*, June 22, 1863; E. A. Paul, "The Cavalry Fight at Aldie," *New York Times*, June 17, 1863.

33. Styple, *Generals in Bronze*, 121.

34. Monaghan, *Custer*, 132–33; Whitaker, *A Complete Life of General George A. Custer*, 1:162–63.

35. Ibid.

36. Monaghan, *Custer*, 135; Whitaker, *A Complete Life*, 1:170.

37. Whitaker, *A Complete Life*, 1:170.

38. Styple, *Generals in Bronze*, 256.

39. Kidd, *A Cavalryman with Custer*, 65–67.

40. Whitaker, *A Complete Life*, 1:172; Monaghan, *Custer*, 134.

41. E. A. Paul, "Our Special Army Correspondence," *New York Times*, July 1, 1863; "The Michigan Cavalry of the Army of the Potomac," *Detroit Free Press*, 10 July 10, 1863.

42. Wert, *Custer*, 83.

43. Ibid., 87, 102.

44. "The Invasion," *New York Herald*, July 2, 1863; W. Young, "Despatch of Mr. W. Young," *New York Herald*, July 3, 1863.

45. Wert, *Custer*, 88–89; E. A. Paul, "The Cavalry Service," *New York Times*, 21 July 21, 1863.

46. Carhart, *Lost Triumph*, 267.

47. Riggs, *East of Gettysburg*, 46; Kidd, *A Cavalryman with Custer*, 80–81.

48. Urwin, *Custer Victorious*, 77.

49. Kidd, *A Cavalryman with Custer*, 86–87.

50. Ibid., 87–88.

51. Urwin, *Custer Victorious*, 78; Carhart, *Lost Triumph*, 236, 238; Utley, *Cavalier in Buckskin*, 23.

52. Kidd, *A Cavalryman with Custer*, 89.

53. Whitaker, *A Complete Life*, 1:177–78.

54. Ibid., 178.

55. Wert, *Gettysburg*, 269.

56. Perry, *A Bohemian Brigade: The Civil War Correspondents*, 204–5, 216.

57. Mueller, "Missing the Story at Gettysburg: Reporters Ignore a Possibly Decisive Cavalry Fight."

58. Agate, "The Great Battles of Gettysburg," *Cincinnati Gazette*, July 8, 1863. The dispatch was dated July 1, so part of the story was written before the battle, but it was published as one long piece including information to the end of the battle.

59. "The Great Victory on Friday," *New York Tribune*, July 6, 1863.

60. Mueller, "Missing the Story at Gettysburg."

61. E. A. Paul, "Doings of the Cavalry," *New York Times*, July 8, 1863; Martin, *Kill-Cavalry*, 12, 49, 54.

62. W. Young, "Seven Days in Captivity," *New York Herald*, July 17, 1863. A number of reporters were taken prisoner by both sides. See Carlson, *Junius and Albert's Adventures in the Confederacy* for one such dramatic tale.

63. "A Fight with Stuart," *Cleveland Morning Leader*, July 11, 1863.

64. E. A. Paul, "Doings of the Cavalry," *New York Times*, July 8, 1863.

65. E. A. Paul, "The Cavalry Service," *New York Times*, July 21, 1863.

66. "Our Cavalry," *New York Times*, July 21, 1863.

67. Walker, *The Cavalry Battle That Saved the Union*, 146.

68. Kidd, *A Cavalryman with Custer*, 90.

69. See Carhart, *Lost Triumph*; and Walker, *The Cavalry Battle That Saved the Union*.

70. Hall, *Last Stand of the U.S. Army at Gettysburg*, 289, 298.

71. Trudeau, *Gettysburg*, 474, 514.

72. Catton, *Gettysburg*, 84.

73. Monaghan, *Custer*, 148.

74. Morelock, *Generals of the Bulge*, 261–62.

75. Mueller, "'Custar' in the News: George Armstrong Custer in the Gettysburg Campaign."

76. Ibid.

CHAPTER 4: BOY GENERAL OF THE GOLDEN LOCKS

1. Wert, *Custer*, 101.

2. H., "From the Michigan Cavalry Brigade," *Detroit Free Press*, July 30, 1863.

3. H. "From the Michigan Cavalry Brigade," *Detroit Free Press*, August 8, 1863.

4. "From the Fifth Cavalry," *Detroit Free Press*, August 30, 1863.

5. "News from Washington," *New York Times*, July 13, 1863.

6. Robert C. Hill, "The Last Peace Story," *New York Times*, September 20, 1863. The letter was addressed to the "Editor of the Sentinel."

7. T. M. N., "From the Army of the Potomac," *New York Tribune*, August 4, 1863.

8. "Our Cavalry Officers," *Harper's Weekly*, August 22, 1863, 541–42.

9. Wert, *Custer*, 108–9.

10. "From the Army of the Potomac," *New York Tribune*, September 15, 1863.

11. "Latest News Received by Telegraph," *Baltimore American & Commercial Advertiser*, September 15, 1863; "The Army of the Potomac," September 14, 1863.

12. L. L. Crounse, "General Pleasanton's Advance," *New York Times*, September 15, 1863.

13. "The Army of the Potomac," *New York Times*, September 23, 1863.

14. N. Davidson, "Meade's Army," *New York Herald*, September 15, 1863.

15. "The Situation," *New York Herald*, September 15, 1863.

16. A. R. Waud, "The Army of the Potomac," *Harper's Weekly*, October 3, 1863, 632–33, 635.

17. Stephen W. Sears, "The Wilderness Revisited," *The Civil War Monitor*, 56–63, 75.

18. Agassiz, *Meade's Headquarters 1863–1865*, 19, 17.

19. Crary, *Dear Belle: Letters from a Cadet*, 214–15, 237.

20. E. B. Custer., "Account of Monument Unveiling," June 1910, Box 3, Folder 8, FC; Hatch, *Glorious War*, 211.

21. Frost, *General Custer's Libbie*, 75; Wert, *Custer*, 113.

22. Nan to Darling Billie, undated ca. July 1863, Box 2, Folder 9, FC. Billie was a nickname for Libbie.

23. Leckie, *Elizabeth Bacon Custer and the Making of a Myth*, 32–33.

24. Thomas Ward to Custer, November 2, 1863, FC.

25. "Custer and the Child," *Kalamazoo Telegraph*, March 18, 1894, FC.

26. Ann Reed to Custer, July 25, 1863, Box 2, Folder 11, FC.

27. Ann Reed to Custer, June 23, 1863, Box 2, Folder 11, FC.

28. Maggie Custer to Custer, October 26, no year given, but probably 1863, Box 2, Folders 3–4, FC. Official Data Foundation, "Inflation Calculator," http://www.in2013dollars.com/us/inflation/1863?amount=5, accessed January 7, 2020.

29. David Donovan to Custer, September 4, 1863, FC.

30. Merington, *The Custer Story*, 67.

31. Hatch, *Glorious War*, 211.

32. Daniel Bacon to Custer, October 22, 1863, Box 1, Folder 1, FC.

33. Hatch, *Glorious War*, 199.

34. Ibid., 200. See also Monaghan, *Custer*, 166–67, and Wert, *Custer*, 116–17.

35. Hatch, *Glorious War*, 202; Wert, *Custer*, 117.

36. "Army of the Potomac," *Baltimore American & Commercial Advertiser*, October 13, 1863.

37. "Army of the Potomac," *Baltimore American & Commercial Advertiser*, October 15, 1863. See also "The War in Virginia," *Chicago Times*, October 14, 1863, and "The War in Virginia," *Chicago Times*, October 17, 1863, for examples of coverage that emphasizes Kilpatrick's role.

38. Wert, *Custer*, 121–22.

39. J. H. K., "From the Sixth Cavalry," *Detroit Free Press*, October 30, 1863.

40. "The Latest by Telegraph," *Chicago Times*, October 22, 1863.

41. E. A. Paul, "The Cavalry Fight on Monday," *New York Times*, October 20, 1863.

42. E. A. Paul, "The Cavalry Advance to Buckland Mills," *New York Times*, 21 October 1863.

43. E. P. R., "A Cavalry Review Movements of the Harris Light Cavalry," *New York Times*, October 25, 1863.

44. Wert, *Custer*, 125.

45. Daniel Bacon to My Young Friend, December 12, 1863, Box 1, Folder 1, FC.

46. Merington, *The Custer Story*, 78–79.

47. Ibid., 79–80.

48. Hatch, *Glorious War*, 216–17; Wert, *Custer*, 132–33; Monaghan, *Custer*, 176–77.

49. Hutton, *The Custer Reader*, 18–19.

50. "Sons of Michigan," *Washington Evening Star*, January 27, 1864.

51. Wert, *Custer*, 135; Leckie, *Elizabeth Bacon Custer and the Making of a Myth*, 37.

52. "Personal Intelligence," *New York Herald*, February 14, 1864; "Personal," *Burlington* (Vt.) *Free Press*, February 26, 1864;

53. Merington, *The Custer Story*, 81.

54. Daniel Bacon to Sister, April 13, 1864, Box 1, Folder 1, FC.

55. Holmes, *Acts of War*, 93–100.

56. Wert, *Custer*, 136–37; Monaghan, *Custer*, 179–80.

57. Ibid.

58. Frost, *General Custer's Libbie*, 94.

59. Ibid.; Barefoot, *Gaslight Melodrama*, 77; Andrew Maunder, "Mrs Henry Wood," *The Literary Encyclopedia*.

60. Merington, *The Custer Story*, 87–89.

CHAPTER 5: THEN YOU'LL REMEMBER ME

1. Carroll, *Custer in the Civil War*, 18–20.

2. "Mr. N. Davidson's Despatch," *New York Herald*, March 3, 1864.

3. "The Newspaper Despatches," *New York Herald*, March 3, 1864.

4. Ray, "*Our Special Artist*," 43–46.

5. Monaghan, *Custer*, 187.

6. "Personal," *Cleveland Morning Leader*, February 11, 1864.

7. Merington, *The Custer Story*, 85.

8. Ibid., 92–94.

9. Ibid., 87–89.

10. Ibid.

11. Ibid.

12. Merington, *The Custer Story*, 90–92.

13. Ibid., 92–94.

14. Ibid.

15. Ibid.; Leckie, *Elizabeth Bacon Custer and the Making of a Myth*, 44–45.

16. Merington, *The Custer Story*, 89.

17. Wert, *Custer*, 155–56.

18. Merington, *The Custer Story*, 97.

19. S. T. Bulkley, "Sheridan!" *New York Herald*, May 17, 1864.

20. Merington, *The Custer Story*, 99.

21. "Sheridan's Expedition," *Chicago Tribune*, May 20, 1864.

22. Carroll, *Custer in the Civil War*, 30.

23. Urwin, *Custer Victorious*, 159.

24. N. Davidson, "Sheridan," *New York Herald*, June 21, 1864.

25. Ibid.

26. Wert, *Custer*, 164; Kidd, 66.

27. Merington, *The Custer Story*, 103–5.

28. Ibid., Wert, *Custer*, 165.

29. Carroll, *Custer in the Civil War*, 31.

30. Catton, *A Stillness at Appomattox*, 275.

31. Hatch, *Glorious War*, 276.

32. Stiles, *Custer's Trials*, 187; Hatch, *Glorious War*, 278–79; Rafuse, "Measure for Measure," *America's Civil War*, 32–39.

33. Merington, *The Custer Story*, 118.

34. Ibid.

35. Ibid., 118–19.

36. I. P. Christiancy to Custer, September 6, 1864, Box 1, Folder 3, FC.

37. "Patriotic Letter from Gen. Custer—Wholesome Reading for Loyal Men," September 16, 1864, unidentified newspaper clipping, FC.

38. I. P. Christiancy to Custer, September 22, 1864, Box 1, Folder 3, FC.

39. I. P. Christiancy to Custer, September 21, 1864, Box 1, Folder 3, FC.

40. See for example, E. H. Custer to Custer, Sept. 1, 1864, and Sept. 6, 1864, Box 1, Folder 20, FC.

41. E. H. Custer to Custer, September 22, 1864, Box 1, Folder 20, FC.

42. "Inflation Calculator," http://www.in2013dollars.com/us/inflation/1864?amount =200, accessed January 7, 2020.

43. David Reed to Custer, September 14, 1864, Box 2, Folder 12, FC.

44. Urwin, *Custer Victorious*, 173; Wert, *Custer*, 173.

45. Merington, *The Custer Story*, 114.46. Hatch, *Glorious War*, 276.

47. Hatch, *Glorious War*, 271.

48. Urwin, *Custer Victorious*, 198–99; Wert, *Custer*, 189–91.

49. Carroll, *Custer in the Civil War*, 41.

50. Urwin, *Custer Victorious*, 201–2; Merington, *The Custer Story*, 122.

51. Urwin, *Custer Victorious*, 210–11.

52. Carroll, *Custer in the Civil War*, 46.

53. Urwin, *Custer Victorious*, 215.

54. Wert, *Custer*, 196–97; Monaghan, *Custer*, 216–17; Frederick L. Ray, "America's Civil War."

55. Alberts, *General Wesley Merritt*, 146.

56. Carroll, *Custer in the Civil War*, 49.

57. Ibid., 47; "Sheridan's Cavalry," *New York Times*, November 6, 1864.

58. Carroll, *Custer in the Civil War*, 50; Urwin, *Custer Victorious*, 217.

59. "Visit of General Custer to Newark," *New York Herald*, October 26, 1864. This story was reprinted from the *Newark Advertiser*.

60. Cutler, *The North Reports the Civil War*, 586–89.

61. Walsh, *To Print the News and Raise Hell!*, 176.

62. Andrews, *The North Reports the Civil War*, 545–48.

63. R. S. H. "The Battle of Cedar Creek—Fair Play," *New York Times*, October 28, 1864; E. A. Paul, "The Weather," *New York Times*, November 8, 1864.

64. "Presentation of the Captured Flags to the War Department," *New York Times*, October 27, 1864.

65. "Gen. Custer upon Peace Propositions, *New York Times*, October 27, 1864; "Gen. Custer in Newark, N.J.," *New York Times*, October 27, 1864.

66. E. A. Paul, "The Battle of Cedar Creek," *New York Times*, October 27, 1864.

67. "News Jottings," *Evening* (Philadelphia) *Telegraph*, October 27, 1864.

CHAPTER 6: A HEART TOO FULL FOR UTTERANCE

1. Monaghan, *Custer*, 225.

2. Daniel Bacon to Custer, February 8, 1865, Box 1, Folder 1, FC.

3. E. H. Custer to Custer, Feb. 20, 1865, Box 1, Folder 20, FC.

4. E. A. Paul, "The Great Cavalry Raid," *New York Times*, March 21, 1865.

5. Ibid.

6. Ibid.

7. Ibid.

8. Carroll, *Custer in the Civil War*, 57.

9. E. A. Paul, "The Great Cavalry Raid," *New York Times*, March 21, 1865.

10. E. A. Paul, "From Gen. Sheridan," *New York Times*, March 20, 1865.

11. Urwin, *Custer Victorious*, 228.

12. "Presentation of Sheridan's trophies to the War Department," *New York Herald*, March 22, 1865; "An Interesting Scene," Washington, D.C., *Evening Star*, March 21, 1865.

13. Merington, *The Custer Story*, 145.

14. Ibid.

15. Merington, *The Custer Story*, 144.

16. Ibid., 142.

17. Ibid., 142, 144.

18. Ibid., 141; E. A. Paul, "Leaves from a Raider's Diary," *New York Times*, March 26, 1865.

19. Merington, *The Custer Story*, 141.

20. Wert, *Custer*, 212.

21. Merington, *The Custer Story*, 141.

22. E. A. Paul, "The Great Cavalry Raid," *New York Times*, March 21, 1865.

23. Charles H. Farrell, "Sheridan," *New York Herald*, March 10, 1865.

24. E. A. Paul, "The Great Cavalry Raid," *New York Times*, March 21, 1865; "Rebel Accounts," *New York Herald*, March 15, 1865.

25. "Rebel Accounts," *New York Herald*, March 15, 1865.

26. E. A. Paul, "The Great Cavalry Raid," *New York Times*, March 21, 1865.

27. "Inflation Calculator," http://www.in2013dollars.com/us/inflation/1865?amount =165, accessed January 7, 2020; E. A. Paul, "The Great Cavalry Raid," *New York Times*, March 21, 1865

28. E. A. Paul, "The Great Cavalry Raid," *New York Times*, March 21, 1865

29. E. A. Paul, "Leaves from a Raider's Diary," *New York Times*, March 26, 1865.

30. E. A. Paul, "The Great Cavalry Raid," *New York Times*, March 21, 1865; Merington, *The Custer Story*, 141.

31. E. A. Paul, "The Cavalry Operations," *New York Times*, April 3, 1865.

32. "The Rebel Rout," *New York Times*, April 7, 1865.

33. E. A. Paul, "Another Brilliant Affair by Gen. Custer," *New York Times*, April 20, 1865.

34. E. A. Paul, "The Pursuit of Lee," *New York Times*, April 7, 1865; E. A. Paul, "The Battle of Harper's Plantation," *New York Times*, April 14, 1865; E. A. Paul, "Capture of a Wagon Train," *New York Times*, April 14, 1865.

35. Merington, *The Custer Story*, 146.

36. Wert, *Custer*, 222; Stiles, *Custer's Trials*, 205.

37. E. A. Paul, "Capture of a Wagon Train," *New York Times*, April 14, 1865.

38. Merington, *The Custer Story*, 151.

39. Urwin, *Custer Victorious*, 245.

40. E. A. Paul, "Capture of a Wagon Train," *New York Times*, April 14, 1865.

41. E. A. Paul, "The Pursuit of Lee," *New York Times*, April 7, 1865; E. A. Paul, "Details of the Surrender of Lee's Army," *New York Times*, April 20, 1865.

42. Longstreet years later wrote an account in which he claimed he intimidated Custer, who in a blustering way demanded the surrender of the whole rebel army. This author agrees with Monaghan, *Custer*, 244, that Longstreet's account is doubtful. The author instead relies on Monaghan and E. A. Paul, "Details of the Surrender of Lee's Army," *New York Times*, April 20, 1865; and Merington, *The Custer Story*, 156–57.

43. Merington, *The Custer Story*, 159.

44. Ibid., 160.

45. Carroll, *Custer in the Civil War*, 64–65.

46. George Custer to Elizabeth Custer, April 11, 1865, Box 1, Folder 2, EBCP.

47. E. A. Paul, "Capture of a Wagon Train," *New York Times*, April 14, 1865.

48. *New York Times*, April 14, 1865.

49. *New York Times*, April 15, 1865.

CHAPTER 7: RECONSTRUCTION

1. Hatch, *Glorious War*, 202.

2. Merington, *The Custer Story*, 162.

3. "Maj.-Gen. Custer on the Punishment of the Rebel Leaders," *New York Times*, May 7, 1865.

4. "The Vt. Cavalry," *Rutland Herald*, May 25, 1865.

5. Ibid.

6. "Serenade to Gen. Custer," *New York Times*, May 23, 1865.

7. "The Grand Review in Washington," *Cadiz Sentinel*, May 31, 1865.

8. "The Review," *New York Herald*, May 24, 1865.

9. "Our Cavalry," *New York Times*, May 9, 1865.

10. "Gen. Custer Going West," *New York Times*, May 26, 1865.

11. Wert, *Custer*, 231.

12. E. B. Custer, *Tenting on the Plains*, 21–22.

13. Ibid., 34–35.

14. Ibid., 36–38.

15. Ibid., 24.

16. Ibid., 168.

17. Carroll, *Custer's Cavalry Occupation of Hempstead & Austin, Texas*, 14.

18. Wert, *Custer*, 233.

19. E. B. Custer, *Tenting*, 63–67.

20. Ibid.

21. "Barbarities in Texas," *Weekly Ottumwa* (Iowa) *Courier*, October 26, 1865.

22. Roderick, "Cruelty to Soldiers," *Rock Island* (Ill.) *Daily Argus*, October 18, 1865.

23. Ben C. Truman, "Condition of Texas," *New York Times*, March 5, 1866.

24. "Gen. George A. Custer," *National* (Washington, D.C.) *Tribune*, April 28, 1892; E. B. Custer, *Tenting*, 71; Wert, *Custer*, 234.

25. Joseph Connor, "Let There Be Light," *World War II*, March/April 2017, 36–45.

26. Carroll, *Custer's Cavalry Occupation*, 17–18.

27. Ibid., 156.

28. E. B. Custer, *Tenting*, 139–40.

29. Merington, *The Custer Story*, 175.

30. Truman, "Condition of Texas," *New York Times*, March 5, 1866.

31. Carroll, *Custer in Texas*, 167–68. Italics in original; "Custer," Washington, D.C., *National Republican*, February 24, 1866.

32. Merington, *The Custer Story*, 171; Barnett, *Touched by Fire*, 74.

33. E. B. Custer, *Tenting*, 181.

34. "Soldiers for Office," *Frank Leslie's Illustrated Newspaper*, Sept. 23, 1865, 2.

35. Carroll, *Custer in Texas*, 272–73.

36. Ibid., 275–76.

37. Merington, *The Custer Story*, 177–79.

38. Sherwood, *Labor of Love*, xvii, 6–7, 23–24.

39. Vinnie Ream Hoxie to Elizabeth Custer, December 4, 1907, Box 1, Folder 14, FC.

40. Merington, *The Custer Story*, 177–79.

41. Ibid.

42. Ibid., 179.

43. Ibid., 181.

44. Ibid., 182.

45. Wert, *Custer*, 242–43; Frost, *General Custer's Libbie*, 153.

46. Boulard, *The Swing Around the Circle*, 14–15; Jay Monaghan, *Custer*, 264, 270.

47. Monaghan, *Custer*, 269–70; Schroeder-Lein and Zuczek, *Andrew Johnson*, 203–5.

48. Boulard, *The Swing Around the Circle*, 35.

49. "Washington," *New York Herald*, August 22, 1866.

50. "Washington," *New York Tribune*, August 21, 1866.

51. "Then and Now," *Cleveland Daily Leader*, August 24, 1866.

52. G. A. Custer, "The Philadelphia Convention," *New York Times*, August 22, 1866.

53. Ibid.

54. Boulard, *The Swing Around the Circle*, 36; Monaghan, *Custer*, 272.

55. Ibid., 37.

56. Schroeder-Lein and Zuczek, *Andrew Johnson*, 287.

57. *New York Times*, September 3, 1866, 5; Boulard, *The Swing Around the Circle*, 105.

58. "The Tour," *New York Herald*, September 4, 1866; "The President's Mistake, *"New York Times*, September 7, 1866.

59. Boulard, *The Swing Around the Circle*, 134.

60. "The Radical Riot at Indianapolis—the Facts as Stated by Gen. Custer," *National Intelligencer*, September 18, 1866, 2; Boulard, *The Swing Around the Circle*, 135.

61. Boulard, *The Swing Around the Circle*, 138.

62. "The Tour," *New York Herald*, September 14, 1866.

63. Ibid.

64. "The Cleveland Convention," *New York Tribune*, September 18, 1866.

65. "The Cleveland Convention," *New York Tribune*, September 19, 1866.

66. "Nasby," *Western Reserve (Warren, Ohio) Chronicle*, October 10, 1866.

67. "The Radicals and the Soldiers," *National Intelligencer*, September 24, 1866.

68. "Union," *New York Herald*, September 19, 1866.

69. "A Pen Picture of Custer," *Daily (Columbus) Ohio Statesman*, October 2, 1866. Reprinted from the *Boston Advertiser*.

70. Ibid.

71. Dafoe, Willem, "Willem Dafoe," interview by Cal Fussman, *Esquire*, 141.

72. "Ungrateful Custer," *Detroit Free Press*, October 9, 1866.

73. "Major General Custer's Letter," *Detroit Free Press*, October 6, 1866.

74. G. A. Custer, "The Soldiers," *New York Herald*, August 23, 1866.

75. "Letter from the Army," *Ashland* (Ohio) *Union*, October 4, 1865.

CHAPTER 8: THE HANCOCK EXPEDITION

1. Merington, *The Custer Story*, 180–82.

2. Ibid., 182.

3. Ibid., 190.

4. E. B. Custer, *Tenting*, 218.

5. Monaghan, *Custer*, 280; E. B. Custer, *Tenting*, 218–19.

6. Lawrence Barrett, "Personal Recollections of General Custer," in Whitaker, *A Complete Life: Volume 2*, 2:631.

7. Barrett, "Personal Recollections of General Custer," 633.

8. E. B. Custer, *Tenting*, 219.

9. Barrett, "Personal Recollections of General Custer," 633.

10. Ibid.; Tarnoff, *The Bohemians*; Wert, *Custer*, 245.

11. Barrett, "Personal Recollections of General Custer,"632.

12. E. B. Custer, *Tenting*, 231–32.

13. Ibid., 232–33.

14. Ibid., 233.

15. Monaghan, *Custer*, 281–83.

16. Utley, *Frontier Regulars*, 118–19; 137–38.

17. Wert, *Custer*, 254; G. A. Custer, *My Life on the Plains*, 32–33.

18. George Custer, *My Life on the Plains*, 37–39.

19. Ibid., 40–43. Other sources suggest the girl was white or Cheyenne, and that she was assaulted by the troops who captured the village. See Chalfant, *Hancock's War*, 184–86.

20. Wert, *Custer*, 255.

21. George Custer, *My Life on the Plains*, 49–52.

22. Ibid., 56–57.

23. Merington, *The Custer Story*, 199.

24. Burkey, *Custer, Come at Once!*, 17.

25. Nicholas Lezard, "The Book to End All Books," *Guardian*, August 17, 2001.

26. Merington, *The Custer Story*, 203–4.

27. Nathan "N. R." Gaddis, "Nathan 'N. R.' Gaddis's Reviews: The Anatomy of Melancholy," https://www.goodreads.com/review/show/272228483, accessed January 11, 2020.

28. Burkey, *Custer, Come at Once!*, 21.

29. Merington, *The Custer Story*, 203–4.

30. Ibid., 204.

31. Burkey, *Custer, Come at Once!*, 13–14.

32. Ibid., 14.

33. George Custer, *My Life on the Plains*, 44–45.

34. Burkey, *Custer, Come at Once!*, 14.

35. Ibid., 23–24.

36. Frost, *The Court-Martial of General George Armstrong Custer*, 45.

37. Mueller, "Stanley before Livingstone: Henry Morton Stanley's Coverage of Hancock's War against the Plains Tribes in 1867," 5–14.

38. Stanley, "The Indian War," *Missouri Democrat*, June 8, 1867.

39. Stanley, "Hancock's Indian Expedition," *Missouri Democrat*, May 14, 1867.

40. Stanley, "The Indian War," *Missouri Democrat*, June 10, 1867.

41. Stanley, *My Early Travels and Adventures in America and Asia*, 107.

42. Merington, *The Custer Story*, 199–200.

43. Frost, *Court-Martial*, 43.

44. Merington, *The Custer Story*, 204–6; Monaghan, *Custer*, 291–92. Cooper's brevet rank was colonel.

45. Frost, *Court-Martial*, 46–47.

46. Ibid.

47. Wert, *Custer*, 258; Monaghan, *Custer*, 293.

48. Custer, *My Life on the Plains*, 79–84.

49. Wert, *Custer*, 259–60.

50. Custer, *My Life on the Plains*, 103–4.

51. Monaghan, *Custer*, 296.

52. Custer, *My Life on the Plains*, 105; Merington, *The Custer Story*, 206.

53. Custer, *My Life on the Plains*, 109–11.

54. Ibid. 112.

55. Ibid.

56. Ibid., 113–14.

57. Frost, *Court-Martial*, 190–93.

58. Custer, *My Life on the Plains*, 116–17.

59. Ibid., 118.

60. Frost, *Court-Martial*, 226–27.

61. Ibid.

62. Frost, *Court-Martial*, 214–15.

63. E. B. Custer, *Tenting*, 400.

64. Ibid., 401.

65. Monaghan, *Custer*, 300–301.

66. Merington, *The Custer Story*, 211.

67. Frost, *Court-Martial*, 89–91; Klokner, *The Officer Corps of Custer's Seventh Cavalry*, 106–7.

68. Frost, *Court-Martial*, 91.

69. Ibid., 216–17.

70. Ibid., 217.

71. Ibid., 219.

72. Ibid., 234.

73. Ibid., 233.

74. Ibid., 236.

75. Ibid., 236–37.

76. Ibid., 237–44.

77. Ibid., 246–47.

78. "Sentence of General Custer Approved," *New York Times*, November 30, 1867. The story, which was originally published in the St. Louis *Republican*, was carried by newspapers around the country.

79. Merington, *The Custer Story*, 213–14.

80. Ibid., 214–15; Frost, *Court-Martial*, 260.

81. I. P. Christiancy to Custer, October 13, 1867, Box 1, Folder 3, FC.

82. Frost, *Court-Martial*, 87.

83. Ibid., 256–57.

84. "Red Tape," *Urbana* (Ohio) *Union*, December 18, 1867.

85. Russell, "From the Plains," *New York Times*, December 7, 1867.

86. Ibid.

87. Ibid.

88. Merington, *The Custer Story*, 212.

89. Frost, *Court-Martial*, 256.

90. Receipt, Harper & Brothers Publishers, New York, December 6, 1867, Box 3, Folder 10, FC.

91. Frost, *Court-Martial*, 265.

92. Merington, *The Custer Story*, 215.

CHAPTER 9: WASHITA

1. George Custer, *My Life on the Plains*, 182.

2. Ibid.

3. Ibid.

4. Hoig, *The Battle of the Washita*, 66.

5. Ibid., 70–74.

6. George Custer, *My Life on the Plains*, 183.

7. Ibid.

8. George Custer, *My Life on the Plains*, 184.

9. Ibid., 189–90, 198.

10. Hutton, *The Custer Reader*, 106.

11. George Custer, *My Life on the Plains*, 191.

12. The description of California Joe comes from George Custer, *My Life on the Plains*, 191–98.

13. Ibid., 185.

14. Ibid., 206–7.

15. Ibid., 207–8; Klockner, 50–51. "Dundreary" came from a character named Lord Dundreary in the play *Our American Cousin*, which was the play Lincoln was watching when he was assassinated. In Britain Dundrearies were called Piccadilly Weepers.

16. Stiles, *Custer's Trials*, 310.

17. Utley, *Life in Custer's Cavalry*, 204–5.

18. George Custer, *My Life on the Plains*, 208–9.

19. Ibid., 209.

20. Monaghan, *Custer*, 308.

21. Frost, *General Custer's Libbie*, 176.

22. Barnett, *Touched by Fire*, 187–88.

23. Wert speculated Custer was sterile because he had been treated for syphilis while at West Point. Frost attributed it to the hard riding of the cavalry. It's impossible to know for certain.

24. See, for example, GAC to Mrs. Reed, February 24, 1862, Reel 1, Frames 0405–0411, GACC. There are several such letters in the collection.

25. Frost, *General Custer's Libbie*, 177.

26. Ibid., 178; Barnett, *Touched by Fire*, 188–90.

27. Merington, *The Custer Story*, 218.

28. Ibid., 309.

29. George Custer, *My Life on the Plains*, 270.

30. Frost, *General Custer's Libbie*, 174.

31. Wert, *Custer*, 269.

32. George Custer, *My Life on the Plains*, 205.

33. Wert, *Custer*, 296.

34. Frost, *General Custer's Libbie*, 175–76.

35. George Custer, *My Life on the Plains*, 214.

36. Ibid., 215.

37. Ibid.

38. Utley, *Life in Custer's Cavalry*, 213–15; George Custer, *My Life on the Plains*, 216–18.

39. George Custer, *My Life on the Plains*, 218–20.

40. Ibid., 219–20.

41. Utley, *Life in Custer's Cavalry*, 215.

42. George Custer, *My Life on the Plains*, 223.

43. Ibid., 224.

44. Ibid., 225.

45. Hoig, *The Battle of the Washita*, 119–20; George Custer, *My Life on the Plains*, 227.

46. George Custer, *My Life on the Plains*, 228–31.

47. Ibid.

48. Ibid., 231–33.

49. Ibid., 233.

50. Utley, *Life*, 218–19; George Custer, *My Life on the Plains*, 234–35.

51. George Custer, *My Life on the Plains*, 234–35.

52. Ibid., 237.

53. Ibid., 237–40

54. Ibid.

55. The song is mentioned about five times in *Charles O'Malley, The Irish Dragoon*, including a scene in which the characters rewrite the lyrics. Lever, *Charles O'Malley*, *(Part 1)*, 353.

56. George Custer, *My Life on the Plains*, 237–40.

57. Hoig, *The Battle of the Washita*, 128.

58. Greene, *Washita: The U.S. Army and the Southern Cheyennes*, 109, 129.

59. Hoig, *The Battle of the Washita*, 93; Greene, *Washita*, 204.

60. George Custer, *My Life on the Plains*, 241–43; Hoig, *The Battle of the Washita*, 93, Greene, *Washita*, 204

61. Ibid.

62. Hardorff, *Washita Memories*, 154–55.

63. George Custer, *My Life on the Plains*, 244–46.

64. Ibid.

65. Ibid.

66. Ibid., 249.

67. Ibid., 250.

68. Ibid., 258.

69. Hoig, *The Battle of the Washita*, 143; George Custer, *My Life on the Plains*, 267–68

70. George Custer, *My Life on the Plains*, 267–68; Lever, *Charles O'Malley, (Part 1)*, 302.

71. Knight, *Following the Indian Wars*, 69–70; "The Indian War," *New York Herald*, December 24, 1868. De B. Randolph Keim wrote the story but did not get a byline.

72. "The Indian War."

73. Keim, *Sheridan's Troopers on the Borders*, 81; "The Indian War."

74. "The Indian War."

75. Ibid.

76. George Custer, *My Life on the Plains*, 269.

CHAPTER 10: A HERO AND A VILLAIN

1. Mueller, "Little Big Myth," unpublished paper.

2. Ibid.; "The Indians," *Chicago Times*, Dec. 16, 1868.

3. "Federal and Confederate," *Chicago Times*, Dec. 18, 1868; "Let us have peace!" *Missouri* (St. Louis) *Democrat*, Dec. 12, 1868.

4. "The United States Indian Commission," *New York Herald*, Dec. 24, 1868; Hoig, 189.

5. "The Indian Fight," *Missouri* (St. Louis) *Democrat*, Dec. 10, 1868.

6. "The Contrast," *Missouri* (St. Louis) *Democrat*, Dec. 23, 1868.

7. "News Items," *Fremont* (Ohio) *Journal*, Dec. 11, 1868.

8. "Sheridan's Indian Campaign," *Green Mountain* (Montpelier, Vt.) *Freeman*, Dec. 9, 1868.

9. "The latest Indian intelligence," *Chicago Tribune*, Dec. 25, 1868.

10. "Sheridan's Winter Campaign," *New York Times*, Dec. 4, 1868.

11. "Fight with Indians," *Santa Fe* (N.Mex.) *Weekly Gazette*, Dec. 12, 1868.

12. *Chicago Times*, Dec. 12, 1868.

13. *Chicago Times*, Dec. 10, 1868.

14. "The Indian bill in Congress," *Chicago Times*, Dec. 24, 1868.

15. "The Late Indian Murder by General Custer," (Woodsfield, Ohio) *Spirit of Democracy*, Feb. 23, 1869.

16. "Indian Murder," *Sweetwater* (Tenn.) *Forerunner*, Jan. 7, 1869.

17. "The Battle of the Washita," *Athens* (Tenn.) *Post*, Feb. 10, 1869.

18. "The Indians," *Charleston* (S.C.) *Daily News*, Dec. 24, 1868.

19. Hutton, *Phil Sheridan & His Army*, 98–99.

20. Ibid., 99.

21. Frost, *Custer Legends*, 131–32.

22. Ibid., 132–33; Stiles, *Custer's Trials*, 326–27. Stiles doubts Benteen actually challenged Custer in this fashion. To this author it is believable given the personalities and the tension of the campaign.

23. George Custer, *My Life on the Plains*, 282.

24. Ibid., 286.

25. Ibid., 289–90.

26. Wert, *Custer*, 279.

27. George Custer, *My Life on the Plains*, 290.

28. Ibid., 293.

29. Hutton, *Phil Sheridan*, 19, 83–84; George Custer, *My Life on the Plains*, 250-254.

30. Ibid., 84–85.

31. Keim, *Sheridan's Troopers*, 156.

32. Stanley, *My Early Travels*, 241.

33. Keim, *Sheridan's Troopers*, 156.

34. Hoig, *The Battle of the Washita*, 165–66.

35. Ibid.; George Custer, *My Life on the Plains*.

36. George Custer, *My Life on the Plains*, 300–301.

37. Ibid., 313.

38. Ibid.

39. Hutton, *Phil Sheridan*, 103.

40. Hoig, 169; George Custer, *My Life on the Plains*, 314–16.

41. George Custer, *My Life on the Plains*, 318.

42. Ibid., 322.

43. Ibid., 321.

44. Ibid., 322.

45. Ibid., 324–30.

46. Ibid., 327. Fort Sill was also called New Fort Cobb, Fort Elliott, and "the camp on Medicine Bluff Creek" before Sheridan gave it the formal name it has today. See Hoig, *The Battle of the Washita*, 169.

47. Ibid., 354–57.

48. According to Cheyenne history, when they finished the smoke, Medicine Arrow tapped the ashes from the pipe on Custer's boots and cursed him that if he betrayed the Cheyenne, he and all his soldiers would die. This story has become part of the Little Bighorn lore as it foreshadows neatly Custer's death. But Custer did not write about it in his account of the meeting in *My Life on the Plains*. Someone like Custer, who was constantly studying Indian culture, likely would have noticed such an action and would have asked the interpreter about it. As a natural storyteller, he would have put it in his book. See Wert, *Custer*, 284–85, for a standard account of this episode.

49. Custer, *My Life on the Plains*, 360.

50. Ibid.

51. Ibid., 359–62.

52. Ibid.; Custer, *My Life on the Plains*, 362–63.
53. Spotts, *Campaigning with Custer and the Nineteenth Volunteer Cavalry*, 158.
54. Custer, *My Life on the Plains*, 364–68.
55. Ibid., 369–70.
56. Spotts, *Campaigning with Custer*, 157–58.
57. Hoig, *The Battle of the Washita*, 179. Actually, two brothers survived the Indian raid, see Hoig, *The Battle of the Washita*, 67.
58. Custer, *My Life on the Plains*, 371–73.
59. Ibid.; Spotts, *Campaigning with Custer*, 158–59.
60. Custer, *My Life on the Plains*, 374.
61. Kraft, *Custer and the Cheyenne*, 180.
62. Ibid., 376.
63. E. B. Custer, *Following the Guidon*, 85, 95–96; Burkey, *Custer, Come at Once!*, 68; Custer, *My Life on the Plains*, 377–78.
64. E. B. Custer, *Following the Guidon*, 96.
65. Ibid., 109–11.

CHAPTER 11: EXPLORING NEW PATHS

1. Dippie, *Nomad*, 6.
2. Frost, *General Custer's Libbie*, 179.
3. Betts, "Sporting Journalism in Nineteenth-Century America," *American Quarterly*, 39–56.
4. Hutton, *Phil Sheridan*, 164.
5. Abrahamson, *Magazine-Made America*, 56–57.
6. Dippie, *Nomad*, 48.
7. Ibid.
8. Saxon, *P. T. Barnum*, 226–27.
9. Dippie, *Nomad*, 60–62.
10. Ibid., 44–45; 134–35; Burkey, *Custer, Come at Once!*, 83–84; "Henry Anson Cavendish, 4th Baron Waterpark," *The Peerage*.
11. Dippie, *Nomad*, 44–45.
12. Ibid.
13. Ibid., 44, 49; 138; Monaghan, *Custer*, 332.
14. Pohanka, *A Summer on the Plains with Custer's 7th Cavalry*, 66–67.
15. Ibid., 8–10.
16. Ibid., 12–13, 17.
17. Ibid., 57.
18. Ibid., 58–61.
19. Ibid., 154.
20. Olson, "A Bit of Custer Humor."
21. Pohanka, *A Summer on the Plains*, 154.
22. Ibid., 156–57.
23. McKay, *Little Pills*, 9–10.
24. E. B. Custer, *Following the Guidon*, 160.
25. Frost, *General Custer's Libbie*, 183; Wert, *Custer*, 289.

26. Utley, *Cavalier*, 109; Wert, *Custer*, 294.

27. Merington, *The Custer Story*, 229–31; Winter, *The Life and Art of Joseph Jefferson*, 183; "'The Liar' at Wallack's Theatre," *New York Times*, April 16, 1871.

28. Merington, *The Custer Story*, 237;

29. Kellogg, *Memoirs of an American Prima Donna*, 57–58.

30. Merington, *The Custer Story*, 235–36.

31. Barnett, *Touched by Fire*, 197–200.

32. Ibid.; Merington, *The Custer Story*, 234.

33. Merington, *The Custer Story*, 234.

34. Ibid., 235.

35. Monaghan, *Custer*, 333.

36. Merington, *The Custer Story*, 239. The phrase translates to "knight without fear and without reproach."

37. Ibid.

38. Ibid., 235.

39. "Col. W. C. Church, Editor, Dies at 80, *New York Times*, May 24, 1917.

40. Stiles, *Custer's Trials*, 351; Ian Webster, CPI Inflation Calculator, http://www.in2013dollars.com/us/inflation/1871?amount=100, accessed January 17, 2020.

41. Merington, *The Custer Story*, 239.

42. Ibid., 240–41.

43. Ibid.

44. "1812, Reunion of Veterans—Survivors of the Raisin Massacre—Dinner, Toasts and Speeches," *Monroe Commercial*, June 22, 1871.

45. Frost, *General Custer's Libbie*, 200–201.

46. Scott, Bleed, and Damm, *Custer, Cody, and Grand Duke Alexis*, 22–24.

47. Frost, *General Custer's Libbie*, 199. Accidental shootings of horses and even riders during the wild and dangerous buffalo hunts were not uncommon, particularly with novices involved. See Dippie, *Nomad*, 138, note 19. Sheridan was nearly shot by Custer and Alexis, prompting him to severely curse his favorite general and his international guest. See Hutton, *Phil Sheridan*, 213.

48. Frost, *General Custer's Libbie*, 198–99; Hutton, *Phil Sheridan*, 213–16; Wert, *Custer*, 296.

49. Whitaker, *A Complete Life*, 2:633.

50. Monaghan, *Custer*, 338.

51. Whitaker, *A Complete Life*, 2:633.

CHAPTER 12: WARRIOR AND WRITER

1. E. B. Custer, *Boots and Saddles*, 4–6.

2. Dippie, *Nomad*, 103.

3. Monaghan, *Custer*, 341–42.

4. Ibid., 342.

5. Frost, *Custer's 7th Cav and the Campaign of 1873*, 61.

6. Ibid.

7. Merington, *The Custer Story*, 265–66.

8. Ibid., 249.

9. Dippie, *Nomad*, 161–62; Wert, *Custer*, 306–7

10. Ibid. Custer is identifying his brother by his brevet rank of lieutenant colonel. His regular Army rank was captain.

11. Wert, *Custer*, 306–7; Monaghan, *Custer*, 346–47.

12. Frost, *Custer's 7th Cav*, 75.

13. Ibid., 83–86; Wert, *Custer*, 308.

14. Frost, *Custer's 7th Cav*, 83–86; Utley, *Cavalier*, 122.

15. Frost, *Custer's 7th Cav*, 87.

16. Wooten, "Did You Know That Custer was a Taxidermist? Gen. George A. Custer and his Last Battle," *Breakthrough* 54, undated, Box 7, CC.

17. Merington, *The Custer Story*, 261.

18. Ibid., 258–59.

19. E. B. Custer, *Boots*, 122.

20. Merington, *The Custer Story*, 253.

21. Ibid., 267.

22. E. B. Custer, *Boots*, 92–95; Wert, *Custer*, 311.

23. E. B. Custer, *Boots*, 256.

24. Ibid., 144–47.

25. Ibid., 144.

26. Ibid., 149.

27. Katz, *Custer in Photographs*, xiii.

28. Monaghan, *Custer*, 332, 336.

29. E. B. Custer, *Boots*, 123–24.

30. Barry, "Barry Remembers Custer."

31. Barnett, *Touched by Fire*, 364.

32. E. B. Custer, *Boots*, 123–24.

33. Smyth, *The Gilded Age Press*, 72.

34. Ibid., 72–85; Hunter S. Thompson, "Hunter S. Thompson Quotes," https://totallygonzo.org/gonzowriting/wisdom-from-the-good-doctor/.

35. Stanley, *My Early Travels*, 5; Stanley, "Gen. Hancock's Expedition," *Missouri Democrat*, April 12, 1867.

36. Custer, *My Life on the Plains*, 44.

37. Ibid., 7.

38. Ibid., 322–23.

39. Ibid., 237.

40. Ibid., 51.

41. Dippie, *Nomad*, xv.

42. Utley, *Cavalier*, 54.

43. Ibid., 125.

44. Merington, *The Custer Story*, 244.

45. Custer, *My Life on the Plains*, 22.

46. Ibid., 313.

47. Ibid., 381.

48. Utley, *Cavalier*, 132–35.

49. Wert, *Custer*, 314.

50. Merington, *The Custer Story*, 272, 274.

51. Ibid.
52. Utley, *Cavalier*, 141–43; Jackson, *Custer's Gold*, 113–14.
53. Utley, *Cavalier*, 144–45.
54. Bergeron, *The Papers of Andrew Johnson*, vol. 16, 695.

CHAPTER 13: GILDED AGE CRUSADER

1. Merington, *The Custer Story*, 276.
2. Ibid., 276.
3. E. B. Custer, *Boots*, 208.
4. "The Story of Theatre," Victoria and Albert Museum, https://www.vam.ac.uk /articles/the-story-of-theatre, accessed February 24, 2020.
5. E. B. Custer, *Boots*, 208.
6. Utley, *Cavalier*, 163–64; Hutton, *Phil Sheridan*, 134–38.
7. Merington, *The Custer Story*, 277.
8. McKivigan, *Forgotten Firebrand*, 120–21.
9. I used an inflation calculator to estimate how much the contract would be worth today. http://www.in2013dollars.com/us/inflation/1876?amount=200, retrieved on December 9, 2018. According to the calculator, $200 in 1876 is worth $4,803.25 in 2020. Five nights a week is about twenty days per month, or 100 days for a five-month contract. Multiply that by a rounded 4,800 gives 480,000.
10. Merington, *The Custer Story*, 277.
11. Monaghan, *Custer*, 280; Frost, *General Custer's Libbie*, 217 and 219.
12. "Wild Bill Hickok," *All About History Book of the Wild West*, 85.
13. Whitaker, *A Complete Life*, 1:635–36.
14. Monaghan, *Custer*, 364.
15. Stiles, *Custer's Trials*, 420–22; Wert, *Custer*, 320; Utley, *Cavalier*, 155.
16. Custer, *My Life*, 166.
17. Ibid., 167–68.
18. Ibid., 152–53.
19. Mueller, *Shooting Arrows*, 18.
20. Utley, *Cavalier*, 159.
21. "The Iniquity of Belknap," *New York Sun*, March 30, 1876.
22. (Washington, D.C.) *Eastern Star*, March 30, 1876.
23. "The Iniquity of Belknap," *New York Sun*, March 30, 1876.
24. *New York Herald*, March 31, 1876.
25. "Rice vs. Custer," *Washington National Republican*, March 31, 1876.
26. "Washington," *Chicago Tribune*, April 5, 1876.
27. Merington, *The Custer Story*, 284.
28. Ibid., 289. Alexander Roby Shepherd was a prominent Republican politician in Washington and an associate of Grant's.
29. Merington, *The Custer Story*, 285.
30. Ibid., 289.
31. Ibid., 290.
32. Ibid., 289–91.
33. Mueller, *Shooting Arrows*, 8.
34. Merington, *The Custer Story*, 293.

35. Wert, *Custer*, 323.

36. Ibid.

37. Merington, *The Custer Story*, 292–93.

38. Wert, *Custer*, 323.

39. Ibid., 323–24.

40. Victor Davis Hanson, "The Bigmouth Tradition of American Leadership," *National Review*.

41. "Custer," *Los Angeles Herald*, May 3, 1876.

42. "Custer Sacrificed, *New York Herald*, May 6, 1876.

43. Wert, *Custer*, 324.

44. Mueller, *Shooting Arrows*, 18–19.

45. Utley, *Cavalier*, 162.

46. Wert, *Custer*, 324–25; Utley, *Cavalier*, 162–63.

47. "Grant and Custer," *Los Angeles Herald*, May 5, 1876.

48. "Custer Sacrificed," *New York Herald*, May 6, 1876.

49. "President Grant's Latest Mistake—Custer Punished," *New York Herald*, May 6, 1876.

50. "Custer Sacrificed, *New York Herald*, May 6, 1876.

51. Stiles, *Custer's Trials*, 439.

52. *Dallas Daily Herald*, May 9, 1876.

CHAPTER 14: CUSTER'S LAST STAGE

1. Utley, *Cavalier*, 163.

2. Ibid.

3. E. B. Custer, *Boots*, 217.

4. Ibid., 217–18.

5. Ibid., 220.

6. E. B. Custer, *Boots*, 219.

7. Utley, *Cavalier*, 165; Frontier, "Terry's Expedition," *Bismarck* (Dakota Territory) *Weekly Tribune*, May 17, 187. Kellogg usually used "Frontier" as a byline.

8. Mueller, *Shooting Arrows*, 33.

9. Monaghan, *Custer*, 371.

10. Merington, *The Custer Story*, 277; Mueller, *Shooting Arrows*, 16.

11. Holmes, *Acts of War*, 204–5; Windolph, *I Fought with Custer*, 53.

12. Mueller, *Shooting Arrows*, 15; Holmes, *Acts of War*, 136–38.

13. Holmes, *Acts of War*, 208; 213–18.

14. Barrett, "Personal Recollections of General Custer," 634. The passage quoted is in Barrett's essay but is attributed to an unidentified "intimate friend of General Custer."

15. Stewart, *Custer's Luck*, 181; Utley, *Cavalier*, 163–64.

16. Merington, *The Custer Story*, 289.

17. Utley, *Cavalier*, 172.

18. Merington, *The Custer Story*, 301–2.

19. Frontier, "Big Horn Expedition," *Bismarck* (Dakota Territory) *Weekly Tribune*, June 14, 1876.

20. Merington, *The Custer Story*, 303–4.

21. Ibid.

22. Mueller, *Shooting Arrows*, 21–22.

23. Ibid.

24. Philbrick, *The Last Stand*, 69–70.

25. Ibid.

26. Hutton, *Phil Sheridan*, 311–12.

27. Brinnistool, *Troopers with Custer*, 218.

28. Frontier, "Big Horn Expedition," May 24, 1876, *Bismarck* (Dakota Territory) *Weekly Tribune;* "Big Horn Expedition," *Bismarck* (Dakota Territory) *Weekly Tribune,* June 21, 1876.

29. Frontier, "Big Horn Expedition," May 24, 1876, *Bismarck* (Dakota Territory) *Weekly Tribune.*

30. Wert, *Custer*, 328; Merington, *The Custer Story*, 300–302.

31. Utley, *Cavalier*, 171. Such rough teasing might sound horrific to twenty-first-century readers, but mainstream American humor in Custer's day was quite rough. See Mueller, *Shooting Arrows*, 169–92, for a detailed discussion of humor and the Little Bighorn.

32. Utley, *Cavalier*, 172–73; Merington, *The Custer Story*, 305.

33. Donovan, *A Terrible Glory*, 195. Custer made the remark later to Lt. Charles Varnum.

34. Merington, *The Custer Story*, 305.

35. Utley, *Cavalier*, 174–76; Donovan, *A Terrible Glory*, 182–83.

36. Hatch, *The Custer Companion*, 208–9.

37. Merington, *The Custer Story*, 307.

38. Donovan, *A Terrible Glory*, 176–77.

39. Merington, *The Custer Story*, 309.

40. Ibid., 306.

41. Donovan, *A Terrible Glory*, 177–78; Stewart, 248; Wert, *Custer*, 332.

42. Donovan, *A Terrible Glory*, 183.

43. Godfrey, *The Godfrey Diary*, 65–67

44. Ibid.

45. Ibid., 67–68.

46. Mueller, *Shooting Arrows*, 23–24; Utley, *Cavalier*, 180; Godfrey, *The Godfrey Diary*, 67.

47. Godfrey, *The Godfrey Diary*, 68–69; Utley, *Cavalier*, 180–81.

48. Godfrey, *The Godfrey Diary*, 69–70.

49. Donovan, *A Terrible Glory*, 207.

50. Ibid., 207.

51. Merington, *The Custer Story*, 307.

52. Utley, *Cavalier*, 181.

53. Mueller, *Shooting Arrows*, 21–22.

54. Utley, *Cavalier*, 181–82.

55. Mueller, *Shooting Arrows*, 24. The creek is now named Reno Creek.

56. Linderman, *Plenty-Coups*, 97.

57. The warrior had been killed in the Battle of the Rosebud with Crook, but no one in the command knew that, or even that Crook had fought the Sioux.

58. Utley, *Cavalier*, 182.

59. Ibid., 183.

60. Mueller, *Shooting Arrows*, 25.

61. Utley, *Cavalier*, 185.

62. Donovan, *A Terrible Glory*, 220.

63. Ibid., 225–26; Utley, *Cavalier*, 186.

64. Donovan, *A Terrible Glory*, 226.

65. Ibid., 231.

66. Utley, *Custer*, 188.

67. Donovan, *A Terrible Glory*, 253.

68. Mueller, *Shooting Arrows*, 26.

69. Godfrey, *The Godfrey Diary*, 79.

70. Donovan, *A Terrible Glory*, 260.

71. Godfrey, *The Godfrey Diary*, 80.

72. Mueller, *Shooting Arrows*, 26.

73. Utley, *Cavalier*, 187–91. Utley, a National Park Service administrator and one of the most famous Custer scholars, wrote that this description is a "plausible theory" of Custer's movements and plans. The following description of the battle is based largely on Utley's account, the author's study of the battlefield, and other sources as noted. No soldiers survived from Custer's command. Indian accounts provide some information about what happened, but of course nothing about Custer's plans. The account is, as Utley wrote of his own interpretation, "informed speculation."

74. Holmes, *Acts of War*, 234–35.

75. Custer's body was found with about twenty rifle shells around it. A roadside marker on the battlefield indicates a warrior was shot in the forehead from Last Stand Hill. Of course, no one can know who fired the fatal shot, but it's reasonable to think that Custer, with his fine weapon, shooting skills, and long combat experience, was the one who did it.

76. "Sitting Bull Talks," *New York Herald*, November 16, 1877. This account of Custer's death comes from an interview Sitting Bull gave to the *Herald* after he had escaped with his band to Canada. He did not witness the events he described but heard them from warriors immediately after the battle; Donovan, *A Terrible Glory*, 276.

77. "Sitting Bull Talks"; Pohanka, *A Summer on the Plains*, 155.

78. Utley, *Cavalier*, 192; Godfrey, *The Godfrey Diary*, 95.

79. Hall, *The Oxford Book of Children's Verse in America*, 41–42.

CHAPTER 15: FORGOTTEN HONOR

1. Rosenberg, *Custer and the Epic of Defeat*, 2.

2. Peter Baker, "Days of Darkness, with Death Outside the Door," *Washington (D.C.) Post*, April 14, 2003.

3. "Telegraphic Progress," *Alta (San Francisco) California*, June 26, 1876.

4. Mueller, *Shooting Arrows*, 37–42.

5. Ibid., 42; Donovan, *A Terrible Glory*, 322; Hutton, *Phil Sheridan*, 317–18.

6. Mueller, *Shooting Arrows*, 66–67.

7. Ibid., 74–76.

8. Richter, "'A Better Time Is in Store for Us,'" *Military History of Texas and the Southwest*, 47.

9. Kellogg, *Memoirs of an American Prima Donna*, 42; Wright, "Nym Crinkle: Gadfly Critic and Male Chauvinist," *Educational Theatre Journal*, 370–82.

10. Nym Crinkle, "Custer as an Author," *New York World*, July 9, 1876.

11. Mueller, *Shooting Arrows*, 212, 172.

12. "A Monument to Custer," *New York Herald*, July 12, 1876.

13. Leckie, *Elizabeth Bacon Custer and the Making of a Myth*, 190–91. Legend has it the same hymn was played by the band on the Titanic thirty-five years later as that ship slid beneath the Atlantic.

14. Leckie, *Elizabeth Bacon Custer and the Making of a Myth*, 190–91.

15. Ibid.; E. B. Custer, *Boots*, 222.

16. Leckie, *Elizabeth Bacon Custer*, 119, 198, 203; Frost, *General Custer's Libbie*, 232; "Mrs. Custer in Chicago," *New York Herald*, August 7, 1876.

17. Ian Webster, CPI Inflation Calculator, http://www.in2013dollars.com/us/inflation/1876?amount=30, accessed January 23, 2020; Barnett, *Touched by Fire*, 355.

18. Leckie, *Elizabeth Bacon Custer*, 208; Frost, *General Custer's Libbie*, 239.

19. "Gen. Custer," *Chicago Tribune*, December 23, 1876.

20. *Bismarck Weekly Tribune*, January 3, 1877.

21. Leckie, *Elizabeth Bacon Custer*, 217–19; "Funeral of General Custer," *Harper's Weekly*, October 27, 1877.

22. "General Custer's Funeral," *New York Herald*, October 11, 1877.

23. School Girl, letter to the editor, *New York Herald*, July 13, 1876, in Mueller, *Shooting Arrows*, 5.

24. Leckie, *Elizabeth Bacon Custer*, 224; Ian Webster, CPI Inflation Calculator, http://www.in2013dollars.com/us/inflation/1876?amount=1795; accessed on January 23, 2020; Grossman, *A Spectacle of Suffering*, 6, 183–84.

25. Leckie, *Elizabeth Bacon Custer*, 224–27, 233–35, 246. An illustration in Frost, *General Custer's Libbie*, 251, shows the ridiculousness of the design.

26. Leckie, *Elizabeth Bacon Custer*, 214.

27. Ibid., 212–13; 231.

28. Ibid., 231; Frost, *General Custer's Libbie*, 240.

29. Frost, *General Custer's Libbie*, 257.

30. "New Publications," *New-York Daily Tribune*, April 24, 1885.

31. *Portland* (Maine) *Daily Press*, April 24, 1885.

32. Leckie, *Elizabeth Bacon Custer*, 240.

33. Ibid., 22, 254–55.

34. Ibid., 278.

35. "Edward Potter"; Leckie, *Elizabeth Bacon Custer*, 280.

36. Ibid.

37. E. B. Custer, "Account of Monument Unveiling," June 1910, unpublished manuscript, 304, Box 3, Folder 8, FC.

38. "General Custer's Memory Is Eulogized by President," *Daily Missoulian* (Montana), June 5, 1910; "Custer's Widow Unveils Statue," *San Francisco Call*, June 5, 1910.

39. E. B. Custer, "Account of Monument Unveiling," June 1910, 20-21, Box 3, Folder 8, FC.

40. Leckie, *Elizabeth Bacon Custer*, 246–47; Letter from EBC to Pathé Moving Picture Co., undated, Reel 1, Frames 0259–0260, GACC.

41. "Mrs. Custer Turns Pages of History," *Washington* (D.C.) *Evening Star*, June 25, 1929.

42. Remarque, *All Quiet on the Western Front*, 5.

43. Donovan, *A Terrible Glory*, 348.

44. Ibid., 395; Leckie, *Elizabeth Bacon Custer*, 251–52.

45. Donovan, *A Terrible Glory*, 394–95.

46. Klokner, *The Officer Corps of Custer's Seventh Cavalry*, 65–67.

47. Paul Andrew Hutton, introduction to *Glory-Hunter*, by Frederic Van de Water, 12–14.

48. Langellier, *Custer: The Man, the Myth, the Movies*, 45–47; Glancy, "Warner Bros Film Grosses, 1921–51," *Historical Journal of Film, Radio and Television*, 55–73.

49. Doyle, "The Lightness of Errol Flynn," *The American Scholar*.

50. Peter Valenti, *Errol Flynn*, 86, 89

51. Ibid., 82.

52. Holmes, *Acts of War*, 267–68; Dippie, *Nomad*, 139–40.

53. Nomin Ujiyediin, "In Response to Backlash, Sonic Withdraws Commercial Featuring General Custer," KGOU.org, May 4, 2017, http://www.kgou.org/post/response -backlash-sonic-withdraws-commercial-featuring-general-custer.

Bibliography

MANUSCRIPT COLLECTIONS

Custer Collection, Monroe County Historical and Museum Association Archives, Monroe, Michigan.

General George A. Custer Collection, Monroe County (Michigan) Library System.

Elizabeth Bacon Custer Papers, Beinecke Rare Book & Manuscript Library, Yale University, New Haven, Conn.

Dr. Lawrence A. Frost Collection of Custeriana, Monroe County Historical and Museum Association Archives, Monroe, Michigan.

BOOKS AND ARTICLES

Abrahamson, David. *Magazine-Made America: The Cultural Transformation of the Postwar Periodical*. New York: Hampton Press, 1996.

Agassiz, George R., ed. *Meade's Headquarters 1863–1865: Letters of Colonel Theodore Lyman from The Wilderness to Appomattox*. Boston: Massachusetts Historical Society, 1922.

Alberts, Don E. *General Wesley Merritt: Brandy Station to Manila Bay*. Columbus, Ohio: The General's Books, 2001.

Ambrose, Stephen E. *Crazy Horse and Custer: The Parallel Lives of Two American Warriors*. Garden City, N.Y., 1975.

———. *Duty, Honor, Country: A History of West Point*. Baltimore: Johns Hopkins University Press, 1999.

Andrews, J. Cutler. *The North Reports the Civil War*. Pittsburg: University of Pittsburg Press, 1985.

Barefoot, Guy. *Gaslight Melodrama: From Victorian London to 1940s Hollywood*. London: Bloomsbury Publishing Co., 2016.

Barnett, Louise. *Touched by Fire: The Life, Death, and Mythic Afterlife of George Armstrong Custer.* New York: Henry Holt, 1996.

Barrett, Lawrence. Personal Recollections of General Custer. In *A Complete Life of General Custer: Volume 2: From Appomattox to the Little Big Horn*, Lincoln: University of Nebraska Press, 1993.

Barry, John M., "John M. Barry Remembers Custer." *Newsletter of the Little Big Horn Associates* 24 (February 1995). Tom O'Neil, ed. Originally published in the *New York Evening Post*, May 28, 1910. FC.

Beemer, Rod. "The Unknown Custer." *Greasy Grass* 31 (May 2015).

Bergeron, Paul H., ed. *The Papers of Andrew Johnson*, vol. 16. Knoxville, Tenn.: University of Tennessee Press, 2000.

Betts, John Rickards. "Sporting Journalism in Nineteenth-Century America." *American Quarterly* 5, no. 1 (1953): 39–56. doi:10.2307/3031289.

Boulard, Gary. *The Swing Around the Circle: Andrew Johnson and the Train Ride That Destroyed a Presidency.* Bloomington, Ind.: iUniverse, 2008.

Brininstool, E. A. *Troopers with Custer: Historic Incidents of the Battle of the Little Big Horn.* Lincoln, Nebraska: Bison Books, 1989.

Burkey, Blaine. *Custer, Come at Once!* Fort Hays, Kans.: Society of Friends of Historic Fort Hays, 1991.

Carhart, Tom. *Lost Triumph: Lee's Real Plan at Gettysburg—and Why It Failed.* New York: G. P. Putnam's Sons, 2005.

Carlson, Peter. *Junius and Albert's Adventures in the Confederacy: A Civil War Odyssey.* New York: PublicAffairs, 2013.

Carroll, John M., ed. and compiler. *Custer in the Civil War: His Unfinished Memoirs.* San Rafael, California: Presidio Press, 1977.

———. *Custer's Cavalry Occupation of Hempstead & Austin, Texas; The History of Custer's Headquarters Building.* Glendale, Calif.: The Arthur H. Clark Co., 1983.

Catton, Bruce. *Gettysburg: The Final Fury.* Garden City, N.Y.: Doubleday & Company, Inc., 1974.

———. *Mr. Lincoln's Army: The Odyssey of General George Brinton McClellan and the Army of the Potomac.* Garden City, N.Y.: Double Day and Company, 1956.

———. *A Stillness at Appomattox.* New York: Doubleday & Co., Inc., 1956.

Cayton, Andrew R. L. *Ohio: The History of a People.* Columbus: Ohio State University Press, 2002.

Chalfant, William Y. *Hancock's War: Conflict on the Southern Plains.* Norman: University of Oklahoma Press, 2014.

Coddington, Ronald S. "Custer and His Roommate Part Ways." *New York Times*, February 15, 2012.

Connor, Joseph. "Let There Be Light." *World War II*, March/April 2017, 36–45.

Cooper, William. "James Buchanan: Campaigns and Elections." University of Virginia Miller Center. http://millercenter.org/president/buchanan/essays/biography/3, accessed June 16, 2015.

Crary, Catherine S. ed., *Dear Belle: Letters from a Cadet & Officer to his Sweetheart 1858–1865.* Middletown, Conn.: Wesleyan University Press, 1965.

Custer, Elizabeth B. *Boots and Saddles: Or Life in Dakota with General Custer.* New edition with an introduction by Jane R. Stewart, Norman: University of Oklahoma Press, 1961.

————. *Following the Guidon*, 1890. Reprint, with an introduction by Shirley A. Leckie, Lincoln: University of Nebraska Press, 1994.

————. *Tenting on the Plains: Or General Custer in Kansas and Texas*, 1895. Reprint, with an introduction and notes by Jane R. Stewart, 1971, and forward by Shirley A. Leckie, Norman: University of Oklahoma Press, 1994.

————. "A Tribute of Love." Unidentified newspaper clipping. December 11, 1892. FC.

Custer, George Armstrong. *My Life on the Plains: Or, Personal Experiences with Indians*. Norman: University of Oklahoma Press, 1988.

Dafoe, Willem. "Willem Dafoe." Interview by Cal Fussman. *Esquire*, March 2012, 141.

Dippie, Brian W., ed. *Nomad: George A. Custer in Turf, Field and Farm*. Austin: University of Texas Press, 1980.

Donovan, James. *A Terrible Glory: Custer and the Little Bighorn—the Last Great Battle of the American West*. New York: Little, Brown and Company, 2008.

Doyle, Brian. "The Lightness of Errol Flynn." *The American Scholar*, December 5, 2016. https://theamericanscholar.org/the-lightness-of-errol-flynn/#.XX6erehKiM8, accessed September 15, 2019.

"Edward Potter." https://en.wikipedia.org/wiki/Edward_Clark_Potter.

Farley, Joseph Pearson. *West Point in the Early Sixties*. Troy, N.Y.: Pafraets Book Co., 1902.

Ford, Worthington Chauncy, ed. *A Cycle of Adams Letters, Vol. 2*. Boston: Houghton Mifflin Co., 1920.

Frost, Lawrence A. *The Court-Martial of General George Armstrong Custer*. Norman: University of Oklahoma Press, 1968.

————. *Custer Legends*. Bowling Green: Bowling Green University Popular Press, 1981.

————. *Custer's 7th Cav and the Campaign of 1873*. El Segundo, Calif.: Upton & Sons, Publishers, 1986.

————. *General Custer's Libbie*. Seattle: Superior Publishing Co., 1976.

————. *Let's Have a Fair Fight!* Monroe, Mich.: Monroe County Historical Association, 1965.

Gaddis, Nathan "N.R." "Nathan 'N.R.' Gaddis's Reviews: The Anatomy of Melancholy." *Goodreads.com*. https://www.goodreads.com/review/show/272228483, accessed July 19, 2018.

Glancy, H. Mark. "Warner Bros Film Grosses, 1921–51: the William Schaefer ledger." *Historical Journal of Film, Radio and Television* (1995): 55–73.

Godfrey, Edward Settle. *The Godfrey Diary: The Field Diary of Lt. Edward Settle Godfrey*. Middletown, Del.: Big Byte Books, 2016.

Greene, Jerome A. *Washita: The U.S. Army and the Southern Cheyennes, 1867–1869*. Norman: University of Oklahoma Press, 2008.

Grossman, Barbara Wallace. *A Spectacle of Suffering: Clara Morris on the American Stage*. Carbondale: Southern Illinois University Press, 2009.

Grossman, Dave. *On Killing: The Psychological Cost of Learning to Kill in War and Society*. New York: Back Bay Books, 2009.

Hall, David, ed. *The Oxford Book of Children's Verse in America*. New York: Oxford University Press, 1985.

Hall, Jeffrey C. *Last Stand of the U.S. Army at Gettysburg*. Bloomington: Indiana University Press, 2003.

Hanson, Victor Davis. "The Bigmouth Tradition of American Leadership." *National Review,* December 27, 2017. https://www.nationalreview.com/2017/12/american-history-leadership-temperamental-omar-bradley-george-s-patton-dwight-d-eisenhower-harry-s-truman/, accessed March 16, 2019.

Hardorff, Richard G. *Washita Memories: Eyewitness Views of Custer's Attack on Black Kettle's Village.* Norman: University of Oklahoma Press, 2006.

Hatch, Thom. *Clashes of Cavalry: The Civil War Careers of George Armstrong Custer and Jeb Stuart.* Mechanicsburg, Pa.: Stackpole, 2001.

———. *The Custer Companion: A Comprehensive Guide to the Life of George Armstrong Custer and the Plains Indian Wars.* Mechanicsburg, Pa.: Stackpole, 2002.

———. *Glorious War: The Civil War Adventures of George Armstrong Custer.* New York: St. Martin's Press, 2013.

Haydon, F. Stansbury. *Military Ballooning during the Early Civil War.* Baltimore: The Johns Hopkins University Press, 2000.

"Henry Anson Cavendish, 4th Baron Waterpark." *The Peerage.* http://www.thepeerage.com/p14607.htm#i146061, accessed November 19, 2018.

Hoig, Stan. *The Battle of the Washita.* Lincoln: University of Nebraska Press, 1979.

Holmes, Richard. *Acts of War: The Behavior of Men in Battle.* New York: The Free Press, 1986.

Hunter, Robbins. *The Judge Rode a Sorrel Horse.* New York: E. P. Dutton & Co., 1950.

Hutton, Paul Andrew. Introduction to *Glory-Hunter: A Life of General Custer,* by Frederic Van de Water. Lincoln: University of Nebraska Press, 1988.

———. *Phil Sheridan and His Army.* Norman: University of Oklahoma Press, 1999.

———, ed. *The Custer Reader.* Lincoln: University of Nebraska Press, 1992.

Jackson, Donald. *Custer's Gold: The United States Cavalry Expedition of 1874.* Lincoln: University of Nebraska Press, 1972.

Jordan, David M. *Winfield Scott Hancock: A Soldier's Life.* Bloomington: Indiana University Press, 1996.

Katz, D. Mark. *Custer in Photographs: A Visual Portrait of One of America's Most Intriguing Civil War Heroes.* New York: Bonanza Books, 1985.

Keegan, John, and Richard Holmes. *Soldiers: An Illustrated History of Men in Battle.* New York: Konecky & Konecky, 1985.

Keim, De B. Randolph. *Sheridan's Troopers on the Borders: A Winter Campaign on the Plains.* New York: George Routledge and Sons, 1885.

Kellogg, Clara Louise. *Memoirs of an American Prima Donna.* New York: G. P. Putnam's Sons, 1913.

Kidd, J. H. *A Cavalryman with Custer: Custer's Michigan Cavalry Brigade in the Civil War,* 1908. Abridged edition, with an introduction by Robert M. Utley, New York: Bantam Books, 1991.

Klokner, James B. *The Officer Corps of Custer's Seventh Cavalry: 1866–1876.* Atglen, Pa.: Schiffer Military History, 2007.

Knight, Oliver. *Following the Indian Wars: The Story of the Newspaper Correspondents among the Indian Campaigners.* Norman: University of Oklahoma Press, 1960.

Kraft, Louis. *Custer and the Cheyenne: George Armstrong Custer's Winter Campaign on the Southern Plains.* El Segundo, Calif.: Upton and Sons, 1995.

Langellier, John Phillip. *Custer: The Man, the Myth, the Movies.* Mechanicsburg, Pa.: Stackpole Books, 2000.

Leckie, Shirley A. *Elizabeth Bacon Custer and the Making of a Myth.* Norman: University of Oklahoma, 1993.

Lever, Charles. *Charles O'Malley, The Irish Dragoon (Part 1).* Wildside Press. Reprint of 1894 edition.

———. *Charles O'Malley, The Irish Dragoon (Part 2).* Wildside Press. Reprint of 1894 edition.

Lezard, Nicholas. "The Book to End All Books." *Guardian,* August 17, 2001.

Linderman, Frank B. *Plenty-Coups: Chief of the Crows.* Lincoln: University of Nebraska Press, 2002.

McClellan, B. Edward. Introduction to *The Hoosier Schoolmaster,* by Edward Eggleston Bloomington: Indiana University Press, 1984.

McKay, R. H. *Little Pills: An Army Story.* Pittsburg, Kans.: Pittsburg Headlight, 1918.

McKivigan, John R. *Forgotten Firebrand: James Redpath and the Making of Nineteenth-Century America.* Ithaca: Cornell University Press, 2008.

Mahon, John K. *History of the Militia and the National Guard.* New York: Macmillan Publishing Co., 1983.

Martin, Samuel J. *Kill-Cavalry: The Life of Union General Hugh Judson Kilpatrick.* Mechanicsburg, Pa.: Stackpole Books, 2000.

Maunder, Andrew. "Mrs Henry Wood." *The Literary Encyclopedia.* First published July 18, 2001. https://www.litencyc.com/php/speople.php?rec=true&UID=4790, accessed 13 March 2019.

Merington, Marguerite, ed. *The Custer Story: The Life and Letters of General George A. Custer and His Wife Elizabeth.* New York: Barnes & Noble Books, 1994.

Michie, Peter. "Reminiscences of Cadet and Army Service," 183–97. *Personal Recollections of the War of the Rebellion.* Ed. A. Noel Blakeman. New York: G.P. Putnam's Sons, 1897.

Monaghan, Jay. *Custer: The Life of General George Armstrong Custer.* Lincoln: University of Nebraska Press, 1971.

Morelock, Jerry D. *Generals of the Bulge: Leadership in the U.S. Army's Greatest Battle.* Mechanicsburg, PA: Stackpole, 2015.

Mueller, James E. "Custar" in the News: George Armstrong Custer in the Gettysburg Campaign." In Sachsman, David B., editor. *A Press Divided: Newspaper Coverage of the Civil War.* Piscataway, N.J.: Transaction Publishers, 2014.

———. "Little Big Myth: Press Coverage of George Armstrong Custer at the Washita." Paper presented at the Symposium on the 19th Century Press, Chattanooga, Tenn., November 2016.

———. "Missing the Story at Gettysburg: Reporters Ignore a Possibly Decisive Cavalry Fight." Paper presented at the annual meeting of the Association for Education in Journalism and Mass Communication, Minneapolis, August 2016.

———. *Shooting Arrows & Slinging Mud: Custer, the Press, and the Little Bighorn.* Norman: University of Oklahoma Press, 2013.

———. "Stanley before Livingstone: Henry Morton Stanley's Coverage of Hancock's War against the Plains Tribes in 1867." *Journalism History* 42 (Spring 2016): 5–14.

Official Data Foundation. "Inflation Calculator." http://www.in2013dollars.com/us /inflation/1863?amount=5, retrieved on March 13, 2019.

Olson, Gordon L. "A Bit of Custer Humor." *Chronicle*, Winter 1977–1978.

Paul, E. A. "Doings of the Cavalry." *New York Times*, July 8, 1863.

Perry, James M. *A Bohemian Brigade: The Civil War Correspondents—Mostly Rough, Sometimes Ready.* New York: John Wiley & Sons, 2000.

Philbrick, Nathaniel. *The Last Stand: Custer, Sitting Bull, and the Battle of the Little Bighorn.* New York, Viking, 2010.

Pohanka, Brian C., ed. *A Summer on the Plains with Custer's 7th Cavalry: The 1870 Diary of Annie Gibson Roberts.* Lynchburg, Va.: Schroeder Publications, 2004.

Rafuse, Ethan F. "Measure for Measure." *America's Civil War*, November 2015, 32–39.

Ray, Frederic E. *"Our Special Artist": Alfred R. Waud's Civil War.* Mechanicsburg, Pa.: Stackpole Books, 1994.

Ray, Frederick L. "America's Civil War: George Custer and Stephen Ramseur," July 2003. http://www.historynet.com/americas-civil-war-george-custer-and-stephen -ramseur.htm, accessed June 16, 2018.

Remarque, Erich Maria. *All Quiet on the Western Front.* New York: Fawcett Crest, 1958.

Richter, William L. "'A Better Time Is in Store for Us'": An Analysis of the Reconstruction Attitudes of George Armstrong Custer." *Military History of Texas and the Southwest* 11 (1973): 31–50.

Riggs, David F. *East of Gettysburg: Custer vs. Stuart.* Fort Collins, Colo.: Old Army Press, 1970.

Roberts, John. *Buckeye Schoolmaster: A Chronicle of Midwestern Rural Life, 1853–1865.* Ed. J. Merton England. Bowling Green: Bowling Green State University Press, 1996.

Ronsheim, Milton. *The Life of General Custer.* Monroe, Mich.: Monroe County Library System, 1991.

Rosenberg, Bruce A. *Custer and the Epic of Defeat.* University Park, Pa.: Pennsylvania State University Press, 1974.

Saxon, A. H. *P. T. Barnum: The Legend and the Man.* New York: Columbia University Press, 1989.

Schaff, Morris. *The Spirit of Old West Point, 1858–1862.* London: Forgotten Books, 2012.

Schroeder-Lein, Glenna R., and Richard Zuczek. *Andrew Johnson: A Biographical Companion.* Santa Barbara, Calif.: ABC-CLIO, 2001.

Scott, Douglas D., Peter Bleed, and Stephen Damm. *Custer, Cody, and Grand Duke Alexis: Historical Archaeology of the Royal Buffalo Hunt.* Norman: University of Oklahoma, 2013.

Sears, Stephen W. *George B. McClellan: The Young Napoleon.* New York: Da Capo Press, 1999.

———. "The Wilderness Revisited." *The Civil War Monitor*, Spring 2016, 56–63, 75.

Sherwood, Glenn V. *Labor of Love: The Life & Art of Vinnie Ream.* Hygiene, Colo.: Sunshine Press Publications, Inc., 1997.

Slotkin, Richard. *The Fatal Environment: The Myth of the Frontier in the Age of Industrialization, 1800–1890.* Norman: University of Oklahoma Press, 1998.

Smythe, Ted Curtis. *The Gilded Age Press, 1865–1900.* Westport, Conn.: Praeger, 2003.

Spotts, David L. *Campaigning with Custer and the Nineteenth Volunteer Cavalry on the Washita Campaign, 1868–69.* Ed. E. A. Brinninstool Lincoln: University of Nebraska Press, 1988.

Stanley, Henry M. *My Early Travels and Adventures in America and Asia*. London: Duckworth, 2001.

Stewart, Edgar I. *Custer's Luck*. Norman: University of Oklahoma Press, 1989.

Stiles, T. J. *Custer's Trials: A Life on the Frontier of a New America*. New York: Alfred A. Knopf, 2015.

"The Story of Theatre." Victoria and Albert Museum. http://www.vam.ac.uk/content /articles/0-9/19th-century-theatre/, accessed February 23, 2020.

Styple, William B., ed. *Generals in Bronze: Interviewing the Commanders of the Civil War*. Kearny, N.J.: Bell Grove Publishing Co., 2005.

Tarnoff, Benjamin. *The Bohemians: Mark Twain and the San Francisco Writers Who Reinvented American Literature*. New York: Penguin Books, 2014.

Thompson, Hunter S. "Hunter S. Thompson Quotes." https://totallygonzo.org/gonzo writing/wisdom-from-the-good-doctor/, accessed December 2, 2018.

Trudeau, Noah Andre. *Gettysburg*. New York: Harper Collins, 2002.

Ujiyediin, Nomin. "In Response to Backlash, Sonic Withdraws Commercial Featuring General Custer." KGOU.org, May 4, 2017. http://www.kgou.org/post/response -backlash-sonic-withdraws-commercial-featuring-general-custer, accessed February 3, 2019.

Urwin, Gregory J. W. *Custer Victorious: The Civil War Battles of General George Armstrong Custer*. East Brunswick, N.J.: Associated University Presses, 1983.

U.S. Census Bureau. "Resident Population and Apportionment of the U.S. House of Representatives.   https://www.census.gov/dmd/www/resapport/states/ohio.pdf, accessed May 25, 2017.

Utley, Robert M. *Cavalier in Buckskin: George Armstrong Custer and the Western Military Frontier*. Norman: University of Oklahoma Press, 1988.

———. *Frontier Regulars: The United States Army and the Indian, 1866–1890*. New York: Macmillan Publishing Co., 1973.

———, ed. *Life in Custer's Cavalry: Diaries and Letters of Albert and Jennie Barnitz, 1867–1868*. Lincoln: University of Nebraska Press, 1987.

Valenti, Peter. *Errol Flynn: A Bio-Bibliography*. Westport, Conn.: Greenwood Press, 1984.

Van de Water, Frederic. *Glory-Hunter: A Life of General Custer*. Lincoln: University of Nebraska Press, 1988.

Village of Hopedale. "Our History." http://www.hopedaleohio.com/our-history.html, accessed January 31, 2018.

Walker, Paul. D. *The Cavalry Battle That Saved the Union: Custer vs. Stuart at Gettysburg*. Gretna, La.: Pelican Publishing Co., 2002.

Wallace, Charles B. *Custer's Ohio Boyhood: A Brief Account of the Early Life of Major General George Armstrong Custer*. Cadiz, Ohio: Harrison County Historical Society, 1993.

Walsh, Justin E. *To Print the News and Raise Hell!* Chapel Hill: The University of North Carolina Press, 1968.

Warner, Ezra J. *Generals in Blue: Lives of the Union Commanders*. Baton Rouge: Louisiana State University Press, 2002.

Wert, Jeffry D. *Custer: The Controversial Life of George Armstrong Custer*. New York: Simon & Schuster, 1996.

———. *Gettysburg: Day Three*. New York: Simon & Schuster, 2001.

"Wild Bill Hickok." *All About History Book of the Wild West*. London: Future, 2018.

Whisker, James B. *The Rise and Decline of the American Militia System.* Selinsgrove, Pa.: Susquehanna University Press, 1999.

Whitaker, Frederick. *A Complete Life of General George A. Custer: Volume 1: Through the Civil War.* Reprint, 1876, with an Introduction by Gregory J. W. Urwin. Lincoln: University of Nebraska Press, 1993.

————. *A Complete Life of General George A. Custer: Volume 2: From Appomattox to the Little Big Horn.* Reprint, 1876, with an introduction by Robert M. Utley, Lincoln: University of Nebraska Press, 1993.

White, Richard. *"It's Your Misfortune and None of My Own": A New History of the American West.* Norman: University of Oklahoma Press, 1993.

Wilson, James Harrison. *Under the Old Flag: Recollections of Military Operations in the War for the Union, the Spanish War, the Boxer Rebellion, Etc.* New York: D. Appleton and Company, 1912.

Windolph, Charles. *I Fought with Custer: The Story of Sergeant Windolph, Last Survivor of the Battle of the Little Big Horn as Told to Frazier and Robert Hunt.* Lincoln: University of Nebraska Press, 1987.

Winter, William. *The Life and Art of Joseph Jefferson: Together with Some Account of His Ancestry and of the Jefferson Family of Actors.* New York: MacMillan and Co., 1894.

Wooten, Dickie. "Did You Know That Custer was a Taxidermist? Gen. George A. Custer and His Last Battle. *Breakthrough* 54.

Wright, Thomas K. "Nym Crinkle: Gadfly Critic and Male Chauvinist." *Educational Theatre Journal* 24, no. 4 (1972): 370–82. doi:10.2307/3205931.

Yu, Amy Zhao, Shahar Ronen, Kevin Hu, Tiffany Lu, and César A. Hidalgo (2016). Pantheon 1.0, a Manually Verified Dataset of Globally Famous Biographies. *Scientific Data* 2:150075. https://doi.org/10.1038/sdata.2015.75.

NEWSPAPERS

Ashland (Ohio) *Union*, 1866.

Athens (Tenn.) *Post*, 1868.

Baltimore American and Commercial Advertiser, 1863–1876.

Bismarck (N. Dak.) *Tribune*, 1876–1877.

Burlington (Vt.) *Free Press*, 1864.

Cadiz (Ohio) *Sentinel*, 1844–1865.

Charleston (S.C.) *Daily News*, 1868.

Chicago Times, 1863–1876.

Chicago Tribune, 1864–76.

Cincinnati Gazette, 1863.

Cleveland Daily Leader, 1866.

Cleveland Morning Leader, 1863–1864.

Dallas Daily Herald, 1876.

Detroit Free Press, 1863–1866.

Frank Leslie's Illustrated Newspaper, 1865.

Freemont (Ohio) *Journal*, 1868.

Green Mountain Freeman (Montpelier, Vt.), 1868.

Hartford Courant, 1876.

Harper's Weekly, 1861–1877.
Los Angeles Herald, 1876.
Missoulian (Missoula, Mont.), 1876–1910.
Missouri Democrat (St. Louis, Mo.), 1867–1868.
Monroe (Mich.) *Commercial*, 1871–1876.
National Intelligencer (Washington, D.C.), 1866.
National Republican (Washington, D.C.), 1866, 1876.
National Tribune (Washington, D.C.), 1892.
New York Herald, 1862–1877.
New York Sun, 1876.
New York Times, 1863–1876.
New York Tribune, 1866–1876, 1885.
Portland (Maine) *Daily Press*, 1885.
Rock Island (Ill.) *Daily Argus*, 1865.
San Francisco Call, 1910.
Santa Fe (N. Mex.) *Weekly Gazette*, 1868.
Spirit of Democracy (Woodsfield, Ohio), 1868.
Sweetwater (Tenn.) *Forerunner*, 1868.
Washington Evening Star, 1864–1876, 1929.
Weekly Ottumwa (Iowa) *Courier*, 1865.

Index

Page numbers in *italic* typeface indicate illustrations.